Palgrave Studies in the History of Finance

The study of the history of financial institutions, markets, instruments and concepts is vital if we are to understand the role played by finance today. At the same time, the methodologies developed by finance academics can provide a new perspective for historical studies. Palgrave Studies in the History of Finance is a multi-disciplinary effort to emphasise the role played by finance in the past, and what lessons historical experiences have for us. It presents original research, in both authored monographs and edited collections, from historians, finance academics and economists, as well as financial practitioners.

More information about this series at
http://www.palgrave.com/gp/series/14583

Gisela Huerlimann • W. Elliot Brownlee
Eisaku Ide
Editors

Worlds of Taxation

The Political Economy of Taxing, Spending, and Redistribution Since 1945

palgrave
macmillan

Editors
Gisela Huerlimann
ETH Zurich Institute of History
Zürich, Switzerland

W. Elliot Brownlee
University of California, Santa Barbara
Santa Barbara, CA, USA

Eisaku Ide
Keio University
Tokyo, Japan

Palgrave Studies in the History of Finance
ISBN 978-3-030-07978-9 ISBN 978-3-319-90263-0 (eBook)
https://doi.org/10.1007/978-3-319-90263-0

Cover illustration: Jackof, iStock / Getty Images Plus

Printed on acid-free paper

This Palgrave Macmillan imprint is published by the registered company Springer International Publishing AG part of Springer Nature.
The registered company address is: Gewerbestrasse 11, 6330 Cham, Switzerland

Preface and Acknowledgments

It is the nature of books with several editors and authors to have a complicated history, one that transcends the solitary studying and writing exercises of scholars. Often, this history starts with a happy episode and thus with contingency, much to historians' taste. In this case, it was a conference in Cologne in May 2013 that brought two of the three editors into their first contact and led them to discover their mutual acquaintance with the third editor. It must have been over a *Koelsch* that the Swiss tax historian recklessly suggested to her American counterpart that they author a common book on taxation. The idea was met with amusement instead of rejection, and quickly induced the co-organization of an international workshop in the bigger Sister Republic's capital. The conference "Taxation for and against Redistribution since 1945: Historical Trajectories and Comparative Outcomes" took place on December 5–6, 2014, and was hosted by the German Historical Institute in Washington DC. The second and third conference, devised to continue our common intellectual project, both took place in Japan. Eisaku Ide and Seiichiro Mozumi from Keio University organized "The Changing Fortune of the Fiscal State" in Odawara from July 31 to August 1, while all three editors jointly organized the panel "Internationalization, Globalization, and their Effects on Taxation and Redistribution in OECD-nations since 1945" at the World Economic History Conference 2015 in Kyoto.

Nine out of the ten authors of this volume were chosen from a larger group of scholars who participated in one or more of these three conferences and who agreed to adapt their contributions to the questions outlined by the editors. We are very grateful for their stimulating discussions and for their commitment to this adventure. Thanks to another happy encounter, this time in Basel in December 2016, the tenth author for the Greek case study was won over, thus strengthening our attention of the often-neglected "Southern rim" of European tax and welfare states. Other than to our authors, we as editors are deeply indebted to Maya Wohlgemuth, who has diligently assisted the production of this volume since the Zurich editorial meeting in February 2017, to Ruth Willats, who meticulously edited several of the chapters and rendered them into fluent English, and to Juri Dossenbach, who lent us his support on our last mile. Their assistance was made possible through the generous sponsoring by the Chair for the History of Technology at ETH Zurich, David Gugerli.

Our thanks, naturally, go to our partners at Palgrave Macmillan, Aimee Dibbens, Tula Weis, Natasha Denby and Ruth Noble as well as to Divya Anish at SPi Global, for making the production of this volume possible and for patiently accompanying our work. We would like to express our thanks to the Keio Economic Society and the MEXT-Supported Program for the Strategic Research Foundation at Private Universities for funding research and conference activities in Japan. And we would like to conclude by thanking Catherine Schenk who, then in Glasgow, now in Oxford, had suggested we should publish in the Palgrave History of Finance series, after another lucky encounter at a conference in Bern in summer 2016.

Zürich, Switzerland	Gisela Huerlimann
Santa Barbara, CA	W. Elliot Brownlee
Tokyo, Japan	Eisaku Ide

Contents

The Political Economy of Taxing, Spending, and Redistribution Since 1945: An Introduction 1
Gisela Huerlimann, W. Elliot Brownlee, and Eisaku Ide

How Employers and Conservatives Shaped the Modern Tax State 17
Alexander Hertel-Fernandez and Cathie Jo Martin

How They All Came to Love the VAT: Consumption Taxes, Big Business, and the Welfare State in Sweden 49
Gunnar Lantz

Working-Class Power and the Taxation of Current Earnings: Danish Pay-As-You-Earn Income Tax in Comparative Perspective 73
Isaac W. Martin

Universalism and Tax Consent in Denmark 99
Shintaro Kurachi

The Powerlessness of Employees in France: The Spread of Income Taxation, 1945–1980 131
Frances M. B. Lynch

Tax Policy in the United States: Was There a "Neo-Liberal" Revolution in the 1970s and 1980s? 155
W. Elliot Brownlee

Tax Reformers' Ideas, the Expenditure-Taxation Nexus, and Comprehensive Tax Reform in the United States, 1961–1986 187
Seiichiro Mozumi

The Rise and Fall of the Industrious State: Why Did Japan's Welfare State Differ from European-Style Models? 217
Eisaku Ide

A Reverse-Functioning System: Japan's Social Security System and Tax Progression in the Early Twenty-First Century 245
Mari Osawa

A Fair Case for Tax Relief: Swiss Tax Policy, 1940s to 1960s 269
Gisela Huerlimann

Unfairness, Inequality, and Tax Evasion: An Analysis of the Distribution of the Tax Burden in Greece, 1955–1989 301
Zoi Pittaki

Limits to Redistribution in Late Democratic Transitions: The Case of Spain 321
Sara Torregrosa Hetland

Index 349

Notes on Contributors

W. Elliot Brownlee is Emeritus Professor of History at the University of California, Santa Barbara. His publications include his award-winning *Federal Taxation in America: A Short History,* Third Edition (2016) and—edited with Eisaku Ide and Yasunori Fukagai—*The Political Economy of Transnational Tax Reform: The Shoup Mission to Japan* (2013). He is about to complete a book on the financing of the First World War in the United States.

Alexander Hertel-Fernandez is Assistant Professor of International and Public Affairs at Columbia University. He studies the political economy of the United States, with an emphasis on the politics of organized interests, especially business and labor, and public policy. His book *Politics at Work* (2018) examines how employers are increasingly recruiting their workers into politics to change elections and policy. He is about to complete a manuscript entitled *State Capture: How Conservative Activists, Big Businesses, and Wealthy Donors Reshaped the American States—and the Nation*, with Oxford University Press.

Gisela Huerlimann is a senior assistant and senior researcher at the ETH Zurich Institute of History, Chair for the History of Technology. Her research and teaching focus on Swiss economic, business and social history in transnational perspective, transportation and mobility, technological innovation, migration, the history of psychiatry and asylums, public finance and social inequality. Her publications on tax history include *Swiss Worlds of Taxation: The Political Economy of Fiscal Federalism and Tax Competition* (edited by Buggeln, Daunton and Nützenadel).

Eisaku Ide is Professor of Economics at Keio University. His publications include (with W. Elliot Brownlee) "Fiscal Policy in Japan and the United States since 1973: Economic Crises, Taxation and Weak Tax Consent," in *The Political Economy of Public Finance: Taxation, State Spending and Debt since the 1970s*, ed. Marc Buggeln et al. (2017), 57–82; (ed. with Gene Park) *Debt and Deficits in Industrialized Democracies* (2015); and (ed. W. Elliot Brownlee and Yasunori Fukagai) *The Political Economy of Transnational Tax Reform: The Shoup Mission to Japan in Historical Context* (2013). He has served on many governmental commissions and committees for agencies of the Japanese government including the Ministry of Finance, the office of the Cabinet, and the Ministry of Internal Affairs and Communication. His current research focuses on the development of the Japanese welfare state in the postwar era.

Shintaro Kurachi is a researcher at the Tokyo Institute for Municipal Research, specializing in public finance. His works on tax and welfare policy in Nordic countries (especially Denmark) include "The interrelationship between the tax policies in Nordic countries: the introduction of dual income taxation in Denmark and Sweden," published in Japanese in *Public Finance after the Comprehensive Reform of Social Security and Tax in Japan* (Yuhikaku, 2014).

Gunnar Lantz is a PhD candidate in Economic History at Umeå University. His doctoral thesis deals with how the expansion of the Swedish welfare state was financed. It includes studies of the policy processes that shaped these fiscal strategies and of how they affected the distribution of tax payments across income levels.

Frances M. B. Lynch is Reader in History at the University of Westminster, London, United Kingdom. She has published extensively on the economic history of France since 1945 and the history of taxation. Her best-known publications are *France and the International Economy from Vichy to the Treaty of Rome* (1997), and "Restoring France: the road to integration," in Alan S. Milward, Frances M.B. Lynch, Ruggero Ranieri, Federico Romero and Vibeke Sørensen, *The Frontier of National Sovereignty. History and Theory, 1945–1992*, First Edition (1993). She has also produced a database with Noam Weingarten, *EuroPTax. Who Pays for the State? The Evolution of Personal Taxation in Post-War Europe, 1958–2007* (UK Data Archive: Study No. 6358).

Cathie Jo Martin is Professor of Political Science at Boston University, President of the Comparative Politics Section of the American Political Science Association (APSA) and former Chair of the Council for European Studies. Her book with Duane Swank, *The Political Construction of Business Interests* (2012), received the APSA Politics and History Book Prize. In 2013–2014, she co-chaired with Jane Mansbridge an APSA presidential task force on political negotiation, which produced *Negotiating Agreement in Politics* (2015). Martin is also the author of *Stuck in Neutral: Business and the Politics of Human Capital Investment Policy* (2000), *Shifting the Burden: The Struggle Over Growth and Corporate Taxation* (1991) and articles in the *American Political Science Review*, *World Politics*, and *British Journal of Political Science* among others. She has held fellowships at the Radcliffe Institute for Advanced Study, the Russell Sage Foundation, and the University of Copenhagen. She holds affiliated professor positions with Southern Danish University and the Copenhagen Business School. She received her PhD from the Massachusetts Institute of Technology in 1987.

Isaac W. Martin is Professor of Sociology at the University of California, San Diego. His books on the political sociology of taxation include the award-winning *The Permanent Tax Revolt: How the Property Tax Transformed American Politics* (2008) and *Rich People's Movements: Grassroots Campaigns to Untax the One Percent* (2013), along with the edited volumes *After the Tax Revolt: California's Proposition 13 Turns 30* (with Jack Citrin, 2009) and *The New Fiscal Sociology: Comparative and Historical Perspectives on Taxation* (with Ajay Mehrotra and Monica Prasad, 2009).

Seiichiro Mozumi teaches economic policy in the Department of Economics at Yokohama National University. He specializes in public finance, social theory of fiscal science, and US fiscal history. His articles appear in several journals and editorial volumes: for example, "The Kennedy–Johnson Tax Cut of 1964, the Defeat of Keynes, and Comprehensive Tax Reform in the United States," *Journal of Policy History*, 30(1) (2018), 25–61.

Mari Osawa specializes in comparative gender analysis of social policies. She holds a PhD in Economics, she is a Professor at the Institute of Social Science, and she serves as Executive Director and Vice President of the University of Tokyo. Mari Osawa is also a member of the Science Council of Japan, and a Mercator Fellow of the Deutsche Forschungsgemeinschaft (DFG). Her English publications include *Social Security in Contemporary Japan, A Comparative Analysis* (2011).

Zoi Pittaki holds a PhD in Economic and Social History from the University of Glasgow. She is an affiliate of the Centre for Business History in Scotland and Graduate Teaching Assistant in Economic and Social History at the University of Glasgow School of Social and Political Sciences. Her research interests include entrepreneurship, business history, institutions, business environment and business ethics.

Sara Torregrosa Hetland is an economic historian and a postdoctoral researcher at Lund University, Sweden. Her main interests are taxation, inequality and political economy. She has worked extensively on Spain and is now analyzing other cases in Europe and Latin America.

List of Figures

How Employers and Conservatives Shaped the Modern Tax State

Fig. 1 The puzzle of tax and welfare systems. Note: Authors' analysis of OECD data. Tax progressivity refers to the concentration coefficient of household taxes (computed in the same way as the Gini coefficient), so that a value of zero means that all groups pay an equal share of taxes. Tax payments based on household surveys 20

Fig. 2 Two models of tax politics. State-building tax politics in countries with industrial and political coordination. Crisis-mobilization tax politics in countries without industrial and political coordination 24

Fig. 3 The persistent legacy of early employer organization on tax progressivity. Note: Authors' analysis of OECD data and Martin and Swank (2012) data. Tax progressivity refers to the concentration coefficient of household taxes (computed in the same way as the Gini coefficient), so that a value of zero means that all groups pay an equal share of taxes. Tax payments based on household surveys 39

How They All Came to Love the VAT: Consumption Taxes, Big Business, and the Welfare State in Sweden

Fig. 1 General consumption tax as a share of total tax revenue, 1960–2010. Source: OECD and Swedish National Accounts 52

Working-Class Power and the Taxation of Current Earnings: Danish Pay-As-You-Earn Income Tax in Comparative Perspective

Fig. 1 Date of adopting PAYE income tax, by participation in World War II and left political power, in 15 developed countries 76

Universalism and Tax Consent in Denmark

Fig. 1 Trends in the tax structure and perceptions in Denmark. Note: The ratio of each question includes the sum of those who answered "strongly agree" and "agree." Source: *Danske vaelggere 1971–2011*; Denmark Statistics 101

Fig. 2 The Danish people's perception of tax burdens and governmental services for immigrants and refugees. Note: The answers are the weighted average between -5 and +5 (0–10 converted). The lower points represent the higher ratio of answers the immigrants tended to receive. (Question: Most people who come to live here work and pay taxes. They also use health and welfare services. Do you think people who come here take out more than they put in or put in more than they take out?). Source: European Social Survey 2002, 2008, 2014 118

The Powerlessness of Employees in France: The Spread of Income Taxation, 1945–1980

Fig. 1 Number of households paying proportional income tax and progressive income tax, 1948–1963. Source: AEF B-1457, Étude présentée par M. André Furst, June 16, 1964 138

Fig. 2 Effective income tax rates paid by a single worker on average earnings in France, the United Kingdom, West Germany, and Italy. Source: Lynch and Weingarten, *EuroPTax* 147

Fig. 3 Effective tax rates paid by different French households. Source: Lynch and Weingarten, *EuroPTax* 148

The Rise and Fall of the Industrious State: Why Did Japan's Welfare State Differ from European-Style Models?

Fig. 1 Social expenditures of GDP for elderly and working generation. Source: OECD stat. "For Elderly" means "Old Age" expenditures in OECD stat of GDP and "For Working Generation" means "Family" "Housing" "Unemployment" "Active Labor Market Programs" of GDP 221

Fig. 2 Rate of developed paddy fields and agricultural working hours. Source: http://www.maff.go.jp/j/wpaper/w_maff/h27/h27_h/trend/part1/chap2/attach/xls/c2_2_00-1.xls 223

Fig. 3 Government expenditures and employment in government in OECD countries in 2015. Source: https://data.oecd.org/gga/general-government-spending.htm, https://doi.org/10.1787/888933532048 225

Fig. 4 Spending on public works and social security in general account and FILP. Source: Chapter 5 "Public Finance," Historical Statistics of Japan 227

A Reverse-Functioning System: Japan's Social Security System and Tax Progression in the Early Twenty-First Century

Fig. 1 Net burden of single parents with two children, 2000–2016. Source: OECD.Stat taxing wages data. Notes: Net burden refers to income tax plus the employer's contribution to social insurance premiums minus social security cash benefits. This figure shows the ratio (percent) of net burden to gross wage income set at 67 percent of average wage 256

Fig. 2 Trends of net burden rates for two-child household, in Japan and Denmark, 2000–2016. Source: OECD.Stat Taxing wages data. Note: Vertical axis: Ratio of net burden to gross wage income 258

Fig. 3 2016 Net burden rates for two-child (single parent, one-earner couple) households. Source: OECD.Stat: Taxing wages data. Note: Vertical axis: Ratio of net burden to gross wage income. Horizontal axis: Gross wage income in percent of average wage 260

A Fair Case for Tax Relief: Swiss Tax Policy, 1940s to 1960s

Fig. 1 "Barrel without bottom?—Tax bill: No". Postcard for the popular referendum vote on the Federal Decree on the Constitutional Reorganization of the Federal Financial Regime, December 6, 1953, designed by Peter Birkhaeuser, Swiss Social Archives Zurich, F Ka-0001-493 277

Fig. 2 Evolution of federal financial statements, 1955–1965. Data: Federal Finance Administration: Financial statements federal, cantonal and local governments, 1938–2007 283

Fig. 3 Evolution of tax burden: workers and employees, 1939–1961. Average tax burden für married men without children in the 10 largest Swiss cities. Data: Bundesamt für Industrie, Gewerbe und Arbeit [BIGA]. "Steuerbelastung des Arbeitseinkommens der Arbeiter und Angestellten 1939–1961." In *Die Volkswirtschaft* 35:5 (May 1962), 231 286

List of Tables

How Employers and Conservatives Shaped the Modern Tax State

Table 1	Hypotheses	21
Table 2	Determinants of national tax systems (1900–2000), no covariates	28
Table 3	Determinants of top income tax rates (1900–2000)	29
Table 4	Determinants of reliance on production and sales taxes (1900–2000)	30
Table 5	Summary statistics for main analysis	40

How They All Came to Love the VAT: Consumption Taxes, Big Business, and the Welfare State in Sweden

Table 1	Causal factors for postwar regressive taxation	53

Universalism and Tax Consent in Denmark

Table 1	The number/percentage of individuals who had experienced adverse social circumstances or who had applied to social services under the Social Assistance Act	113

A Reverse-Functioning System: Japan's Social Security System and Tax Progression in the Early Twenty-First Century

Table 1	Net burden on single-parent/two-child households, 2016	257

A Fair Case for Tax Relief: Swiss Tax Policy, 1940s to 1960s

Table 1	Relative importance of different federal taxes and tax groups for the Swiss federal treasury, 1950	272
Table 2	Evolution of Swiss tax quota, 1915–1970	273

Unfairness, Inequality, and Tax Evasion: An Analysis of the Distribution of the Tax Burden in Greece, 1955–1989

Table 1 Ratio of total special allowances to taxable profits of domestic corporations 306
Table 2 Income tax scale (1955–85) 310
Table 3 Tax rates for incomes up to DRS 1 m 310

Limits to Redistribution in Late Democratic Transitions: The Case of Spain

Table 1 The impact of taxation on inequality in Spain, 1970–1990 326
Table 2 Parties benefiting from the electoral rules, 1977–1986 330
Table 3 Main tax proposals, 1977–1979 331

The Political Economy of Taxing, Spending, and Redistribution Since 1945: An Introduction

Gisela Huerlimann, W. Elliot Brownlee, and Eisaku Ide

The prolonged aftermath of the 2007–2009 financial and fiscal crisis has revealed how crucially tax policy reverberates with the socio-economic structures and the political system of a nation state. Across the industrial economies of the world, governments face growing challenges to their ability to set fiscal policies that fund welfare services and public investment and address the increasing inequality of wealth and income. Examples abound.

G. Huerlimann (✉)
ETH Zurich Institute of History, Zürich, Switzerland
e-mail: huerlimann@history.gess.ethz.ch

W. E. Brownlee
University of California, Santa Barbara, Santa Barbara, CA, USA
e-mail: brownlee@history.ucsb.edu

E. Ide
Keio University, Tokyo, Japan
e-mail: ask_ide@econ.keio.ac.jp

G. Huerlimann et al. (eds.), *Worlds of Taxation*,
Palgrave Studies in the History of Finance,
https://doi.org/10.1007/978-3-319-90263-0_1

In 2014, Japanese citizens chose the kanji (Chinese character) for *zei* (tax) as the one best describing the public mood in a year that saw the first value-added tax (VAT) reform for almost two decades. The tax increase, designed to expand the Japanese welfare state, produced the highest growth rate of consumer prices since 1991 and a large decline in personal consumption. In the United States, many public finance experts suggest that significant tax increases will be necessary for that nation to provide adequate social investment and return public debt to the levels achieved during the late 1990s. Meanwhile, the tax cuts proposed by President Donald Trump and enacted by the Republican Congress in 2018 appear likely to worsen the concentration of income and wealth while increasing deficits. Republicans may then seek to use the deficits to create pressure to shrink domestic spending even further, particularly in the realms of public investment, environmental protection, education, science, and welfare. But intense partisan conflict over fiscal policy seems likely in the 2018 and 2020 elections.

In France, as in the United States, reductions in the corporate tax rate have become the center of controversy. Beginning in 2018, the French Corporate income tax rate will be gradually reduced until it reaches 25 percent in 2022. This reform will be accompanied by other cuts including a reduction in taxes on dividends. The promise of tax cuts for the sake of international competitiveness and in order to relieve the average French household proved controversial during Emanuel Macron's successful presidential campaign in 2017, leaving both the traditional right and left political camps in ruins. The reform includes such divergent measures as a comprehensive flat tax for financial income and a reduced wealth tax for the benefit of the well-off, while the abolition of local property taxes and the reduction of social contributions are intended to "reinforce" the spending power of the working population.

In the United Kingdom, as in the United States, conflicting fiscal currents have disturbed political waters. On the one hand, in 2015 growing uneasiness over the widening income distribution helped to propel Jeremy Corbyn, a stern advocate of a more progressive and redistributive taxation, to the leadership of the British Labour Party. On the other hand, the outcome of the referendum on European Union (EU) membership in 2016 served the conservative camp as an argument for dramatic corporate tax cuts for the sake of fiscal competition. Tax fairness issues are prominent in the post-Brexit tax reform debate: Should the income tax and national insurance contributions be combined to simplify the tax system?

Should a surcharge on investments be introduced again to promote the equal treatment of earnings from investments and wage income, or should a revived Manchester-liberalism promote the neutrality and linearity of taxation? Some of the British reform proposals are, like President Trump's and Macron's tax cuts, devised to meet the challenges of globalization's latest wave.

The purpose of this book is to provide background for understanding of such current debates. We do so by taking an historical and comparative approach to the study of what we call the "Worlds of Taxation."[1] Our specific topic is the comparative history of the fiscal regimes that the so-called advanced nations have employed since World War II. More specifically, the contributors to this volume analyze the way in which these nations have used taxation, spending, and borrowing to balance the sometimes conflicting goals of economic growth, equity, and stability, particularly during periods of economic crisis, and, in the process, often reformed their fiscal systems. They focus on significant episodes of policy history and ask the central question of how choices in fiscal policy have constrained and shackled, but in some instances also expanded, redistribution and social integration during the second half of the twentieth and the early years of the twenty-first centuries.

In studying major shifts in fiscal policy, the authors rely on the theoretical approaches developed by the growing number of interdisciplinary scholars who, beginning in the 1990s, have made significant contributions to fiscal history. Such scholars, often remembering the work of both fiscal sociologists like Rudolph Goldscheid and Joseph Schumpeter and political economists like Richard Musgrave, responded to the call of political scientist and sociologist Theda Skocpol in 1985 for "Bringing the State back in."[2] In so doing, this new generation of fiscal sociologists, political economists, and economic historians has established the comparative fiscal analysis of capitalist welfare regimes as a productive research field. Scholars in this new generation usually concentrated on the fiscal history of a particular nation, most frequently the United States, but virtually all worked within theoretical frameworks based on implicit comparisons across national boundaries.

The pioneering scholars of the generation that took shape during the 1990s included historians Richard Bonney, Patrick K. O'Brien, and W. Mark Ormrod, whose studies of early modern statehood moved beyond Joseph Schumpeter's "tax state" model to incorporate debt finance and thus encompass the crucial linkages between successful national states and financial markets.[3] The political scientist Sven Steinmo innovated by using differences in democratic institutions, particularly electoral structures, to explain national variations in both tax systems and the welfare systems the taxes funded during the twentieth century.[4] At the same time, a group of interdisciplinary scholars associated with the Woodrow Wilson International Center for Scholars took up the analysis of fiscal history as part of a multifaceted program of exploring the historical relationship between the rise of the modern state and the development of social investigation in the United States and Great Britain. In the process, these scholars embraced what one of them, W. Elliot Brownlee, described as a "democratic-institutionalist" approach to explaining fiscal history. Focusing on the United States since 1945, they broadened the approach of institutionalists like Steinmo by paying close attention to the roles of "social learning," changes in economic structure, and historical contingency.[5] This group studied the fiscal dynamics of a welfare state that, like those in other countries, had, beginning in the 1970s, undergone retrenchment and transformation. Subsequently other scholars further broadened and deepened this kind of institutionalist study of the modern welfare state. Martin Daunton, for example, wrote two volumes on British tax history that highlighted the importance of the issues of tax consent and compliance, and connected them with the rise of Thachterism.[6] Monica Prasad, to take another example, studied the rise of free-market policies across four nations in the post-World War II era. She stressed the importance of political structures that led to conflict between labor and capital and between middle-class and poor.[7] By 2009, the vigorous development of historical institutionalism applied to fiscal systems led Isaac W. Martin, Ajay Mehrotra, and Monica Prasad to declare the arrival of a "new fiscal sociology." The occasion of their announcement was the publication of a conceptually rich volume that included essays presenting novel international comparisons.[8]

The declaration that a "new fiscal sociology" had arrived coincided roughly with the Great Recession of 2007–2009. That economic crisis, and the slow recovery which followed, exposed more clearly the limitations of modern welfare states in addressing issues of economic inequality and inequity. The economists Anthony B. Atkinson, Thomas Piketty, and Emmanuel Saez offered historical context for such limitations by suggesting, in Piketty's words, that, contrary to "the magical Kuznets curve theory … the sharp reduction in income inequality that we observe in all the rich countries between 1914 and 1945 was due above all to the world wars and the violent economic and political shocks they entailed."[9] Partly in response to the economic debacle, students of fiscal history turned to placing greater emphasis on the weaknesses and failures of post-World War II welfare states, and to deepening their study of the interactions of taxation and expenditures within fiscal systems. For example, historian Molly Michelmore sought to explain how, since World War II, the interaction of the American tax system with the welfare system through automatic income tax revenues, Social Security taxes, and tax expenditures has reinforced existing social inequalities.[10] Other scholars stressed the success of class interests in resisting taxes, especially progressive taxes, thereby contributing both to increasing concentration of wealth and to meager social provision. Historian Romain D. Huret charted the history of tax resistance in the United States, arguing that its success resulted from the way in which anti-tax ideas have provided cohesion to a diverse conservative movement.[11] Sociologist Isaac W. Martin analyzed how "movement entrepreneurs," over several generations of experience and social learning, discovered how best to mobilize grass roots support on behalf of wealthy clients. Martin provided one possible resolution to the paradox of how the anti-tax wealthy succeeded within a democratic political system.[12] In the latest edition of his fiscal history of the United States, W. Elliot Brownlee suggested that the roots of the fiscal restructuring undertaken by the federal government from the Reagan through the Trump presidencies lie deep in the fiscal regime created during the New Deal and World War II.[13]

The resurgence of scholarship in fiscal history that followed the guideposts of "fiscal sociology," "political economy," and "democratic institutionalism" has enhanced understanding of the nature of the modern state, and its redistributive power or weakness in response to the demands of civil society, party politics, organized interest groups, and the state itself. In this volume, we seek to contribute further to this scholarship and, thereby, enrich contemporary debates over public finance and its linkages to income and wealth inequalities.

Our approach is to develop an array of case studies focused on significant episodes of policy shift in the fiscal history of Denmark, Sweden, France, Greece, Spain, Switzerland, the United States, and Japan, enriched with comparative data referring to other Organisation for Economic Co-operation and Development (OECD) nations such as Norway, Great Britain, and Germany. Thirteen contributors provide these case studies in 12 chapters. They map what we describe as the varieties of fiscal welfarism in the OECD nations (current definition) since 1945.[14] These varieties include, among other elements, reliance on both progressive income taxation and consumption taxes; on social contributions; on finance by debt or inflation; on public works for providing "welfare-through-incomes"; and on tax competition as a means of raising revenue. The authors examine the sources of the policy shifts with the following questions in mind: Which processes of social and political learning can be identified, retrospectively? What weights are given to specific programmatic and ideological commitments of governments, political parties, and interest groups representing consumers, business, and labor? What understanding of tax justice and fairness underlies the tax measures analyzed and their reception by taxpayers? And what were the redistributive outcomes of old and new fiscal and welfare systems?

The first group of essays (second chapter through sixth chapter) analyzes tax policy in those European nations with social compacts that produced universalistic welfare states funded primarily by relatively broad-based taxes, but only moderately progressive tax systems. In the chapter "How Employers and Conservatives Shaped the Modern Tax State," Alexander Hertel-Fernandez and Cathie Jo Martin argue that these nations have been able to maintain such social compacts through strong political institutions for consensual policymaking. These institutions have been those associated with not only multiparty systems, as emphasized by Sven Steinmo, but also corporatist industrial relations, leading business leaders and the right to become largely supportive of revenue expansions. The relative absence of class conflict has permitted significant reforms to happen under politics as usual, in a relatively stable fashion, in response to economic transformations and expanded need for welfare expenditures. In contrast, the authors suggest, a crisis mobilization model of revenue-system development is common in countries with fewer political institutions for consensual policymaking and with intense class conflict. Significant revenue reforms are delayed until crises (usually wars) demand new fiscal instruments; in these instances, business and the right largely oppose social and fiscal policy expansions. This leads to contentious tax politics that aim to "soak the rich" through progressive levies. The authors support their argument with quantitative data from 1900 to 2000 and qualitative case studies of Denmark and the United States.

The third chapter, by Gunnar Lantz, focuses on a key revenue component—the VAT—of the broad-based taxes of the universalistic welfare states. Lantz's chapter, "How They All Came to Love VAT: Consumption Taxes, Big Business, and the Welfare State in Sweden," examines the development of the political strategies of the industrialists who in the

1960s helped build the Swedish tax state by promoting the adoption of a VAT. Lantz argues that in Sweden the goal of establishing a competitive advantage for exports was more important in the adoption of the VAT than the wish for a political union with the European Economic Community (EEC). In the process, Lantz explains the importance of the process of political learning involved in the "corporatist" cooperation between labor and business.

The next two chapters expand the analysis of broad-based taxation in universalistic welfare states. Isaac W. Martin, in the chapter "Working Class Power and the Taxation of Current Earnings: Danish Pay-As-You-Earn Income Tax in Comparative Perspective," explores the nature of tax consent in Denmark. He asks how and why the Danish government accepted the introduction of pay-as-you-earn (PAYE) income taxation in 1967. He provides a comparative analysis of how PAYE income taxation emerged in other European countries (especially Sweden, Norway, and Germany). Particular conditions associated with World War II seem to explain why Denmark was late in introducing PAYE, compared to its Swedish neighbor, but chose to rely more heavily on PAYE taxation than any other continental nation. Isaac Martin concludes that governing power, exercised through the Social Democratic party, was critical for the introduction and diffusion of this policy instrument.

In the chapter "Universalism and Tax Consent in Denmark," Shintaro Kurachi assesses how the strains of the 1970s recession, new populist movements, and socio-demographic change through migration have affected tax consent and a universalistic approach to welfare state benefits. Kurachi finds significant weakening of the social compact that Hertel-Fernandez and Martin posited in the chapter "How Employers and Conservatives Shaped the Modern Tax State." Kurachi examines in detail the fierce tax revolt that began in December 1973, and subsequent passage of the Social Assistance Act, which was designed to renew citizens' confidence by establishing a policy of "local universalism." His essay examines the effects of the 1970s recession and the fiscal consolidation in the 1980s. Despite the fiscal shackles, Denmark expanded social expenditure by introducing general child benefits and a fixed-level benefit in order to decrease the tax burden on families with incomes in the lower-middle range. Kurachi concludes by analyzing fiscal shifts since 1990, exploring the changes in the tax policy that benefitted middle- to high-income groups as compared to those who were long-term unemployed or new immigrants.

The sixth chapter, and the last in this first group, is "The Powerlessness of Employees in France: The Spread of Income Taxation, 1945–1980," by Frances M. B. Lynch. She suggests important comparisons between France and the Scandinavian nations. As Lynch shows, the revenue raised from taxation in France has been among the highest in Europe, in both absolute and per capita terms. This in principle gave the French state considerable power to redistribute income. Yet the ways in which such revenue has been raised have contributed to growing inequality. Since the introduction of income taxation during World War I, the French state has been reluctant to raise revenue from this source, preferring to rely more on indirect taxes and on social security contributions. Furthermore, the pro-natalist policy adopted after 1945 provided considerable fiscal advantages to large wealthy families, thereby adding to the inequality in French society. It was only in the 1970s, largely due to the high rates of inflation, that many people began to pay income taxes and the regressive nature of the fiscal system rose in political salience. Lynch's research on France supports Hertel-Fernandez and Martin's conclusion that employers and conservatives played a crucial role in shaping the tax state.

These five case studies implicitly explore the question of whether or not the western European nations form a useful class for the purpose of comparative analysis. The seven essays that follow expand the "Worlds of Taxation" by assessing the histories of nations that, since World War II, have relied on less ambitious welfare states and more eclectic tax systems. The first four of these seven essays take up the cases of the United States and Japan, two nations with huge economies, relatively low levels of taxation, and arguably the most fragmented welfare states among the largest OECD nations.

In the chapter "Tax Policy in the United States: Was there a "Neoliberal" Revolution in the 1970s and 1980s?," W. Elliot Brownlee argues that the legacy of the fiscal order created during the New Deal and World War II was the ironic combination of a highly progressive tax system and a badly fragmented welfare state. Through a path-dependent process, the progressive income tax hampered movement toward a universalistic welfare state and created powerful incentives for weakening both the progressivity and the breadth of the tax base. As a result of the lack of debate over tax increases, taxpayers lost consciousness of the connection between their taxes and public expenditures. At the same time, the high progressive tax rates produced great incentives for high-income taxpayers to seek tax cuts and contributed to a bipartisan consensus that eschewed further assaults on corporate finance, and embraced tax cutting as a central fiscal policy. Thus, the erosion of both the progressivity of the tax system and the breadth of the welfare state began well before the economic crises of the 1970s and the Reagan tax cuts of 1981. After 1981, the Reagan administration initiated the most significant string of peacetime tax increases in American history, and the increases continued until 1993 during subsequent administrations. However, during the George W. Bush Presidency, the organized "retro-liberal" movement and the Republican Party finally succeeded in introducing a new fiscal regime, and it became even more firmly entrenched during the administration of President Barack Obama. From Reagan through Obama, spending on discretionary domestic programs stagnated, and this stagnation was a more influential factor in the growing concentration of income and wealth than was Republican tax cutting.

The chapter "Tax Reformers' Ideas, the Expenditure–Taxation Nexus, and Comprehensive Tax Reform in the United States, 1961–1986," by Seiichiro Mozumi, continues the discussion of the United States case by analyzing the three leading episodes since World War II in which Congress seriously considered reforms designed to broaden the base of income taxation, as proposed by experts at the Treasury Department and others who wanted to build a more robust fiscal state. Mozumi explores the reasons for the perplexing defeat of comprehensive tax reform in 1964 and 1978, two instances when Democrats controlled the federal government, and its relative success in 1986, when the Republicans and Democrats shared power. Mozumi argues that the Kennedy-Johnson tax cuts in 1964 signaled the priority of supply-side growth stimulation and the 1978 case revealed the rising influence of neo-liberal tax ideas. But in 1986 Treasury economists and tax attorneys found a way to take these ideas into account while achieving tax reform that strengthened the fiscal state. To Mozumi, the 1986 reforms suggest the potential for bipartisan compacts that both broaden the tax base and increase the progressivity of the fiscal system. His essay suggests the wisdom of harboring some optimism about the long-run future of broad-based taxation in the United States.

The next two chapters turn to the case of Japan. Eisaku Ide's essay, "The Rise and Fall of the Industrious State: Why did Japan Differ from European-Style Models?," clarifies the process of establishing Japan's limited welfarism during the era of high economic growth. After World War II, Japanese conservatives, through the Liberal Democratic Party (LDP), embraced the national virtues of hard work and thrift. The government reduced personal income taxation in return for "industrious" labor in urban areas and increased large-scale public works in order to provide work opportunities, particularly in rural areas. The Japanese welfare system, referred to as the "Construction State," developed into an "Industrious State" through a mix of tax cuts, the use of citizens' savings for public spending, and an expansion of work-related social security. In the late 1970s and 1980s, when the government was met with the growing influence of reformist parties, it increased public works spending although its fiscal flexibility became limited. In the 1990s, faced with long-term economic stagnation, the government undertook major income tax reductions while increasing large-scale public works projects to stimulate the economy. This resulted in historic public debt. The subsequent change of course included drastic cuts in both public works projects and social expenditures following neo-liberal ideas. The cuts deepened the economic distress and aroused political discontent. Ide concludes that the exhaustion of the Japanese welfare system, based on employment and the resulting social insurance premiums and savings, has contributed to social instability and the growth of income inequality in Japan.

In the chapter "A Reverse-Functioning System: Japan's Social Security System and Tax Progression in the Early Twenty-first Century," Mari Osawa expands on Ide's discussion by explaining how the safety net in Japan's social security system has been disintegrating in recent years. Since 2008, panels appointed by the Prime Minister have recognized this problem. However, according to Osawa, Prime Minister Shinzo Abe's administration's "Basic Policies for the Economic and Fiscal Management and Reform" ("Basic Policies") have demonstrated that the political will to strengthen the social security's functions is weak. Drawing on state-of-the-art political science and economic analysis of Japan's fiscal and welfare system, Osawa concludes that the Japanese tax and social security system is not merely dysfunctional or deteriorating, but "reverse-functioning." By that, she means that the system exacerbates the problems of social integration it is supposed to address and solve. Thus, her essay presents a critique, based on hard economic and social data, of the approach of the current administration to the disintegration of social cohesion in Japan.

The last group of essays returns to European nations, each with historic and institutional peculiarities that have profoundly shaped its fiscal welfarism. In the chapter "A Fair Case for Tax Relief: Swiss Tax Policy, 1940s to 1960s," Gisela Huerlimann finds in Switzerland the same strong postwar enthusiasm for cutting taxes that was revealed in the case studies on the United States or Japan. Huerlimann focuses on the stabilization of the federalist fiscal agreement. By that she means the permission extended to the federal government, as well as the Swiss cantons, to levy taxes on incomes and earnings, and to couple those taxes with a turnover-style consumption tax, beyond the exceptional times of World War II. Tax relief was first advocated by the left in various cantons in reaction to the surge in the burden that growing taxes and social contributions placed on workers' households in the 1940s. Once adopted by the bourgeois-liberal camp, in the 1950s the tax relief for fairness gospel spread onto the federal stage when Parliament and organized interest groups debated the permanent anchoring of the federal finance regime. The essay shows how the concept of an unfair "fiscal drag" drove demands for tax cuts on the backdrop of a booming economy, how this pressure counteracted the government's attempt to adopt a neo-Keynesian budget policy, and how limiting the federal tax levying capacity in time and scope became the fiscal rationale until the mid-1960s.

The last two essays shed light on the often-neglected situation of nations in Europe's "Southern periphery." In the chapter "Unfairness, Inequality, and Tax Evasion: An Analysis of the Distribution of the Tax Burden in Greece, 1955–1989," Zoi Pittaki offers an explanation for the rampant tax evasion by Greek citizens that captured international attention in the wake of the last economic, fiscal, and debt crisis that destabilized the Greek party system and ultimately led to a radical political change. Pittaki argues that the postwar Greek tax system was skewed against the interests of the salaried middle- and lower income classes, and was therefore perceived as highly unfair. Thus, to many, tax evasion seemed to be a legitimate means of resistance against a system that benefited businesses with tax exemptions for ineffective investments, privileged high-income earners at the expense of farmers and other self-employed, and prioritized regressive indirect taxation. The perception of fiscal inequity was acerbated by the levy of taxes in favor of third parties: organized professional and interest groups with superior political bargaining power. Pittaki links this fiscal malaise with a political landscape plagued with corruption and the lack of democratic control, and not just during the reign of the military junta.

Spain was another OECD country that was hit hard during the economic and debt crisis of 2008–2011. The turmoil translated into severe challenges for the dominant political parties which had alternated in governing the country since its democratic transition. This historic period is the starting point for the closing essay of this volume. The chapter "Limits to Redistribution in Late Democratic Transitions: The Case of Spain," by Sara Torregrosa Hetland, analyzes fiscal policy in the post-Franco transition to democracy and then in the period of full democratization through the 1980s. This contribution enriches the volume by providing a case study of the experience of a nation that attempted to create a welfare state during a process of democratization after the golden age of Western economic growth, and at the time of the second great wave of globalization. The underlying thesis is that the new economic context made it increasingly difficult to develop redistributive policies where they had been absent before. When equalization demands could be democratically expressed, the tax principles of the twentieth century were introduced in Spain. But their full implications could not be completely realized because of economic distress (stagflation and industrial restructuring), increasing capital mobility (especially in the EEC/EU countries), and the newly dominant tax ideas that emphasized incentives for growth and privileges for capital. These challenges to redistributive taxation arrived in different countries roughly at the same time, but caught them at different stages of economic and also political development. Thus, this chapter examines the challenges that new democracies may face as they use fiscal policy to address problems of distribution. The author warns that dictatorships can cast long shadows, undermining trust in the new institutions set up for political representation, and even accentuating the prevailing levels of inequality.

None of the chapters in this volume focuses directly on the fiscal effects of globalization. But no volume on international fiscal history since World War II would be complete without reference to the various waves of globalization since the 1970s. The crises these waves have created or reinforced have challenged established modes of governing and pushed questions of fiscal reform high up the national and transnational policy agenda. Globalization has influenced socio-economic structures such as income distribution, labor market policies, and standards of living, and it has had important effects on political institutions. According to critics of globalization, international business and mobile capital have increasingly influenced national fiscal and redistributive policies, as an expiatory argument or as provable fact. However, the rich historical findings of the contributors to this volume suggest more balanced interpretations, ones that recognize the importance of contingent political, social, and economic developments and, also, historical peculiarities that have resulted in a path-dependent evolution of national fiscal policies. Such variations lead us to think of our case studies as identifying, on the one hand, certain similarities in the modeling of fiscal and welfare regimes but stressing, on the other hand, significantly different, albeit entangled, "Worlds of Taxation." In any case, it remains to be seen whether the ongoing economic globalization, a surging multipolar world order, and proposals for the creation of international fiscal systems by bodies such as the OECD, the EU, or the G7- and G20-group of countries, will alter the nature and scope of fiscal and redistributive policies in the OECD nations. We are confident that the question will be the subject of future research, and we hope that this volume will contribute to that important project.

Notes

1. This term adapts a concept made famous by Gøsta Esping-Andersen, *The Three Worlds of Welfare Capitalism.*
2. In a volume like this one, devoted to the international study of fiscal policy, it is especially important to take note of the influential comparative work by Richard A. Musgrave in his *Fiscal Systems* and elsewhere. For the most influential of Theda Skocpol's invocations, see her "Bringing the State back in: Strategies of Analysis in Current Research."
3. See, for example, Richard Bonney, *Economic Systems and State Finance* and Richard Bonney ed., *The Rise of the Fiscal State in Europe, c.1200–1815.* For the "tax state" model, see Joseph Schumpeter, "The Crisis of the Tax State."
4. Sven Steinmo, *Taxation and Democracy: Swedish, British, and American Approaches to Financing the Modern State.*
5. See W. Elliot Brownlee, ed., *Funding the American State, 1941–1995: The Rise and Fall of the Era of Easy Finance*, especially Brownlee, "Reflections on the History of Taxation." The other contributors to this volume included historians Edward D. Berkowitz, Carolyn C. Jones, and Julian E. Zelizer, political scientist Cathie Jo Martin, and economists Herbert Stein and C. Eugene Steuerle. See, also, W. Elliot Brownlee, *Federal Taxation in America: A Short History*, First Edition; C. Eugene Steuerle, *The Tax Decade: How Taxes Came to Dominate the Public Agenda*; and Julian E. Zelizer, *Taxing America: Wilbur D. Mills, Congress, and the State, 1945–1975.*

6. Martin Daunton, *Trusting Leviathan, The Politics of Taxation in Britain, 1799–1914* and *Just Taxes: The Politics of Taxation in Britain, 1914–1979.*
7. Monica Prasad, *The Politics of Free Markets: The Rise of Neoliberal Economic Policies in Britain, France, Germany, and the United States.*
8. Isaac William Martin, Ajay K. Mehrotra, and Monica Prasad, *The New Fiscal Sociology: Taxation in Comparative Historical Perspective.*
9. See, for example, Anthony B. Atkinson, Thomas Piketty, and Emmanuel Saez, "Top Incomes in the Long Run of History"; Piketty, *Capital in the Twenty-First Century*; and Piketty and Saez, "How Progressive Is the U.S. Federal Tax System: A Historical and International Perspective." The Piketty quote is from *Capital in the Twenty-First Century*, 15. Kuznets's original delineation of his bell-shaped curve was *Shares of Upper Income Groups in Income and Savings.*
10. Molly C. Michelmore, *Tax and Spend: The Welfare State, Tax Politics, and the Limits of American Liberalism.*
11. Romain D. Huret, *American Tax Resisters.* See, also, Nicolas Delalande and Romain Huret, "Tax Resistance: A Global History?"
12. Isaac William Martin, *Rich People's Movements: Grassroots Campaigns to Untax the One Percent.*
13. W. Elliot Brownlee, *Federal Taxation in America: A History*, Third Edition.
14. In using the term "fiscal welfarism" we should acknowledge our debt to Richard Titmuss and his concept of "fiscal welfare." See Richard Titmuss, *Essays on the Welfare State.*

References

Atkinson, Anthony B., Thomas Piketty, and Emmanuel Saez. 2011. Top Incomes in the Long Run of History. *Journal of Economic Literature* 49: 3–17.

Bonney, Richard. 1995. *Economic Systems and State Finance.* Oxford: Clarendon Press.

———, ed. 1999. *The Rise of the Fiscal State in Europe, c.1200–1815.* Oxford: Clarendon Press.

Brownlee, W. Elliot. 1996a. *Federal Taxation in America: A Short History.* 1st ed. Washington, DC and Cambridge: The Wilson Center Press and Cambridge University Press.

———, ed. 1996b. *Funding the American State, 1941–1995: The Rise and Fall of the Era of Easy Finance.* Washington, DC and Cambridge: The Wilson Center Press and Cambridge University Press.

———. 2003. Reflections on the History of Taxation. In *Funding the American State, 1941–1995*, ed. W. Elliot Brownlee, 3–36. New York: Cambridge University Press.

———. 2016. *Federal Taxation in America: A History*. 3rd ed. Cambridge: Cambridge University Press.

Daunton, Martin. 2001. *Trusting Leviathan: The Politics of Taxation in Britain, 1799–1914*. Cambridge: Cambridge University Press.

———. 2002. *Just Taxes: The Politics of Taxation in Britain, 1914–1979*. Cambridge: Cambridge University Press.

Delalande, Nicolas, and Romain Huret. 2013. Tax Resistance: A Global History? *Journal of Policy History* 25 (3): 301–307.

Esping-Andersen, Gøsta. 1990. *The Three Worlds of Welfare Capitalism*. Princeton: Princeton University Press.

Huret, Romain D. 2014. *American Tax Resisters*. Cambridge: Harvard University Press.

Kuznets, Simon. 1953. *Shares of Upper Income Groups in Income and Savings*. Cambridge: National Bureau of Economic Research.

Martin, Cathie Jo. 1991. *Shifting the Burden: The Struggle Over Growth and Corporate Taxation*. Chicago: University of Chicago Press.

Martin, Isaac William. 2013. *Rich People's Movements: Grassroots Campaigns to Untax the One Percent*. Oxford: Oxford University Press.

Martin, Isaac William, Ajay K. Mehrotra, and Monica Prasad, eds. 2009. *The New Fiscal Sociology: Taxation in Comparative Historical Perspective*. Cambridge: Cambridge University Press.

Michelmore, Molly C. 2012. *Tax and Spend: The Welfare State, Tax Politics, and the Limits of American Liberalism*. Philadelphia: University of Pennsylvania Press.

Musgrave, Richard A. 1969. *Fiscal Systems*. New Haven: Yale University Press.

Piketty, Thomas. 2013. *Capital in the Twenty-First Century*. Cambridge: Harvard University Press.

Piketty, Thomas, and Emmanuel Saez. 2007. How Progressive Is the U.S. Federal Tax System? A Historical and International Perspective. *Journal of Economic Perspectives* 21 (7): 1–24.

Prasad, Monica. 2006. *The Politics of Free Markets: The Rise of Neoliberal Economic Policies in Britain, France, Germany, and the United States*. Chicago: University of Chicago.

Schumpeter, Joseph. 1954. The Crisis of the Tax State. In *International Economic Papers: Translations Prepared for the International Economic Association*, ed. Alan T. Peacock et al., 5–38. London: Macmillan.

Skocpol, Theda. 1985. Bringing the State Back In: Strategies of Analysis in Current Research. In *Bringing the State Back In*, ed. Peter B. Evans et al., 3–43. Cambridge: Cambridge University Press.

Steinmo, Sven. 1993. *Taxation and Democracy: Swedish, British, and American Approaches to Financing the Modern State*. New Haven: Yale University Press.

Steuerle, C. Eugene. 1992. *The Tax Decade: How Taxes Came to Dominate the Public Agenda*. Washington, DC: The Urban Institute Press.
Titmuss, Richard. 1969. *Essays on the Welfare State*. London: Unwin University Books.
Zelizer, Julian E. 1998. *Taxing America: Wilbur D. Mills, Congress, and the State, 1945–1975*. Cambridge: Cambridge University Press.

How Employers and Conservatives Shaped the Modern Tax State

Alexander Hertel-Fernandez and Cathie Jo Martin

According to classical works on fiscal policy, societies face a trade-off between equality (favored by the left) and economic growth (favored by the right). Progressive taxation ostensibly embodies this trade-off: politicians may reduce inequality through redistributive taxes, but will wind up distorting economic incentives to work.[1] Paradoxically, however, it is historically left-leaning nations with generous welfare states and low inequality that tax the masses with comparatively regressive income tax bases, high consumption taxes, and low capital taxes. In contrast, liberal countries with high inequality and limited welfare states embrace progressive taxation (until recently), high tax rates on upper-income people, high taxes on capital, and limited consumption taxes.[2]

Our chapter explores the political origins of these paradoxical "mass" versus "class" tax strategies that date back to the early twentieth century and have created path dependencies for subsequent policy reforms with the

A. Hertel-Fernandez (✉)
Columbia University, New York, NY, USA

C. J. Martin
Boston University, Boston, MA, USA
e-mail: cjmartin@bu.edu

G. Huerlimann et al. (eds.), *Worlds of Taxation*,
Palgrave Studies in the History of Finance,
https://doi.org/10.1007/978-3-319-90263-0_2

expansion of modern welfare states.[3] Thus although this volume generally focuses on the postwar period, our contribution reflects on path dependencies established at the beginning of the twentieth century. We suggest that "mass" and "class" tax strategies come from radically different models of revenue policymaking, organized around the logic of *state-building* versus *crisis mobilization*, and each model is associated with distinctive institutional policymaking processes and coalitional bases. A *state-building model* of revenue system development, which produces the mass tax, transpires in countries with strong political institutions for consensual policymaking (corporatist industrial relations and multiparty systems), and includes broad support by business and the right. Muted class conflict permits significant reforms to happen under politics as usual, in response to economic transformations and expanded need for social and fiscal policies. Employers are incorporated collectively into the policymaking process by their strong associations and dedicated business parties, and participate in the design of social and revenue policies. Consequently, they consent to a large revenue base, wield leverage to shift taxes off capital and onto labor, and facilitate the adoption of broad-based, less progressive tax systems and extensive welfare states.

In contrast, a *crisis-mobilization model* of revenue system development, which produces the class tax, occurs in countries with few political institutions for consensual policymaking and, therefore, with intense class conflict. Significant reforms are delayed until crises (namely war) demand new fiscal instruments, contentious tax politics produces "soak the rich" progressive levies, and business and the right largely oppose social and fiscal policy expansions. We employ comparative qualitative and quantitative evidence to support our claims. Quantitative analyses demonstrate that well-organized employers' groups and multiparty systems are both powerful predictors of the distribution of the tax burden from 1900 to 2000 in the advanced economies. Countries with greater employer coordination and multipartism had lower top income tax rates and relied more on regressive production and sales taxes compared to countries with weak industrial relations organizations and majoritarian electoral rules, even when controlling for other social, political, and economic factors. Consistent with our distinction between crisis-mobilization and state-building politics, war mobilization results in increases in the top income tax rates in majoritarian systems, but not in multiparty governments.

Qualitative case studies of the paradigmatic countries of the United States and Denmark illustrate the causal mechanisms by which crucial tax initiatives were created at critical junctures and set historical paths for the postwar evolution of revenue systems. Political coalitions supporting tax reforms were dramatically different in coordinated Denmark and the liberal United States. Strong Danish industrial relations organizations and multipartism nurtured class consensus. In contrast, weak American industrial relations organizations and fierce competition between the two parties encouraged class warfare. Accordingly, the American national tax system was characterized by a relatively progressive income tax bolstered by progressive levies on capital expanded during moments of crisis, especially war mobilization. These conclusions offer several contributions to comparative political economy. First, we engage with burgeoning research on the long-run determinants of tax systems, offering a new set of explanatory factors—centered on the organization of industrial relations and the structure of party systems—that remain underexplored in previous studies.[4] Moreover, we provide insights into the timing of contemporary variation in tax policies, showing that cross-national differences in tax progressivity were already largely established by the 1950s.

Second, we shed light on debates over the "tax-welfare paradox"[5] by revealing similarity in political coalitions undergirding revenue and social spending initiatives. Both tax and welfare systems were shaped by a common set of political coalitions, involving employers and conservatives as the crucial actors. Our work thus contributes to scholarship on the historical evolution of diverse national political economies.[6] Finally, these findings have bearing on practical concerns about the extent to which countries may achieve equality through progressive taxation versus through social investments with welfare state spending. In the face of rapidly rising inequality, especially at the very top of the income distribution, many politicians, policy experts, and pundits have called for more progressive taxes to facilitate greater redistribution.[7] We share these concerns about inequality, but illuminate the political implications of various coalitional patterns. In particular, we show that broad-based taxation historically was accompanied by buy-in from economic elites and conservatives, and permitted equality-enhancing investments in social spending.

Determinants of Tax Regimes

Tax progressivity and total tax take as a proportion of GDP (together with welfare state spending) are strongly inversely related. Thus Denmark and Sweden have relatively low tax progressivity but raise the highest levels of revenue, while Australia and the United States have the most progressive tax systems and raise the least revenue. Figure 1 demonstrates this relationship,

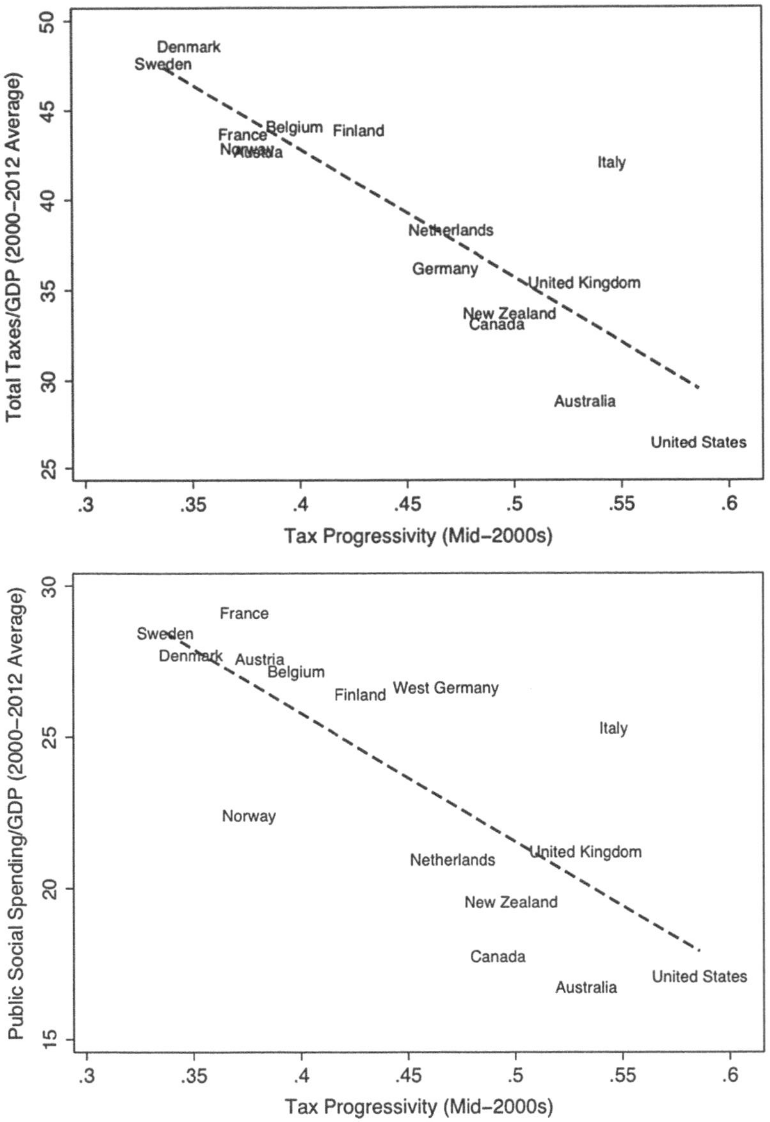

Fig. 1 The puzzle of tax and welfare systems. Note: Authors' analysis of OECD data. Tax progressivity refers to the concentration coefficient of household taxes (computed in the same way as the Gini coefficient), so that a value of zero means that all groups pay an equal share of taxes. Tax payments based on household surveys

showing overall tax progressivity in the mid-2000s plotted against total tax take (upper panel) and public social spending as a share of GDP (lower panel) in the 2000s.[8]

One thus wonders why some countries developed broad-based, somewhat regressive "mass tax" systems (with extensive taxation of labor and consumption, and high levels of revenue), but other countries developed more progressive "class tax" systems (relying on capital and property taxes and having lower levels of revenue). Scholars identify several sets of factors to explain cross-national variation in tax systems, yet most do not anticipate the correlation between high spending levels and somewhat regressive patterns of taxation. Table 1 offers hypotheses based on these causal arguments. First, features of the economy, such as levels of *economic development*, *industrialization*, and *economic openness*, may be associated with preferences for increased revenue levels. GDP growth in industrial economies both allows political leaders to collect higher taxes and motivates state-building to help citizens cope with new social risks.[9] Yet GDP growth addresses levels of revenue, but says little about the composition or progressivity of taxing instruments. Preferences for progressive taxes may rise with industrialization, if rising tensions between agrarian and industrial elites inspire agricultural interests (sometimes with the support of progressive reformers) to shift the tax burden to industry.[10] Economic openness matters, because greater dependence on world markets may motivate politicians to seek alternative revenue sources to tariffs and to taxes on mobile capital. Openness may either dampen enthusiasm for highly progressive tax rates, or spur expanded revenue to fund social protections against risks associated with economic openness.[11] See hypotheses 1, 2, and 3 in Table 1.

Table 1 Hypotheses

Hypothesis #1	Economic development: indeterminate prediction for tax progressivity
Hypothesis #2	Industrialization: greater industrialization will lead to greater tax progressivity
Hypothesis #3	Mass wartime mobilization: greater mass wartime mobilization will lead to greater tax progressivity
Hypothesis #4	Democratization: greater access to the franchise will lead to greater tax progressivity
Hypothesis #5	Power resources: greater control of government by the left will lead to greater tax progressivity
Hypothesis #6	Institutions of economic and political coordination: Stronger institutions of economic and political coordination will lead to lower tax progressivity

Second, *war mobilization* should precipitate rising revenue levels because politicians can capitalize on broad public support for shared sacrifice. For example, the mass mobilization of troops during the World Wars prompted the expansion of US taxes, especially the income tax.[12] Recent research also finds that countries deeply involved in mass military conflicts were more likely to increase the progressivity of their income and estate taxes.[13] See Hypothesis 3 in Table 1. Third, *democratization* and an *expanded franchise* should produce greater demand for public benefits and more revenue; yet these variables do not anticipate our observed pattern. Rather scholars generally surmise that higher levels of democratization should lead to *more rather than less* progressive taxation to satisfy the redistributive preferences of the enlarged electorate.[14] See Hypothesis 4 in Table 1. Fourth, power resources theory similarly suggests that *working class* strength (strongly organized workers and vibrant left parties) produces progressive and redistributive taxation combined with robust social spending.[15] Yet the strong relationship between large welfare states and regressive taxes challenges the expectations of power resources theory. See Hypothesis 5 in Table 1. Finally, important recent fiscal scholarship highlights a crucial requirement of postwar social programs: the need for a robust revenue system. Policymakers recognized that the taxation of the rich was unlikely to reap sufficient revenue for the expansion of social spending after World War II, and turned to new revenue sources, most critically, the value-added tax.[16] The fiscal requisites for the expanding welfare state establish the linkages between large welfare states and broad-based, regressive revenue systems.

We heartily agree with this line of inquiry, yet feel that the story begins earlier and builds on important prewar policy legacies. Although these scholars largely concentrate on postwar reforms, contemporary cross-national patterns of tax progressivity were already well in place by the 1950s. Moreover, these researchers disagree as to whether generous welfare states were made possible by earlier (and unrelated) decisions to institute regressive consumption levies, or whether policymakers chose such tax instruments precisely for their revenue-raising capacities. Additional work is thus required to understand the models of revenue creation that gave rise to different types of revenue *and* social policy regimes. If the strength of labor and the left alone cannot predict the model of progressive spending and regressive taxation, then we must also explore how employers and the right contribute to fiscal regimes.

The Politics of State-Building Versus Crisis Mobilization

We suggest that countries rely on quite different models of revenue development, which we characterize as the *state-building* and *crisis-mobilization* models. These models are associated with distinctive institutional processes for policymaking and incorporate diverse coalitional interests. The state-building model of revenue collection, which produces the mass tax, is associated with consensual political and industrial relations institutions, whereas the crisis-intervention model, which produces the class tax, is associated with more contentious political institutions. The key political institutions shaping the construction of preferences for fiscal policies are political party systems and industrial relations systems. These consensual versus conflictual political institutions incorporate employers and the right differently into the political process and this helps to explain the paradoxical combination of relatively regressive taxation and progressive social spending, or its mirror image. The state-building model of revenue development is more likely found in countries with consensual labor relations organizations and proportional party systems. Conservative parties and their constituent employers have strong incentives to participate in the revenue policymaking process, and enjoy the political leverage to shift much of the tax burden off capital and onto labor and consumption. Figure 2 visualizes this argument, showing the different incentives and access faced by employers and conservative parties in countries with institutions of coordination (top panel) and those without such institutions (bottom panel).

Compared to employers in weakly organized pluralist systems, employers in countries with encompassing business associations and macro-corporatist bargaining systems are more likely to hold preferences for higher levels of social spending and taxation, and to have the political access to realize their preferences. At a basic level, business and labor make a quid pro quo exchange: labor receives higher levels of social spending but in exchange accepts lower taxation of capital, broad-based taxes that lower relative burdens on upper-income taxpayers, and higher consumption taxes.[17] Beyond the logic of quid pro quo exchange, coordinated industrial relations organizations also influence how employers and workers construct their preferences for public policies. In consensual, macro-corporatist industrial relations systems, employers and workers are organized into national, encompassing, and hierarchical peak associations that enjoy the right to present officially the collective business or labor position

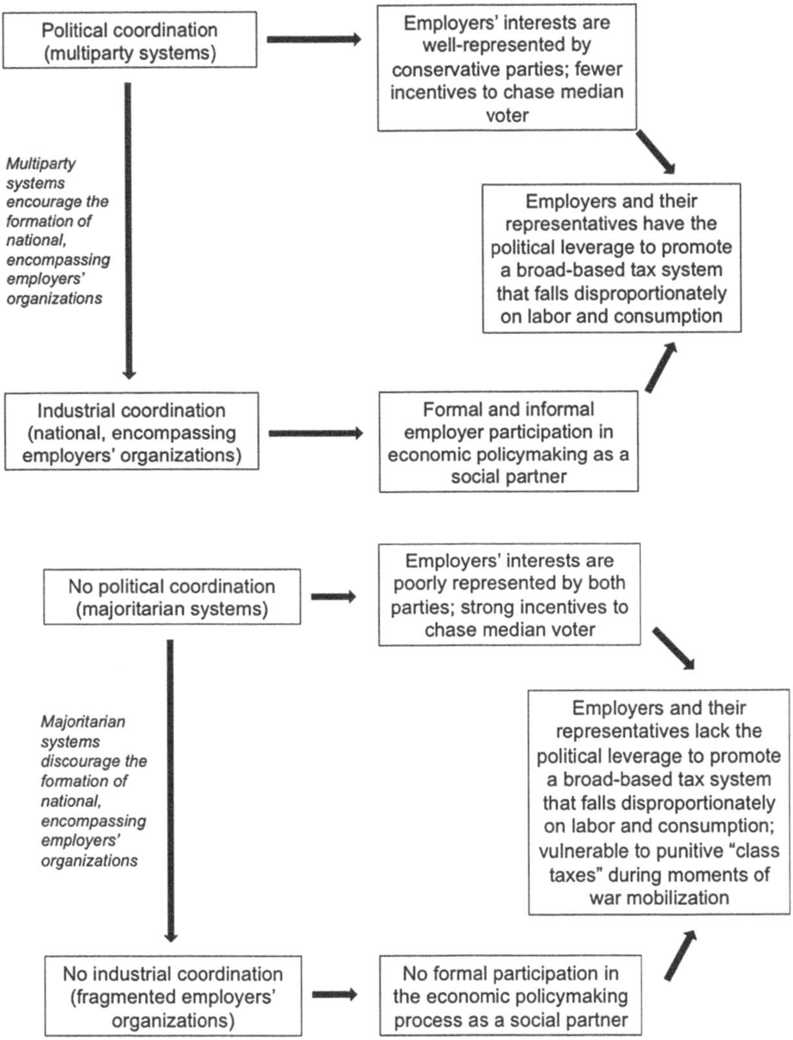

Fig. 2 Two models of tax politics. State-building tax politics in countries with industrial and political coordination. Crisis-mobilization tax politics in countries without industrial and political coordination

on public policy issues. Peak employers' associations and unions actively take part in policy formulation through collective bargaining and tripartite commissions; this brings employers into repeated contact with government and labor policy experts, and increases trust that members will not be punished by the market for supporting human capital investments. This expands employers' feeling of ownership over negotiated policies and augments their tolerance of higher spending levels. In contrast, pluralist organizations found in liberal countries enjoy no monopoly to offer the collective voice of business or labor, rather even the national groups—such as the National Association of Manufacturers and the US Chamber of Commerce—compete for members and influence. Lacking an official, routinized way to engage in policymaking, employers take action more individualistically, often lobby for narrow, sectarian interests, and have limited collective ownership over public policy.[18]

We hypothesize that the well-documented impacts of consensual industrial relations systems on the social partners' preferences for social spending will apply to the politics of revenue collection. Strongly organized employers and workers are more willing to fund policies that they have helped to create, to trust one another and the state, and to pay high taxes in exchange for strong social protections. Both sides accept expert opinion about the long-run benefits for growth of taxing labor and consumption and minimizing taxes on capital and property. Thus, macro-corporatist arrangements also ease productivity pacts combining high taxation of labor and consumption, low taxes on capital, and high spending on social investments and protections. Proportional party systems also increase the likelihood that conservative parties (representing employers) will both support higher overall tax levels and will have the political power to secure broader-based taxes with lower levels of capital taxation, compared to their counterparts in majoritarian, two-party systems. Politicians in proportional, multiparty systems generally represent well-organized economic interests, do not chase the median voter, and participate in coalition governments, and these factors together contribute to their greater willingness to collaborate with other parties and consent to a relatively larger tax take. At the same time, participation in coalition governments in proportional party systems gives conservative parties leverage in policy formation to obtain lower taxes on capital. Finally, proportional multiparty systems are also themselves a significant determinant of strongly organized, macro-corporatist industrial relations systems.[19] In sum, countries with stronger institutions of political and industrial coordination should have more broad-based and less progressive tax regimes in contrast to countries without such institutions. In countries with institutions of coordination, the development of the tax state should occur under consensual politics as usual, in efforts aimed at *state-building*. In contrast, countries without such institutions should rely on moments of *crisis*—especially wartime mobilization—to develop and expand their tax systems and politics should be dominated by intense class and partisan conflict.

The Quantitative Analysis

Our quantitative analysis pools data from 15 advanced industrial countries for the ten decades from 1900 to 2000. These countries include Australia, Canada, Denmark, Finland, France, Ireland, Italy, the Netherlands, New Zealand, Norway, Sweden, Switzerland, the United Kingdom, the United States, and (West) Germany. We examine two outcomes: a country's *Top Income Tax Rate* and *Production and Sales Tax Reliance*. Together, these two variables capture much of the important variation in the design of national tax systems. Top marginal income rates have been used by other scholars to evaluate the demand for tax progressivity, and provide a measure of the degree to which income taxes burden upper-income individuals that is relatively comparable across diverse contexts (although analysts vary in their categorizations).[20] Our data on these top income tax rates come from a variety of sources, beginning with the data collected by Kenneth Scheve and David Stasavage (and for greater detail, please see our technical appendix).[21]

While top income rates provide some sense of the progressivity of a single tax instrument (although effective rates vary across countries), these rates miss the degree to which countries rely more or less on different types of taxes. To measure variation in the *composition* of tax instruments, we examine countries' reliance on production and sales taxes, such as excise, value-added, and sales taxes. Reliance on production and sales taxes is another important determinant of tax progressivity, since such levies generally fall disproportionally on lower-income households. Our data on production and sales tax reliance comes from Peter Flora's volume of cross-national economic statistics, with additional calculations based on data from national statistical agencies and the Organisation for Economic Co-operation and Development (OECD). We operationalize *Production and Sales Tax Reliance* as total tax revenue from production and sales taxes as a share of total central government revenue.[22]

Our main independent variables represent the industrial and political pillars of coordination. *Employer Organization* captures the degree to which firms are mobilized into powerful national peak associations. This variable is a continuous zero to three measure based on three standardized indices, capturing the following aspects of employer organization: whether a country possesses a national and encompassing business organization, the powers held by that peak organization over its members, and the integration of that organization into the policymaking process.[23]

Proportional Representation captures how political coordination in the electoral and party system shapes tax policy. Proportionality is an ordinal variable indicating how votes are translated into seats in the national legislature; 0 indicates a disproportional system; 1 indicates a semi-proportional system; and 2 indicates a proportional representation system.[24]

We also control for various competing explanations set forth in our hypotheses. We use GDP per capita (in 1990 constant dollars) to examine the role of *Economic Development*.[25] To control for the effect of *Economic Openness*, we calculate imports and exports divided by total GDP.[26] To gauge the strength of power resources theory, we include *Left Power*, or the share of votes received by left parties.[27] To test for industrialization, we evaluate the share of the economically active population in the manufacturing sector, *Manufacturing Share of Labor Force*.[28] We use Kenneth Scheve and David Stasavage's variable for *War Mobilization*, a dummy indicating if a country was involved in an interstate war with at least 2 percent of its population mobilized in the military.[29] We indicate the presence of universal *Male Suffrage* with a dummy variable.[30] Lastly, we include a dichotomous measure of *Federalism*.[31] Given limitations on the availability of some variables, the long length of our panel and noisy measurement for several variables, we examine our data at decadal intervals between 1900 and 2000, using averages of the values of each variable throughout each decade. We employ Ordinary least squares (OLS) and compute panel-corrected standard errors, though the results remain similar with other standard error procedures. We include dummies for each decade to account for time-specific shocks to countries that could simultaneously shape tax, electoral, and industrial relations systems.

Because of correlations among the independent variables, we first examine only the relationship between our main explanatory factors (employer organization and electoral proportionality) and tax structure without the covariates (though with the decade effects). As we note below,

Table 2 Determinants of national tax systems (1900–2000), no covariates

	Top income tax rate	*Production and sales tax reliance*
Employer organization	−2.16*	8.31***
	(1.13)	(1.47)
Electoral proportionality	−2.26*	7.13***
	(1.17)	(1.32)

Notes: Table shows the results of four separate regressions. Top values in each cell are OLS coefficients; values in parentheses are panel-corrected standard errors. All four regressions include decade effects. *N* for top income rate models is 111; *N* for production and sales tax models is 104

Panel-corrected standard errors below coefficients

Significance levels: *$p < 0.10$; **$p < 0.05$; ***$p < 0.01$

we find consistent results in both limited and more complete models and this helps to address concerns about the effects of multicollinearity.

Table 2 summarizes the results of these four limited regression models. All four coefficients are signed as expected. Employer organization and electoral proportionality are negatively related to top income tax rates, but positively related to production and sales tax reliance. A move from the minimum to maximum values of employer organization (e.g., from the United States to Denmark) is predicted to reduce a country's top income rate by about 7 percentage points (about a third of a standard deviation), while a move from a disproportional to a proportional representation system is predicted to reduce the top rate by about 5 percentage points (about a fourth of a standard deviation). In contrast, the same shifts are predicted to increase a country's reliance on more broad-based production and sales taxes by 25 percentage points (over one standard deviation) and 14 percentage points (about three-fourths of a standard deviation), respectively.

More complete models, including alternative explanations and potential confounders, yield similar results. Table 3 examines variation in top income tax rates, while Table 4 examines reliance on production and sales taxes. In each table, Models 1 and 2 examine the effects of employer organization and electoral proportionality on tax structures in the same decade, while Models 3 and 4 investigate the effects of these variables on tax structures in the subsequent decade (lagging the dependent variables by one decade).

We find relatively consistent results across all specifications. Greater employer organization and the presence of electoral proportionality lead

Table 3 Determinants of top income tax rates (1900–2000)

	Outcome is top income tax rate			
	Model 1—Same decade	*Model 2—Same decade*	*Model 3—Next decade*	*Model 4—Next decade*
Employer organization	−4.24** (1.76)		−3.49** (1.65)	
Electoral proportionality		−3.34** (1.54)		−2.55* (1.36)
GDP per capita	−0.69 (0.54)	−0.80 (0.54)	−0.11 (0.44)	−0.18 (0.44)
Trade openness	0.06 (0.05)	0.09 (0.06)	0.08** (0.04)	0.10** (0.04)
Left strength	0.13 (0.10)	0.02 (0.08)	0.24*** (0.09)	0.15** (0.07)
War mobilization	−6.51 (5.48)	−4.18 (5.34)	13.08*** (4.21)	15.03*** (4.14)
Manufacturing share of LF	−7.48 (26.89)	−8.35 (26.32)	11.87 (23.70)	13.01 (23.88)
Male suffrage	18.56* (9.72)	20.49** (9.42)	−27.43*** (6.53)	−26.02*** (6.55)
Federalism	1.39 (2.70)	2.50 (2.39)	0.61 (2.38)	1.59 (2.18)
R squared	0.71	0.71	0.66	0.67
Country-decades	108	108	100	100
Decade effects	Yes	Yes	Yes	Yes

Panel-corrected standard errors below OLS coefficients

Significance levels: $*p < 0.10$, $**p < 0.05$, $***p < 0.01$

to lower top income tax rates and a greater reliance on production and sales taxes, both in the short and long run. The results for employer organization indicate that a move from the minimum to maximum levels of organization reduces the top income tax rate by about 11–13 percentage points, while the presence of proportionality reduces the top income tax rate by about 5–7 percentage points. The effects on production and sales tax reliance indicate increases of 26–29 percentage points and 10–12 percentage points, respectively.

We test our prediction that countries without institutions of coordination (proportionality) will rely on moments of crisis to build their tax systems by examining the effect of war mobilization on top income tax

Table 4 Determinants of reliance on production and sales taxes (1900–2000)

	Outcome is production and sales tax reliance			
	Model 1—Same decade	*Model 2—Same decade*	*Model 3—Next decade*	*Model 4—Next decade*
Employer organization	8.71***		9.51***	
	(2.13)		(2.11)	
Electoral proportionality		4.76***		6.16***
		(1.51)		(1.42)
GDP per capita	−0.47	−0.26	−1.07**	−0.98*
	(0.61)	(0.67)	(0.53)	(0.54)
Trade openness	0.12**	0.10*	0.09*	0.05
	(0.05)	(0.06)	(0.05)	(0.05)
Left strength	0.01	0.26**	0.07	0.33***
	(0.13)	(0.10)	(0.12)	(0.09)
War mobilization	−2.03	−6.63	9.43	−1.13
	(8.53)	(8.93)	(13.04)	(16.18)
Manufacturing share of LF	18.31	32.57	8.95	23.16
	(24.01)	(23.35)	(23.12)	(21.02)
Male suffrage	−16.68	−19.45*	−26.57***	−29.57***
	(11.28)	(11.44)	(7.62)	(7.58)
Federalism	4.31	1.47	3.96	1.58
	(2.73)	(2.56)	(2.65)	(2.38)
R squared	0.62	0.59	0.64	0.62
Country-decades	101	101	105	105
Decade effects	Yes	Yes	Yes	Yes

Panel-corrected standard errors below OLS coefficients

Significance levels: *$p < 0.10$, **$p < 0.05$, ***$p < 0.01$

rates in countries with strong institutions of political coordination (PR, multiparty or *Proportional Representation* systems) versus those without such institutions (SMP, majoritarian or *Single Member Plurality* systems). Wartime mobilization *only* leads to higher income tax rates in countries without proportional representation systems.

We find mixed support for our competing hypotheses. Greater trade exposure does not constrain progressivity; rather, it is related to *higher* top income tax rates, although only in subsequent years. In some models, trade openness is also positively related to production and sales taxes reliance, but the effect is not consistent, and is estimated with considerable uncertainty. Male suffrage is positively correlated with top income tax progressivity in the contemporaneous decade, but negatively correlated in the subsequent period, preventing a straightforward interpretation of its effects. Suffrage is also negatively related to production and sales tax reliance, but the estimates are inconsistent across models. War mobilization is related to higher top income tax rates, confirming the work of Kenneth Scheve and David Stasavage, though only in the decade following military mobilization.[32] Having mobilized a large proportion of its population for an interstate war, a country can expect to increase its top income tax rate by 13–15 percentage points over the subsequent decade. War mobilization has no consistent effects on production and sales tax reliance, however. Lastly, we find only modest support for power resource explanations of income tax progressivity. In some specifications (Models 3 and 4 of Table 3), there is a positive correlation between the share of votes received by left-wing parties and top income rates, but this finding is not consistent across Models 1 and 2. Left party strength has no consistent relationship with production and sales tax reliance.

Taxation in Denmark and the United States

Qualitative case studies of Denmark and the United States further illustrate the differences between the state-building and crisis-mobilization models of revenue policymaking.[33] In some ways, these countries—paradigms for coordinated and liberal market economies—created their modern revenue systems in response to similar challenges in the early twentieth century. Tax proposals were motivated in both by shifting economic priorities, and war mobilization prompted similar tax increases. Labor and left-oriented parties supported progressive taxation in both countries. The United States had a much larger domestic economy than Denmark, yet actors in both countries sought alternative sources of revenue to the tariff in the early twentieth century. Employers held similar early preferences for revenue collection: a growing tax burden shared by all social groups, broad-based rates, high reliance on consumption taxes, low corporate rates, and market-supporting tax policies. Yet the countries parted ways in the later reform positions of classes and party coalitions. Danish advances were all legislated during peacetime, and the peak employers' association and right parties joined coalitions supporting income, consumption, and corporate tax reforms. In the United States, the right and left (with their corresponding business and labor constituents) were at loggerheads at each milestone of the emerging tax system.

The Evolution of the Danish Revenue System

Danish legislators created the income tax in 1903 with a top rate of 2.5 percent, and expanded the top marginal rate to 14.5 percent during World War I. In 1922, a Liberal Party government with Conservative support passed a foundational tax law, which codified progressive marginal rates (25 percent for individuals and 15 percent for corporations) and dominated tax law until the late sixties. The act created a significantly lower rate for undistributed corporate profits placed into a dedicated statutory reserve fund for investment capital. The top rate would increase to 50 percent by World War II, and soar to 90 percent after the war; however, from the beginning and in crucial distinction to the United States, the income tax was a mass tax covering nearly all wage earners.[34] Just as important, consumption taxes were an early part of the Danish tax base. Excise taxes were already about a third of the revenue base in the nineteenth century; consumption taxes expanded significantly in the early twentieth century and came to consistently generate a greater share of total central government revenue than income taxes, except for a brief period after World War I.[35] The Danish case gives credence to some alternative hypotheses. Industrialization provided a crucial backdrop to the creation of the new income tax, as participants hoped to reduce both increasingly unpopular tariffs and revenue collected on land, yield, and buildings.[36] Although the crucial acts were passed in peacetime (in 1903 and 1922), Denmark significantly expanded military spending to defend its neutrality during World War I, and the top revenue rate rose to 14.5 percent.[37]

Most crucially, the case demonstrates that the income tax system was created in the spirit of state-building by consensual institutions with cross-class support. Despite its modest beginnings, the broad-based income tax became a crucial source of state revenue for state-building in the early twentieth century. The guiding philosophy behind the income tax was a benefits principle—users of services should bear the costs—and political supporters denied that the measure would enable redistribution. Consensual institutions were essential to the cross-class and cross-party support for the legislation. The income tax's creation in 1903 and expansion in 1922 occurred under the right-oriented Liberal Party leadership with support from the Radical Liberals and Right (subsequently Conservative) Party, which had nearly passed its own income tax in 1898.[38] Right Party constituents supported the income tax to offset taxation of property, to pay for government economic development policies, and to build military capacity. The Liberal Party (representing wealthy farmers), for its part, wanted to curb tariffs and lower land taxes. The encompassing employers' association, the Federation of Danish Employers (DA), also supported the income tax, balanced with a high reliance on consumption taxes, to avoid military cutbacks.[39] Conservative Folk Party politicians and industrialists particularly favored consumption taxes because farmers could not easily avoid these levies. In fact, during the 1903 tax debate, Niels Andersen (the founder of DA and Right party politician) warned that "It will take generations before farmers will understand that taxable income includes bringing in a basket of eggs in from the henhouse or taking sacks of grain to the miller and later baking bread from the flour."[40] This act established a powerful policy legacy for revenue acts in the postwar period: when state-building required additional revenue, cross-class coalitions negotiated the measures within consensual policymaking institutions. Confronted with enormous revenue needs for reconstruction after World War II, government policymakers sought a growth-oriented revenue strategy to meet its somewhat contradictory roster of objectives: to build up inventory, spur consumer demand, promote savings, sustain employment, restrain inflation, increase defense spending, and offset balance of payment deficits.[41] Initially, an income tax surcharge significantly increased the revenue burden of top-income people. While supporting an increased revenue base, the DA deplored the surtax as a "capricious measure," which threatened economic growth and violated principles of equal treatment.[42] The DA therefore called on parliament to form a special commission on corporate taxation.[43]

These fears about the very high income tax levels motivated renewed attention to consumption taxes. Participants across the political spectrum feared that rising taxes on capital and top incomes would distort productive investment and pushed for higher consumption taxes, which reached 63 percent of total tax revenue in 1950–1952. The DA's periodical, *Arbejdsgiveren*, argued that citizens preferred indirect taxes to direct taxes, although tellingly their evidence only applied to upper-income people.[44] A Finance Ministry-led committee, including economists and major industrial relations organizations, produced an influential 1956 government report entitled, "Cooperation Problems in the Danish Political Economy." The report viewed Denmark as falling behind in global exports and risking worsening terms of trade, high unemployment, dangerous inflation, and inadequate investment. The committee found that neither income nor consumption taxes could raise the necessary additional revenue without significant economic distortion and, instead, proposed a "turnover tax" on intermediate goods. The report also urged core stakeholders to cultivate a better-shared understanding of collective goals and proposed a research enterprise to disseminate economic wisdom (Samarbejdsproblemer i Danmarks økonomiske politik). Parties across the political spectrum negotiated closely with one another in the wake of the report, agreeing to limit the direct income tax, to reject tariffs, to protect the revenue base for social and economic needs, and to promote savings and investment. Early versions of the important value-added tax emerged from this committee work.[45] The MOMS tax (comprehensive on all wholesale goods) was legislated in 1967 by a left-dominated government with broad cross-class and multipartisan support. Social Democrats insisted that a measure to withhold income at the source be included in the reform, while the Conservative Party and DA successfully demanded employer representation on the agencies to set tax rules in each industrial sector and a permanent tripartite committee to oversee the implementation of the act, thereby institutionalizing employer participation in future tax policy decisions.[46] Thus Denmark entered the 1970s with the capacity to raise large amounts of revenue through its new system of consumption taxes, which built on a legacy of consensual tax politics and a longstanding tradition of broad-based taxes.

The Evolution of the American Revenue System

Permanent national income taxation in the United States began in 1913 with a top rate of 7 percent, which Congress expanded in 1916 to 15 percent (with additional increases thereafter). The income tax became even more steeply progressive with the New Deal-era Revenue Act of 1935 (the "soak the rich" tax), which created income surtax rates of 75 percent in the top bracket (leading to a total rate of 79 percent) and graduated taxes on corporate income. As in Denmark, the US top tax rate was to rise to 90 percent during World War II, yet it was only comparatively belatedly in 1948 that the class tax—falling on the wealthy—became a mass tax to which most wage earners would contribute. Interestingly, as in Denmark, policymakers also considered expanding consumption taxes in the early twentieth century. Republicans under President Taft considered excise taxes, an inheritance tax, and a small income tax, and subsequently, Congress passed an excise tax on corporate net income and an amendment authorizing the federal government to collect income taxes (thereafter ratified by the states). A national sales tax was first proposed in 1921 to retire the war debt, but was repeatedly rejected. Thus unlike in Denmark, the American early income tax legislation (e.g., in 1916 and 1935) constituted a class tax and consumption taxes were limited at the national level.[47] The American case supports some alternative explanations, too. Dual needs of an industrializing economy and war mobilization clearly drove the development of the income tax, as well as progressivity of that levy. In the early twentieth century, both parties sought revenue alternatives to tariffs, which were particularly burdensome on export-oriented industrial and agricultural sectors. There initially seemed to be some bipartisan support for an income tax; yet this disappeared when President Wilson proposed highly progressive tax legislation and Republicans lobbied instead for a consumption tax. War mobilization also figured heavily in the American story, as the income tax was expanded in 1916 to meet war-induced revenue needs.[48]

Crucially, however, the US case offers strong support for our core hypothesis that the income tax was done under crisis-mobilization conditions through an antagonistic political process with intense class conflict. Unlike Denmark, the United States has no consensual political institutions and few incentives for cross-party and cross-class compromise. In the US majoritarian two-party system, parties were sectionally divided in the late nineteenth century with the Democratic Party dominated by southern agricultural interests and the Republicans dominated by northern manufacturers.[49] Pluralist or highly fragmented employers' associations and unions were quite weak, as they lacked encompassing peak federations to organize constituents' interests collectively. In 1895, employers, inspired by Germany, and with the close collaboration of William McKinley's presidential campaign, sought to form a centralized, peak association to coordinate economy-wide interests, which resulted in the National Association of Manufacturers (NAM). NAM attempted to gain formal powers of representation and self-regulation; however, Democratic legislators rejected these bills and in 1903 NAM was taken over by a strong anti-labor leadership and ended its bid for cooperative labor relations. Labor understandably became more suspicious of organized business after this interlude and class relations became decidedly antagonistic, as they had been before the flirtation with higher levels of cooperation.[50] Lacking political and industrial structures for coordination, tax politics in the United States were fraught with class conflict and this worked against Republican and employers' acceptance of the new revenue measure. Southern agricultural interests formed an alliance with northern Progressives to advocate for the 1916 income tax bill. Democratic agricultural interests sought the income tax to reduce tariffs and to shift the tax burden onto increasingly wealthy manufacturers. Progressive reformers viewed redistributive income taxation as less onerous to the working man than the consumption tax proposed by the Republicans.[51] Because the proposed income tax would fall entirely on upper-income individuals and corporations (unlike the contemporaneous Danish measure), employers railed against the new tax with great vigor. The NAM's official publication viewed the tax measure as part of a larger assault on industry, and the US Chamber of Commerce considered the tax to be a violation of states' rights.[52] Employers preferred consumption taxes and were strong supporters of the national sales tax, proposed first in 1921 to retire war debt. The US Chamber of Commerce visited President Coolidge in October 1923 to request the substitution of war excise taxes with a sales tax.[53] But Democrats opposed the proposed tax because their agricultural constituents were already exempted from the income tax; in like manner, the American Federation of Labor feared that the consumption tax would shift the burden from capital to labor. An alliance of Democrats and Midwestern Republicans defeated the 1921 national sales tax proposals, and similar coalitions stifled tax reforms that would have imposed new federal consumption taxes in 1932 and 1942.[54]

The Revenue Act of 1935, also done under conditions of crisis mobilization, reinforced the spirit of class conflict. Many economists and the Treasury Department favored a Danish-style broad-based system, with tax breaks for the very poor. But this "low-end progressivity" was abandoned in favor of "high-end progressivity" that concentrated the tax burden on the wealthy and corporations.[55] Organized business opposed the tax acts in 1935 and 1936 as punitive and likely to depress economic growth; thus, Roy Osgood wrote in the US Chamber of Commerce publication *Nation's Business* that instead of the sharply progressive income tax structure instituted by the Roosevelt administration, "Business wants taxes which will not retard business stability and … which are sane and rational viewed from the standpoint of their practical application."[56] These early revenue acts created powerful policy legacies for the postwar period: when policymakers sought to mobilize parties and industrial actors against various economic challenges, they met with significant class conflict and lacked consensual policymaking institutions to strike a broader deal to fund the growth of state capacity.[57] As in Denmark, policymakers worried about the tax-distorting impacts of the income tax on productive investment after World War II. Moreover, American policymakers also had serious concerns about unemployment, slow economic growth, balance of payment deficits, and a depleted money supply, which Walter Heller (Chair of the Council of Economic Advisers) described as the "cruel dilemma of economic policy."[58] But whereas Danish parties across the political spectrum converged in support of a non-price distorting consumption tax to fund the revenue needs of the state and encourage investment, American policymakers veered away from expanded consumption taxes (reflecting the earlier rejection of national consumption taxes), and instead embraced tax cuts on top incomes and capital that failed to spur investment or fund the future growth of the public sector. The Kennedy administration responded to economic concerns with two revenue acts. First, the Revenue Act of 1962 created tax expenditures for businesses to spur investment and growth, including the investment tax credit and the accelerated depreciation of assets. Initially proposed reforms to the corporate tax code were abandoned in response to intense lobbying from business, and the final bill was no longer in fiscal balance.[59] The second Kennedy tax bill, the Revenue Act of 1964, was signed into law after the president's death. The initial proposal for across-the-board rate cuts to stimulate economic expansion also included loophole-closing reforms, but these were largely dropped during the legislative process and the administration caved in to business demands for tax reduction aimed at the highest rates.[60]

The legislative histories of these measures illustrate the problems of building cross-class support for tax reform in a context of severe partisan infighting and the absence of an encompassing employer association to organize fragmented and short-sighted business interests. The Democratic administration sought business support for the tax cuts to overcome Republican opposition and gain southern Democratic approval in Congress. But lacking any encompassing employers' association to organize their broad collective interests, business managers remained divided and focused on their own narrow concerns. Many manufacturers, for instance, supported tax reduction as a form of deficit-financed economic stimulus, and Heller reported that 80 percent of a group of business economists favored a substantial tax cut, even if accompanied by a large deficit and increased expenditures.[61] Worried that tax cuts would exacerbate balance of payments deficits, financial interests conversely demanded that rate cuts be concentrated in top brackets (so as to be more favorable to investment) and be conditional on spending reductions. Capital-intensive and labor-intensive sectors benefitted very differently from the investment tax and accelerated depreciation measures, and this exacerbated conflict over the revenue acts.[62]

The United States thus entered the crucial 1970s period poorly equipped to raise new revenue and characterized by a highly contentious tax politics. No expert commission advocated a need for loophole-closing and most such measures were removed from the bills. No broad support for the welfare state motivated corporate participants to widen the revenue base in return for measures limiting the growth of progressive taxation. Instead, income tax reduction within the highest brackets, paradoxically begun by Democratic presidents, served the long-term interests of employers and the right in restraining the growth of the public sector.

Conclusion

Taxation is at the heart of the modern state, yet political scientists remain divided over explanations for why countries have pursued such different means of raising revenue. Especially puzzling is the fact that the countries that have the largest and most redistributive public welfare states rely much more on relatively regressive taxes that fall disproportionately on workers, while countries with the smallest and least redistributive public benefit systems seem to soak the rich. Do regressive taxes lead to generous welfare states, or do canny politicians choose regressive taxes knowing that such levies will bring in substantial amounts of revenue? The answer we offer in this chapter is that *both* generous welfare states and relatively regressive tax systems are found in countries with a state-building model of revenue legislation, whereas limited welfare states and progressive tax systems are found in systems operating under a logic of crisis mobilization. Each of these models is associated with a distinctive set of political institutions and pattern of class engagement. Countries with highly proportional, multiparty political systems and encompassing macro-corporatist employers' organizations tended to implement tax systems dominated by indirect taxes, especially production and sales taxes, as well as relatively less progressive income taxes at the turn of the nineteenth and early twentieth century. As Fig. 3 shows, these patterns have persisted to present day. Thus, countries with a high degree of employer coordination at the turn of the twentieth century to mid-century continue to have relatively less progressive taxes in recent years.

Our quantitative analysis of tax system design confirmed that variables measuring political and industrial coordination were strongly related to countries' choices about income tax progressivity and their reliance on different tax instruments—even after accounting for factors that others

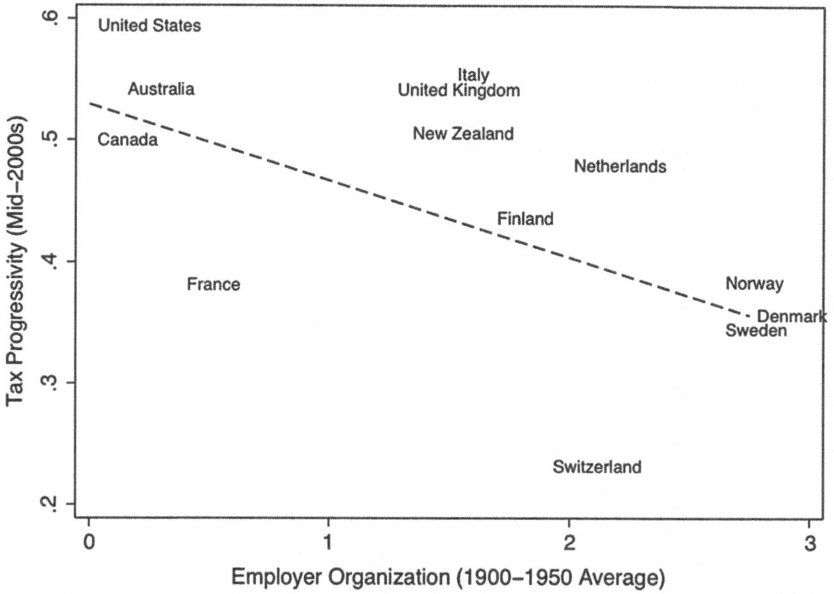

Fig. 3 The persistent legacy of early employer organization on tax progressivity. Note: Authors' analysis of OECD data and Martin and Swank (2012) data. Tax progressivity refers to the concentration coefficient of household taxes (computed in the same way as the Gini coefficient), so that a value of zero means that all groups pay an equal share of taxes. Tax payments based on household surveys

have offered to explain cross-national variation in tax policy. In addition, our case studies spelled out the mechanisms through which greater industrial and political coordination facilitated a consensus around broad-based taxes in Denmark, while weaker coordination in the United States led to a much more contentious and class-based tax politics. In all, this investigation suggests that taxation, an understudied policy area in varieties of capitalism, should be viewed as a crucial—and longstanding—institutional pillar of different systems of capitalism in the advanced economies. Scholars often conclude that the politics of revenue collection are qualitatively different from the politics of spending. For example, a truism about the United States is that direct spending programs are less politically viable than the use of tax expenditures to fund social and economic goals.[63] Our work, however, suggests that coalitions underlying the evolution of taxing policies are quite similar to those undergirding spending choices. Neither tax nor social policies can be viewed in isolation from the political and economic coalitions that characterize different varieties of capitalism. This conclusion has important implications both for how scholars view the tax state, as well as how policymakers and advocates ought to approach the politics of redistribution and taxation.

Technical Appendix

Data Sources for Top Income Tax Rates

For top marginal income tax rates, we started with data from Scheve and Stasavage (2010). These data covered top rates in the United States, the United Kingdom, the Netherlands, Canada, Sweden, and France. We obtained data for Australia and New Zealand from the dataset compiled by Atkinson and Leigh (2010). Data for Denmark was provided by Jakob Engholt Søgaard (from Atkinson and Søgaard 2013). We obtained top rates for Italy from Facundo Alvaredo and Elena Pisano (2010). Data for Belgium's circa 1930 top rate came from Harvard Widener Library's League of Nations Documents (Public Finance Volume, 1929–1935), as did the circa 1920 and 1930 top rates for West Germany and Norway. Data for Belgium's circa 1950 observation was provided by the Belgium Ministry of Finance to the authors. Data for West Germany's circa 1950 top rate was provided to the authors by the German Ministry of Finance. Data for all countries after 1960 are from Piketty, Saez, and Stantcheva 2014.

Table 5 Summary statistics for main analysis

Variable	*Obs.*	*Mean*	*Std. Dev.*	*Min.*	*Max.*
Top income rate	111	50.5	21.2	0	96.8
Production and sales tax reliance	104	33.5	18.6	0	71.3
Employer organization	122	1.6	1.0	0	3
Electoral system	122	1.2	1.0	0	2
GDP per capita	122	11.9	6.6	2.3	30.1
Openness	122	42.3	31.5	2.4	176.1
Left share vote	122	31.5	14.4	0	52.2
War mobilization	120	0.1	0.2	0	1
Manufacturing share LF	121	0.3	0.1	0	0.5
Male suffrage	122	1.0	0.1	0	1
Federalism	122	0.4	0.5	0	1

Source: authors' analysis

Notes

1. Okun, *Equality and Efficiency.*
2. Steinmo, *Taxation and Democracy*; Wilensky, *Rich Democracies*; Kato, *Regressive Taxation*; Lindert, *Growing Public*; Cusack and Beramendi, "Taxing Work"; Ganghof, "Tax Mixes"; Beramendi and Rueda, "Social Democracy Constrained"; Prasad and Deng, "Taxation and the Worlds."
3. For a similar summary of the puzzle focused more on the question of social spending, see Korpi and Palme, "The Paradox of Redistribution."
4. Aidt and Jensen, "Tax Structure, Size of Government"; Flores-Macias and Kreps, "Political Parties at War"; Scheve and Stasavage "Conscription of Mass Wealth," *Taxing the Rich.*
5. Ganghof, "Tax Mixes"; Kato, *Regressive Taxation.*
6. Cusack, Iversen, and Soskice, "Economic Interests and the Origins"; Martin and Swank, *Political Construction of Business Interests.*
7. Perhaps most prominently, see Piketty, *Capital in the Twenty-First Century.* For the consensus on the left for taxing the wealthy as a means of reducing inequality during the 2016 presidential campaign in the United States, see Cohen, "What Could Raising Taxes on the 1% Do?"
8. This data comes from the OECD Income Distribution and Poverty Database. Tax progressivity is measured as the difference between the concentration coefficient of income after transfers but before taxes and the concentration coefficient of income after both taxes and transfers. The definition of taxes includes household taxes and employee social security contributions and is generally from the mid-2000s. Data accessible from https://doi.org/10.1787/421784425386. Despite drawbacks with the OECD measure, studies using different data support this finding. Kenworthy, *Social Democratic America*; Prasad and Deng, "Taxation and the Worlds."
9. Wilensky, *Rich Democracies.*
10. Brownlee, "Wilson and Financing the Modern State"; Prasad, *Land of Too Much.*
11. Bensel, *Sectionalism*; Hays, "Globalization and Capital Taxation"; Rodrik, *Trade, Social Insurance*; Swank and Steinmo, "New Political Economy of Taxation."
12. Flores-Macias and Kreps, "Political Parties at War"; Tilly "Warmaking and Statemaking."
13. Scheve and Stasavage, "Conscription of Wealth," *Taxing the Rich.*
14. Acemoglu and Robinson, *Economic Origins*; Peters, *Politics of Taxation*; but Aidt and Jensen "Tax Structure."
15. Korpi, *Democratic Class Struggle*, but Korpi and Palme, "Paradox of Redistribution."

16. Cusack and Beramendi "Taxing Work"; Ganghof, "Tax Mixes"; Kato, *Regressive Taxation*; Lindert, *Growing Public*; Prasad and Deng, "Taxation and the Worlds"; Steinmo, *Taxation and Democracy*.
17. Beramendi and Rueda, "Social Democracy Constrained."
18. Streeck, *Social Institutions*, 265–84; Martin and Swank, "Does the Organization of Capital Matter?," *Political Construction of Business*; Lindert, *Growing Public*.
19. Martin and Swank, *Political Construction of Business*.
20. Piketty and Saez, "How Progressive"; Scheve and Stasavage, "Conscription of Wealth."
21. Scheve and Stasavage, "Conscription of Wealth."
22. Data from Flora et al., *State, Economy, and Society*, as compiled by Seebohm, "Development of the tax structure."
23. Compiled by Martin and Swank, *Political Construction of Business*.
24. This measure comes from Martin and Swank, "Does the Organization of Capitalism Matter?" and Lijphart, *Patterns of Democracy*. The effective number of political parties as a continuous variable comes from Mackie and Rose, *International Almanac*.
25. Data from Bolt and Zanden, *First Update of the Maddison Project*.
26. Data from Mitchell, *International Historical Statistics*.
27. Data from Mackie and Rose, *International Almanac*.
28. Data from Mitchell, *International Historical Statistics*.
29. Data from Scheve and Stasavage "Conscription of Mass Wealth."
30. Data from Flora et al., *State, Economy, and Society*, as compiled by Seebohm, "Development of the tax structure."
31. Federalism may also shape the demand for redistributive taxes. Obinger, Leibfried, and Castles, *Federalism*.
32. Scheve and Stasavage, "Conscription of Wealth," *Taxing the Rich*.
33. This section draws from material also discussed in Martin, "Labor Market Coordination"; and Martin, *Shifting the Burden*.
34. Udfærdiget gennem Finansministeriet, Lov om Indkomst-og Formueskat til Staten 1922, Rigsdagstidenden for 1921–1922: Folket. Tid. Sp. 2503; Johansen, *Indkomstskatter*, 160–1; Martin "Labor Market Coordination."
35. Glydendals, *Skatter*.
36. Hyldtoft, *Danmarks Økonomiske Historie*, 184–5.
37. Johansen, *Indkomstskatter*, 21–37.
38. The Right Party (later the Conservative Folk Party representing industrialists) and Liberal Party (representing wealthy farmers) anchored the right, and the Social Democrats and Radical Liberals anchored the left. Fearing a loss of power to a labor-farmer coalition, the Right Party helped to form the Federation of Danish Employers (DA) in 1895. Industrial relations

became much more cooperative and employers subsequently became crucial to the evolution of the welfare state. Martin and Swank, Political Construction.

39. Hansen, *Økonomist vækst*, 310; Glydendals, *Skatter*.
40. Johansen, *Indkomstskatter*, 135–6, trans. by Martin.
41. Giltner, "Success of Collaboration," 501; Gersmann, Therkildsen, and Meyer, *Fra Importregulering*.
42. "Efter skatteforliget på rigsdagen"; "Eengangsskatten."
43. "En Henvendelse Vedrørende Forslaget til Skatteudskrivningsloven."
44. Gersmann, Therkildsen, and Meyer, *Fra Importregulering*; "Direkte Eller Indirekte Skatter."
45. Kauffeldt, *Det Konservative Folkepartis*, 115; Fink, *DA i Danmark*, 59–60.
46. "Meroms og skattereform," 14–5; Folketingsårbog, *Lov om almindelig omsætningsafgift*, 77–9.
47. See Martin, "Labor Market Coordination"; Brownlee, "Wilson and Financing," "American Way," *Federal Taxation in America*; Morgan and Prasad, "Federal Taxation"; Thorndike, "Unfair Advantage."
48. Brownlee, "Wilson and Financing," 195–8; Robinson, "Federal Corporation Tax," 693–4; Baack and Ray," Special Interests," 609, 614.
49. Bensel, *Sectionalism and American Political Development*.
50. Martin and Swank, *Political Construction*.
51. Brownlee, "Wilson and Financing," 173–81; Journal of Political Economy, "Washington Notes," 1001; Morgan and Prasad, "Federal Taxation in America"; Mehrotra, "More Mighty Than the Waves of the Sea," 178; Baack and Ray, "Special Interests," 609, 614.
52. Hickey, "Taxation," 11; Nation's Business, "State Income Tax," 1.
53. Nation's Business, "Business Call on Mr. Coolridge," 46.
54. Prasad, *Land of Too Much*, 107.
55. Thorndike, "Unfair Advantage," 29–38.
56. Osgood, "Federal Revenue Policies," 53–4.
57. On class and business backlash to progressive taxation, see especially Martin, *Rich People's Movements*.
58. Heller to JFK 11/28/1961.
59. CQ Press 1962, 478.
60. CQ Press 1964, 518; Mooney, "U.S. Chamber," 1, 47.
61. Heller to JFK, 11/10/1962.
62. Martin, *Shifting the Burden*.
63. Mettler, *The Submerged State*.

References

Acemoglu, Daron, and James A. Robinson. 2009. *Economic Origins of Dictatorship and Democracy*. New York, NY: Cambridge University Press.

Aidt, Toke, and Peter Jensen. 2009. Tax Structure, Size of Government, and the Extension of the Voting Franchise in Western Europe, 1860–1938. *International Tax and Public Finance* 16 (3): 362–394.

Austen-Smith, David, and Jeffrey Banks. 1988. Elections, Coalitions, and Legislative Outcomes. *American Political Science Review* 82 (2): 405–422.

Baack, Bennett D., and Edward John Ray. 1985. Special Interests and the Adoption of the Income Tax in the United States. *The Journal of Economic History* 45 (3): 607–625.

Bensel, Richard Franklin. 1984. *Sectionalism and American Political Development: 1880–1980*. Madison, WI: University of Wisconsin Press.

Beramendi, Pablo, and David Rueda. 2007. Social Democracy Constrained. *British Journal of Political Science* 37 (4): 619–641.

Bolt, Jutta, and Jan Luiten Van Zanden. 2013. The First Update of the Maddison Project; Re-estimating Growth Before 1820. Maddison Project.

Brownlee, Elliott. 1985. Wilson and Financing the Modern State: The Revenue Act of 1916. *Proceedings of the American Philosophical Society* 129 (2): 173–210.

Brownlee, Elliott W. 1989. The American Way. *The Wilson Quarterly* 13 (2): 86–98.

———. 2016. *Federal Taxation in America: A Short History*. New York, NY: Cambridge University Press.

Cohen, Patricia. 2015. What Could Raising Taxes on the 1% Do? Surprising Amounts. *The New York Times*, October 16.

CQ Press. 1962. *Congressional Quarterly Almanac*. Washington, DC: Congressional Quarterly Press.

———. 1964. *Congressional Quarterly Almanac*. Washington, DC: Congressional Quarterly Press.

Cusack, Thomas, and Pablo Beramendi. 2006. Taxing Work. *European Journal of Political Research* 45 (1): 43–73.

Cusack, Thomas R., Torben Iversen, and David Soskice. 2007. Economic Interests and the Origins of Electoral Systems. *American Political Science Review* 101 (3): 373–391.

"Direkte Eller Indirekte Skatter." 7/26/1946. *Arbejdsgiveren* 47 (15): 226.

"Eengangsskatten." 7/26/1946. *Arbejdsgiveren* 47 (15): 226.

"Efter skatteforliget på rigsdagen." 12/1/1950. *Arbejdsgiveren* 51 (23): 337.

"En Henvendelse Vedrørende Forslaget til Skatteudskrivningsloven." 4/1/1949. *Arbejdsgiveren* 50 (7): 87.

Esping-Andersen, Gosta. 1990. *The Three Worlds of Welfare Capitalism*. Princeton, NJ: Princeton University Press.

Faricy, Christopher. 2011. The Politics of Social Policy in America: The Causes and Effects of Indirect versus Direct Social Spending. *Journal of Politics* 73 (1): 74–83.

Fink, Jørgen. 1996. *DA I Danmark*. Copenhagen: DA Forlag.

Flora, Peter, Jens Alber, Richard Eichenberg, Jurgen Kohl, Franz Kraus, Winfried Pfenning, and Kurt Seebohm. 1983. *State, Economy, and Society in Western Europe 1815–1975*. New York, NY: Campus Press.

Flores-Macias, Gustavo A., and Sarah Kreps. 2013. Political Parties at War: A Study of American War Finance, 1789–2010. *American Political Science Review* 107 (4): 833–848.

Folketingsårbog (with Arne Marquard). 1966–1967. *Lov om almindelig omsætningsafgift*. Copenhagen: J.H. Schultz Forlag.

Ganghof, Steffen. 2006a. Tax Mixes and the Size of the Welfare State: Causal Mechanisms and Policy Implications. *Journal of European Social Policy* 11 (1): 360–373.

———. 2006b. Tax Mixes and the Size of the Welfare State: Causal Mechanisms and Policy Implications. *Journal of European Social Policy* 16 (4): 360–373.

Genschel, Philipp, Hanna Lierse, and Laura Seelkopf. 2013. *Autocracy, Democracy and Global Tax Competition*. Presented at the Seminar on the State and Capitalism Since 1800.

Gersmann, Paul, Alf Therkildsen, and Tobiesen Meyer. 1987. *Fra Importregulering Til Moms 1945–1986*. Copenhagen: Toldhistoriesk Selskab.

Giltner, Phil. 2001. The Success of Collaboration: Denmark's Self-Assessment of Its Economic Position After Five Years of Nazi Occupation. *Journal of Contemporary History* 36 (4): 485–506.

Glydendals. n.d. *Skatter, afgifter og andre offentlige indtægter*. Den Store Danske.

Hansen, Svend Aage. 1972. *Økonomisk vækst I Danmark*. Copenhagen: Universitetsforlaget i København.

Hays, Jude C. 2003. Globalization and Capital Taxation in Consensus and Majoritarian Democracies. *World Politics* 56: 79–113.

Heller to JFK. 1961. *The Balance-of-Payments Dilemma*. Presidential Office Files, Box 73, CEA 11/61. JFK Library, November 28.

———. 1962. *Business Views on the Economic Outlook and Tax Cuts*. Presidential office Files, Box 75, CEA 11/7/62-11/14/62, JFK Library, November 10.

Hickey, Michael. 1916. Taxation in Its Relation to Industrial Expansion. *American Industries* XVII (1): 11.

Howard, Christopher. 2007. *The Welfare State Nobody Knows*. Princeton, NJ: Princeton University Press.

Hyldtoft, Ole. 1999. *Danmarks Økonomiske historie 1840–1910*. Aarhus: Systime.

Johansen, Martin. 1985. Arbejderflertallet 1966–1967: Det 'røde' kabinet. *Socialistisk Arbejderavis* 9: 4.

Johansen, Hans Chr. 2007. *Indkomstskatter og offentlig vækst. Dansk skattehistorie*. Vol. VI.

Journal of Political Economy. 1915. Washington Notes. *Journal of Political Economy.* 23 (10): 993–1001.
Kato, Junko. 2003. *Regressive Taxation and the Welfare State: Path Dependence and Policy Diffusion.* New York, NY: Cambridge University Press.
Kauffeldt, Carl. 1966. *Det Konservative Folkepartis Historie I et Halvt Århundrede IV.* Copenhagen: Nyt Nordisk Forlag Arnold Busck.
Kenworthy, Lane. 2014. *Social Democratic America.* New York, NY: Oxford University Press.
Korpi, Walter. 1983. *The Democratic Class Struggle.* London: Routledge Press.
Korpi, Walter, and Joakim Palme. 1998. The Paradox of Redistribution and Strategies of Equality: Welfare State Institutions, Inequality, and Poverty in the Western Countries. *American Sociological Review* 63 (5): 661–687.
Kreuzer, Marcus. 2010. Setting the Rules of the Game. The Choice of Electoral Systems in Advanced Democracies. *American Political Science Review* 104: 269–292.
Lijphart, Arend. 1999. *Patterns of Democracy: Government Forms and Performance in Thirty-Six Countries.* New Haven, CT: Yale University Press.
Lindert, Peter H. 2004. *Growing Public: Social Spending and Economic Growth since the Eighteenth Century.* New York, NY: Cambridge University Press.
Mackie, Thomas T., and Richard Rose. 1981. *The International Almanac of Electoral History.* Strathclyde: University of Strathclyde.
Martin, Cathie Jo. 1991. *Shifting the Burden: The Struggle Over Growth and Corporate Taxation.* Chicago, IL: University of Chicago Press.
Martin, Cathie Jo. 2014. Labor Market Coordination and the Evolution of Tax Regimes. *Socio-Economic Review* 13 (1): 33–54.
Martin, Cathie Jo, and Duane Swank. 2004. Does the Organization of Capital Matter? Employers and Active Labor Market Policy at the National and Firm Levels. *American Political Science Review* 98 (4): 593–611.
———. 2012. *The Political Construction of Business Interests: Coordination, Growth, and Equality.* New York, NY: Cambridge University Press.
Martin, Isaac. 2013. *Rich People's Movements: Grassroots Campaigns to Untax the One Percent.* New York, NY: Oxford University Press.
Martin, Isaac, Ajay Mehrotra, and Monica Prasad, eds. 2009. *The New Fiscal Sociology: Taxation in Comparative and Historical Perspective.* New York, NY: Cambridge University Press.
Mehrotra, Ajay. 2004. More Mighty than the Waves of the Sea: Toilers, Tariffs, and the Income Tax Movement, 1880–1913. *Labor History* 45 (2): 165–198.
"Meroms og skattereform." 7/1/65. *Arbejdsgiveren* 12: 14–5.
Mettler, Suzanne. 2011. *The Submerged State: How Invisible Government Policies Undermine American Democracy.* Chicago, IL: University of Chicago Press.
Mitchell, Brian. 2007. *International Historical Statistics: Europe, 1750–2005.* New York, NY: Palgrave Macmillan.

Mooney, Richard. 1962. U.S. Chamber Asks for Tax Cut Now; Accepts a Deficit. *The New York Times*, June 30.

Morgan, Kimberly J., and Monica Prasad. 2009. Federal Taxation in America: A Short History. *American Journal of Sociology* 114 (5): 1350–1394.

Nation's Business. 1912. The State Income Tax. *Nation's Business* 1 (5): 1.

———. 1923. A Business Call on Mr. Coolridge. *Nation's Business* 11 (11): 46.

Obinger, Herbert, Stephan Leibfried, and Francis Castles. 2005. *Federalism and the Welfare State: New World and European Experiences*. New York, NY: Cambridge University Press.

Okun, Arthur M. 1975. *Equality and Efficiency: The Big Tradeoff*. Washington, DC: The Brookings Institution.

Osgood, Roy. 1936. Federal Revenue Policies. *Nation's Business* 24 (6): 54–55.

Peters, Guy B. 1982. *Politics of Taxation*. New York, NY: Wiley.

Piketty, Thomas. 2014. *Capital in the Twenty-First Century*. Cambridge, MA: Belknap Press.

Piketty, Thomas, and Emmanuel Saez. 2007. How Progressive Is the U.S. Federal Tax System? A Historical and International Perspective. *Journal of Economic Perspectives* 21 (1): 3–24.

Prasad, Monica. 2012. *The Land of Too Much: American Abundance and the Paradox of Poverty*. Cambridge, MA: Harvard University Press.

Prasad, Monica, and Yingying Deng. 2009. Taxation and the Worlds of Welfare. *Socioeconomic Review* 7 (3): 431–457.

Robinson, Maurice. 1911. The Federal Corporation Tax. *The American Economic Review* 1 (4): 691–723.

Rodrik, Dani. 1997. *Trade, Social Insurance, and the Limits to Globalization*. Cambridge, MA: National Bureau of Economic Research.

Rogowski, Ronald. 1987. Trade and the Variety of Democratic Institutions. *International Organization* 41: 203–223.

Samarbejdsproblemer i Danmarks økonomiske politik. 1955. Rapport fra Formandskabet for det af Finansministeren den 14.12.1955 i henhold til Folketingsbeslutning af 25.11.1955 nedsatte udvalg. http://docplayer.dk/7971469-Samarbejdsproblemer-i-danmarks-oekonomiske-politik.html. Accessed 20 Feb 2018.

Scheve, Kenneth, and David Stasavage. 2010. The Conscription of Wealth: Mass Warfare and the Demand for Progressive Taxation. *International Organization* 64 (4): 529–561.

———. 2016. *Taxing the Rich: A History of Fiscal Fairness in the United States and Europe*. Princeton: Princeton University Press.

Seebohm, Kurt. 2009 [1983]. Development of the Tax-Structure in Western European Countries 1815 to 1875. GESIS Data Archive, Cologne.

Steinmo, Sven. 1993. *Taxation and Democracy: Swedish, British, and American Approaches to Financing the Modern State*. New Haven, CT: Yale University.

Streeck, Wolfgang. 1992. *Social Institutions and Economic Performance*. Beverly Hills, CA: Sage Press.

Swank, Duane. 2013. Comparative Political Parties Dataset: Electoral, Legislative, and Government Strength of Political Parties by Ideological Group in 21 Capitalist Democracies, 1950–2011. http://www.marquette.edu/polisci/documents/PARTY19502011.xls. Accessed 5 Jan 2014.

Swank, Duane, and Sven Steinmo. 2002. The New Political Economy of Taxation in Advanced Capitalist Democracies. *American Journal of Political Science* 46 (3): 642–655.

Thorndike, Joseph. 2009. 'The Unfair Advantage of the Few': The New Deal Origins of Soak the Rich Taxation. In *The New Fiscal Sociology: Taxation in Comparative and Historical Perspective*, ed. Isaac Martin, Ajay Mehrotra, and Monica Prasad, 29–47. New York, NY: Cambridge University Press.

Tilly, Charles. 1985. Warmaking and Statemaking as Organized Crime. In *Bringing the State Back In*. New York, NY: Cambridge University Press.

Udfærdiget gennem Finansministeriet. Lov om Indkomst- og Formueskat til Staten. 1922. Se Rigsdagstidenden for 1921–22: Folket. Tid. Sp. 2503, 2766; Landst. Tid. Sp. –, –; Till. A. Sp. 3111; Till. B. 669, –; Till. C. Sp. –, –. https://www.retsinformation.dk/Forms/r0710.aspx?id=63303. Accessed 2 Feb 2018.

Wilensky, Harold L. 2002. *Rich Democracies: Political Economy, Public Policy, and Performance*. Berkeley, CA: University of California Press.

How They All Came to Love the VAT: Consumption Taxes, Big Business, and the Welfare State in Sweden

Gunnar Lantz

The most extensive welfare states, according to a number of studies, have been financed by taking a considerable percentage of their revenue from the lower- and middle-income strata.[1] Somewhat counterintuitively, nations with smaller welfare states have tended to rely relatively more on progressive income taxation. In Peter Lindert's explanation to how Sweden managed to combine a high tax levy with strong economic growth, the value-added tax (VAT) has a central role. This chapter traces the roots of this fiscal solution. In an analysis of documents from the policy process, the role of welfare state formation, business–labor agreements, and influences from international processes are evaluated. The main conclusion is that broad taxes on consumption were a purposeful component of Swedish social democratic policy for achieving a comprehensive welfare state. Resistance was answered with promises of compensation for low-income households. Right-wing and business groups continuously appealed

G. Lantz (✉)
Department of Geography and Economic History, Umeå University, Umeå, Sweden
e-mail: gunnar.lantz@umu.se

G. Huerlimann et al. (eds.), *Worlds of Taxation*, Palgrave Studies in the History of Finance,
https://doi.org/10.1007/978-3-319-90263-0_3

for reliefs from this new charge on companies' inputs and this had a pivotal role in the subsequent transition from sales tax to VAT. This chapter refutes the notion that the direct influence of international organizations is the principal explanation for this transition. Appeals from the Swedish business community about keeping up with international competition are given more weight.

Overall, a generally negative attitude on the part of policymakers to consumption taxes changed during the 1960s. The political left began to reframe the general consumption tax as indispensable for public welfare and equitable policy, whereas the center-right reframed it as indispensable for lowering direct taxation and reducing progressivity. This laid the groundwork for repeated increases of VAT rates throughout the postwar period.

First, the historical context and main events are summarized. The next section elaborates on causal explanations given in previous analyses. This is followed by a section on the procedure for evaluating the potential explanatory factors by studying documents related to the policy process. The results are incorporated into an account of the processes concerning general taxes on consumption in postwar Sweden. A discussion of the findings concludes this chapter.

An Era of Transformation

The rapid economic growth and expansion of public welfare that began in the middle of the twentieth century increasingly seem like remarkable exceptions in human history. Economic gains began to be channeled into much of society, instead of only to a minority elite. Many western countries experienced this to some degree, but one group stood out in terms of performance in both these areas. These were countries marked by corporatism, labor market coordination and a political dominance of social democratic parties.

Several reasons have been proposed to explain how their fiscal structure was formulated and what consequences it had in terms of welfare and growth. These concern the mobilization of interest groups, the structure of political institutions, capital mobility, pressure from supranational organizations, and economic efficiency, among other aspects.[2] According to Lindert, the Nordic countries managed to combine growth with high taxation and public welfare by taxing lower-income earners comparatively harder than in other countries. Allegedly, this allowed incentives for economic advancement to remain intact. Lindert takes Sweden as a representative of this group as it offers an extreme example of this policy. The question that remains is: How did it get there? Swedish postwar politics was dominated by a strong labor movement, which would want to tax its own constituency as lightly as possible.

The first step in this direction was the adoption of a sales tax during World War II as an extraordinary measure.[3] It was heavily criticized and consequently repealed a few years after the war. The left opposed the tax because it increased the price of goods that workers and poor people spent a large fraction of their income on. The right opposed it because it added to business costs. The social democratic government's general direction for tax policy at this point was to consolidate progressive direct taxation. The Communists had gained ground in the most recent elections, and in general support for a radical stance was strong in the labor movement. Toward the end of the 1950s, the Social Democrats achieved a major feat in pushing through an earnings-related supplement to the public pension, which transformed this benefit into something far more than the last resort for the destitute. The Liberals had lost ground in the 1958 parliamentary elections following a public debate dominated by the pension issue, which indicated that there was some support among professionals and middle-class voters for the reform. At the same time, the controversial general sales tax returned to the agenda. After a dramatic turn of events in 1959, when the prime minister declared that the government would resign if they lost the vote, the Communists abstained and allowed a general sales tax to come into effect. Despite initial broad opposition, the rate increased sharply in the years that followed from 4 percent in 1960 to 10 percent in 1968, and the sales tax was replaced by VAT at the same rate in the following year at the initiative of a social democratic minority government. Its share of public revenue rose accordingly and continued to do so after this first formative period (see Fig. 1).

Common Explanations for Postwar Regressive Taxation

The major studies of these developments have focused on one or more of the following factors: How interests were organized; how the political system offered incentives; and the role of economic forces, such as the timing of tax reforms in relation to when severe budget deficits first appeared. Studies covering other postwar social democracies, or advanced

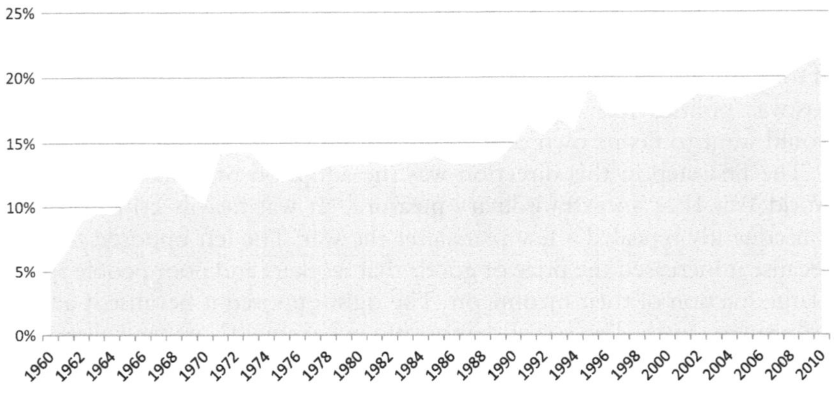

Fig. 1 General consumption tax as a share of total tax revenue, 1960–2010. Source: OECD and Swedish National Accounts

industrial countries more generally, emphasize other factors, such as international relations, economic efficiency, technocratic rationality, and the risk of capital flight. Table 1 organizes these factors according to the meta-categories of institutional versus economic on one axis, and domestic versus international on the other. Earlier studies differ in terms of where on this matrix they place their emphasis.

The first type of explanation frames tax reform as a struggle between interest groups at the domestic level. In his detailed work on Swedish tax politics, Nils Elvander emphasizes how parties and interest organizations interacted to form policy.[4] The underlying notion is that they had considerable room for maneuver and that causality was mainly endogenous to the actors. An extreme version of this position is the partisan approach, which attributes total control to the political group in power at a given point in time.[5] A criticism that could be raised is that generally there are constraints on the agency of governments, such as the division of power, exogenous pressure, and institutional inertia.

This perspective undoubtedly has some relevance, as the domestic actors who formulated economic policy had a direct influence on the minutiae of the decisions taken. However, what is lacking is a conceptualization of the conditions and structures within which these organizations and individuals operated. The comparative literature has moved the spotlight to illuminate how such structural features constrain or

Table 1 Causal factors for postwar regressive taxation

	Institutional factors	*Economic factors and exogenous shocks*
Domestic	Organization of interests Political structure Corporatism as a constraint	Economic development Wars and other crises The efficiency of a tax Growth impossible to combine with a high-tax welfare state without VAT
International	Supranational organizations Inspiration from options tested in other countries	Capital mobility Competition in international markets

favor these organizations and political parties, which makes the question more complex than merely the political weight of labor versus capital. As Sven Steinmo points out, the Nordic countries were not the only ones where labor movements exerted influence, but there it led to a universal welfare state.[6] Similar interest groups and parties could be found in the other industrialized democracies. Although not as strong, they still worked in the same direction. For Steinmo, the main factor that explains the differences between Sweden and the Anglo-Saxon countries is the character of the structure for exercising political decision-making. The electoral process in the Swedish parliament, where seats were divided proportionally according to the election results, meant that no single party was likely to form the majority. This resulted in incentives for negotiation and compromise between the political parties compared to political systems like those found in the United Kingdom, which promoted majority rule, or in the United States with its decisive division of power.

What the emphasis on political structure cannot tell us is why change occurs. That approach is valuable for comparing economies that correspond in some respects but show different outcomes. However, it does not help us explain why a country with a given political system abruptly switches path even when nothing has changed in the structure of this system. An example of incorporating both structural aspects and notions of group agency is Cathie Jo Martin's study of the role of employer organization in forming public welfare and regressive taxation regimes.[7]

Economic Forces and Constraints

An alternative position is to emphasize factors that arise outside of domestic politics: economic development, war, crises, or international processes.[8] One example is Enrique Rodriguez, who in his study of taxation in Sweden sets out to arrive at a general explanation of what drives the expansion of public revenue.[9] His principal conclusion is that the ambitions of government activity determine how much revenue is raised in the long run. This ambition in turn is constrained by citizens' willingness to pay. The factors that decide change include crises, economic shocks, and changes in citizens' demands. His focus on the importance of crises can, however, be contrasted with Hertel-Fernandez and Martin's chapter "How Employers and Conservatives Shaped the Modern Tax State" of this volume. They show that crisis mobilization has greater weight in countries where institutions are more fragmented and organizations less coordinated, which would make this mechanism relatively less important in postwar Sweden.

Rodriguez favors pragmatism as the other main component of his explanatory model. He argues that changes in the structure of the tax system and the levels of individual taxes are decided independently of the total level. According to Rodriguez, policymakers treat this as a technical problem and tend to favor the option that yields the most revenue with the least taxpayer resistance.

Junko Kato likewise departs from the focus on partisanship and ideological preference. According to Kato, the key factor that explains why some industrial democracies managed to build an extensive welfare state supported by regressive taxes while others did not is timing. It comes down to whether these taxes were introduced before or after the chronic budget deficits that first appeared in the 1970s and continued thereafter. Kato argues that her comparison between Sweden and France "demonstrates that the very early institutionalization of the VAT, regardless of policy makers' original intentions, led to the same result in two countries with a distinct tradition of government partisanship."[10] Japan adopted VAT in 1989, two decades later than Sweden. Since then, attempts to increase the rate have been met with mass protests and difficulties in carrying it through. In the United States, it has never been possible to overcome resistance to a national VAT. Sales taxes are levied at the state and local levels, but differ considerably in terms of rate and design.

This explanation is in line with Rodriguez's claims about the role of pragmatism, citizens' attitude, and exogenous events such as the unexpected series of budget deficits, which the architects of tax systems have to adapt to and counter. If the willingness to pay is low, any such attempts will fail. Taxpayers' unwillingness to pay might be mitigated if taxes are less visible and more automatic, such as employers' social security contributions and consumption taxes. It is more likely that a government will be able to introduce taxes such as these during a period of prosperity and optimism about the future than when stagnation and budget deficits are experienced.

Technocracy and the Role of Supranational Organizations

An alternative account holds that there was a technocratic logic to the expansion of a generalized consumption tax in Sweden. After an initial struggle, everyone involved settled for going further in the same direction simply because they realized that it was the best and most efficient option. A view of technocratic rationalism as the key factor became widespread, according to Kathryn James, because the International Monetary Fund (IMF) and other organizations actively promoted it.[11] This "conventional" approach, as James calls it, attributes the spread of VAT to policymakers and experts jointly developing a view of this tax as a useful tool; it succeeded simply because it was superior. There is a certain degree of determinism in this explanation, at least concerning the possibility of influencing events at the domestic level. Steinmo and Elvander express this view to some extent when explaining the developments after the introduction of the general sales tax.[12]

Another interpretation stresses that international relations—in particular the dawning economic cooperation in Europe—obliged all countries in this sphere to adopt VAT.[13] This explanation is challenged by Frances Lynch, who does not identify a direct link between decisions at the European level and implementation in the respective countries.[14] James connects this to her critique of the conventional approach and highlights the resistance found at the political level below the European Economic Community (EEC):

> This resistance to reform, at a minimum, shows that the good is not self-evident to all actors in the policy process—a point that requires further exploration, not diminution. However, rather than explore these and other issues that draw on the VAT's rise, and subsequent resistance, the conventional approach ignores and minimizes them.[15]

In conclusion, there appears to have been a link between the supranational and the national. A desire to synchronize taxation of trade in Europe is expressed in the 1957 Treaty of Rome which established the EEC, but to what extent this mattered for the individual countries is open to debate.

Necessary for Public Welfare?

A common argument is that regressive taxation was central to constructing the Swedish welfare state. Steinmo was one of the first to develop this idea in the early 1990s.[16] The established view of earlier decades had been to associate Sweden with exceptionally progressive taxation of income. Kato continued this investigation and concluded that regressive taxation was necessary for the construction of the welfare state. Lindert focused on the question of what enabled Sweden to combine high economic growth with a high tax levy. His answer is that regressive taxes, such as VAT, have contributed to a tax mix that is compatible with growth, even at high tax-to-GDP ratios. This argument was quite influential, but did not go unchallenged.

Steffen Ganghof criticized the idea that consumption taxes and social security contributions in themselves are necessary for the construction of a welfare state.[17] According to him, the mechanism of interest is that they allow for a lower taxation of capital. This is useful for minimizing the risk of capital flight. According to Ganghof, a state aiming for a high tax levy will find it difficult to extract a large percentage from capital owners. To avoid flight while maintaining a high aggregate level of revenue it needs to rely heavily on capital-friendly taxes such as VAT and social security contributions. Pablo Beramendi and David Rueda propose that, for labor parties, regressive taxes were an important, but not an indispensable, solution to the problem of how to finance a generous welfare state, thus relativizing Kato's claims.[18] Their conclusion is that the postwar era's corporatist agreement between labor and employers imposed a constraint on the possibility of decreasing regressive taxes, as the business community opposed any increase of taxes on wealth, high incomes, and corporations. Beramendi and Rueda argue that, as a result, countries with a low degree of corporatism have more fiscal options open to labor parties.

A weak spot in their explanatory model is that it implies a counterfactual scenario where social democracy and corporatist institutions were not intertwined. In their literature overview, on the other hand, Beramendi and Rueda acknowledge that the historical roots of this institutional setting are usually associated with left-wing governments. Their main point, however, is not to criticize Kato's historical analysis but her normative implication that regressive taxes will remain necessary to expand and maintain the welfare state. Beramendi and Rueda's alternative view is that after a weakening of the corporatist agreement in traditional social democracies starting in the late 1980s, their labor governments are unconstrained and can finance public welfare with other taxes. This could be countered with Ganghof's argument that the main constraint is capital mobility, which means that a high tax ratio will continue to require regressive taxes regardless of the extent of business–labor agreement.

How to Evaluate the Potential Explanatory Factors

In conclusion, early explanations of postwar reform for regressive taxation cover factors that can be roughly categorized within the four-field matrix shown in Table 1. We find institutionalist approaches that focus on the political system versus those that dwell on economic and other factors exogenous to the legislative process. The other division is between the domestic and the international levels. The following analysis of parliamentary sources focuses on the main tensions between the different modes of explanation. An evaluation of how these apply to Sweden's significant reliance on general consumption taxes for welfare funding forms the basis of the analysis.

In order to make this concrete and investigable, the explanatory factors are narrowed down to a set of key topics, terms, and types of arguments. These are analyzed as they appear in statements made by politicians, stakeholders, and experts. A first category contains arguments that promote the interests of low-income earners and workers versus the interests of capital owners, high-income earners, and businesses when discussing motives for supporting or opposing a reform. These include welfare state expansion and social policy on the one hand, and arguments about business conditions and limiting the taxation of high incomes and wealth on the other. The second category concerns statements that attempt to define what must be done and what the limits to action are. This is intended to capture not only the labor–capital dimension, but aspects in all the fields shown in Table 1 including technocracy, economic factors, and international influences. The third category comprises all other types of reference to international developments in the debate on generalized consumption taxes.

Before moving on to this analysis, an introduction to the parliamentary sources is apposite. The role of the policy actors is highly contingent on the context of the country in this era. For this reason, some background data are given next.

A Corporatist Legislative Process

The Social Democrats and the labor movement in general dominated the Swedish political scene from the late 1930s to the end of the 1960s. The main opposition consisted of the Conservatives and the Liberals.[19] The Agrarians were part of coalitions formed on both sides. The Social Democrats occupied the main position in all governments in this period. Sometimes they were able to form a government on their own; at other times they formed a coalition with other parties. They rarely had a parliamentary majority; instead, there was either a social democratic minority government, tacitly supported by the Communists, or a coalition between the Social Democrats and the Agrarians. An exception came in 1968 when Sweden briefly experienced social democratic majority rule.

A distinctive feature of Swedish and, from a broader perspective, Scandinavian politics in this period was the central role of national labor market organizations.[20] The most important representative of labor in Sweden, the LO (Confederation of Trade Unions), was closely linked to the Social Democrats. The corresponding organization for employers was the SAF (Swedish Employers' Association). Much of the responsibility for minimum wage levels and worker safety regulations had been left to these organizations to determine through negotiation, without government intervention. It was customary for governments to ask them, and a wide range of other stakeholders, for their opinions during an official commission of inquiry preparing new legislation. The government was expected to take their input into consideration before presenting a bill on the topic in question.

The official documents from the tax policy process contain statements from all these spheres. The main sources studied here are documents produced by the tax committee (*Bevillningsutskottet*), which was composed of a proportionally representative number of members of parliament (MPs). The other main type consists of reports (*Statens offentliga utredningar*) from commissions of inquiry appointed in the preparatory stage of a reform in order to expand the knowledge base and gather input from interest groups.

The standard tax policy process can be summarized as follows. First, an initiative to prepare new legislation was taken from within government, which then appointed a commission of inquiry. The commission consisted of MPs, outside experts, or both. Their report was sent to selected organizations and authorities, which were given the opportunity to express their opinion. The government was expected to take their opinions into account before presenting a bill. MPs could then prepare motions on the issue. The majority of the tax committee agreed on a statement and delivered a revised proposal for new legislation for parliament to take a stand on. If all MPs remained loyal to their party, the proposal would be accepted because the composition of the committee reflected the outcome of the parliamentary elections. Members of the tax committee could submit their own statements and voice reservations if they disagreed or wished to add something. In this way, the opposition could present alternative proposals for parliament to vote on. Finally, the majority's proposal and any alternatives were debated in parliament and put to the vote.

The tax committee included MPs from all the elected parties, presumably individuals who were familiar with tax issues. Documents from the committee covered everything from expert inquiries to stakeholder opinions, government bills, and motions from MPs who were not members of the committee. Consequently, this source can be used to analyze the positions of the most influential groups in the process. It is complemented by other parliamentary sources, such as bills and commission reports, when deemed necessary for clarification. The part about international influences is based on expert statements presented in official commissions of inquiry.

General Taxes on Consumption in Sweden

The most intense and formative period concerning general consumption taxes in Sweden began with the preparation for the 1959 decision to adopt a permanent sales tax. It ended with the transition to VAT around a decade later. It is also worth noting that a temporary general sales tax was imposed during World War II.

In more detail, the core decisions came into effect as follows. 1941 was the first year of the temporary general sales tax (*allmän omsättningsskatt*), which was withdrawn in 1947. In 1960 a new general sales tax (*allmän varuskatt*) came into effect. In 1962 the rate was increased from 4 to 6 percent of the final price including tax, in 1966 to 9.1 percent, and in 1968 to 10 percent. Finally, in 1969, the sales tax was replaced by VAT (*mervärdesskatt*).

The analysis of welfare state formation versus business interests focuses on the 1959 sales tax decision and the path to the decision in 1968 to replace it with a VAT. This is when both the expansion of the welfare state and economic growth took off. The first part of the empirical account addresses this theme. The focus is mainly on MPs' statements. The last part concerns international influences. We then return to 1940 and preparation for the wartime sales tax decision. This is less tied to the timing of corporatism and welfare state expansion. International influences are equally likely to have played a role at any stage. The focus is on how these aspects were discussed in expert commissions during the preparatory stages of the reforms in question. This complements the analysis of internationally oriented arguments by MPs in the earlier part.

The Fiscal Setting of the 1950s

The first few years of the postwar period solidified the system of progressive direct taxation initiated at the beginning of the twentieth century.[21] The aim was explicitly redistributive. During the war, in contrast, a temporary general sales tax had been adopted. However, in Rodriguez's words, it became "politically impossible" to keep it after the war.[22] Criticism regarding the problems it caused for low-income earners became difficult for the social democratic government to ignore. Repeal of the tax was in the spirit of the sharpening of direct taxation. The pressure for such reforms coincided with the Communists gaining ground in the elections and, overall, labor organizations gaining strength. There was broad support for openly targeting high-income earners. Decreasing the burden on low-income earners by removing the general sales tax followed the same logic.

During the late 1950s, a heated debate emerged over a suggested earnings-related supplement to the basic public pension.[23] This became an emblematic reform for the Swedish-style welfare state. Unlike much previous welfare policy, it was not directed at the lowest income stratum, but it would benefit those who demanded and expected a considerably larger pension than the bare minimum.[24] Unions and employers of the better-off white-collar workers had until then made their own agreements to cover this. The new pension proposal offered an alternative solution and would protect less affluent wage earners who had not previously enjoyed these perks. Now everyone would get a supplement to the minimum pension based on the level of their earnings during their working life.

The center-right opposition did not support this. In the 1958 parliamentary elections, following a public debate dominated by the pension issue, the Liberals received a severe blow. Parts of their constituency seemed to back the Social Democrats' position. With this additional electoral support, the new pension system could come into effect in 1960. It marked a symbolic breakthrough for the new alliance between white-collar workers and the labor movement.[25] This can be contrasted with developments in the United States, which did not reform their pension scheme. Instead, private insurance remained the main option for the middle class. Gøsta Esping-Andersen, among others, describes the situation in Sweden as the middle class becoming loyal to the welfare state, while in the United States a basic pension was considered a residual factor meant only to provide for the destitute.[26]

At the same time that the new pension system was being prepared, a parallel process concerning the revenue side of public finances was taking place. The government assessed the possibility of launching a new general sales tax. According to the leaders of the Social Democrats, this was necessary to finance the welfare reforms. As before, the possibility of a general sales tax was generally not well received. Left-wing critics opposed it for social policy reasons, while right-wing opponents saw it as bad for business and growth, and feared it would open the gates to expanding the state.

An early initiative had come from an LO union economist, whose point of departure was that it would not be possible to gain much revenue from further increasing the progressivity of direct taxes.[27] He argued that, unlike before, compensatory measures such as child benefits and tax deductions would ensure that low-income earners would not be worse off under a general consumption tax, and the increased revenue was intended to cover the planned reforms for pension and health insurance and to restore the real value of existing social benefits. This view, however, was not shared by the majority of the LO or by the rest of the labor movement, and the LO's official submission to a commission of inquiry in 1957 dismissed the introduction of a general sales tax.[28]

A recurring tendency to resort to circular reasoning about social policy, as in the example above, can be discerned among proponents of the sales tax. They argued that an increase in this regressive tax was introduced because it allowed social welfare to improve. In turn, this led to a need to compensate low-income earners for the increased cost of living. A few years later, they could argue that the costs of these new compensatory measures had to be covered by increasing indirect taxation, and so on.

Consolidating the Sales Tax While Satisfying Business Interests

The launch of the sales tax had been controversial. In spite of this, less than two years later the government proposed an increase in order to allow new reliefs for low-income earners to be made, such as upward adjustments to the income tax brackets and larger deductions for those on low incomes.[29] These measures would reduce public revenue and so needed to be covered by other means. A range of compensatory arrangements for low-income households, among them increased child allowances and reduced social security charges for the disadvantaged, would need to be covered too. Increased indirect taxation was referred to as inevitable.

The reactions from the opposition reveal a different perspective on inevitability and aims in fiscal policy. The leader of the Conservatives indicated that his party had dropped their opposition to the general sales tax. Their present stance was that the need to reduce the high marginal tax rates, along with direct taxation in general, outweighed the negative consequences of a general consumption tax.[30] By shifting the tax levy in the direction of indirect taxes, a deduction of direct taxes could be achieved. And this was what they would aim for.

In mid-decade, the government proposed a second increase. The same socio-political criticism was countered with promises of more generous deductions for low-income earners, increased child allowances, and lower pension contributions.[31] The same applied to the 1967 bill which would allow a third increase, with compensation achieved by adjusting the income tax deductions for those on low incomes. In the bill, the Minister of Finance simply noted that the country's financial situation required a consolidation of public revenue, without discussing the possibility of reconsidering public expenditures. The tax committee's response was that while reducing the tax burden on low-income earners was desirable, it was impossible at that time. The demands on the public sector to contribute in many areas had greatly restricted the scope for tax reliefs.

This was echoed in part by the Conservative committee members. They expressed concern about Sweden being among the highest taxed countries in the OECD (Organisation for Economic Co-operation and Development), something they argued was an impediment to entrepreneurial activity.[32] They noted nonetheless that previous parliamentary decisions on expenditure had imposed certain commitments on the state.

In the absence of opportunities to reduce the overall tax rate, the Conservatives wanted to focus on shifting the balance from direct to indirect taxes. For these reasons, they endorsed the bill increasing the sales tax.

In the initial debate over a generalized consumption tax, the main right-wing counterargument had been that it would slow down the economy.[33] This was a general concern related to the overall tax level. Other arguments were directed specifically at the sales tax. The proposal to levy it at the retail level meant that some categories of raw materials and capital goods would be subject to this tax and result in increased costs for the individual company. There would also be a cumulative, or cascade, effect as one item passed through several stages of production, being taxed at each step. According to right-wing and business representatives, this would stand in the way of free competition.

When the first increase of the general sales tax was proposed in 1961, the non-socialist parties had started to show reluctant acceptance of this new indirect tax. At the same time, they expressed dissatisfaction with its design and wanted to modify those parts that negatively impacted the business community.[34] One demand was that all purchases made by companies should be exempt from sales tax. This would improve conditions for them and minimize price increases for consumers. The Liberals, who were now more amenable to general consumption taxation as a way to reduce the total tax levy, believed that the solution was to let companies subtract the sum of purchases from their taxable revenue.

In two joint motions, a group of Conservatives and Liberals called for the same treatment of taxation of factory-made building materials and the equivalent products made directly on construction sites. As things were, the tax system favored the latter by taxing it more lightly. They argued that it skewed competition and encouraged "irrational," onsite work over the "modern" and efficient factory production of concrete and other components. Here we see an example of cascade-type consumption taxes providing incentives for the vertical integration of production, sometimes at the expense of productivity, due to less division of labor. The opposition's solution was to move tax collection from retailers to an earlier stage of production for these products. They based their argumentation on what would be good for business, but also on how this would benefit society in general. The Conservatives argued that any additional cost of production caused by the sales tax was passed on so that ultimately it was the consumer who bore the burden. They also suggested turning the sales tax into a VAT on the grounds that this would permit a decrease in the progressivity of direct taxes.

In light of this discussion, the social democratic government added a concession for businesses to the 1965 bill on raising the statutory rate for a second time. No more than 60 percent of a company's costs for machinery and other equipment with a depreciation period of more than three years would be subject to tax.[35] This was not enough to satisfy the opposition in full though. Conservative motions recalled that the problems in the construction sector remained.[36] They wanted factory-made building materials to be subject to the 60 percent rule as well. They argued that efficient innovations, such as modular building systems and pre-fabricated concrete, should not be discriminated against in favor of less efficient, onsite production, which at the time was not subject to sales tax at the final stage. The tax committee majority did not cave in to all the opposition's demands, but did agree to make an exception for factory-made concrete and include it in the category "capital goods," which was subject to the 60 percent rule.

Committee members from the three non-socialist parties submitted a set of motions and a joint reservation to the committee's statement, where they pleaded for even more reliefs for capital goods.[37] They stated that it had become common practice in other countries to reimburse companies for all indirect taxes when exporting, and emphasized the rise of international dependence and foreign trade. Consequently, they argued that the Swedish tax system needed to be better adapted to other countries' regulations and should accept the proposal of the preceding official commission of inquiry[38] to replace the general sales tax with VAT. Otherwise, Swedish companies would encounter difficulties when competing abroad. They argued that VAT was advantageous in being neutral with regard to consumer choice, since the price is not affected by how the components of the product are taxed at different stages of production. They repeated the goal of reducing direct taxation, particularly marginal taxes, and argued that consumption taxes were the only viable way to get there.

A bill to replace the sales tax with VAT was presented in 1968. It provided a more permanent solution to the problems that the business community and center-right parties had raised. The main line was that this was nothing more than a "technical" change.[39] Not everyone agreed. Communist MPs argued that shifting the tax burden from businesses to consumers had distributional consequences.[40] The government's response was to propose a new "general employer's contribution" as a counterweight. It was set to 1 percent of wage costs and was intended to match what the companies would gain from sales tax reliefs. Other employer's contributions were already in place, but were mainly linked to the social security system. This was framed as an all-purpose payroll tax. The government's rationale was that the reform should not lead to a redistribution of tax burden onto consumers, in line with how the Communists argued. The Conservatives criticized the proposal and claimed that the government was overcompensating. Insofar as consumers had previously carried the burden of "hidden" sales taxes accumulated during the production process, VAT should be seen as a relief for consumers. In the Conservatives' opinion, employer's contributions were an unjustifiable burden on the business community.

International Relations

This process was not unique to Sweden. Similar changes could be found throughout the industrialized world, some sooner, some later, some more far-reaching, others less so. The EEC actively promoted the harmonization of consumption tax policy, which later meant opting for VAT. How developments abroad were approached in official inquiries, and how this in turn was received by Swedish policymakers, gives us an insight into the role of the international dimension as an explanatory approach.

The commission preparing for the first general sales tax discussed developments abroad extensively in their 1940 report.[41] They stated that between the two world wars almost all developed countries had adopted some form of general turnover tax, mainly to deal with financial difficulties arising during World War I. In no time it had become central to the public finances of many states. The commission gave an overview of different types of general turnover tax, using examples of what other states had done. Their interpretation is summarized next.

The cumulative type, where one good is taxed at several stages of production, was pioneered in Germany. An advantage was that the authorities were spared from distinguishing between who is liable to pay and who is not. One disadvantage was the large number of taxpayers; non-neutrality was another, since the final amount of tax depended on the number of firms in the production chain. The tendency of German firms to pursue vertical integration had been clear, according to the commission, giving rise to imbalances and difficulties for producers of intermediate goods.

A non-cumulative tax could be levied either at the retail level or at the producer and wholesale level. Canada was seen as setting an example for the latter kind. This solution was neutral in terms of vertical integration. The number of firms liable to pay was relatively small, which made administration and control easier. However, the rates had to be much higher than with a cumulative tax. The authors of the report expressed concern that it would be difficult to assess how consumer prices would be affected.

The only other alternative, a retail sales tax, had been successfully introduced in a number of US states and in Denmark. The authors described it as the "final step" in the evolution of the turnover tax thus far. This alternative avoided most of the problems associated with the producer, wholesaler and cumulative alternatives. The tax could be designed to create an equal burden on different fields of private consumption and minimize disruptions within production. There would be the least number of transition problems, according to the commission. The only real disadvantage was the challenge of efficiently ensuring compliance among the many retailers, but examples from the United States showed that this was not impossible. This was the option chosen by the Minister of Finance, Ernst Wigforss. Even though he acknowledged valid arguments against introducing the tax with regard to social policy, administrative difficulties, and the effects on production and prices, he argued that it was needed to cover increased public expenses pertaining to the war.

International developments were similarly considered when preparing the next major sales tax reform. The commission's report of 1957 included an assessment of general consumption taxes in foreign countries.[42] It covered a range of single-stage alternatives, such as the one employed in Sweden during the war, as well as the option of only taxing the value added. The main lesson learned from previous experiences was that with a single-stage tax there is no simple way of distinguishing who is liable to pay. The commission noted that, in practice, there are no clear-cut categories, such as retailer, wholesaler, and producer. If this tax were selected, the authorities would have to be prepared to devote a great deal of time to solving the issue of borderline cases that would inevitably appear.

A lesson they took from countries with cumulative solutions was that there are generally some adverse effects that have to be countered by special arrangements, such as deductions or reimbursements. The value-added alternative was greeted with some enthusiasm by the commission. However, they saw its benefits as more relevant under conditions of very high revenue from this type of taxation. Under current conditions, they considered a low-rate sales tax would be more advantageous. But when the report was written in the late 1950s there was no full-fledged model to turn to, as no European country had adopted a VAT that covered all sectors and all stages of production.

In its 1964 report, the next major commission for tax reform included an assessment of VAT in France and of the West German and UK governments' positions.[43] Since the British had dismissed VAT, most of the discussion concerned France and West Germany. In France, indirect taxation had become complex. The so-called VAT on production was combined with a municipal retail sales tax, a service tax, and numerous excises. There was some movement toward unifying these, but nothing had been agreed at that stage. An important influence motivating France was the idea of creating a common market within Europe, which involved taxing commerce in a similar way in this area. The German VAT proposal of 1963 contributed to making this question all the more urgent. After a long planning process there was now a proposal to abandon the cumulative turnover tax in favor of a VAT levied at all stages from producer to final consumer. A central argument in the German debate, according to the commission, was that the VAT was neutral in terms of consumer choice. Another crucial aspect was the pressure for a solution that would not increase the tax burden on businesses. The German VAT was expected to come into effect in 1966 at the earliest.

Regarding international competition, the commission noted that the Swedish sales tax had been criticized for not offering domestic producers conditions equal to those of producers exporting to Sweden.[44] The same was true of Swedish export industries regarding their ability to compete in the international market. The commission dismissed the alternative of adjusting this through customs duties, since it would go against the General Agreement on Tariffs and Trade (GATT) and the European Free Trade Association (EFTA). In other countries, this problem had been solved through restitution to domestic firms threatened by cheap imports. However, this had been a source of conflict at home and abroad. The EEC had made it clear that it would monitor these arrangements and possibly even ban them in order to achieve the common market. The commission further noted that the EEC was processing a proposal for a joint transition to VAT, though the details were still a matter of debate. The reason given by the commission for considering this was that the EEC member states were important industrial competitors. The Swedish government had applied for "associate membership" to the EEC in 1961,[45] but the prime minister made clear that he was not interested in full membership. The application was not approved.

As has been shown earlier, these inquiries were echoed in the subsequent parliamentary process in arguments concerning international competition and equal treatment of businesses. The MPs and experts involved referred to external pressure as a constraint on domestic policy. What is clear though is that certain crucial details were still open to debate. This is underscored by the diverse paths that were taken by European countries. The hands-on matter of international competition, however, was clearly present in the Swedish policy process.

Conclusions Regarding the Swedish Path to VAT

Unlike what the technocratic rationality type of explanation implies, making tax policy in this period was far from uneventful. There were examples of distributional clashes between business and capital versus labor groups. This was also the period in which VAT and the general employer's contribution were established. Both of these taxes would keep on growing in importance thereafter.

Concerning the mechanisms behind the rise of VAT in Sweden, two main features can be discerned. There was an unequivocal connection between the formation of universal welfare systems, redistributive spending, and the expansion of this generalized form of taxation on consumption. Second, the business community played a part in fashioning the design of consumption taxes, though not in setting overall tax revenue. Corporations were granted lower sales tax rates for certain inputs and equipment. When the transition to VAT was agreed on, a major argument was that this would make matters easier for corporations. The hallmarks of a long corporatist tradition are plain to see. This is in line with Steinmo's argument that the structure of the political system fostered compromise and long-term collaboration.

In the struggle between labor and employer interests, both sides framed the general consumption tax to accord with their respective political narratives. They moved beyond the traditional left- and right-wing views regarding VAT as either bad for the poor or bad for business and growth. The first steps are explained by the desire of social democratic leaders to use this regressive tax to maintain and expand the welfare state. The continuous consolidation and, eventually, broad support for this tax was made possible by the two extremes of the political spectrum managing to see it from a different angle. The left could focus on this tax as a revenue machine for the government, and the right could concentrate on the fact that it was regressive and a lesser evil than increased direct taxes and high progressivity. Throughout this process, we can see concessions being made to avoid worsening conditions for business. This was advocated more directly by the right-wing representatives, but the Social Democrats proved willing to adapt their policies in this direction.

It should be recognized that international developments also played a role. The idea of experimenting with a general sales tax was inspired by respective attempts in other countries. Their experiences provided a learning base, which demonstrated the strengths and weaknesses of the various solutions. When an urgent need for increased public revenue arose, these options were considered by Swedish politicians and experts. International developments were frequently referred to in order to provide a rationale for this generally unpopular tax. There was to some extent a willingness to move closer to Europe, but more in terms of maintaining trade relations with these important export markets than to become a member of the EEC. European influences can explain the Swedish transition from general sales tax to VAT only indirectly. The concerns and demands of the Swedish business community exerted a more direct influence. We can see a willingness on the part of social democratic politicians to meet these demands, at least in part. In that light, the transition to VAT stands out as part of a larger package of policies concerning the business sphere and the overall goal of enabling the continued expansion of the welfare state and economic growth.

Notes

1. Lindert, *Growing Public*; Kato, *Regressive Taxation*; Steinmo, *Taxation and Democracy*; Prasad and Deng, "Taxation and the Worlds of Welfare."
2. Martin, "Labour Market Coordination"; Steinmo, *Taxation and Democracy*; Ganghof, "Tax Mixes"; Beramendi and Rueda, "Social Democracy Constrained"; James, *Rise of the Value-Added Tax*; Kato, *Regressive Taxation*; Lindert, *Growing Public.*
3. This account of general fiscal developments is based on Elvander, *Svensk skattepolitik.*
4. Ibid.
5. Hibbs Jr., "Partisan Theory"; Allan and Scruggs, "Political Partisanship."
6. Steinmo, *Taxation and Democracy*; Andersson, *Politics of Taxation*, is a more recent contribution that also demonstrates the importance of electoral systems.
7. Martin, "Labour Market Coordination."
8. Rodriguez, *Offentlig inkomstexpansion.*
9. Ibid.
10. Kato, *Regressive Taxation*, 31.
11. James, *Rise of the Value-Added Tax.*

12. Steinmo, *Taxation and Democracy*, 124, states that "tax politics in the 1950s and 1960s can largely be summarized in one word: boring" in reference to this as a period of consensus-oriented technocratic rule.
13. Ebrill et al., *Modern VAT*, make this association of European integration fueling the spread of VAT. It is contested by Lynch, "Harmonization through Competition?"; and James, *Rise of the Value-Added Tax.*
14. Lynch, "Harmonization through Competition?"
15. James, *Rise of the Value-Added Tax*, 177, 237f.
16. Steinmo, *Taxation and Democracy*; Steinmo, "Political Institutions." He was followed by Kato, *Regressive Taxation*; and Lindert, *Growing Public.*
17. Ganghof, "Tax Mixes."
18. Beramendi and Rueda, "Social Democracy Constrained."
19. The Liberals are categorized as part of the political right, and the center-right opposition more broadly, relative to a socialist left-wing consisting of the Social Democrats and Communists, during the period in question.
20. Elvander, *Intresseorganisationerna i dagens Sverige.*
21. Rodriguez, *Offentlig inkomstexpansion*; Kato, *Regressive Taxation.*
22. Rodriguez, *Offentlig inkomstexpansion*, 109. This and other quotes translated from Swedish by the author of this chapter.
23. *Allmänna tilläggspensionen* (ATP).
24. Kato, *Regressive Taxation*, 65.
25. This refers to the coalition-building hypothesis (Esping-Andersen, *Worlds of Welfare*) in which this alliance succeeds the old one between workers and agrarians, which had been key to building the Scandinavian welfare states, but had since diminished in importance.
26. Ibid. Loyalty to the welfare state also forms part of the argument concerning Sweden in Lindert, *Growing Public.*
27. Elvander, *Svensk skattepolitik*, 303–14.
28. Ibid., 135–8.
29. Prop 1961:188, 27–8.
30. BeU 1961:79, 31.
31. BeU 1965:16, 63–4; Prop 1967:7, 13–16.
32. BeU 1967:2, 48–9.
33. BeU 1959:60.
34. BeU 1961:79.
35. Prop 1965:14.
36. BeU 1965:16, 51–2, 81–3.
37. BeU 1965:16, 52, 81, 101–5.
38. SOU 1964:25.
39. Prop 1968:100.
40. BeU 1968:45, 37–8, 40–2.
41. Prop 1940:U3, 77–94, appendix (P. M. angående omsättningsskatt).

42. SOU 1957:13, 154–64, 359–96.
43. SOU 1964:25, 779–98.
44. SOU 1964:25, 102–3, 106–7.
45. Bergquist, *Sverige och EEC.*

References

Swedish Parliamentary Resources

BeU (*Bevillningsutskottet*, Tax Committee) 1959:60, 1961:79, 1965:16, 1967:2, 1968:45.

Prop (*Proposition*, Government Bill) 1940:U3, 1961:188, 1965:14, 1967:7, 1968:100.

SOU (*Statens offentliga utredningar*, Official Commissions of Inquiry) 1957:13, 1964:25.

Secondary Literature

Allan, James P., and Lyle Scruggs. 2004. Political Partisanship and Welfare State Reform in Advanced Industrial Societies. *American Journal of Political Science* 48 (3): 496–512.

Andersson, Per F. 2017. *Essays on the Politics of Taxation*. Lund: Lund University.

Beramendi, Pablo, and David Rueda. 2007. Social Democracy Constrained: Indirect Taxation in Industrialized Democracies. *British Journal of Political Science* 37 (4): 619–641.

Bergquist, Mats. 1970. *Sverige och EEC: En statsvetenskaplig studie av fyra åsiktsriktningars syn på svensk marknadspolitik 1961–1962*. Stockholm: Norstedt.

Ebrill, Liam, Michael Keen, Jean-Paul Bodin, and Victoria Summers. 2001. *The Modern VAT*. Washington, DC: International Monetary Fund.

Elvander, Nils. 1969. *Intresseorganisationerna i dagens Sverige*. Lund: Gleerup.

———. 1972. *Svensk skattepolitik 1945–1970: en studie i partiers och organisationers funktioner*. Stockholm: Rabén & Sjögren.

Esping-Andersen, Gøsta. 1990. *The Three Worlds of Welfare Capitalism*. Cambridge: Polity.

Ganghof, Steffen. 2006. Tax Mixes and the Size of the Welfare State: Causal Mechanisms and Policy Implications. *Journal of European Social Policy* 16 (4): 360–373.

Hibbs, Douglas A., Jr. 1992. Partisan Theory After Fifteen Years. *European Journal of Political Economy* 8 (3): 361–373.

James, Kathryn. 2015. *The Rise of the Value-Added Tax*. New York: Cambridge University Press.
Kato, Junko. 2003. *Regressive Taxation and the Welfare State: Path Dependence and Policy Diffusion*. Cambridge: Cambridge University Press.
Lindert, Peter H. 2004. *Growing Public: Social Spending and Economic Growth Since the Eighteenth Century*. Cambridge: Cambridge University Press.
Lynch, Frances Florian B. 2007. Harmonization Through Competition? The Evolution of Taxation in Post-War Europe. In *Global Debates About Taxation*, ed. Holger Nehring and Florian Schui, 116–133. London: Palgrave Macmillan.
Martin, Cathie Jo. 2015. Labour Market Coordination and the Evolution of Tax Regimes. *Socio-Economic Review* 13 (1): 33–54.
Prasad, Monica, and Yingying Deng. 2009. Taxation and the Worlds of Welfare. *Socio-Economic Review* 7 (3): 431–457.
Rodriguez, Enrique. 1980. *Offentlig inkomstexpansion: En analys av drivkrafterna bakom de offentliga inkomsternas utveckling i Sverige under 1900-talet*. Lund: Gleerup.
Steinmo, Sven. 1989. Political Institutions and Tax Policy in the United States, Sweden, and Britain. *World Politics* 41 (4): 500–535.
———. 1993. *Taxation and Democracy: Swedish, British and American Approaches to Financing the Modern State*. New Haven: Yale University Press.

Working-Class Power and the Taxation of Current Earnings: Danish Pay-As-You-Earn Income Tax in Comparative Perspective

Isaac W. Martin

The pay-as-you-earn (PAYE) income tax is one of the most important tools of macroeconomic governance in twenty-first-century capitalist states. One hundred years ago, income taxes were rare and cumbersome revenue instruments that affected only a few of the world's richest people. Few states levied income taxes. Those that did typically taxed annual income only after the year was done, with the result that they could collect tax only from those who saved the money to pay it; sometimes two years might elapse in between when income was paid and when the taxes came due; and no government in the world had yet attempted to tax the incomes of the majority of wage earners. Today, PAYE taxation enlists the assistance of employers in assessing the provisional income tax liability and withholding it from paychecks of a majority of the labor force even before the income year is up. This procedure for taxing current income on a continuous basis permits states to collect resources from wage earners who

I. W. Martin (✉)
University of California, San Diego, CA, USA
e-mail: iwmartin@ucsd.edu

G. Huerlimann et al. (eds.), *Worlds of Taxation*,
Palgrave Studies in the History of Finance,
https://doi.org/10.1007/978-3-319-90263-0_4

have little savings. It also acts as an automatic stabilizing device that moderates extremes of the business cycle by dampening fluctuations in aggregate demand (since current income tax revenues increase automatically as incomes rise and decrease automatically when incomes fall). The importance of PAYE taxation can be seen in comparative revenue statistics: in 2014, personal income tax yielded revenues equivalent to an average of 11% of GDP in rich democratic countries. In quantitative terms, no other single fiscal instrument compares.[1]

But considered as a social institution, PAYE taxation presents a puzzle. This form of taxation is designed to meet two goals that are fundamentally in tension: taxing personal income *comprehensively* and taxing personal income *continuously*. As the economist Robert Murray Haig famously defined income, it is "the money value of the net accretion of one's economic power between two points in time."[2] Personal income, in this comprehensive sense, can only be known, and measured, by examining all of a person's economic circumstances after a definite period has elapsed, and, from the standpoint of measurement, the longer the period, the better. The most distinctive advantages of personal income tax, however—as an elastic source of public revenue, an effective tool of Keynesian demand management, and a convenient way to tax people who have little savings and who may not keep careful accounts—are achieved by frequent collection that approximates a continuous stream of revenue. The resolution of this tension between infrequent measurement and continuous collection involves a collective feat of social construction. To tax, say, annual income before the tax year is up, states enlist employers in withholding income tax from wages before the definitive tax liability is known; and, to make this continuous taxation at the source possible, states and taxpayers stipulate to provisional measures of current income even before the tax period has concluded. These provisional numbers are, in effect, polite fictions maintained with the cooperation of everyone involved. This cooperation is all the more remarkable because the rituals for producing these provisional numbers, for collecting tax on the basis of these provisional numbers, and for reconciling them with the definitive tax liability computed at the end of the tax period, all are the outcomes of negotiated social arrangements among groups with potentially opposing interests—employers, employees, and the state.[3]

Why would any wage earner ever consent to these arrangements, or participate in upholding these provisional numbers? The existence of PAYE is puzzling because the dominant tradition in historical sociology has taught us that rulers must struggle to extract resources from society over the resistance of their subjects.[4] The increasing sophistication of tax assessment since the fourteenth century, including a dramatic increase in the power of states to measure taxable resources and monitor taxpayer compliance, sparked many of the most dramatic tax rebellions in early modern Europe. Even into the late twentieth century, technical improvements in tax assessment—rather than the adoption of new taxes—caused most of the best known taxpayer rebellions, from the Poujadist movement of postwar France to the property tax revolt of the 1970s United States.[5] Tax assessment, this literature tells us, facilitates predatory rule. The institutionalization of a new and agreed-upon social procedure for tax assessment and collection that requires the active collaboration of the taxpayer would appear to be a puzzle.

The solution to the puzzle lies in the observation that not everyone resists tax assessment, and indeed, that some taxpayers have historically welcomed innovation in tax assessment in order to secure fair and convenient means of paying for public goods that they value. This account draws on the "new fiscal sociology" that treats the rise of the modern fiscal state as an implicit social contract in which subjects agree to be taxed in exchange for collective protection from armed assault and from market failure. In this case, the crucial historical condition for the adoption of PAYE in the rich democratic countries—beginning in the 1920s, spreading rapidly during World War II, and continuing into the first three postwar decades—was the active pursuit of PAYE by labor parties that were elected with working-class votes.[6] This finding may seem surprising: wage earners were the most burdened by the adoption of PAYE because this was the technique that transformed the income tax from a tax on the rich few to a tax on the mass of wage earners. But wage earners were not only passive objects of PAYE taxation. They were the agents of its creation—and they pushed for the adoption of PAYE for very good reasons. Workers—and labor-based political parties—supported PAYE taxation because they saw it as an improved administrative means to achieve collective protection from the risks of military defeat and market failure.

A Brief Comparative Overview

The conventional history of the origins of mass income taxation is the so-called militarist theory that emphasizes the causal importance of mass mobilization for war.[7] The urgent and unprecedented costs of World War II, it is said, overwhelmed all other political considerations and impelled governments to adopt the new practice of taxing the current incomes of wage earners. The comparative evidence appears to support this stylized account as a theory of the adoption of PAYE taxation. Figure 1 presents a timeline that summarizes the years when 15 developed countries finally adopted PAYE taxation, defined operationally as (a) comprehensive tax on personal income, (b) assessed on income in the current year, and (c) levied on the majority of wage earners by withholding wage income at the source. This definition excludes what is sometimes called "withholding tax" on the wages or capital income of foreigners. It also excludes payroll taxes withheld at the source if they were not comprehensive taxes on personal income. (Thus, e.g., France and Switzerland, both of which adopted pension schemes financed by payroll tax on employees of large firms in the 1930s, are not counted as having thereby adopted PAYE taxation.)[8] The focus of this figure is on the adoption of PAYE as a mechanism for assessing and collecting comprehensive personal income tax at the national level from the majority of wage earners.

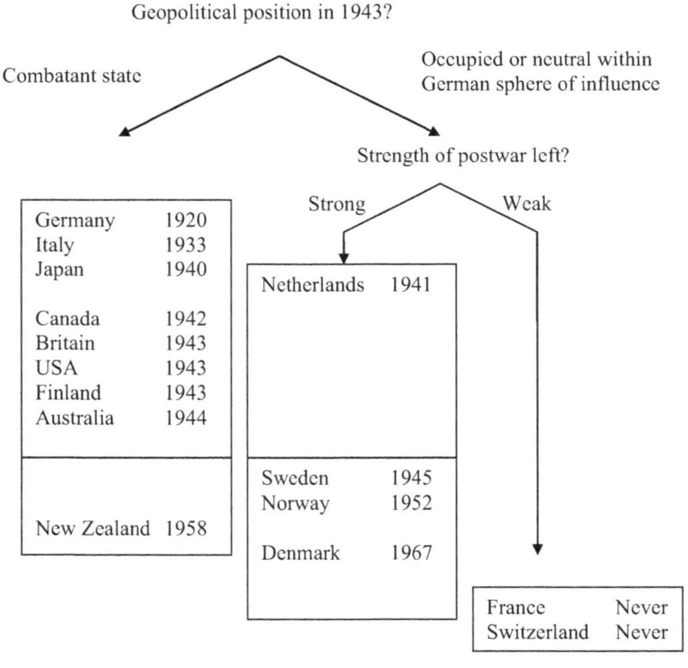

Fig. 1 Date of adopting PAYE income tax, by participation in World War II and left political power, in 15 developed countries

The figure illustrates the importance of military costs. The earliest states to adopt PAYE taxation—Germany, Italy, and Japan—were all militaristic states with authoritarian legacies. Six of the remaining 12 were belligerent states or armed neutrals that adopted PAYE to support their own defense apparatus during World War II. In fact, of the ten countries in this sample that still supported their own professional military during the peak years of the war, nine had adopted PAYE before the conflict ended. Of the five countries in this sample that did *not* support their own professional soldiers in 1943—either because they were already conquered or, like Switzerland, because they relied on unique geographic and diplomatic advantages to preserve their neutrality—only one adopted PAYE before the end of the war. That exception was the Netherlands, which was more closely fiscally integrated into the German state than other occupied countries, and which adopted PAYE under external influence.[9]

But was it simply the expense of war that drove the spread of PAYE? Consider the other occupied countries listed in Fig. 1. Some of these states bore heavy burdens of tribute; they did not pay for their own military defense after they were conquered, but they paid for the support of the occupying military.[10] Conquest and occupation foreclosed the adoption of PAYE *not* by exempting the conquered countries from the costs of war, but instead by removing their political autonomy, and in particular by suppressing working-class political participation. Conversely, the feature of World War II that facilitated the adoption of PAYE was not only the expense of the war, but also its mass-mobilizing character.[11] This was a total war that required the active participation of the working class in every belligerent state. Elites' dependence on workers' participation increased workers' political leverage even in contexts where they were not formally enfranchised—and that leverage led to the adoption of forms of taxation that were favorable to wage earners. This theory—that labor's influence was the most important condition for the adoption of PAYE—might even account for the timing of PAYE even in Germany. Note that Germany did *not* adopt PAYE at the height of any military conflict but instead at the high water mark of its interwar democracy. Germany had long been a militaristic state with substantial administrative capacity, and many German states had imposed income tax on wages in the second half of the nineteenth century.[12] But Germany adopted PAYE taxation—including compulsory withholding at source of tax assessed on the current year's income—only in 1920. The precipitating condition was the inaugural election of the Weimar Republic, which, in 1919, brought Social

Democrats to political power for the first time in history, including a plurality of legislative seats and the leadership of the multiparty coalition government.

The crucial test of this hypothesis that working-class political influence led to the adoption of PAYE taxation lies in the comparative record of the postwar era. If war and militarism alone were crucial, we might expect the most militaristic states to adopt PAYE soonest after the end of the war, even in the absence of immediate military pressure. What we observe instead is that the states where the working class had the most political influence were the quickest to adopt PAYE. Figure 1 sorts the postwar timeline into states where the postwar left was "strong" and states where it was "weak," operationalized by the cumulative annual share of cabinet seats held by parties of the left allied with organized labor from 1945 to 1973. This is a conventional measure of the persistence of social democratic power; it is known to be associated with the implementation of other policies requiring long-term planning that improve the income security of wage earners.[13] (Where the cumulative left cabinet share was greater than 15, I coded the left as strong; where it was less than 8, I coded the left as weak.) The pattern illustrates that the strength of the postwar left distinguishes between states that adopted PAYE, such as Denmark and Norway, and states that still do not impose personal income tax on the majority of wage earners by taxing their income at the source, such as France and Switzerland.

The comparative evidence is consistent with the hypothesis that labor's influence was critically important. But would this hypothesis stand up to qualitative examination of the historical record? In the remainder of the chapter, I turn my attention to a historical case study of efforts to enact PAYE taxation in Denmark. This case presents a particular puzzle for the militarist theory of taxation, because it is a state with a long pacifist tradition, and yet it currently relies more heavily on PAYE taxation than any other state in the history of the world: the personal income tax claimed almost 27% of Danish GDP in 2014.[14] By tracing the history of efforts to adopt PAYE taxation in Denmark—and by comparing successful and failed efforts in Denmark and other Nordic countries, following a most-similar-cases design—I show that the puzzle can be resolved with attention to the power resources of the working class. Only when the Social Democratic Party had an extraordinary degree of political power in the late 1960s did it become possible to adopt PAYE taxation.

How a Small State Got a Big Income Tax

Although Denmark was relatively late to adopt a national income tax, the tax had a long history as a source of revenue for Danish local governments. The State Tax Law of 1903 that established Denmark's first peacetime national income tax built on the administrative basis of the existing local authorities. Boards appointed jointly by local and national governments were responsible for assessing the income and wealth of residents, and required individuals to submit annual income statements (*selvangivelser*) for this purpose. Like most other industrialized countries, Denmark levied income tax against the previous year's income, and collected the tax directly from the taxpayers by means of semi-annual bills. By 1939, central government taxes on personal income yielded 36% of central government revenues; these central government income taxes claimed less than 3% of GDP.[15]

Danish tax administration was not especially distinctive before World War II, and if not for the exigencies of war, it might have been expected to develop in parallel with tax administration in other northern European states. But in April 1940, an unanticipated German invasion (the so-called *Weserübung*) shunted Danish tax administration onto a different track. The German force was overwhelming, and Denmark's armed forces capitulated after two hours of earnest but futile combat. The German government saw Denmark only as a stepping stone to Norwegian ports and Swedish iron ore, however, and otherwise saw little strategic or economic value in Denmark itself. The invaders installed an occupying authority, and attempted to commit only minimal military and administrative resources to maintaining order on Danish soil.[16]

It proved possible for the occupying power to maintain order at little cost to Germany. The Danish parliament quickly formed a grand coalition government, and, after two months of increasingly tense negotiations, assumed a collaborative posture that aimed to preserve some freedom of maneuver by avoiding direct confrontation with the occupying German authorities. Germany, in turn, found it convenient to maintain the legal fiction that Denmark was an independent "protectorate" with its own police powers. Denmark was to be an international propaganda showcase for the benevolence of German imperialism; the occupying authorities went so far as to allow regularly scheduled elections to take place in early 1943.[17]

The comparatively light administrative presence of the occupation did not, however, exempt Denmark from the fiscal pressures of war. To the contrary, the occupying power extracted resources far in excess of the cost of occupation. Germany imposed a substantial burden of tribute on Denmark, amounting in one estimate to an average 19% of Denmark's national income per year during the period of occupation. Most of this tribute was not imposed directly on Danish people, but was paid indirectly through the Danish state, which was presented with inflated bills for "occupation costs," and was forced under German trade policy to pay Danish exporters for their exports to Germany (on the pretense that accounts would be cleared after the war). Thus, Denmark, like the combatant states, faced urgent and burdensome new fiscal pressures as a result of the war. The expansion of personal income tax by adopting PAYE might have seemed an obvious way to distribute the burden.[18]

Denmark also might have been expected to adopt PAYE as an anti-inflation measure. The Danish government had deliberately used taxes as an anti-inflation measure from the earliest days of the war. Because Britain and Germany were Denmark's two greatest trading partners, the outbreak of the war in 1939 immediately restricted international trade and drove consumer prices skyward, even before the German forces invaded. Danish anti-inflation policy began in 1939 with price controls, but it broadened in March 1940 to encompass sharp increases in income and consumption tax rates.[19] Inflation continued under German rule, and the Ministry of Finance subsequently convened a special task force of economists—the so-called Professors' Commission (*professorudvalget*)—to recommend a comprehensive anti-inflation policy. The committee was familiar with Keynesian thinking by way of Sweden, and it issued a report in early 1943 that followed broadly Keynesian lines. The report called on the government to abandon the balanced budget principle, and instead adopt a counter-cyclical policy of balancing the budget over the business cycle; in the context of wartime inflation, this meant cultivating a deliberate budget surplus by increasing taxes further. The committee's specific recommendations included a significant increase in the rates of the personal income tax, the land tax, and a variety of consumption taxes. In July 1943, the *Riksdag* rejected most of the proposals in favor of a special temporary tax on surplus income resulting from the war (*krigskonjunkturskat*), a capital gains tax, and a forced savings plan.[20]

It was the political exclusion of wage earners that rendered PAYE unthinkable. Just as many belligerent powers were implementing PAYE to fund their ongoing war effort, Germany was disarming the Danish military and dissolving the government. The anti-inflation bill of July 1943 passed amid an escalating series of confrontations between the Danish people and the German occupation forces. The sabotage of a German ship in the Odense harbor in June provoked Germans to post armed guards in the shipyards, which in turn provoked a strike that rapidly spread throughout the provincial centers of Denmark.[21] On 29 August, German forces answered the strike by imposing martial law. The *Riksdag* disbanded. For the rest of the occupation, administration was left in the hands of the Danish bureaucracy.[22] This shadow government was in no position to undertake significant fiscal policy initiatives, particularly if they might inflame industrial conflict that would provoke further repressive measures by the occupying power.

A comparison with Sweden will serve to test the hypothesis. Sweden was similar to Denmark in many ways. The pre-war Swedish income tax, like the Danish one, was levied on prior years' income, assessed by local boards that had been appointed by communal authorities, and collected in two installments, with the last payment taking place as much as a year and a half after the last of the income was earned. Withholding of provisional tax was instituted in 1929 on a voluntary basis for civil servants with postal savings accounts. This was an important precedent for PAYE taxation that had no counterpart in Denmark, but a far cry from mandatory withholding of tax on current income for all wage earners.[23] As in Denmark, the flow of income tax revenue from most wage earners was discontinuous, and the system of communal assessment and collection in two installments made it difficult to tax small earners and savers. Although Sweden re-armed earlier and more effectively than Denmark, its defense policy was similarly based on the combination of formal neutrality and trade with the belligerent powers.[24] After the invasion of Denmark and Norway, Swedish neutrality was abandoned in all but name. In the face of overwhelming German force, Sweden's government agreed to permit German supplies and troop trains to use Swedish territory on their way to and from Norway and, later, the Russian front.[25] The fiscal and geopolitical context, in short, was similar.

In contrast to Denmark, however, Sweden was never occupied, and it retained representative institutions and effective working-class suffrage for the duration of the war. It also retained the ability to make policy under a coalition government led by the Social Democratic Prime Minister Per Albin Hansson. By the end of 1941, the Swedish tax department had issued a report calling for taxation of current income with compulsory collection at the source for all wage earners. The proposal relied on employers to withhold income tax from wages, a suggestion that was met with resistance from employers, who complained of the administrative costs involved. Social democrats nevertheless persisted, and hammered out the details in several parliamentary commissions, including the so-called 1944 Tax Collection Working Group (*1944 års uppbördsberedning*), which finally delivered the draft legislation on 31 May 1945. The law was passed on 31 December 1945.[26]

Danish Employer Resistance to PAYE After World War II

The reconstruction of the Danish state after World War II laid the groundwork for one of the most extraordinary bursts of welfare state growth in the history of the world. In 1946, the government began a massive program of subsidized housing construction. In 1956, Denmark replaced means-tested pensions with universal, flat-rate benefits for the elderly. In 1958, the Danish government raised the general level of schooling in rural areas, authorized the construction of larger central schools serving multiple towns, and laid the fuse for the "educational explosion" of the coming decades. In 1960, the state established universal, public health insurance. All of these initiatives—and others, touching on poor relief, child benefits, and unemployment insurance—were financed with income taxes to a degree that was unusual even for Scandinavia, where income tax financing was the norm. Throughout this period of extraordinary growth in income-tax-financed public spending, however, the adoption of PAYE was delayed by employer resistance.[27]

The first plan for the taxation of current income was the work of the Tax Law Commission (*Skattelovskommissionen*), which Finance Minister H. P. Hansen had appointed in 1937 to survey the tax system as a whole and recommend changes. The commission had suspended its work on the income tax during the German occupation, confining its attention to tariff revisions and a proposal to tax lottery winnings, but it resumed its main task with apparent enthusiasm after the war. It issued its first major report in 1948. This *Report on the Taxation of Income and Wealth* included a comprehensive overview of problems with central and local income taxation, including the long delay between income and the realization of revenues, the complexity of the various definitions of taxable income, and the difficulty of taxing small earners and savers. It also included recommendations and over 150 pages of draft legislation. The last of the legislative proposals was designed to implement PAYE income taxation by having employers withhold taxes from wages.[28]

The proposal went nowhere. In a curious display of ambivalence, the commission recommended against introducing its own legislative draft. The reasons for this about-face are obscure, though the report cited reservations held by a majority of commissioners about "the scope of the administrative work that would be demanded of employers and tax authorities" if the proposal were to be adopted.[29] These were considerable. PAYE required employers to act as assessors, tax collectors, and record-keepers. These tasks were complicated by the fact that each individual taxpayer was potentially liable for the national income tax, separate local income taxes for his or her community of residence and place of work, and a special income tax for the "inter-local equalization fund." Employers would thus have had to implement multiple income taxes with different rules, procedures, and even definitions of taxable income. It would then have fallen to the government to coordinate their efforts. All of this was made more difficult by the prevalence of family farms and other small employers in Denmark's economy—few of which could be assumed to have sophisticated payroll or record-keeping systems, and some of which, according to the commission, paid wages partly in kind.[30]

The technical barriers to incorporating small employers, although real, were nevertheless surmountable. The proposed law would have simplified the complicated web of income taxes by eliminating the local income tax that non-residents paid to their place of business (*erhvervskommuneskat*), and by flattening out the rate schedules of the remaining local income taxes. It would have made it easier to compute provisional tax liability by eliminating several deductions, so that workers whose wages were identical could be expected to have similar final tax liabilities, too.[31] It also included an ingenious stamp-book system to simplify record-keeping for employers. They were simply to purchase stamps from the government, and distribute these to workers with their pay. The stamps would represent the taxes that had been withheld from workers' wages; like postage stamps, they would come in multiple denominations. Employees, in turn, would paste these stamps into stamp-books that they would then turn over to the tax authorities at the end of the year to prove that they had paid their taxes. The commission noted that Finland used a similar stamp-book system, where it made PAYE technically feasible even for employers who had little bookkeeping competence.[32]

The barrier to PAYE seems to have been political as much as technical. Small employers were not only numerous, but they were also united in the Danish employers' association (*Dansk arbejdsgiverforening* or DAF) and in their opposition to income tax withholding.[33] At one point in the commission's work, the DAF exercised a direct veto over the implementation of withholding. When it seemed clear that even a stamp-book system could not persuade the parliament to legislate a PAYE system with compulsory withholding, the commission attempted to broker a compromise under which income tax withholding would have been implemented on a voluntary basis. Under the plan, a worker could request that his or her employer withhold taxes. The tax authorities would then work with the employer to calculate the appropriate tax liability, which the employer would deduct from the worker's weekly or monthly paycheck and remit directly to the state. The key to this plan was a national agreement between the employers' association and the national labor association (*De samvirkende fagforbund* or DSF). The unions supported the plan, but the employers balked at the administrative hassle, thereby killing it.[34]

Social Democratic Power and PAYE

The postwar development of the welfare state ultimately put PAYE back on the agenda. The late 1950s were a period of great programmatic innovation in the Danish welfare state. Universal, tax-financed pensions became law in 1956. The National Health Insurance Act of 1960 established universal public health insurance, although premiums and benefits were still income graduated. Further growth was in the offing, driven in part by partisan competition. All four major parties were coming to terms with the fact that the universal social policy was popular with the self-employed and white-collar workers. Although the Liberals and Conservatives took a joint stand in 1959 against increased state intervention in the economy, electoral concerns led the Liberal party to reverse itself in 1963 and call for a coordinated system of grants to insure all individuals against loss of income, whatever the cause.[35] The Social Democrats sensed a threat to their claim to leadership in the field of social policy, and they responded with a series of new initiatives.

In the 1964 elections, the Social Democratic Party presented PAYE to voters as a way to pay for the newly expanded welfare state. The party's campaign promises included legislation to reduce the workweek, expand public housing construction, and establish earnings-graduated pensions that were indexed for inflation. By implementing PAYE taxation at the source, or ***kildeskat***, Denmark would put the finances of the welfare state on secure footing with an elastic and continuous flow of revenues. The Social Democrats also anticipated other benefits from the implementation of PAYE. The principle of taxation at the source was perceived to be popular with the party's working-class base, because paycheck withholding would shift many of the transaction costs of income taxation—including the administrative hassle of keeping records, making calculations, filing forms, budgeting to save the necessary funds, and remitting taxes—from workers to their employers. If workers had non-wage income, PAYE would not discharge their final liability, but a new, centralized tax directorate would prepare a final assessment that would reconcile provisional estimated tax with the final liability. Perhaps most importantly, academic and party economists also argued that PAYE would act as an automatic stabilizer on the economy, moderating the extremes of inflation and unemployment that might otherwise accompany the business cycle.[36]

The Social Democrats emerged from elections in 1964 with their position as the largest parliamentary party unscathed, but without either a majority of seats or a willing coalition partner in any of the so-called bourgeois parties. They formed a minority government. This was a precarious position, since losing a vote on any piece of legislation would have required the cabinet to dissolve itself and call new elections. Despite the government's shaky mandate, the Social Democratic finance minister, Poul Hansen, put forward over 40 ambitious finance proposals, including a proposal for PAYE taxation that he introduced in the last week of May 1965. The government did not schedule negotiations over the PAYE proposal right away. The bourgeois parties had received it coldly, and it was not the Social Democrats' highest priority. The government shelved the proposal indefinitely when Hansen was hospitalized for exhaustion in August.[37] Hansen resigned, and the legislature recessed in September without action on PAYE.

The party persisted because PAYE was popular with its working-class base. A Gallup poll in June 1965 showed that 55% of voters—and 75% of Social Democrats and left-wing Socialist People's Party (*Socialistisk Folkeparti*) voters—favored PAYE.[38] Hansen's successor, Henry Grünbaum, reintroduced the proposal in October 1965. The Social Democrats did not have the votes to pass it on its own, and Grünbaum intended the proposal as a trial balloon to see if a compromise could be negotiated. The balloon sank quickly, as debate revealed little common ground among the parties that could serve as the basis for negotiations. The Liberals flatly rejected income tax withholding as an unfair and unnecessary administrative burden on employers. Liberal spokesman Jens Foged sniffed that workers in *other* countries might need assistance filling out their tax forms, but the well-educated Danish workforce had no need of such coddling. On behalf of the Conservatives, Ninn-Hansen read a long list of objections, beginning with the observation that the proposal would eliminate a tax deduction cherished by high-income taxpayers, the so-called *skattefradragsret*, or deduction for prior years' income and wealth taxes. He also argued that the compulsory withholding of income tax from wages unfairly subjected workers to a more prompt and effective tax collection regime than other taxpayers, and proposed instead that a parliamentary commission be established to investigate an ill-defined proposal for "*voluntary* taxation at source." The Social Democrats' traditional partners in government, the agrarian Radicals, did not have a coherent position on PAYE in general, but they did not support the government's PAYE proposal. Indeed, the government's only vocal supporters outside of the Social Democratic Party came from two small splinter groups. The first was a pair of isolated former Liberal party members who called themselves Liberal Center (*Liberalt Centrum*), and the second was the Socialist People's Party, a minor party that had split from the Communists in 1959.[39] After two rounds of fruitless debate, the government shelved the PAYE proposal rather than put it to a vote and risk losing.

Undeterred, Grünbaum introduced the proposal again in July 1966. This was the third time the Social Democratic government had proposed PAYE taxation, and this time it was a tactical move. Prime Minister Jens Otto Krag was counting on the intransigence of the bourgeois opposition. He intended the *kildeskat* proposal to fail once again, so that he could use the impasse as an excuse to call for elections. Polls and party meetings in the intervening year had revealed a wellspring of support for the idea of a *kildeskat*, and Social Democrats were gambling that a new election would strengthen their shaky mandate. The first part of the plan worked splendidly: when the proposal came up for debate in October, the bourgeois parties took up their customary positions in opposition to PAYE. Although the Conservative opposition had begun to soften, revealing some room to negotiate, the Liberals were intransigent. As debate closed, Krag announced his intention to call for elections.[40]

The election that followed was so dominated by the issue of PAYE taxation that it is sometimes called "the tax-at-source election" (*kildeskattevalget*).[41]

The Social Democrats based their campaign almost entirely on the issue of income tax reform. They packaged taxation at source together with elimination of several tax deductions, and proposed to redefine the income tax unit so that individuals, rather than married couples, were liable for tax. The party framed these as egalitarian and modernizing reforms, but they were also practical measures that eased the way for implementation of PAYE, insofar as they would diminish the difference between the provisional tax withheld from wages and final tax liability. One widely reproduced election poster featured a picture of a trash can overflowing with crumpled income tax forms. "Who wouldn't like to see the end of the tax return—symbol of an archaic, byzantine [*indviklet*] tax system?" it asked rhetorically. The poster continued:

> And it is well on its way. When we get taxation at the source [*kildeskat*], most wage earners will escape from the nightmare of the tax return.
>
> Social Democracy has proposed: taxation at source—the repeal of joint taxation of married couples—a greater tax-free basic income—an increased child benefit—and a fixed, low tax percentage for a larger share of income.
>
> But we still have to put up with the old, antiquated tax system—because the Social Democratic Party does not have a majority in parliament. The other parties have talked about tax reform for thirteen years, and they will keep talking. They have not been able to come to agreement yet.
>
> Only a stronger Social Democratic government can pass the necessary tax reform—not someday, but NOW. And that is why your vote is needed.
>
> Do you want more talk, or do you want results? *That* is your choice on 22 November.[42]

The election polls confirmed a popular mandate for income tax reform. The results were otherwise not at all what the Social Democrats had anticipated. The greatest gains went to the Socialist People's Party, which threatened to outflank the Social Democrats on the left. When the dust had settled, the Social Democrats had lost seven seats, but the Socialist People's Party had gained ten, and socialists of one stripe or another were a majority in parliament for the first time in Danish history. The Social Democrats again formed a minority government, this time with the support of the Socialist People's Party. Although talks between the two parties did not bring the Socialist People's Party into the executive, the two parties established an informal coordinating body that came to be called "the Red Cabinet."[43]

It was this extraordinary socialist majority coalition that was finally able to get the *kildeskat* proposal through parliament. In a deft bit of policy packaging, Grünbaum proposed to couple PAYE taxation and income tax withholding with a value-added tax (VAT). The latter was a general consumption tax that was collected from businesses, and levied against the difference between their sales and the goods and services that they purchased. The VAT was passed on to consumers in the purchase price of goods, and it was understood to be a regressive tax. Social Democrats nevertheless supported it because of its capacity to generate revenue. They planned to compensate for its regressive effects by reducing income tax rates on the lower brackets.[44]

The Social Democrats also had two tactical goals in packaging PAYE together with a VAT. The first was to buy some support for PAYE among the bourgeois parties, who approved of consumption taxes. The second was to undercut the Socialist Peoples' Party by forcing it to take a position in favor of the VAT, a tax that was highly unpopular with its leftist base. Once the Socialist People's deputies had alienated their supporters by voting for the VAT, the theory went, they would be particularly unlikely to vote against the government on other issues, since this would be equivalent to a vote of no confidence and a call for new elections in which they would be likely to lose support.[45]

It worked more or less as planned. The Socialist People's Party reluctantly supported the VAT, and the Conservatives came around to support PAYE. The debate began on familiar ground. The Social Democrats argued for PAYE on the grounds that it was necessary to a modern welfare state. The Liberal speaker Henry Christensen replied that it imposed an unfair administrative burden on small employers. The Conservatives, however, began to signal a new willingness to compromise. Ninn-Hansen announced that his party would concede to the majority on PAYE in hopes of winning concessions on the tax rate. The ***kildeskat*** law passed on 31 March 1967 by a vote of 123 to 35, with 19 abstentions and two absent. The vote was almost exactly along party lines. Socialists and Conservatives supported the bill. All the Liberals, and only the Liberals, voted against the bill. The abstentions consisted of the Radicals, plus one defector each from the Conservative party and the Socialist People's Party, and a nonpartisan deputy from Greenland.[46]

In the end, the condition that enabled the passage of PAYE was the governing influence of socialist parties, supported by working-class votes, in an election that had appealed to workers *explicitly* for support of PAYE. After 1968, the income tax burden on the Danish working class increased dramatically. By 1973, Denmark had the heaviest income tax burden in the history of the world, and it fell largely on wage earners.[47]

The rapid growth of income taxation would lead to an income tax revolt described elsewhere in this volume. The new technique that enabled this expansion of income tax, however, was not foisted on wage earners unwilling or unawares. The idea came from working-class organizations, and a majority of working-class voters supported it at the polls. In short, they asked for it.

Comparative Conclusions[48]

PAYE income taxation is the form in which most of the rich democratic countries collect income tax from working-class adults. But as this case study of Denmark shows, it was precisely working-class political power—as exemplified, in this case, by the legislative influence of the Social Democratic Party—that provided the crucial condition for the adoption of PAYE. Workers and their representatives favored PAYE because it was part of a fiscal bargain. Taxes on current income support protections for workers and the techniques of provisional assessment and income tax withholding associated with PAYE taxation shift the burden of assessment and administration from workers to their employers and the state.

A brief side trip to Norway will provide a final comparative check on this political interpretation. Much like Denmark, Norway had appointed an expert commission to revise its tax structure in the late 1930s. The Norwegian "Tax Committee of 1936" (*Skattekomittéen av. 1936*) had considered PAYE taxation, but recommended against it mainly on the grounds that rural conditions and variations in the local income tax made it administratively impractical. The commission's report was circulating in 1940, when the German invasion and occupation put the work of the Finance Department on hold. After the war, the government appointed the "Tax Commission of 1946" (*Skatteutvalget av. 1946*), which dusted off earlier proposals and recommended PAYE taxation, despite the acknowledged difficulties of administering a current income tax in rural areas where wage earnings were often combined with in-kind income from fishing and agriculture.[49] The commission had already issued its report by 1948, but the Norwegian *Storting* did not enact PAYE taxation until 1952—after the 1949 elections gave the Norwegian Labor Party (*Det Norske Arbejderparti*) an absolute majority of seats for the first time in Norwegian history.[50] The similarity between Norwegian and Danish developments provides further evidence that the political power of labor, rather than economic efficiency or military necessity, dictated the timing of PAYE reforms in postwar Scandinavia and perhaps elsewhere as well.

The implications of this case study extend far beyond Denmark. The historical sociology of the state has labored for too long under the influence of a libertarian discourse that conceptualizes taxation as the extraction of resources by rulers from unwilling subjects. But this comparative study shows that those subjects, once enfranchised, may in fact demand that it be made *easier* for them to contribute to public goods. PAYE allowed governments to extract resources from the paychecks of the working class, but the working class was the electoral constituency that most supported PAYE. The lesson of this case is that taxation in modern, democratic states should be conceptualized not as predation, but as part of a social contract in which subjects exchange contributions for protection from the risks of market society. Taxation is more than extraction. At least sometimes, taxation is how we prefer to pay for security.

Notes

1. The figure of 11% is the average for the 15 countries listed in Fig. 1, computed from OECD, *Revenue Statistics*, 80. The comparable figure for general consumption taxes, including value-added tax, is 6%: idem., 124.
2. Haig, "Concept of Income," 7. If annual income is an annual rate of change between year t and year $t + 1$, we might conceptualize *current* income as an instantaneous rate of change, on analogy to the derivative of a continuous function. But no actually existing income tax system defines current income in this fashion, for two reasons. First, no government is capable of collecting information about every individual's economic power on a truly continuous basis. Second, even if this were possible, "current income" would be unobservable even in principle: given that the future is not observable, the present defines a point on the curve of economic power with respect to time at which the slope is literally undefined. Much more could be said about the ritual processes by which certain provisional numbers come to be accepted as representations of "current income." But for the purposes of this paper, I am focused on the conditions under which *any* such approximation is institutionalized as an appropriate basis for collecting taxes.
3. See, Lampland, "False Numbers," 378.
4. See, inter alia, Tilly, "War Making and State Making"; idem., *Coercion, Capital, and European States*; idem., "Extraction and Democracy."
5. Martin, *Permanent Tax Revolt*, 151–153.

6. Martin, Mehrotra and Prasad, "The Thunder of History," 14. The theoretical assumptions of this chapter may also remind a reader of Walter Korpi's "power resources theory"; see Korpi, "Power Resources and Employer-Centered Approaches." Two important differences are (a) the greater importance here accorded to the geopolitical interests of states and their citizens, and (b) the assumption that workers and their organizations sometimes struggle not only to realize redistributive goals but also to realize particular cultural ideals of just administration.
7. Steinmo, *Taxation and Democracy*; Levi, *Of Rule and Revenue*; see also Scheve and Stasavage, *Taxing the Rich.*
8. See Leimgruber, "Protecting Soldiers, Not Mothers."
9. Sources include Board of Inland Revenue, *Income Taxes Outside the Commonwealth*; idem., *Income Taxes Outside the United Kingdom*; Commerce Clearing House, *Tax Systems of the World*; Herler, "Den svenske Skatteopkrævningsreform"; Levi, *Of Rule and Revenue*; Leibfritz and O'Brien, "The French Tax System," 33; Lent, "Collection of Personal Income Tax at the Source"; Neumark, *Theorie und Praxis*; and Torgersen, "Skatt av. årets inntekt."
10. On the economic organization of occupation in Western Europe generally, including comparative data on levels of exploitation, see Liberman, *Does Conquest Pay?*, Chap. 3; Eichholtz, "Institutionen und Praxis," 29–62.
11. On mass-mobilizing war and taxation, see Scheve and Stasavage, *Taxing the Rich.*
12. See Seligman, *The Income Tax*, 243–250.
13. Data from Huber et al., "Comparative Welfare States Data Set." For details of the measure of cumulative left cabinet share, and its role in predicting welfare state development, see Huber and Stephens, *Development and Crisis.*
14. OECD, *Revenue Statistics*, 106.
15. On early income tax administration in Denmark, see Skattedepartementet, "Oversigt"; Philip, Skattepolitik, Chap. 9. The figures for 1939 are my calculations from Mitchell, *International Historical Statistics*, 935, 1013.
16. Petrick, "Das deutsche Okkupationsregime," 755–774; idem., "Einleitung," 18–61; Nissen, "Adjusting to German Domination," 98–138; Liberman, *Does Conquest Pay?*, Chap. 3; Giltner, *"In the Friendliest Manner,"* Chap. 1.
17. Some scholars have suggested that this rare concession was attributable to the special place the Danes and other Nordic peoples enjoyed in Nazi racial ideology (see, e.g., Liberman, *Does Conquest Pay?*, 39). The record suggests, however, that more pragmatic considerations of state were paramount. Consider the comparative evidence: in the first place, other Nordic states did not get off so easily. At Hitler's orders, the Nazi state drew a

sharp distinction between the "friendly" occupation policy toward Denmark and harsher rule in Norway, which was considered "enemy territory." In the second place, the initial terms that the German government offered to the other small, neutral countries of Europe—which were below Scandinavians in the hierarchy of races envisioned by Nazi ideologues—resembled the terms that it offered to Denmark (Giltner, *"In the Friendliest Manner,"* 6, 33, 170–174). Indeed, it was precisely for this reason that a lenient approach to Denmark was valuable to the German imperial project: the privileges accompanying the "protectorate" status could be held up before the other small neutrals as an example of the benefits that collaboration could bring (Petrick, "Das deutsche Okkupationsregime," 774).

18. See Liberman, *Does Conquest Pay?*, 41, 43.
19. Wendt, *Besættelse og Atomtid*, 20–21; Hansen Henriksen, *Velfærdsstaten*, 17.
20. Gelting, "Pengepolitiken," 238–239; Wendt, *Besættelse og Atomtid*, 245; Hansen and Henriksen, *Velfærdsstaten*, 20.
21. Kaarsted, *Krise og Krig*, 239; Kirchhoff, "Danish Resistance," 260.
22. Kaarsted, *Krise og Krig*, 241–243; Wendt, *Besættelse og Atomtid*, 165–177.
23. Herler, "Den svenske Skatteopkrævningsreform," 7.
24. Böhme, "Principal Features of Swedish Defence Policy," 119–134; Fritz, "A Question of Practical Politics," 95–118.
25. Molin, "Parliamentary Politics during World War II," 305–331; Nissen, "Adjusting to German Domination."
26. Herler, "Den svenske Skatteopkrævningsreform," 14–16; Rodriguez, *Offentlig inkomstexpansion*, Chap. 6.
27. Nørby Johansen, "Denmark," 203, 214–218; Hansen and Henriksen, *Velfærdsstaten*, 220–223; Esping-Andersen, *Politics against Markets*, 168–169.
28. On the history of the commission, see Skattelovskommissionen, *Betænkning, 1. Del*, 5–7; on PAYE, see ibid., 151–162, 181.
29. Skattelovskommissionen, *Betænkning, 1. Del*, 60.
30. Skattelovskommissionen, *Betænkning, 1. Del*, 174; idem., "Referat til finansministeren," 3–4; Philip, *Skattepolitik*, 262. For comparative data on the size of the Danish *petit bourgeoisie* in this period, see Esping-Andersen, *Politics against Markets*, 53.
31. Skattelovskommissionen, *Betænkning, 1. Del*, 174–175.
32. Skattelovskommissionen, *Betænkning, 1. Del*, 153, 183; Herler, "Den svenske skatteopkrævningsreform," 19–20. A similar system was also proposed in the United States in 1938 as a solution to the administrative problems of collecting social security payroll taxes for agricultural workers (Lieberman, *Shifting the Color Line*, 97–98).

33. The Danish employers' association, unlike its Swedish counterpart and in contradistinction to the stereotype of Scandinavian corporatism, was dominated by small employers. The average number of employees for its member firms at the end of World War II was just over ten (see Dansk Arbejdsgiverforening, *Arbejdsgiver foreningen*, 2, 363).
34. Skattelovskommissionen, "Referat til Finansministeren," 2; idem., *Betænkning, 1. Del*, 60–61.
35. Johansen, "Denmark," 200–203; Baldwin, *Politics of Social Solidarity*, 152–153, 226–227; Christensen, *Socialpolitiske strategier*, 106–107.
36. Krag and Andersen, *Kamp og Fornyelse*, 275; Lidegaard, *Jens Otto Krag*, 162. Kaarsted, *De Danske ministerier*, 299, suggests that in addition to these motives, social democrats may have also favored PAYE taxation because it would provide an excuse to abolish the *skattefradragsret*, a deduction that many in the party saw as a violation of the principle of taxation according to the ability to pay. Although this was doubtless a motivating factor for some party activists, the party's original proposal for PAYE taxation did not propose to eliminate the *skattefradragsret*. Finance minister Poul Hansen judged that a hard line against the popular deduction was either too provocative to put before the public, or else too extreme to demand as a starting point for negotiation with the bourgeois parties. See Krag and Andersen, *Kamp og Fornyelse*, 257–258.
37. *Folketingsårbog* (1964–1965): 425; Kaarsted, *De Danske ministerier*, 299–300; Krag and Andersen, *Kamp og Fornyelse*, 278–282.
38. Kaarsted, *De Danske Ministerier*, 299.
39. *Folketingstidende* (1965–1966): cols. 671, 682–683, 688, 690–691, 695–697, 711–713. Kaarsted, *De Danske ministerier*, 299, 310; Krag and Andersen, *Kamp og Fornyelse*, 316. On the origins of these minor parties, see Nissen, *Landet blev by*, 217–218, 307–308.
40. Kaarsted, *De Danske ministerier*, 324–325; Krag and Andersen, *Kamp og fornyelse*, 311, 325.
41. See, for example, Krag and Andersen, *Kamp og fornyelse*, 305, 321.
42. Lidegaard, *Jens Otto Krag*, 307, my translation from the Danish; the poster is also reproduced in Hammerich, *Det store flip*, 19. See also Nissen, *Landet blev by*, 315.
43. Mader, *SF under "det røde kabinet,"* Chap. 5; Rasmussen and Rüdiger, *Tiden efter 1945*, 195–197.
44. Krag and Andersen, *Kamp og fornyelse*, 289.
45. Kaarsted, *De Danske ministerier*, 299, 334–339.
46. *Folketingstidende* (1966–1967): cols. 364, 368–370, 375, 377–378, 3109; Kaarsted, *De Danske ministerier*, 339.
47. Indeed, some estimates imply that more than 100% of the personal income tax burden was borne by wage earners, inasmuch as personal income tax

deductions rendered the aggregate personal income tax yield from capital income negative, at least until tax reforms of the 1990s. See Ganghof, "The Political Economy of High Income Taxation," 1068.

48. This measure is calculated by computing left party cabinet seats as a proportion of all cabinet sets, and then summing over years. So, for example, if left parties held 0.5 of the cabinet seats this year, and 0.75 next year, then the cumulative annual share over the two year period would be 1.25. This measure is thought to combine the extent and duration of left party rule. I employ it here to facilitate comparison of these results with the quantitative literature on social policy development in rich democratic countries.
49. K. Torgersen, "Skatt av. årets inntekt," 1–2, 5.
50. *Tillæg A til Folketingstidende* (1966–1967): 112–160; see Mackie and Rose, *International Almanac of Electoral History*, 367, 371.

References

Baldwin, Peter. 1990. *The Politics of Social Solidarity: Class Bases of the European Welfare State, 1945–1975*. New York: Cambridge University Press.

Board of Inland Revenue. 1956–1966. *Income Taxes Outside the Commonwealth*. London: H. M. Stationery Office.

———. 1967–1983. *Income Taxes Outside the United Kingdom*. London: H. M. Stationery Office.

Böhme, Klaus-Richard. 1984. The Principal Features of Swedish Defence Policy 1925–1945. *International Review of Military History* 57: 119–134.

Christensen, Jacob. 1998. *Socialpolitiske strategier 1945–1972*. Odense: Odense Universitetsforlag.

Commerce Clearing House. 1938. *Tax Systems of the World*. 7th ed. New York: Commerce Clearing House.

Danmarks Statistik. 1932. *Statistisk Aarbog*. Danmarks Statistik: Copenhagen.

Dansk Arbejdsgiverforening. 1946. *Arbejdsgiver foreningen gennem 50 aar, 1896–1946*. Langkjærs Bogtrykkeri: Copenhagen.

Eichholtz, Dietrich. 1997. Institutionen und Praxis der deutschen Wirtschaftspolitik im NS-besetzten Europa. In *Die "Neuordnung" Europas: NS-Wirtschaftspolitik in den besetzten Gebieten*, ed. Richard J. Overy, Gerhard Otto, and Johannes Houwink ten Cate, 29–62. Berlin: Metropol.

Esping-Andersen, Gøsta. 1985. *Politics Against Markets: The Social Democratic Road to Power*. Princeton: Princeton University Press.

Folketingsårbog. 1964–1965. Copenhagen: J. Schultz.

Folketingstidende. 1965–1966. Copenhagen: J. Schultz.

Fritz, Martin. 1984. A Question of Practical Politics: Economic Neutrality During the Second World War. *International Review of Military History* 57: 95–118.

Ganghof, Steffen. 2007. The Political Economy of High Income Taxation: Capital Taxation, Path Dependence, and Political Institutions in Denmark. *Comparative Political Studies* 40 (9): 1059–1084.

Gelting, Jørgen. 1948. Pengepolitiken. In *Danmarks Økonomiske Forhold 1939–1945*, ed. Vilhelm Buhl, 221–240. Odense: A. C. Normanns Forlag and Forlaget Arnkrone Gelting.

Giltner, Philip. 1998. *"In the Friendliest Manner": German-Danish Economic Cooperation during the Nazi Occupation of 1940–1945*. New York: Peter Lang Publishing.

Haig, Robert M. 1921. The Concept of Income – Economic and Legal Aspects. In *The Federal Income Tax*, ed. Robert M. Haig, 1–28. New York: Columbia University Press.

Hammerich, Poul. 1984. *Det store flip, 1968–1972, vol. 6 of Danmarkskrønike*. Copenhagen: Gyldendal.

Hansen, Svend Aage, and Ingrid Henriksen. 1980. *Velfærdsstaten 1940–1978*. Copenhagen: Gyldendal.

Herler, Poul. 1945/1947. Den svenske Skatteopkrævningsreform ('Skatt vid Källan') i Henhold til Uppbördsförordning Nr. 896 af 31. In Rigsarkivet, Skattedepartementet, Skattelovkommissionen af 1937, Record Series 39/199/50, Box 4, Folder "Lønskat."

Huber, Evelyne, and John D. Stephens. 2001. *Development and Crisis of the Welfare State: Parties and Policies in Global Markets*. Chicago: University of Chicago Press.

Huber, Evelyne, Charles Ragin, John D. Stephens, David Brady, and Jason Beckfield. 2004. *Comparative Welfare States Data Set*. Northwestern University, University of North Carolina, Duke University and Indiana University.

Kaarsted, Tage. 1991. *Krise og Krig, vol. 13 of Gyldendal og Politikens Danmarkshistorie, ed. Olaf Olsen*. Copenhagen: Gyldendalske Boghandel and Politikens Forlag.

———. 1992. *De Danske ministerier 1953–1972*. Odense: Odense Universitetsforlag.

Kirchhoff, H. 1990. The Danish Resistance. In *Europäischer Widerstand im Vergleich: Die Internationalen Konferenzen Amsterdam*, ed. Ger van Roon, 249–270. Frankfurt: Siedler Verlag.

Korpi, Walter. 2006. Power Resources and Employer-Centered Approaches in Explanations of Welfare States and Varieties of Capitalism: Protagonists, Consenters, and Antagonists. *World Politics* 58 (2): 167–206.

Krag, J.O., and K.B. Andersen. 1977. *Kamp og fornyelse: Socialdemokratiets indsats i dansk politik 1955–1971*. Copenhagen: Fremad.

Lampland, Martha. 2010. False Numbers as Formalizing Practices. *Social Studies of Science* 40 (3): 377–404.

Leibfritz, Willi, and Paul O'Brien. 2005. The French Tax System: Main Characteristics, Recent Developments, and Some Considerations for Reform. *OECD Economics Department Working Papers*, no. 439.

Leimgruber, Matthieu. 2010. Protecting Soldiers, Not Mothers: Soldiers' Income Compensation in Switzerland During World War II. *Social Politics* 17 (1): 53–79.

Lent, George E. 1940. Collection of Personal Income Tax at the Source. *Journal of Political Economy* 50 (5): 719–737.

Levi, Margaret. 1985. *Of Rule and Revenue*. New York: Cambridge University Press.

Liberman, Peter. 1996. *Does Conquest Pay? The Exploitation of Occupied Industrial Societies*. Princeton: Princeton University Press.

Lidegaard, Bo. 2002. *Jens Otto Krag, 1962–1978*. Copenhagen: Gyldendal.

Lieberman, Robert C. 1998. *Shifting the Color Line: Race and the American Welfare State*. Cambridge: Harvard University Press.

Mackie, Thomas T., and Richard Rose. 1991. *The International Almanac of Electoral History*. Washington, DC: Congressional Quarterly, Inc..

Mader, Erik. 1979. *SF under "det røde kabinet" 1966–1968*. Odense: Odense Universitetsforlag.

Martin, Isaac William. 2008. *The Permanent Tax Revolt: How the Property Tax Transformed American Politics*. Stanford: Stanford University Press.

Martin, Isaac William, Ajay K. Mehrotra, and Monica Prasad. 2009. The Thunder of History: The Origins and Development of the New Fiscal Sociology. In *The New Fiscal Sociology: Comparative and Historical Approaches to Taxation*, ed. Isaac W. Martin, Ajay K. Mehrotra, and Monica Prasad, 1–27. New York: Cambridge University Press.

Mitchell, Brian. 2007. *International Historical Statistics: Europe, 1750–2005*. 6th ed. London: Palgrave Macmillan.

Molin, Karl. 1975. Parliamentary Politics During World War II. In Sweden's Development from Poverty to Affluence 1750–1970, ed. Steven Koblik, trans. Joanne Johnson and Steven Koblik, 305–331. Minneapolis: University of Minnesota Press.

Neumark, Fritz. 1947. *Theorie und Praxis der modernen Einkommensbesteuerung*. Bern: A. Francke.

Nissen, Henrik S. 1983. Adjusting to German Domination. In *Scandinavia During the Second World War*, ed. Henrik S. Nissen, trans. Thomas Munch-Petersen, 98–138. Minneapolis: University of Minnesota.

———. 1991. *Landet blev by, 1950–1970, vol. 14 of Gyldendal og Politikens Danmarkshistorie*. Copenhagen: Gyldendal and Politikens Forlag.

Nørby Johansen, Lars. 1987. Denmark. In *Growth to Limits: The Western European Welfare States since World War II, Volume 4: Appendix (Synopses, Bibliographies, Tables)*, ed. Peter Flora, 191–246. Berlin and New York: Walter de Gruyter.

Organization for Economic Cooperation and Development (OECD). *Revenue Statistics of OECD Member Countries, 2015 edition*. Paris: OECD.

Petrick, Fritz. 1991. Das deutsche Okkupationsregime in Dänemark 1940 bis 1945. *Zeitschrift für Geschichtswissenschaft* 19 (8): 755–774.

———. 1992. Einleitung. In *Die Okkupationspolitik des Deutschen Faschismus in Dänemark und Norwegen (1940–1945)*, ed. Fritz Petrick, 18–61. Berlin: Bundesarchiv and Hüthig Verlagsgemeinschaft.

Philip, Kjeld. 1965. *Skattepolitik*. Copenhagen: Gyldendal.

Rasmussen, Hanne, and Mogens Rüdiger. 1990. *Tiden efter 1945, vol. 8 of Danmarks historie*. Copenhagen: Gyldendal.

Rodriguez, Enrique. 1980. *Offentlig inkomstexpansion: En analys av drivkrafterna bakom de offentliga inkomsternas utveckling i Sverige under 1900-tallet*. Uppsala: CWK Gleestrup.

Seligman, Edwin R.A. 1911. *The Income Tax: A Study of the History, Theory and Practice of Income Taxation at Home and Abroad*. New York: Macmillan.

Skattedepartementet. 1953. Oversigt over den gældende indkomst-og formuebeskatning i Danmark. Rigsarkivet (Denmark), Skattedepartementet, Skattelovkommissionen af 1937, Record Series 39/199/50, Box 9.

Skattelovskommissionen. 1948. *Betænkning om Beskatningen af Indkomst og Formue m.v., 1. Del*. Copenhagen: J. H. Schultz.

———. n.d. Referat til finansministeren angående lønskat. Rigsarkivet, Record Series 39/199/50, Box 4, folder "Lønskat."

Steinmo, Sven. 1993. *Taxation and Democracy: Swedish, British, and American Approaches to Financing the Modern State*. New Haven: Yale University Press.

Tillæg A til Folketingstidende. Copenhagen: J. Schultz, 1966–1967.

Tilly, Charles. 1985. War Making and State Making as Organized Crime. In *Bringing the State Back In*, ed. Peter Evans, Dietrich Rueschemeyer, and Theda Skocpol, 169–191. New York: Cambridge University Press.

———. 1992. *Coercion, Capital, and European States, A.D. 990–1992*. Cambridge, MA: Blackwell.

———. 2009. Extraction and Democracy. In *The New Fiscal Sociology*, ed. Isaac W. Martin, Ajay K. Mehrotra, and Monica Prasad, 173–182. New York: Cambridge University Press.

Torgersen, K. 1948. Skatt av årets inntekt. Foredrag holdt i Skattejuridisk forening 19. November. Skattejuridisk Forening (Norway), Foredrag Nr. 3/48, in Rigsarkivet, Record Series 39/199/50, Box 4, folder "Lønskat."

Wendt, Fritz. 1966. *Besættelse og Atomtid, 1949–1966*. Vol. 14 of *Danmarks Historie*. Ed. John Danstrup and Hal Koch. Copenhagen: Politikens Forlag.

Universalism and Tax Consent in Denmark

Shintaro Kurachi

Introduction

According to a number of studies, the Nordic countries are characterized by a high degree of universalism in their welfare systems. Rothstein argues that universalism has several dimensions.[1] One pertains to how many people, services, and cash benefits are covered; another is how benefits and services are distributed. There is an important difference between universalism and selectivism. Under a universal system state benefits (i.e., for illness and disability, unemployment, and old age support) are needs-tested; under selectivism, they are means-tested (i.e., the service and cash benefits are available to certain income groups only). Therefore, flat cash benefits which are not means-tested (e.g., child benefits) are universal. Regarding eligibility and allocation,[2] Denmark has a universal welfare system, mainly because national pensions and child benefits are set at flat rates and paid in kind. They are funded by local governments, despite universal national pensions having been gradually eroded.[3] Historically, benefit equality was adopted by agricultural coalitions and the working class in the Nordic countries.[4] Therefore, universal welfare placed the socioeconomic situation of all citizens on a par and helped forge social solidarity as a class-free coalition.

S. Kurachi (✉)
Research Department, Tokyo Institute for Municipal Research, Tokyo, Japan
e-mail: mail@shintarokurachi.org

G. Huerlimann et al. (eds.), *Worlds of Taxation*,
Palgrave Studies in the History of Finance,
https://doi.org/10.1007/978-3-319-90263-0_5

The Nordic countries are known for their low inequality thanks to their universal welfare systems. Korpi and Palme point out the "paradox of redistribution," namely, the paradoxical effect by which social policy targeted specifically at the poor leads to more inequality than universal social policies.[5] Korpi and Palme's argument, however, is controversial. Using their analysis, Marx and colleagues show that targeted policies, such as tax credits, can have the effect of reducing inequality.[6]

One of the reasons why these findings are controversial is that the scale of governmental expenditure is based on having sufficient tax revenue. Universal welfare systems can reduce inequality because countries adopting this system tend to have a high tax burden, as is the case in the Nordic countries. In other words, the universal welfare system is based on having enough tax revenue to enable these countries to distribute benefits generously, regardless of recipients' income, in order to reduce income inequality.

This chapter focuses on the historical development of, and the relationship between, universal welfare and a high tax burden since the 1970s to explain how Denmark has built its welfare system in recent years. The Danish welfare system in the early 1970s was not universal but selective, and Denmark has experienced the largest tax revolts in Europe.[7]

Figure 1 shows the historical changes in the tax rate structure and the support for taxation. Danish income taxation consists of a central progressive income tax and local (municipality and county) propositional income taxes. The local income tax rate is not fixed at the national level; instead, local governments set their own rate. The government introduced value-added tax (VAT) in 1967. The Danish election study survey (*Valgundersøgelsen*) provides data on parliamentary election results: In 1973, over 90 percent of the electorate agreed that politicians wasted taxpayers' money, but this percentage had decreased to 34 percent by 2007. In 1973, 89 percent of the electorate considered that too many people received social benefits despite not needing them; this had fallen to 51 percent by 2007. These results show that dissatisfaction with the use of tax revenue rose initially and led to the 1973 tax revolt, but declined gradually thereafter. The majority of taxpayers in Denmark now support their welfare system.

This raises two questions: How did the government overcome the tax revolts, and how did the Danish welfare system became universal? This chapter details how Denmark came to embrace a universal welfare system following the tax revolt, and how it was able to keep a high tax burden in the wake of the tax revolts of the 1970s. By examining government and

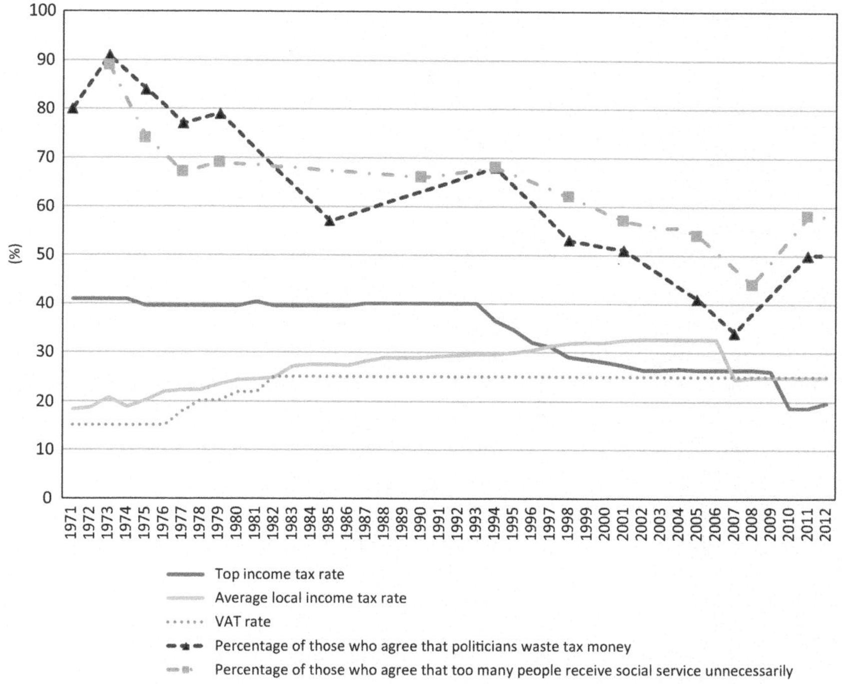

Fig. 1 Trends in the tax structure and perceptions in Denmark. Note: The ratio of each question includes the sum of those who answered "strongly agree" and "agree." Source: *Danske vaelggere 1971–2011*; Denmark Statistics

committee documents, poll survey data, newspaper articles, and other sources, we also look at the historical development of consent to taxation in Denmark.

This chapter is organized as follows. Section "Reform in the 1970s: Social Reform and the Social Assistance Act" discusses the tax revolts in Denmark during the 1970s as well as the process of building a universal welfare system through social policy reforms. Section "The 1980s Reform: Under Globalization" focuses on the welfare and tax reforms of the 1980s under globalization and a financial crisis. Section "Flexicurity: Active Labor Market Policy in the 1990s" analyzes the backlash against the universal welfare system since the 2000s. Finally, Section "After the 2000s: Universalism Is Overturned" suggests areas for future research.

Reform in the 1970s: Social Reform and the Social Assistance Act

In 1891, Denmark became the first country to introduce social assistance in the form of a non-contributory pension scheme (*Alderdomsunderstøttelsen*) that did not entail a loss of civil rights (the right to vote, etc.) or a revolutionary institution. However, social democracy was not fully established, because the unions were weak.

Trade union and management relations formed when the conflict between the *Landsorganisation I Danmark* and the *Dansk Arbejdgiversforeningen* ended with the "September Agreement" of 1899, which contained "not the written rules in the agreement, but the premises on which they were based and their interpretation."[8] In the 1924 general election, the Social Democratic Party (*Socialdemokraterne*) won, and in 1933, the social welfare minister, Karl Kristian Steincke, declared that the state was responsible for providing minimum benefits and services, which meant the government guaranteed the citizens' right to life.[9]

The Danish government began expanding its welfare state in the 1950s. In 1956, it introduced a universal pension (*Folkepension*) for those aged over 67 and its benefits increased consistently, beginning in 1964 and peaking in 1970. Unemployment benefit was also revised several times. In 1946, it was increased to a maximum of 80 percent of average income for those employed in the same trade or profession. The upper limit was increased, and the 80 percent level was calculated according to income from 1967 onward.[10] Following the enactment of the Public Assistance Act of 1961, social assistance was no longer tied to the loss of rights (e.g., the right to vote). Its benefits were set at the same basic level as the national pension,[11] with poverty relief and local benefits reaching similar levels.[12]

Social services also expanded during the 1950s and 1960s. "Housewife relief" (*Husmoderafløsning*), which provided short-term employment for homemakers, was introduced in 1951. It was the municipalities that were responsible for "housewife relief" and housekeeping, both of which were considered regular employment from 1968 onward. Although the municipalities had always borne some of the costs, taxpayers only began to complain about the local tax burden after "housewife relief" was introduced.[13] Altogether, government expenditure increased rapidly during that decade, raising questions about the best way to allocate social welfare funds.[14]

The tax system developed rapidly with the expansion of the welfare state. In January 1967, the Social Democratic government adopted a pay-as-you-earn (PAYE) system[15] to fund the welfare state and resolve the problem of horizontal equity between taxpayers whose income was increasing and taxpayers on a fixed income. This had been complicated due to the time lag in estimating taxable income. The introduction of a withholding tax added rapidly to the actual tax burden because any undeclared taxable income was now included by collecting tax revenue from the employee.

VAT was also introduced and replaced sales tax. It yielded more tax revenue and was in line with the European Community (EC) countries' tax systems.[16] Employer associations, such as the Danish Employers' Association (*Dansk Arbejdgiversforeningen*, DAF) backed these reforms, as did several other parties, although the Liberal Party (*Venstre*) opposed them. This was because PAYE posed a number of technical problems, such as the local tax authority's inability to compute the local taxable income correctly.[17] Furthermore, the Danish people were against the withholding tax. According to the Danish Electorate Studies of October 1968, only 8.9 percent of the population favored the system, while 74.3 percent were against it. In spite of this, the government had no choice but to increase the tax burden further to fund the welfare system.

Moreover, local taxes were also overhauled and transformed from a progressive to a proportional system, with the tax bases of central and local income taxation integrated. The local tax system was standardized to some extent, and the total local income tax burden increased rapidly from the late 1960s due to the large increase in tax rates, in spite of the abolition of progressive taxation, increasing by 7.67 percent between 1969 and 1971. The local income tax increase was higher than that of the national tax rate.

These significant tax reforms resulted in severe problems under adverse economic conditions. First, high inflation and interest rates increased both the tax burden and government expenditure. The inflation rate was 3.9 percent in 1961, but had increased to 7.4 percent by 1970. The wage coordination agreements between the trade unions and DAF, adopted in the 1980s and based on the inflation rate, became the standard coordination models and led to "bracket creep" (when inflation drives income into the higher tax brackets).[18] At the same time, government expenditure increased owing to the high inflation rate, because cash benefits were also based on inflation.

Second, tax administration faced serious problems, owing to technical and human factors. Although parliament decided to introduce PAYE in 1967, this was delayed until 1970 due to technical problems and a change of government. Moreover, the head of the finance ministry (*Skatteministeriet*), which was in favor of the withholding tax (*Kildeskattedirektorat*), warned all employees in writing of their obligation to comply with the new tax laws. However, the finance minister, Poul Møller, apologized and promised not to repeat this mistake. In the late 1970s, local governments made numerous errors in estimating taxable income, and problems surfaced when these were addressed.[19] In October 1971, the local tax authorities overcharged because the local governments had estimated their taxable income incorrectly. In addition, the municipalities had an incentive to estimate their taxable income, because they did so earlier than the central government. If the municipalities' estimates were higher than the actual cost, they had access to short-term, interest-free revenue.[20]

It was not only tax administration, but also government services that faced problems. In the Institute of Social Research's (*Socialforskningsinstitut*, SFI) 1968 and 1972 reports, an interview survey determined the nature of clients' "social events" (*Social Begivenhed*, or social needs). The survey highlighted the applicant's "social events," which were not determined according to income, but according to special needs, such as unemployment, illness, pregnancy, divorce, separation, or the death of a spouse.[21] According to this survey, about 20 percent of "social events" applicants did not improve their status for more than three months, and public services were not accessible to nearly half the applicants.[22]

Cooperation between social institutions and offices in the municipalities did not function well, since information was not shared and each party resorted to their own measures. Those who applied to the social institutions were sent from one department to another. Each institution estimated needs individually and benefit levels differently.[23] Bent Rold Andersen summarized the causes of this difficulty as follows: "The division of tasks between the research institutions of the authorities was hampered somewhat by the fact that the bases for the various assistant organizations privileges were highly variable."[24]

Social workers were extremely formal, conventional, and biased, and if they were unable to understand an applicant's status, they shared the information among the authorities. Attitudes like these could be found in the national health insurance and unemployment benefit offices, as well as in the social committees. However, among maternity benefit workers, rehabilitation center workers, and family consultants' such attitudes were less pronounced.[25]

Most taxpayers were dissatisfied with the welfare distribution system. According to the Danish Election Study of 1973 (*Danske Vælgere*), the question ($N = 531$) asked was whether people favored universal or selective services. They could select either of two answers: "More discretion is needed before providing assistance to people" or "Welfare benefits should be given to anyone who has a right to them." Around 86.3 percent ($N = 458$) of respondents chose the former, and around 9 percent ($N = 48$) the latter, indicating that selective welfare services were widely supported in 1973.[26] Of the former, around 94 percent agreed that "politicians waste taxpayers' money."[27] Even more dissatisfaction was reflected in favoring selective welfare services, making it difficult to break the vicious circle of tax protests and selective welfare services.

While many Danish taxpayers expressed opposition to increasing the tax burden, in a TV interview in January 1971, tax lawyer Mogens Glistrup compared paying taxes to having toothache, and claimed that "paying tax is immoral." He added, "To increase a single krona in taxes paid to the government would lead the country to ruin."[28] The "toothache" that Glistrup described meant people felt they were disadvantaged, with high-income groups resorting to tax avoidance and thus giving rise to inequality.[29] He appealed to taxpayers who resented the ability of the wealthy to take advantage of the tax deduction laws which should have benefited the low- to middle-income sectors. Blue-collar workers and poor families supported him. As far as Glistrup was concerned, taxation was an infringement on private ownership. On the other hand, he also believed that tax avoidance, resorted to by high-income earners, should be accessible to the low- to middle-income groups by means of tax reduction measures. All this led to a national movement, the Progress Party, established on August 22, 1972, with Glistrup as its leader. The aims of the Progress Party can be outlined as follows:

First, personal income tax was to be abolished by the 1980s. In fact, the Progress Party advocated introducing large income deductions for low-income groups and adopting high tax rates once a certain level of income had been reached. Second, the party was opposed to scrapping housing expenditure deductions, which the government had introduced in 1965, owing to high inflation. The party believed the deductions should have been maintained at the 1972 level as many middle-income groups benefited from the deductions when buying a new home. Third, Glistrup and his party demanded more generous pensions and medical care, to replace the existing welfare services. State-employed social workers were to be replaced by private employees, while doctors, business persons, and engineers were to be given public service employment.[30] They insisted on "not self-responsibility, but increased assistance to citizens" with respect to social services, but were against expanding general social services with government grants. Moreover, the number of teachers, nurses, and childcare assistants employed by the state should be reduced and replaced with those in the private sector. Their number would be determined by how much welfare support each municipality needed.[31] The party, fourth, proposed that the number of MPs and officials be reduced by 40. And fifth, media and state schools should be apolitical.

Most politicians found these proposals unrealistic. However, they were based on distrust of the existing political parties and civil service; protests against vested interests and high-income groups; and favoring cash benefits for all except public officials. Progress Party supporters came mostly from the low- to middle-income labor pool (i.e., blue-collar workers), who were vehemently opposed to and criticized social workers, teachers, and officials alike. The Progress Party faced several management problems, since it was set up at short notice. Established in the fall of 1972, the Progress Party accelerated the development of the movement throughout 1973. However, many members quit and membership fluctuated. The party was more centralized than other parties, and although Glistrup was charismatic and exerted power within the association,[32] the Progress Party was not able to maintain internal cohesion. In the 1973 election, the Progress Party did well, becoming the second-largest party in parliament (the Social Democratic Party remained the largest party). The Progress Party demanded abolishing or at least reducing the income tax burden, but was unsuccessful because it did not reach out to other parties to form a coalition.

The tax reform of 1975 was the first of its kind following the 1973 election. The government planned to implement a central income tax reduction, which included a decrease in the top marginal income tax rate (DKK[33] 70 billion) and an increase in local income tax. At the same time, the Progress and the Radical Liberal Parties criticized the government's proposition and suggested increasing personal income deductions for the low- to middle-income groups in order to achieve vertical equity and social equality.[34] The Progress Party's proposition included a substantial reduction in income tax. This plan was more unrealistic than others, according to Knud Heisen of the Social Democrat Party, who criticized the "Progress Party's assumption of reducing personal income taxation", because of the large lack of tax revenue.[35]

The Liberal government tried to implement a tight fiscal policy, reducing central income tax and VAT. In particular, resolving the external payment deficits and stagflation was urgent. In May 1974, the government suggested a third long-term plan, which combined income tax reductions and expenditure cuts. Support from members of the Progress Party or other parties was necessary for the plan to get through. The Progress Party opposed it, although at the last moment some of its members came out in support. It was at this point that Glistrup faltered. Members of the party did not support the party's plan at a meeting, with Niels Eriksen declaring he was backing the government; three other members followed him. The Progress Party was thus unable to exercise any influence in parliament because of this organizational issue.[36]

During the 1975 tax reform, the lowest income tax rate was cut, the highest rate was increased, and the medium income tax bracket was abolished altogether. This reduced the tax burden on the middle-income group. At the same time, the local (proportional) income tax rate rose from 18.8 percent to 22.2 percent. As a result, tax revenue sources were transferred from the central government to local governments. The tax burden of the low- to middle-income groups fell and more taxpayers paid proportional income tax.[37]

Social policy reform, in the form of the Social Assistance Act (*Bistandsloven*), was reviewed after the 1973 election. It integrated seven welfare laws: social benefit, child support, youth support, maternity benefit, rehabilitation, care of the elderly, and home help. Since all service "windows" were integrated, each municipality's welfare services became familiar to all Danes. Under the Social Assistance Act, each municipality set a discretionary service level, following a social worker assessment. Under the law (known as the "framework law"), the central government decided the general direction of the service, while local governments determined its level, content, and quality.[38]

Contrary to the optimism prevalent before the 1973 oil shock, Bent Rold Andersen's support for reducing need, as well as concern for the considerable social costs that would be incurred were the government to regulate social care, became more pressing, with rising unemployment and greater social spending. Support for the Social Assistance Act declined. Only the Liberal Radicals (*Radikale Venstre*), Social Democrats, and Right Union (*Retsforbundet*) Party, as well as a single member from the Center Democratic Party, continued to support it; they did, though, keep a low public profile. The Left voted against the

Act and the other parties abstained. Palle Simonsen,[39] a Conservative People's Party (*Det Konservative Folkeparti*) member (1968–1975, 1977–1989), argued that his party was opposed to the law as, in their opinion, there was a risk that the cost would be higher than the government's projections. Moreover, Inge Krogh[40] of the Christian People's Party[41] (*Kristeligt Folkeparti*) and the Central Democrat Erhard Jacobsen[42] pointed out that no members had received a summary of the statutory financial consequences.[43]

The main criticism was that it would result in an additional fiscal burden due to tight fiscal pressure following the oil shocks. The Social Assistance Act was intended to move burden-sharing from the state government to local governments, and how the calculations were made changed significantly. The process of replacing specific grants with block grants had gradually proceeded through five steps, starting in 1970. As a result, local government discretion had increased in line with the increasing ratio of block grants, and this in spite of public opinion, which was not in support of selective local government services.[44]

Before introducing the Social Assistance Act, there was inter-party controversy with regard to the intergovernmental fiscal burden, the reimbursement rate ratio (the specific grants rate), and the change to block grants. The center-right government tried to increase block grants, while the former social minister, Eva Gredal, was against the increase, telling the Social Committee on March 13, 1974, that "continuing this way [the government trying to replace reimbursement with block grants], preventive and outreach social work in municipalities will fail," and "we will maintain a government where there has to be state reimbursement."

The Social Reform Commission reported that "the Minister of the Social Affairs Committee had expressed the view that a significant extension of a block grant scheme for the Social Assistance Act requires very careful distribution."[45] A block grant would undoubtedly involve inequality among the municipalities; for example, the Copenhagen county would incur extra expenditure (DKK 200 million), as would the Copenhagen municipality (DKK 360 million), if they considered block grants. The social minister, Jacob Sørensen, claimed that it was not possible to separate assistance from other administrative expenditures.[46]

Local governments were also against how the Social Assistance Act was funded. At the Social Committee on May 28, 1973, the Local Government Association[47] (*Kommunernes Landsforening*) vehemently criticized the law: "The law leads with a threat, pointing out obligations and with directions in refunding. The people above all are aware of the restrictions, not the rights."[48] They were furious that they had to pay for social workers' training (in certain subjects) because of the heavy burden it placed on them. The Social Workers Association Education Committee countered that "the municipal proposal would simply mean lowering the professionalism of social workers."[49]

In the government's first proposal for the funding system, the counties were assigned a function in the reimbursement system (a type of specific grant) because they operated with a reimbursement rate of 67 percent paid by the county to the municipality. However, this was not adopted, following municipal protests. In the Social Committee, the Ministry of Social Affairs responded to the Act as follows: "Resistance from the Local Government Association against funding in which counties are involved, is built essentially on the view that such a system would result in conflicts between counties and municipalities, and injures the desired cooperation in the implementation of social reform."[50] Reimbursement was not required to ensure the quality of social workers, according to the minister.

Responsibility for giving advice and guidance was assigned to the Social Committee, and the social and health administration. As the Ministry of Social Affairs confirmed, the central government would set stringent rules on how the municipalities would run the social services. If provisions were made for granting reimbursements from the state for expenditure on consultancy work, provision would be needed to regulate both the consulting companies and the criteria by which these expenses were distinguished from other administrative expenses.[51] In other words, a fiscal state guarantee to cover the cost of advice and guidelines would create fixed and strict criteria for the municipalities. The Ministry of Social Affairs wanted the municipalities to bear the cost to avoid strict rules being imposed.

The government increased the revenues for the Social Assistance Act, even though the law was criticized for its lack of financial support and the high ratio of block grants and reimbursement. The Act, now supported by the Social Democrat Party and the four government coalition parties, was adopted on June 13, 1974, and came into force on April 1, 1976, integrating the previous seven laws, with municipalities becoming the single point of contact for services and given significant discretion in determining client needs.

First, "safety and robust development" meant that "people should not be worried about their 'social circumstances,' or needs changing, and should be assured that they would be supported (according to income loss)."[52]

Social circumstances determined the needs. Regarding the relationship between normal income and social circumstances, Bent Rold Andersen analyzed pre-retirement income and estimated the total number of "normal days" (*normaldage*; i.e., days of work) lost due to social circumstances.[53]

Second, regarding "prevention and measures to identify problems (so-called seek-out measures, *forebyggelse og søge-out foranstaltninger*)," the commission emphasized that "prevention in the long run could be a less expensive way to implement social policy than to pay the costs" (according to the first report; Betænkning No. 543)[54]; "prevention should be accompanied by 'seek-out' activities [*søge-out aktiviteter*]" (second report; Betænkning No. 664).[55] The aim of "seek-out activities" was "to undertake preventive steps ... and as far as possible ensure that treatment and rehabilitation are offered to those who need it."[56]

Third, the "whole family principle" meant that "it was necessary to look at the whole family and see if there was something in their situation which needed to be investigated."[57]

Fourth, the "income-loss principle" (*Indkomst tab*) meant that benefits would be based on need, and that the welfare system would no longer be selective but universal. The framework for needs assessment was based on the client's current situation (estimates principle), because it was expected that the social "circumstance," or crisis, in question would be brief.[58]

Finally, the "unity principle" (*Enhedsprincippet*) was a general approach to resolving clients' social problems. Under the earlier one-tier system (*det enstrengede system*),[59] the municipalities were responsible for coordinating clients' assistance in one place.

Thus, with the introduction of the Social Assistance Act, social policy changed from selective to universal, with the result that the same service would be provided to clients with similar needs and that each local government would provide services based on different needs.

The 1980s Reform: Under Globalization

In the early 1980s, in the aftermath of the oil shocks, the economy faced issues such as a deterioration in its current account balance, cost–push inflation, a deteriorating fiscal balance, and a higher unemployment rate—in a word, stagflation. Consequently, a Keynesian demand policy became ineffective, and in the 1980s, the government turned to currency devaluation to improve the current account balance and keep pace with the European Community's financial deregulation, such as deregulation of overseas financial transactions made in Denmark. High inflation had limited the previous corporatist model between labor and management. By the early 1970s, wage adjustment agreements between labor and management (*Dyrtidsregulering*) had been adapted to an automatic rule based on price changes. Nevertheless, they often could not conclude wage agreements due to high inflation.

There were fewer tax revolts in the early 1980s. Mogens Glistrup was arrested on charges of tax evasion in 1983 and the influence of the Progress Party evaporated. According to the Danish Municipality Election Survey (*Kommunalvalgsvundersøgelse*), in 1978 local taxation evaluation was better than central government taxation evaluation. The number of people who agreed with or were partly in favor of cutting local taxes even if it led to a reduction in local services was higher than in 1981, and people who supported the status quo on municipal taxes and the way the municipality spent were the majority in 1993 and 2005. Consequently, each local government was able to maintain or even increase the local income tax rate, which was the highest of all the Organisation for Economic Co-operation and Development (OECD) countries; the burden on the middle-income group, for example, was 58.2 percent in 1980.[60]

However, the income tax system still had a large loophole due to a plethora of generous income deductions, because vociferous protests by taxpayers had blocked any adjustment to many or scrapping altogether all deductions in the 1970s. The marginal tax rate for capital income varied, depending on the type of taxation and holdings. As a result, the capital income tax system had large inequalities. Furthermore, the liberalization of international capital regulations to improve current account balances caused by currency devaluation continuously enlarged the capital income tax deductions loophole. Both increases to tax deductions due to high inflation and tax evasion reduced net taxable capital income and the tax revenue of capital income taxation.[61] To avoid a repetition of the 1970s tax revolts, in the 1980s the government attempted to introduce a complex tax deduction system for total tax burdens and tax revenue.

In 1982, Kristensen (Finance Ministry) Committee proposed the introduction of "general proportional capital income taxation," a discrete form of taxation with a progressive labor income tax rate and an integrated proportional capital income tax rate, as the prototype of dual income taxation (DIT) based on this committee's reports. The Kristensen Committee also considered introducing inflation-adjusted expenditure and general proportional capital income taxation.[62] This, however, was postponed when inflation fell, and introducing expenditure taxation in Denmark alone would have resulted in profound fiscal problems, incentivizing consumption abroad.[63] The committee abandoned the idea of a comprehensive income tax, and now proposed "general proportional capital income taxation."

The Social Democrat government had intended to introduce tax reforms, but following a change of government, this plan was postponed because the opposition party was strongly against the policy as they believed it would increase the fiscal debt. In 1982, a right-wing centrist government led by Prime Minister Poul Schlüter came to power. It too proposed reforming the tax system by introducing proportional capital taxation. However, the Social Democrat Party was against the proposal because it benefited high-income taxpayers. The party proposed an additional gross income tax (*Bruttobeskatning*) for high taxpayers only.[64]

The Tax Reform Act was passed in 1985, and DIT was introduced, in addition to gross income tax (labor income plus net capital income) for high-income taxpayers. This meant that the principle of separate taxation was not achieved. The 1987 tax reforms maintained large tax revenues thanks to progressive labor income taxation and ensured the horizontal equality of income taxation, with additional taxation under the activation of international capital flow, which was one result of globalization. According to poll surveys (*Den politiske troværdighed i Danmark, 1991*), the greater the proportion of high-income respondents, the higher the ratio of answers stating that the tax burden had increased after the tax reform, as it had boosted the vertical equality of income taxation.

New child benefits were also introduced to compensate for the smaller benefits for the low- to middle-income sectors under DIT. A low birth rate was another social problem.[65] The child benefit level was flat regardless of the number of children in a family and the parents' income. The social assistance benefits for households with dependent children also increased substantially.[66] Moreover, all cash benefits[67] now became fixed taxable income (*Fast Skattepligtigydelse*). It is thus easy to understand the relationship between the tax burden and cash benefits, and to compare the value of each cash benefit.

To determine the effect of introducing the Social Assistance Act in the context of conflict within parties and an economic downturn, the Institute of Social Research conducted an interview survey in 1982.[68] According to the results, from January to April 1982, almost half the population (49 percent) had experienced one or more emergencies. Illness was the most common (21 percent), followed by unemployment (12 percent), loss of income and higher expenditures (11 percent), and others (15 percent). More than half (52 percent) experienced economic loss, with unemployment being the most serious, with three out of four of the unemployed suffering financial loss. Low-income groups in particular were vulnerable to these emergencies.[69]

Table 1 shows how social events in Denmark changed and how determining need according to municipalities changed in 1966 (1474 families with 2381 family members), 1977 (3409 people), and 1982.

The number of people experiencing adverse social circumstances increased by 5 percent between 1966 and 1977, and then decreased by 13 percent. The number of unemployed, the amount of income loss and

Table 1 The number/percentage of individuals who had experienced adverse social circumstances or who had applied to social services under the Social Assistance Act

Event	*Year*	*Social event*		*Access to social services*	
		Number of individuals	*Percentage*	*Number of individuals*	*Percentage of access*
18–66 years old					
	1966	788,000	26	1,01,000	12
	1977	1,454,000	46	2,08,000	14
	1982	1,262,000	40	2,87,000	23
Disease/accident					
	1966	636,000	21	89,000	14
	1977	928,000	30	1,12,000	12
	1982	655,000	21	98,000	15
Unemployment					
	1966	63,000	2	9000	15
	1977	2,26,000	7	53,000	23
	1982	3,96,000	12	1,07,000	27
Income decrease/expenditure increase					
	1966	61,000	2	3000	5
	1977	2,47,000	8	32,000	13
	1982	3,24,000	11	69,000	20
Divorced					
	1966	11,000	0	0	0
	1977	23,000	1	3000	12
	1982	30,000	1	13,000	44

Source: Plovsing, *Socialreformens idealer og praksis*, 1985, 512

expenditure increase, and housing problem categories increased in particular between 1977 and 1982. The ratio of social adverse circumstances was constant; however, the number of adverse circumstances fell.[70]

As Table 1 shows, access to social services changed. Seventy-three percent had applied to at least one social service department for municipal social and health services, unemployment benefit, employment services, their trade union, general practitioners/medical consultants, and hospitals, clinics, or sanatoria. The frequency of access to social services depended on department and need.[71]

From 1966 to 1977, there was a 106 percent increase in the number of people who turned to social services; between 1977 and 1982, the increase was 38 percent. Consultation rates rose from 12 percent in 1966 to 23 percent in 1982. Despite the decline in the number of people under social event between 1977 and 1982, the number of those who turned to social and health services increased. The reason was twofold[72]: first, the duration of income loss; and second, people's greater likelihood to turn to social services for help.[73] Thus, the municipalities could better capture the needs of clients under the Social Assistance Act.

However, social circumstances in the municipalities showed differences in the services responsible for responding to emergencies. Of every 100 clients receiving assistance through the Act nationwide, 10.1 percent received cash. The largest municipality gave 9.15 percent in cash benefits, and the smallest, 5.4 percent. Overall, the proportion of welfare recipients was lowest in the small municipalities and highest in large cities. There were 5.1 cases of long-term (i.e., more than five weeks) illness per 100 inhabitants. The most densely populated municipality had 72 cases per 100 inhabitants, while the least populated had 3.5 cases, with the share of long-term sickness cases lowest in small municipalities and highest in Copenhagen. Distribution of needs was thus based on the size of the municipality, in line with the fiscal burden. The costs were borne by the municipality, regardless of the 50 percent reimbursement rate and so was an onerous burden for municipalities coping with large numbers of clients with diverse needs.

The number of social workers who received training increased; nevertheless, their ratio decreased[74] and the smaller the municipality, the more time case workers and social commissions spent on individual cases.[75] The Socialist People's Party had criticized this problem before the Act came into effect. It attracted more critics against the backdrop of deteriorating fiscal conditions in the weak municipalities.

In 1982, Bent Rold Andersen, addressing the Social Ministry, criticized the Act: "That the Social Ministry has not done well enough with the Social Help Act is a matter of rebellion against the traditional way of performing work.[76] The result is that municipalities are in a hole, because they are used to legal work." He called for preventive advice and guidance as well as the need for social workers with a higher professional status than the outgoing ones.[77]

To overcome these criticisms, the center-right government ran social trials in a number of municipalities in 1984–1985. In these, applicants received not directional benefits based on block grants, but flat benefits. After implementation, applicants were given fixed benefits by household type. These improved their living conditions, and the criteria changed from an estimates principle to a rights principle (*Retprincip*). The level of benefits was fixed in 1987 and benefits were decided on by a reasonable cost-per-family principle through political negotiation.[78] Undermining this reform were the unduly long time it took to establish the need for a social worker, causing recipients to suffer some losses; abuse of the system; and the large discrepancy between benefit levels in the municipalities.[79] To address these, the Act had to be reformed.

The 1987 reform restricted discretion in benefit levels. The criteria for fixed benefits were based on common and basic needs for the entire country, which the central government estimated based on the result of the trials undertaken in the municipalities. In other words, the benefits for various needs in each municipality were replaced with those for basic needs nationwide.

In this way, the universalization of cash benefits was reinforced in the 1980s, increasing the number of beneficiaries of cash benefits, while the tax burden structure flattened. Most taxpayers paid only local income taxes and VAT, and received statutory services based on need.

Flexicurity: Active Labor Market Policy in the 1990s

In the early 1990s, the collapse of the bubble economy had not damaged the economy in Denmark any more than it had in the other Scandinavian countries. The unemployment rate topped 10 percent.[80] The reason was the economic downturn, but how long unemployment persisted was due to the semi-permanent unemployment insurance benefits available before 1994. Throughout the 1980s, the center-right government cut unemployment benefits. Nevertheless, expenditure on unemployment benefits continued to rise. As part of the unemployment insurance funded by state subsidiaries, both the fiscal-to-GDP ratio and the primary balance worsened from 1989 onward, and the incoming Social Democrat government had to implement tight finance policies (starting in 1993).

To improve the incentives to work and rein in state subsidiaries, the labor market policy reform introduced in 1994 limited the receipt of benefits to four years and made job training mandatory. In the 1998 reform, employment policy management was separated from social policy management (*Lov om aktivsocialpolitik*), and the Social Assistance Act was repealed. The government called these labor market policies "flexicurity"—a hybrid of flexibility and security. The aim of the policy did not change, but training was made mandatory. The Danish welfare state ceased to be a tolerant system and now became one that imposed welfare-conditioned obligations, such as job training.

The 1990s reforms reduced cash benefits at the expense of in-kind benefits. Healthcare services were now tax-funded, although the waiting lists (*Ventetidsproblematik*) became a major political issue from the 1980s to the 1990s. Both outpatient and inpatient care had been received only in county hospitals, but the introduction of choice in 1993 enabled people to attend any and as many hospitals as they liked.[81] As a result, waiting times decreased and access to medical services improved.

Tax reforms were implemented in 1994, 1996, and 1998 in conjunction with the labor market policy reforms, which reduced the top marginal tax rate for earned income, introducing employee contributions rather than decreasing the income tax burden, and environmental taxation. These reforms promoted work for the unemployed and cut taxes for the middle- and high-income groups. Although DIT assumed that the corporate tax rate adopted the same labor and capital income tax rates to avoid tax planning, the corporate tax rate had been incrementally reduced starting in the 1990s under the pressure of globalization. However, tax revenue from corporate taxation remained constant as the tax base of corporate taxation expanded. Tax reforms in the 1990s were revenue-neutral (i.e., the income tax burden decreased although the total tax burden remained constant due to environmental taxation, e.g., CO_2 taxation [*grønne afgifter*] in 1992, under the "green tax reform"). Despite its popularity in 1992,[82] the environmental tax burden on households increased relative to corporations due to a large tax deduction for the latter. Acceptance from the low- and middle-income sectors declined after the 1990s due to several tax reforms which, due to their regressive burden structure,[83] increased the tax burden on the low- to middle-income sectors. However, it was difficult to increase the total tax burden any further without incurring protests and negative effects on the supply of labor. Since then, the tax system has maintained similar tax burdens and tax structures.

The unemployment rate halved and periods of unemployment were briefer. Additionally, economic and fiscal performance improved radically. This was known as the "Danish miracle,"[84] with many European countries (e.g., the Nordic countries, the Netherlands, and Germany) adopting Denmark's labor market policy.

After the 2000s: Universalism Is Overturned

In the 2000s, the Danish welfare state faced the challenges of mass immigration, rising nationalism, and the global economic downturn. The Danish Extreme Right became the most successful party of any in Europe. With respect to political influence,[85] the Danish People's Party (*Dansk Folkeparti*) has held the deciding vote in parliament since 2001. The party was founded in 1995 by Pia Kjærsgaard as a successor to the Progress Party. It insisted that welfare benefits were for Danish nationals alone, with limited cash benefits and tax cuts for immigrants and refugees.

Denmark had been tolerant of immigration in the 1970s because the labor was in short supply,[86] but in the 1980s the integration policy was amended to strictly manage the increasing number of immigrants and refugees, particularly from non-European countries.[87] The number of second-generation immigrants also increased.[88] Now, the government refused entry to Tamil refugees from Sri Lanka. However, an independent research committee, made up inter alia of a Supreme Court judge, declared this measure was illegal and the government resigned in 1993.

The economic and social differences between non-European and Danish residents were evident. The unemployment rate of non-European immigrants was 17 percent, that of refugees was 23 percent, and that of Danish nationals was just 5 percent (the difference in the unemployment rate of Danes and immigrants/refugees decreased from 28 percent to 14 percent between 1994 and 1999).[89] The high unemployment rate resulted in considerable dependence on cash benefits on the part of immigrants and refugees. The change of net cash transfers (tax burden—total cash benefits) in 1991–1997 represented an increase of DKK 9100 for the Danish people,[90] whereas the decrease for non-European immigrants was DKK 11,300.[91] Therefore, the latter received more net transfers than the

Danish and depended on social assistance or unemployment benefits in the long term.[92]

These inequalities had a negative effect on tax compliance. Figure 2 shows support by political parties according to European Social Survey (2002, 2008, and 2012) data on whether immigrants and refugees received more benefits than tax burdens. From 2002 to 2014, Danish People's, Liberal, and Conservative Parties' supporters replied that immigrants and refugees received more benefits than tax burdens. Others surveyed concurred. Distrust of immigrants and refugees led to criticism of social policy for immigrants and refugees.

Around 2001, the collapse of the IT bubble economy negatively affected the Danish economy due to a decrease in exports. Growing nationalism followed; adoption of the euro was rejected in a national ref-

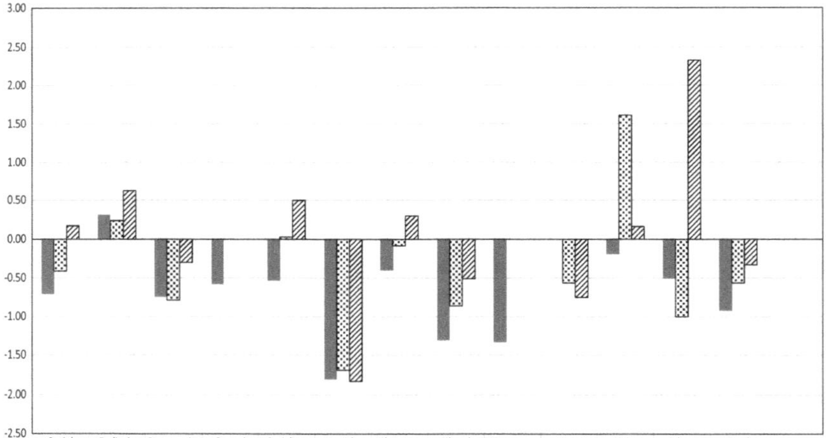

	Social Democratic (N=362; 344;190)	Radicale Liberals (N=61; 88;83)	Conservative (N=88; 129;51)	Central Democrats (N=21)	Socialists (N=95; 180;93)	Danish People (N=89; 122;162)	Christian People (N=23; 12;10)	Liberal (N=402; 356;260)	Progress (N=9)	New Alliance (N=36;50)	Unity (N=6; 18;82)	Others (N=6;5;3)	Total (N=1172; 1290;984)
2002	-0.70	0.31	-0.74	-0.57	-0.53	-1.80	-0.39	-1.31	-1.33	0.00	-0.18	-0.50	-0.92
2008	-0.41	0.24	-0.78	0.00	0.03	-1.69	-0.08	-0.85	0.00	-0.56	1.62	-1.00	-0.56
2014	0.18	0.63	-0.29	0.00	0.50	-1.82	0.30	-0.51	0.00	-0.74	0.17	2.33	-0.33

Fig. 2 The Danish people's perception of tax burdens and governmental services for immigrants and refugees. Note: The answers are the weighted average between −5 and +5 (0–10 converted). The lower points represent the higher ratio of answers the immigrants tended to receive. (Question: Most people who come to live here work and pay taxes. They also use health and welfare services. Do you think people who come here take out more than they put in or put in more than they take out?). Source: European Social Survey 2002, 2008, 2014

erendum, and large-scale terrorist attacks have occurred since the 9/11 terrorist attack in the United States. Most of the political parties had supported the introduction of the euro, with the exception of the Danish People's Party and the left-wing Social Democrats. Its rejection was accompanied by an increase in the number people supporting the Danish People's Party, which insisted on immigration regulations.[93]

After the 2001 elections, the Conservative Party has won the most seats, overtaking the Social Democrat Party, which had held its place since 1920. The Danish People's Party also won and became the second party. The Danish People's Party used its casting vote on immigration policy thanks to the large number of seats and support from outside the Cabinet.

The 2004 reforms benefited Danish nationals almost exclusively, institutionally discriminating against only the unemployed and foreigners. Social support was divided between social care and start-up assistance[94] (*Starthjælp*). The latter was aimed at immigrants owing to the need to fulfill several working criteria and years of residence in order to receive regular social assistance. Start-up benefit was equal to half regular social assistance, and as such was criticized by opposition parties and experts in the field for not meeting minimum living standards. The Social Committee (*Socialudvalget*) of 2012–2013 demonstrated that the recipients of start-up benefits did not have enough to engage in such things as "[buying] birthday presents for friends," "having their hair cut," or "going to the dentist."[95]

The 2004 tax reform also introduced benefits for the elderly (*Ældrecheck*), which were paid in addition to the national pension for the low-income sector. However, not all older people were eligible because it depended on years of residence. Therefore, most refugees and immigrants were ineligible. These means-tested cash benefits were introduced at the insistence of the Danish People's Party.[96] Party leader Kristian Thulesen Dahl declared, "We can agree on this fiscal law with the government, if reform for the most vulnerable pensioner is implemented," which the government accepted.[97]

Tax policy changed from 2000 onward. In the 1990s, it consisted of a flat tax structure due to an increase in the local income tax rate and a decrease in the national progressive income tax. The center-right government from 2001 onward viewed the high waged income tax as an issue and implemented a tax freeze (*Skattestoppe*) in 2002, which prevented the increasing tax burden becoming an "absolutely central factor in tax policy."[98]

Tax reforms in the 2000s continued, involving (1) a reduction in the income tax rate; (2) the enlargement of the income tax bracket for the middle-income sector; (3) the introduction of an employee allowance (*Beskæftigelsesfradrag*); (4) a decrease in the corporate tax rate; and (5) an increase in environmental taxation. The decrease in the income tax rate and the introduction of employee allowances, which offered an income tax deduction for employees, was aimed at increasing the labor supply.[99]

Employees and employers both benefited from the reforms, while the unemployed enjoyed few benefits, as the period for receiving unemployment benefits was cut.

The government also had to resolve the inconsistencies between the increase in the labor supply, a decrease in the income tax rate, and fiscal reconstruction by implementing a fiscal reconstruction program based on the tax freeze (*Denmark 2010*), which achieved a fiscal surplus in 2010. Fiscal reconstruction was based on an estimate of the increase in income tax revenue resulting from an increase in the labor supply, employment creation, and real, continuous economic growth, all of which occurred naturally.

However, any estimate was negatively affected by the financial crisis of 2008 (the "Great Recession"). The Danish economy suffered more than that of the other Nordic countries because the tax freeze created a property bubble, as taxable income on property was fixed to some extent, rendering the property tax burden insufficient in light of the increase in property prices. The tax freeze was vulnerable in that it suffered from the rigidity of tax policy toward globalization and could not provide economic stability during the crisis.[100] Consequently, tax revenues dropped markedly, and the government had to implement severe fiscal reconstruction (*Reformpakken 2020*). This consisted of a shorter period for receiving unemployment benefit and the phasing-out of early retirement benefits. The universal welfare system also cut cash benefits concentrated in government services for immigration.

More recently, the Danish People's Party has won more seats in parliament. In February 2015, there were terrorist attacks in Copenhagen, and the immigration policy was further reinforced after the 2016 elections, although it had previously been reconsidered by the Social Democrat government. The Danish People's Party won the 2015 elections, with the second-largest number of seats in parliament. The party attempted to implement a stricter immigration policy. In one example, the government passed a bill allowing the government to seize refugees' assets if they were to achieve the level of need required to be eligible for assistance, as stipulated by the party.

Thus, anyone who contributed to tax revenue by paying onerous income taxes could receive universal welfare benefits, while those receiving state cash benefits were subject to different conditions. In other words, while the welfare system superficially looks universal, it is in fact selective when it comes to immigrants.[101]

The Danish economy and society have adopted globalization through the introduction of DIT and by taking in immigrants and refugees since 1980. At the same time, the universal welfare system was created as a solution to tax revolts in the 1970s. However, support for a universal welfare system depended on a homogeneous society with regard to income or race. If the income inequality between the Danish people and immigrants continues to rise, the divided and selective system will grow increasingly popular, and societal rifts will widen.

Conclusion

This chapter traces how Denmark maintained its high benefit levels with a high tax burden under globalization. In the early 1970s, Denmark experienced large tax revolts against the increase in tax burdens. Taxpayers were dissatisfied with the high tax burden under the welfare system, which comprised a serious problem on the supplier's side. The local governments did not provide services based on applicants' needs. From the viewpoint of a universal welfare system, the system at the time was not universal in the sense that it was not based on applicants' needs and did not cover the people in need of governmental services.

In 1976, the welfare system was transformed into a decentralized and universal system under the Social Assistance Act. Access to government services improved when various service "windows" were amalgamated and assistance was based on need. The welfare system was now truly universal and was favorably rated by taxpayers.

Starting in the early 1980s, in response to the oil shock, the government imposed a tight fiscal policy, which led to criticism of the Social Assistance Act and its massive costs. In 1987, the Act was reformed, and variable benefits determined at the local government level were replaced by fixed benefits set at the national level. Supplementary, flexible benefits to control the increase in social expenditure at the local government level were also permitted. At the same time, universal child benefits were introduced because DIT gave smaller benefits to the low- and middle-income sectors; it was also intended to encourage larger families as the low birth rate had become a social problem. Child benefits were fixed and flat regardless of household income, and other benefits were also treated as taxable income, so that cash benefits were flat and transparent. This ensured a universal system.

In the 1990s, social policy became active, which meant that anyone applying for cash benefits was encouraged to undergo job training and look for work to fill the needs of the active labor market policy. The right to receive cash benefits was accompanied by obligations. "Flexicurity" radically decreased the unemployment rate, and both the economy and fiscal performance improved. The scale of in-kind benefits widened in the 2000s and access to health services improved.

Since then the welfare system has come under strain with the increase in the number of immigrants and refugees who received more benefits than Danish nationals, something that caused extreme social tension and dissatisfaction, although the presence of immigrants has never created financial problems. Since the mid-2000s, an anti-immigration party, the Danish People's Party, has won more seats in parliament, and the center-right government has implemented a tighter immigration policy by cutting cash benefits for immigrants and limiting entry into Denmark. Now immigrants receive different benefits under stricter criteria for eligibility. The universal welfare system is open to Danish nationals, while immigrants are subject to a selective system.

The meaning of universalism has thus changed. It is generally understood that the development of a universal welfare system is related to a country's total tax revenue. Although universal welfare is theoretically possible under small governments, historically, large governments are needed to secure tax consent in order to ensure sufficient revenue to fund it. Support for a universal welfare system on the part of Danish nationals depended on a homogeneous society with regard to income and race. Opinion was divided over whether immigrants contributed enough to tax revenue. The division between Danish nationals and foreigners deepened. Future research will determine how the welfare system can become inclusive and how tax consent can be achieved in Denmark.

Notes

1. Rothstein, *Just Institutions Matter*.
2. Kildal and Kuhnle, "The Nordic Welfare Model and the Idea of Universalism," 13–33.

3. Greve, "Denmark: Universal or not so Universal Welfare State," 156–69.
4. Esping-Andersen, *The Three World of Welfare Capitalism.*
5. Korpi and Palme, "The Paradox of Redistribution and Strategies of Equality."
6. Marx et al., "The Paradox of Redistribution Revisited: And that it May Rest in Peace?"
7. Kato, *Regressive Taxation and the Welfare State.*
8. Hasselbalch, *Labour Law in Denmark*, 24.
9. Christiansen and Petersen, "The Dynamics of Social Solidarity," 182ff.
10. Greve, "The Danish Welfare State," 50.
11. Christiansen and Petersen, "The Dynamics of Social Solidarity," 177–96.
12. Greve, "The Danish Welfare State," 48.
13. Kruse, "The Relief Housewife in Denmark."
14. Marcussen, *Danish Information Handbooks: Social Welfare in Denmark*, 22.
15. See for the PAYE system the contribution by Isaac Martin in this volume.
16. Some opposed the introduction and subsequent increase of VAT, because the tax did not adopt the reduced rate due to the need for more tax revenue. As a result, the VAT burden on the low- to middle-income sectors increased rapidly. Many taxpayers took part in demonstrations to demand repeal of the increased tax rate; Shoup, *Experience with the Value-Added Tax in Denmark*, 237.
17. Politiken, "Danmark sidste civiliserede land der indfører kildeksat," 4.
18. At that time, the Danish income tax system was highly progressive. If income increased, the tax rate increased automatically. This is known as bracket creep.
19. Martin, *The Permanent Tax Revolt*, 159.
20. Politiken, "Tusinder betaler for meget i skat," 2.
21. Andersen, "A Danish Study of the Functioning of the System of Social Security," 337; Socialreformkommissionens, *Det sociale tryghedssystem Service og Bistand, Betænkning nr. 664.*
22. Socialreformkommissionens, *Det sociale tryghedssystem Service og Bistand, Betænkning nr. 664.*
23. Marcussen, *Danish Information Handbooks: Social Welfare in Denmark*, 23–4.
24. Christiansen, *1970'ernes socialreform*, 10.
25. Ibid., 15.
26. About 4.7 percent ($N = 25$) of respondents chose "Do not know, it depends."

27. Kurachi, "The Process of Universalism in the Danish Welfare System."
28. Aarhus Universitet, "Mogens Glistrup sammenligner skattesnydere med jernbanesabotører under besættelsen."
29. Nielsen, "Glistrup: Vor skattelovgivning er en sump," 19.
30. Wilensky, *Rich Democracies*, 377.
31. Fremskridtspartiet, *De er jo enig med os Fremskridts partiet*; Wilensky, *Rich Democracies.*
32. Larsen, "En studie af Fremskridtspartiets organisation."
33. The abbreviation for the Danish Krone.
34. Politiken, "Skattereform uden social balance," 5.
35. Politiken, "Glistrup gjorde minister usikker," 5; Dabelsteen, "Klart nej til afskaffelse af indkomstskat," 4.
36. Johansen, *Indkomstskatter og offentlig vækst 1903–2005*, 222ff.
37. Danmarks Statistik, *Skatter og Afgifter Oversigt 1976.*
38. Greve, "The Danish Welfare State," 52f.
39. Palle Simonsen was a member of the Conservative Party (Det Konservative Folkeparti) from 1965 to 1975 and 1977 to 1989, and chairman of the Social Committee (Socialudvalget) from 1974 to 1975.
40. Inge Krogh was an MP from 1973 to 1984 representing the Kristeligt Folkeparti.
41. Kristelig Folkeparti (since 2003 known as Kristendemokraterne) was set up on April 13, 1970. The party won its first seat in parliament in December 1973.
42. Erhard Jacobsen resigned from Socialdemokratiet on November 6, 1973, and set up Centrum Demokraterne. In the December 1973 election, this party won 14 seats.
43. Kolstrup, "Fra forsorgslov til b election," 227f.
44. Lundtorp, *Udviklingen i de kommunale udligningsordninger*, 10–11.
45. Socialministeriet, *Rapport om finansering*, 38.
46. Politiken, "Socialt virke svigtes ikke," 12.
47. Kommunernes Landsforening is the association of municipalities. It was set up in 1970 when local administration reform was implemented, playing a role in coordinating expenditure and revenue in the municipalities through negotiation between the state and the Local Governments Association.
48. Politiken, "Trusler i bistandslov," 9.
49. Politiken, "Vi skal bare sidde og forklare folk de ingen penge kan få," 5.
50. Socialministeriet, *Rapport om finansering*, 39.
51. Ibid.
52. Greve, "The Danish Welfare State," 52.
53. Bengtsson, *Social service til alle*, 53.
54. Socialreformkommission, 1. *Betænkning, Det sociale tryghedssystem Struktur og Dagpenge, Betænkning nr. 543*, 1969.

55. Socialreformkommissionens, *Det sociale tryghedssystem Service og Bistand, Betænkning nr. 664.*
56. Greve, "The Danish Welfare State," 52.
57. Ibid.
58. Ibid.
59. Ibid.
60. Sørensen, "Reforms of Danish Capital Income Taxation in the 1980s," 46.
61. Sørensen, "Recent Tax Reform Experiments in Scandinavia," 18.
62. Nordiska skattevetevetenskapliga forskningsrådets, *Skattereformer Rapporter och inlägg vid NSF: seminarium i Hønefoss i oktober 1988*, 9.
63. Renteskatteudvalgt, *Den skattemassige behandling af renter og andet kapitalafkast, Betænkning 949*, 11.
64. Socialdemokratiets, *For nye fremgang*, 23–4.
65. The average minimum tax rate of DIT was set at 50 percent.
66. Households with dependent children were eligible for general child benefits.
67. Except for social allowance, for example, child benefit and housing allowance.
68. January–April, 1644 persons.
69. Pruzan et al., *Socialreform undersøgelserne 5 social problemer 1966–1982*, 12.
70. Ibid., 23.
71. Ibid., 17f.
72. Plovsing, "Socialreformens idealer og praksis."
73. Plovsing, "Socialreformundersøgelserne," 149.
74. Petersen et al., *Velfærdsstaten i tidehverv Dansk velfærdshistorie bd. 5.*
75. Plovsing, "Socialreformundersøgelserne," 4–14.
76. Bent Rold Andersen (1929–2015) was a Social Democrat politician (1956–1999). From 1972 to 1975, he was professor of social policy and labour market policy at Roskilde Universtitet. He became social minister in 1982.
77. Petersen et al., *Velfærdsstaten i tidehverv Dansk velfærdshistorie bd. 5*, 141f.
78. Jappe, *Håndbog i Bistandshjælp; Plovsing, Socialpolitik.*
79. Kurachi, "Social Assistance in Denmark."
80. The introduction of DIT caused the collapse of the bubble economy in the Nordic countries. However, the effect of the bubble economy was small, as Denmark entered the EC economy community early and implemented relaxation of monetary regulations in advance.
81. Sato et al., "An International Comparative Study of Financing Healthcare," 30–1.
82. Andersen, "Green Tax Reform in Denmark," 139–45.

83. Klok et al., "Ecological Tax Reform in Denmark," 905–16.
84. Pedersen, "Minority Governments and Party Politics," 53–70.
85. Widfeldt, Extreme Right Parties in Scandinavia.
86. From the mid-1970s to the mid-1980s the number of immigrants was small, consisting mainly of Turkish guest-workers.
87. Among those fleeing the war in Bosnia many migrated to Denmark, and the municipality has been responsible for the integration of immigrants/refugees in local society.
88. Pedersen and Smith, "International Migration and Migration Policy in Denmark," 3–5.
89. Dansk Arbejdsgiverforening, *Integration & Arbejdsmarkedet*, 74f.
90. Except for the parents of immigrants.
91. Wadensjö, "Immigration, the Labour Market, and Public Finances in Denmark," 67.
92. Pedersen and Smith, "International Migration and Migration Policy in Denmark."
93. Widfeldt, *Extreme Right Parties in Scandinavia*, 134ff.
94. Start-up assistance was introduced in 2004 in order to motivate immigrants and refugees with few years' residence in Denmark to find a job.
95. Socialudvalget 2012–2013, *En danskfattigdomsgrænse analyser og forslagtilopgørelsesmetoder*.
96. Politiken, "Lavere ældrecheck til indvandrere."
97. Politiken, "Dansk Folkeparti vil indføre ældre-check."
98. Skatteministeriet, *Skat April 2002*, 49
99. Skatteministeriet, *Skat April 2004*, 115–31.
100. Det Økonomiske Råd, *Dansk Økonomi forår 2002*.
101. Kvist and Greve, "Has the Nordic Welfare Model Been Transformed?"

References

Aarhus Universitet. Mogens Glistrup sammenligner skattesnydere med jernbanesabotører under besættelsen. http://danmarkshistorien.dk/leksikon-og-kilder/vis/materiale/mogens-glistrup-sammenligner-skattesnydere-med-jernbanesabotoerer-under-besaettelsen/. Accessed 10 Feb 2018.

Andersen, Rold Bent. 1972. A Danish Study of the Functioning of the System of Social Security. *Journal of Social Policy* 1 (4): 331–344.

Andersen, Skou Mikael. 1994. Green Tax Reform in Denmark. *Environmental Politics* 3 (1): 139–145.

Bengtsson, Steen. 1999. Social service til alle – om oganisering gennem 30 år. *Socialforsikringsinstituttet* 99: 1.

Christiansen, Terkel. 1975. *1970'ernes socialreform: kilder til belysning af den aktuelle socialpolitik*. Kopenhagen: Gyldendal.

Christiansen, F. Niels, and Klaus Petersen. 2001. The Dynamics of Social Solidarity: The Danish Welfare State, 1900–2000. *Scandinavian Journal of History* 26 (3): 177–196.

Danmarks Statistik. 1976. *Skatter og Afgifter Oversigt 1976*. København: Danmarks Statistik.

Dansk Arbejdsgiverforening. 2001. *Integration & Arbejdsmarkedet*. København.

Det Økonomiske Råd. 2002. *Dansk Økonomi forår 2002*. København: De Økonomiske Råd.

Esping-Andersen, Gøsta. 1990. *The Three Worlds of Welfare Capitalism*. Cambridge: Polity Press.

Fremskridtspartiet. 1975. *De er jo enig med os Fremskridts partie*. København: Fremskridtspartiet.

Greve, Bent. 2002. The Danish Welfare State: The Legislative Framework and Future Prospects. In *The Welfare State, Past, Present, Future*, ed. Henrik Jensen, 41–57. Pisa: Universitá di Pisa.

———. 2004. Denmark: Universal or Not So Universal Welfare State. *Social Policy and Administration* 38 (2): 156–169.

Hasselbalch, Ole. 2009. *Labor Law in Denmark*. Austin: Wolters Kluwer Law & Business.

Jappe, Erik. 1985. *Håndbog i Bistandshjælp – kontanthjælp*, Frydenlund.

Johansen, Christian Hans. 2007. *Indkomstskatter og offentlig vækst 1903–2005. Danske Skattehistorie VI*. København: Told og Skattehistorisk Sleskab.

Kato, Junko. 2003. *Regressive Taxation and the Welfare State: Path Dependence and Policy Diffusion*. Cambridge: Cambridge University Press.

Kildal, Nanna, and Stein Kuhnle. 2005. The Nordic Welfare Model and the Idea of Universalism. In *Normative Foundations of the Welfare State: The Nordic Experience*, ed. Nanne Kildal and Kuhnle Stein, 13–33. London: Routledge.

Klok, Jacob, Larsen Anders, Anja Dahl, and Kirsten Hansen. 2006. Ecological Tax Reform in Denmark: History and Social Acceptability. *Energy Policy* 34: 905–916.

Kolstrup, S. 2012. Fra forsorgslov til bistandslov. In *Velfærdsstatens storhedstid Dansk Velfærdshistorie, bind 4 1956–1973*, ed. Henrik Petersen, Klaus Jørn, and Finn Christiansen Niels, 165–238. Syddansk Universitetsforlag.

Korpi, Walter, and Joakim Palme. 1998. The Paradox of Redistribution and Strategies of Equality: Welfare State Institutions, Inequality, and Poverty in the Western Countries. *American Sociological Review* 63 (5): 661–687.

Kruse, Margrethe. 1951. The Relief Housewife in Denmark. *The American Journal of Nursing* 51 (2): 105–108.

Kurachi, Shintaro. 2014. Social Assistance in Denmark – Method and Criterion of Cash Benefit Level. In *Minimum Life Guarantee and Criterion of Social Assistance – Decision Method and Reference in Eight Developed Countries*, ed. A. Yamada, H. Fukawa, and the Poverty Research Committee, 171–194. Akashi Shoten. (Japanese)

———. 2016. The Process of Universalism in the Danish Welfare System: The Multi-tiered Needs Testing System in Denmark *Keio-IES Discussion Paper Series*, DP2016-006.
Kvist, Jon, and Bent Greve. 2011. Has the Nordic Welfare Model Been Transformed? *Social Policy and Administration* 45 (2): 146–160.
Larsen, Villads Bjarne. 1977. En studie af Fremskridtspartiets organisation. *Politica* 9 (3–4): 59–84.
Lundtorp, Svend. 2004. *Udviklingen i de kommunale udligningsordninger*. AFK Forlaget.
Madsen, Kongshøj Per. 2006. Flexicurity – A New Perspective on Labour Markets and Welfare States in Europe. *CARMA Research Paper 3*.
Marcussen, E. 1980. *Danish Information Handbooks: Social Welfare in Denmark*. Det Danske Selskab.
Martin, Isaac. 2009. *The Permanent Tax Revolt*. Stanford, Stanford University Press.
Marx, Ive, Lina Salanauskaite, and Gerlinde Verbist. 2013. The Paradox of Redistribution Revisited: And That It May Rest in Peace? *IZA DP NO.7414*, Discussion Paper Series.
Nielsen, Sørensen. 1971. Glistrup: Vor skattelovgivning er en sump. *Politiken*, February 8, p. 19.
Nordiska skattevetevetenskapliga forskningsrådets. 1989. Skattereformer Rapporter och inlägg vid NSF:s seminarium i Hønefoss i oktober 1988. In *Nordiska skattevetevetenskapliga forskningsrådets Skriftserie*.
Page, C. Edward, and Michael Goldsmith, eds. 1987. *Central and Local Government Relations: A Comparative Analysis of West European Unitary States*. London: Sage.
Pedersen, C. 2001. Minority Governments and Party Politics: The Political and Institutional Background to the 'Danish Miracle. *Journal of Public Policy* 21 (1): 53–70.
Pedersen, Møller Kjeld. 2009. Udviklingen af et sundhedsvæsen—illustreret ved Vejle Amt. *Health Economics Papers* 1: 1–74.
Pedersen, J. Peder, and Nina Smith. 2001. International Migration and Migration Policy in Denmark. *CLS Working Paper No. 01-05*. Available at SSRN: https://ssrn.com/abstract=298580 or https://doi.org/10.2139/ssrn.298580
Petersen, H. J., K. Petersen, and N. Christiansen, eds. 2013. *Velfærdsstaten i tidehverv Dansk velfærdshistorie bd. 5, 1973–1993*. Syddansk Universitetsforlag.
Plovsing, J. 1985a. Socialreformens idealer og praksis. *Politica* 17 (4): 502–518.
———. 1985b. *Socialpolitik 2000*. Handelshøjskolens Forlag.
Politiken. 1967. Danmark sidste civiliserede land der indfører kildeksat. *Politiken*, March 30, p. 4.
———. 1971. Tusinder betaler for meget i skat. *Politiken*, October 6, p. 2.
———. 1973. Trusler i bistandslov. *Politiken*, May 29, p. 9.

———. 1974a. Klart nej til afskaffelse af indkomstskat. *Politiken*, January 24, p. 4.
———. 1974b. Vi skal bare sidde og forklare folk de ingen penge kan få. *Politiken*, April 17, p. 5.
———. 1974c. Socialt virke svigtes ikke. *Politiken*, March 14, p. 12.
———. 1974d. Skattereform uden social balance. *Politiken*, August 25, p. 5.
———. 1974e. Glistrup gjorde minister usikker. *Politiken*, September 22, p. 5.
———. 2002a. Dansk Folkeparti vil indføre ældre-check. *Politiken*, July 28.
———. 2002b. Lavere ældrecheck til indvandrere. *Politiken*, November 9.
Pruzan, V., et al. 1982. *Socialreform undersøgelserne 5 social problemer 1966–1982*. København: Statens Trykningskontor.
Renteskatteudvalgt. 1982. *Den skattemassige behandling aff renter og andet kapitalafkast, Renteskatteudvalgt*, Betænkning 949.
Rothstein, Bo. 1988. *Just Institutions Matter: The Moral and Political Logic of the Universal Welfare State*. Cambridge: Cambridge University Press.
Sato, Kazuaki, Yui Ohtsu, Shintaro Kurachi, and Leo Shimamura. 2016. An International Comparative Study of Financing Healthcare: The Case of Eight Developed Countries in 1990s–2000s. *Keio-IES Discussion Paper Series*.
Shoup, Carl. 1969. Experience with the Value-added Tax in Denmark, and Prospects in Sweden. *Finanzarchiv* 28: 236–252.
Skatteministeriet. 2002. *Skat April 2002*. København: Skatteministeriet.
———. 2004. *Skat April 2004*. København: Skatteministeriet.
Socialdemokratiets. 1984. *1984: For nye fremgang, Socialdemokratiets arbejdsprogram for 1984–1988*. København: Socialdemokratiet.
Socialministeriet. 1981. *Rapport om finansering*. Betænkning 940.
Socialreformkommission. 1969. *1. Betænkning, Det sociale tryghedssystem Struktur og Dagpenge, Betænkning nr. 543*. København: Statens Trykningskontor.
Socialreformkommissionens. 1972. *2. Betænkning, Det sociale tryghedssystem Service og Bistand, Betænkning nr. 664*. København: Statens Trykningskontor.
Socialudvalget. 2013. *2012–2013, En danskfattigdomsgrænse analyser og forslagtilopgørelsesmetoder*. SOU Alm, delVilag 263 Offentligt.
Sørensen, Birch Peter. 1988. Reforms of Danish Capital Income Taxation in the 1980s. *Finnish Economic Papers* 1 (1): 45–71.
———. 1993. *Recent Tax Reform Experiments in Scandinavia Global Change and Transformation*. Handelsh Øjskolens Forlag.
Wadensjö, Eekil. 2000. Immigration, the Labour Market, and Public Finances in Denmark. *Swedish Economic Policy Review* 7: 59–83.
Widfeldt, Anders. 2015. *Extreme Right Parties in Scandinavia*. London: Routledge.
Wilensky, Harold. 2002. *Rich Democracies: Political Economy, Public Policy, and Performance*. Berkeley: University of California Press.

The Powerlessness of Employees in France: The Spread of Income Taxation, 1945–1980

Frances M. B. Lynch

Since the end of the Second World War, French governments have relied mainly on proportional and thus regressive taxes on goods and services, and on social security contributions to fund one of the largest states in the Organisation for Economic Cooperation and Development (OECD). Income taxes that were introduced in France during the First World War have accounted for a much smaller proportion of total state revenue than in almost any other OECD country. In 1965, personal income tax accounted for 10.6 percent of total tax revenue at a time when the OECD average was 25.9 percent. By 1980, it was no more than 12.9 percent compared with 32 percent in the OECD.[1] Yet, over the 35-year period following the end of the Second World War the number of households paying income tax increased dramatically, rising from 10 percent in 1945 to peak at 64 percent in 1980.[2] This meant that workers on average wages began to pay income tax for the first time at some point over this period. If the worker was single, income tax became a reality in the mid-1950s. If they earned half the average wage, it was not until the late 1970s that they

F. M. B. Lynch (✉)
University of Westminster, London, UK
e-mail: lynchf@westminster.ac.uk

G. Huerlimann et al. (eds.), *Worlds of Taxation*,
Palgrave Studies in the History of Finance,
https://doi.org/10.1007/978-3-319-90263-0_6

began to pay any income tax. If there were two dependent children, income tax was charged in the 1950s, but then, following reforms in 1959, liability for income tax was removed for several years. What remained consistent was that all employees had to pay income tax on the previous year's earnings as French employers successfully resisted any attempt to turn them into tax collectors for the state under a pay-as you-earn (PAYE) system.[3] Why France has maintained the tax structure normally associated with a less democratic and less economically developed country is usually explained in terms of governments not attempting to make personal income taxation a comprehensive system, preferring to rely on less visible revenue sources.[4] In this chapter, we examine the historical record of income tax policy-making over the postwar period in order to expose the motives behind changes in income tax policy in 1948 and 1959 under both the Fourth and Fifth Republics. We also fill a gap in the historical record by using the published tax rules and rates of income tax in order to calculate the outcome of policy changes in terms of the actual income tax paid by different households between 1945 and 1980.[5] Unlike other studies that focus on the marginal rate of tax paid by the highest earners we establish the income tax paid by the majority of households across a range of incomes and family structures[6] in order to determine whether the outcome of the extension of income taxation was a more or less equitable society in France.

The extension of income taxation from a tax that only a minority of the wealthiest households paid to one affecting households on average incomes was a gradual process due in part to the structural changes resulting from the rapid growth and development of the French economy after 1945. These structural changes meant that the number of households whose income was declared by an employer expanded, while the proportion of self-employed or those deriving their income from capital declined. The gradual transformation of income tax into a mass tax was accompanied by persistent accusations that the entire system was unfair, penalizing some socio-economic groups to the advantage of others. Under the parliamentary multi-party system of the Fourth Republic, the protests came from the political Right, the self-employed, small businesses, and traders, who claimed that they were funding a state that no longer looked after their interests. Under the presidential majoritarian system of the Fifth Republic, dominated by conservative governments until 1981, the accusations made by the Left were that it was those who were unable to conceal their actual earnings, whose wages and salaries were recorded by their employer, who were paying more than their fair share of income taxes.

One important consequence of the change in the constitutional regime was that fiscal policy became the prerogative of the government and the president under the Fifth Republic rather than of the National Assembly as it was under the Fourth Republic.[7] While right-wing protests in the 1950s led to reform of the tax system under the new Fifth Republic in 1959, the main problem faced subsequently by the Left was that, in the absence of relevant data, they were unable to demonstrate the inequity of the income tax system. The statistics published each year by the Ministry of Finance showed tax rates as well as macro-economic indicators, such as the percentage of each tax in total tax revenue and in GDP, but not the differential impact of the system of income taxation across the socio-economic groups. This lack of interest in the impact of the tax system on people's lives and livelihoods was symptomatic of the government's distance from the average worker at the time and contributed to the rage that swept across France in 1968. Nevertheless, in terms of tax policy, little changed after 1968.

Preliminaries to a Reform: The Pro-Natalist Agenda Setting of 1945

Even before the first attempt to reform the income tax system in 1948, the provisional government under General Charles de Gaulle had agreed that the first priority of the system should be to boost the birth rate. In the eighteenth century, the population of France had been three times that of Great Britain; by 1946 it was about 20 percent smaller.[8] While concern with the depopulation of France had long been associated with right-wing, pro-natalist and family groups such as the Alliance Nationale and La Plus Grande Famille which had found a receptive ear in the Vichy regime (1940–1944), what was new was that after the Second World War this policy was also supported by the left-wing parties. De Gaulle himself had given the lead in backing the pro-natalist cause by calling in March 1945 for "twelve million beautiful babies" to restore the grandeur of France.[9] In 1945 a National Assembly for which women had voted for the first time passed legislation for the new family quotient system. Under the rules of the new system, the total income of a couple, whether married or not, was divided into a number of parts, with each parent allocated one part and each dependent child half of one part. The tax liability of each part was calculated as if it were a single person applying the same deductions at the base and the same scale of rates. The resulting figure was then multiplied by the number of parts to establish the total income tax liability of the household. It was a system that redistributed income from single and older people to families with dependent children, but it also benefited larger wealthy families more than poorer ones, the primary earner more than the secondary one (even if the couple did not have children), and reduced the revenue from income taxation as well as its progressivity.[10] Thus, paradoxically, one of the most left-wing National Assemblies that France ever had laid the basis for one of the most regressive tax regimes in the OECD. Because the family quotient system reduced the yield from income tax even as the number of households paying that tax grew, the weight of income tax as a proportion of total taxation and of GDP in France remained among the lowest in OECD, with consumption taxes providing a larger and more secure source of revenue.

The other legislation that was to have a bearing on the evolution of income taxes concerned the funding of social security. Unlike in Britain, where the new welfare state was to be funded out of general taxation supplemented by a national insurance fund, in France there was no agreement to merge workplace funds into one national fund or to fund welfare from taxation.[11] What was agreed after the Second World War was that both employers and employees would contribute, on a flat-rate basis, to separate funds for each socio-professional group and that the program as a whole would be self-financing.[12] In this way the funding of social security also contributed to the regressive nature of the tax system.

External Pressure to Increase the Yield from Income Taxation: the 1948 Tax Reform

The small numbers paying income tax and the low yield from the tax owed much to the rules agreed during the First World War when income tax had first been introduced. One of the primary concerns of those drafting the legislation was that, in the interests of equity, there should be different rules for taxing different sources of income. Because this made the system as a whole extremely complicated, it increased the scope for individuals and businesses not to declare, or at least to minimize, the size of some sources of income. As a result of the widespread prevalence of such tax fraud, the French state became more dependent on revenue from indirect taxes. Estimated at anything between 10 percent and 20 percent of revenue in the interwar period, tax fraud then escalated under the German Occupation when for many it assumed the role of a patriotic duty.[13] After the war the practice proved hard to reverse.

By 1947, the proportion of households paying any income tax had fallen to its lowest level since 1924.[14] A committee set up in 1946 to investigate how best to increase the revenue from income taxes and reduce fraud failed to produce a majority report.[15] In the absence of any reform, increased claims on the budget arising from the need for additional public investment to make up for the shortfall of investment in the 1930s, as well as to cover the cost of reconstruction, came from the French franc counterpart of loans and grants from the United States and from advances from the recently nationalized Bank of France. By 1948 following a threat made by the United States not to release further aid until the French parliament had reformed the taxation system, legislation was finally passed in December 1948.[16] The main objective of this legislation was to increase the revenue derived from income tax by simplifying the structure inherited from the First World War, but without compromising the basic principle of equity. That structure, sometimes compared to a Greek temple, had a number of columns, representing flat-rate proportional taxes levied on different sources of income, which supported a horizontal architrave representing a tax on total income levied on a progressive basis.[17] As a first step in reforming this complicated structure, the 1948 legislation separated the income tax levied on households from that of business corporations. It then replaced the different scheduled taxes (the columns) with one flat-rate, proportional tax, set at 18 percent, without any deductions at the base apart from deductions for each dependent child. The only source of income that was exempt from this proportional tax was that earned by employees. This exemption was based on two assumptions: first, that since this was the only income declared by a third party (the employer), it could not be deliberately underestimated, as the income of all the self-employed was judged to be[18]; and second that to have imposed a proportional tax on salaried income would have led to a demand for higher wages thereby fueling the inflationary cycle that the tax reform was designed to break. Instead of levying a proportional tax of 18 percent on wages and salaries, a 5 percent payroll tax was levied on employers. Whether this would be passed on in the form of higher prices and thereby become an indirect tax was never resolved.[19]

In deference to the large agricultural vote, no change was made to the system introduced during the First World War of allowing the income tax liability of agriculture to be assessed according to a number of objective indicators, such as the location, size, and use of land. Known as the *forfait* system, it was generally acknowledged that it greatly underestimated farmers' tax liability.

Superimposed on this proportional tax was a progressive surtax (the architrave) with rates ranging from 10 percent to 60 percent after a basic deduction had been applied. This covered all incomes, including wages and salaries, and was subject to the rules of the family quotient. Indeed, since the calculations of the proportional tax also gave allowances for dependent children, the advantages of having a larger family were greater than under the family quotient system alone. Because of the tax advantages given to large families and to the agricultural sector, the yield of the new income tax system was reduced from the outset.

The Battle Against Fraud

A further weakness of the 1948 reform was that, in acknowledging the reality of tax fraud and penalizing those who were in a position to under-declare their income by imposing a flat-rate proportional tax on them, it made those self-employed who declared their actual earnings look like fools. The result was that, far from reducing fraud, the reform increased it. By 1952, one official estimate put fraud at between 20 percent and 25 percent of tax receipts.[20] When US aid ended that year, this shortfall became an even more acute problem. Following the rejection by the National Assembly of a proposal to increase all taxes by 15 percent the way that the shortfall was dealt with by the new center-right government headed by the conservative Antoine Pinay, was to try to improve how taxes were collected rather than raise rates.[21] At the same time Pinay, a co-founder of the National Center of Independents and Peasants, granted an amnesty for all previous tax offenses going back to the Second World War and German Occupation. However, the hope that fraud could be detected by sending out, or threatening to send out, teams of tax inspectors across rural France to check both the income tax and indirect tax returns of all small, self-employed workers proved illusory. Instead of bringing in more money, word of the fraud squad sparked a revolt, spearheaded by a small shopkeeper, Pierre Poujade, which attracted a mass following across the less industrialized regions of France. As a result, the numbers of people paying the proportional tax plummeted and it was not until 1958 that the 1951 level was restored.

The government's immediate response was to replace Pierre Allix, the General Inspector of Taxes, with Robert Blot, who was known to be more sympathetic to the self-employed.[22] The government then reverted to its previous practice of using advances from the Bank of France to cover public spending rather than cutting expenditure or raising tax rates. Taking advantage of the fact that prices had risen as a result, the government then deliberately and surreptitiously kept the thresholds of each band of the progressive surtax at their 1953 levels until 1959. This meant that many people began to pay surtax for the first time, the numbers rising from 3.37 million in 1952 to 5.05 million in 1959.[23] Because of the progressive rates of the surtax, it also meant that the tax burden of those who were already paying taxes also increased. Blot calculated that a household on average earnings with two dependent children would have paid 3.91 percent of their income in surtax in 1953. If the purchasing power of this household did not change between 1953 and 1959, its surtax liability would have risen to 4.71 percent of its gross wage. But if over that period the head of household had been promoted so that his/her income in 1959 was 66 percent higher than in 1953, then the household's tax would have risen to 8.19 percent of the worker's gross wage. In other words, this tax would have increased by 109 percent at a time when income increased by only 66 percent.[24]

But if inflationary financing penalized many wage and salary earners, it worked to the advantage of those who paid the proportional tax since the value of that tax had fallen in real terms by the time it was paid in the following year. Inflationary financing also had the effect of stimulating structural changes in the economy. As much publicly funded investment poured into industry and agriculture, millions left low-productivity employment in agriculture to work in higher productivity jobs in industry and services. The impact of these structural changes on receipts from income taxes was significant since the greater number of salaried jobs created in manufacturing and services increased income from the surtax relative to that from proportional tax. The widening gap between the numbers paying the flat-rate proportional tax (the self-employed and professional groups) and the numbers paying the progressive surtax (waged and salaried earners, as well as some of the self-employed) can be seen clearly in Fig. 1.

A further effect of the structural changes taking place in the economy was that revenue from direct taxes rose faster than national income and faster than receipts from indirect taxes.[25] Thus, despite the very vocal protests of the self-employed, it was in fact salaried workers who were paying more in income tax. Yet as opinion polls showed, half the people surveyed in 1957

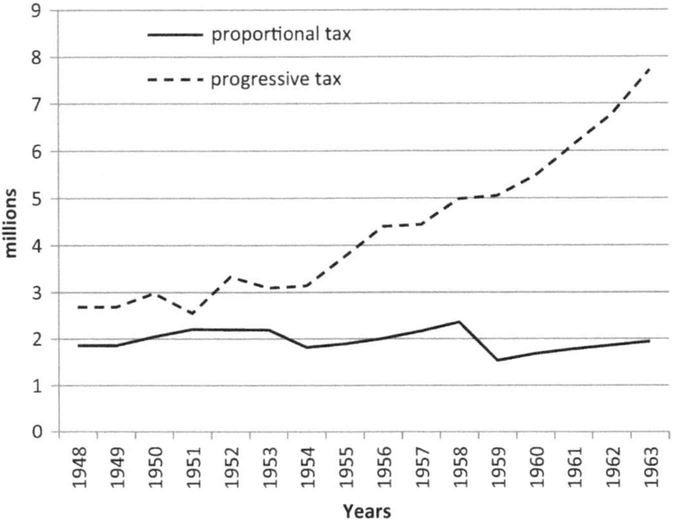

Fig. 1 Number of households paying proportional income tax and progressive income tax, 1948–1963. Source: AEF B-1457, Étude présentée par M. André Furst, June 16, 1964

were happy with the increased weight of income taxes in the tax system compared with 35 percent who thought that income taxes should be replaced by indirect taxes. The main concern of the majority (59 percent) of salaried workers was that employers continued to block the introduction of a PAYE system.[26] But if income taxes had acquired greater legitimacy among more of the population than before the Second World War, half the people surveyed in 1957 were dissatisfied, as, in their opinion, they were being left behind by the rapid changes in the economy which were being funded by their taxes.[27] The Fourth Republic, they maintained, had placed an excessive tax burden on incomes other than wages and salaries.[28]

Victory for the Self-Employed: de Gaulle's Reform of Income Taxation in 1959

Under the Fifth Republic, led by President Charles de Gaulle, the intention was to reduce and ultimately remove the apparent penalty imposed on the self-employed by phasing out the entire proportional taxation system. Under the tax reform law of December 1959, and supposedly in the interests of equity, the proportional tax and progressive surtax were abolished and replaced by a single tax levied on a progressive basis on the total income of the physical person (IRPP). To make up for any loss arising from the removal of the proportional tax which had risen to 22 percent, each of the surtax rates was increased by 5 percent. As an interim measure non-salaried incomes which had previously paid the proportional tax had to pay a flat-rate tax—now called a complementary tax—on a sliding scale from 6 percent to 9 percent on their 1959–1961 incomes. All allowances for dependent children were removed from this complementary tax. At the same time, it was stipulated that when the complementary tax was abolished in full, it was not to result in a transfer of the tax burden from non-salaried to salaried households.[29] In order to forestall an expected outcry from salaried households who had not paid any proportional tax but were now faced with a 5 percent increase on each of the tax bands of the IRPP, their allowances were raised from 15 percent to 19 percent in 1960 and to 20 percent thereafter. Skilled and craft workers were also given a range of allowances in the transitional period. The *forfait* system for taxing agriculture was retained, as was the payroll tax.[30] To compensate for any loss in revenue as a result of the change in structure of the income tax the rate of corporation tax was raised from 36 percent to 50 percent, although some concessions were given in permitted depreciation schedules and in special stock revaluation taxes following the devaluation of the franc in 1958. According to the General Inspector of Taxes, the new system was fair to both salaried and non-salaried households. Blot calculated that waged and salaried employees thus enjoyed the first reduction in income taxes in many years and, as a result of the increase in the threshold of the IRPP, the numbers paying income tax fell by about 400,000. The self-employed also benefited because the proportional tax rate was cut from 22 percent to 6 percent. The result of both measures was a reduction in the total yield from income taxes: from 36,989 million francs to 33,700 million and an expected reversal in the practice under the Fourth Republic when the weight of income taxes as a proportion of GDP had been slowly increasing. Whereas that proportion had increased from 2 percent to 3.08 percent of GDP between 1956 and 1959, Blot estimated that it would fall to 2.82 percent in 1960 and decline further still in the future.[31]

The concern raised by this reduction in income tax receipts was not that it would make the system more regressive and socially unjust, but that it might make it harder for the government to raise enough revenue to cover its needs in the new, more open regime of the European Economic

Community (EEC). One of the last decisions taken by the Fourth Republic before it collapsed under the strains of the Algerian War was to sign the Treaty of Rome, which took France into a customs union with the member states of the European Coal and Steel Community (ECSC). Under article 99 of the Treaty of Rome it was proposed that indirect taxes should be harmonized in order to remove any potential barriers to trade arising from different forms of taxes on production and consumption in member states. France had been the first member state to replace its production tax, levied on a cumulative basis, with a new tax (VAT) on value added. Because VAT was economically neutral, not discriminating between forms of production, size of firm, or between domestic and export markets (unlike the cumulative taxes on production, which was retained in other member states), the French government argued that VAT should become the common form of indirect tax throughout the EEC. The risk was that if the rates of the new tax were harmonized, they might be lower than the VAT rate in France at that time. The potential problem for France, one that was identified by the tax authorities, was that it would probably not be able to increase receipts from VAT to compensate for the fall in income tax receipts arising from the 1959 tax reform, since it already raised more revenue from indirect taxes than any member state, apart from Italy, regardless of whether the 5 percent payroll tax was included as an indirect tax.

At a time when income from tariffs was to fall as a result of the formation of the customs union, Blot raised the possibility that the French government might have to increase revenue from income taxes. Once again it was potential external pressure rather than any concern for greater equity in the French tax system that led to the question of what scope there was for raising more revenue from direct taxes. The rate of corporation tax was comparatively high, as was the top rate of income tax. However, as Blot told a parliamentary committee, comparison of top rates was meaningless since they bore no relation to the actual tax paid by households. Since no other member state had a system like that of the French family quotient it would be necessary, he said, to calculate what households earning similar incomes with similar family structures were paying in income tax across the member states. He selected three family types for the exercise: one without children, one with two children, and one with four children in West Germany, Britain, and Italy. In the French case he made two calculations, one where the payroll tax was included as a tax on income and the second where it was passed on as a tax on consumption.

Blot's calculations revealed that because exemption from income tax was greater in France than in West Germany, Britain, or Italy, low and medium wage earners paid less income tax in France. On similar incomes the tax rates were between two and three times higher in West Germany and Britain than in France. Because income tax started at a higher income in France than in other countries, the degree of progressivity was more rapid. For a household without children the highest income group in France paid ten times more tax than the lowest one, the actual rates being 28.63 percent compared with 2.78 percent. In Britain, they paid six times more: 59.7 percent compared with 9.9 percent. In West Germany, they paid four times more: 38.5 percent compared with 9.7 percent; and in Italy three times more: 19 percent compared with 6.69 percent. But for a household with children the effect of the family quotient system in France reduced this progressivity dramatically. Blot calculated that for a family with two children in the highest income group the difference in tax between the highest income and the lowest was 8.5 percent in France, 7.1 percent in West Germany, 15.6 percent in Britain, and 3.2 percent in Italy. The conclusion he drew was that there was scope to increase income tax rates in France since the effect of the family quotient reduced the actual tax paid considerably.[32] Whether that would work politically was a different matter.

Blot's account of France as a country where the average household paid less income tax than elsewhere in Europe, and much less than wealthier households, did not correspond with popular perception. An article in the American magazine *Time* was nearer the mark:

> France in theory imposes higher income taxes than almost any other country and in practice collects less: a mere 14 percent of government revenue v. 60 percent in the United States. The injustice of the system is that hapless wage earners, whose incomes are recorded on company payrolls and are thus easily available to '*le fisc*' shell out two thirds of all the income taxes collected in France. While the rich get richer, thanks to an economic boom and the native genius for fiscal camouflage, rich and poor alike must shoulder massive consumer taxes.[33]

An Increasingly Unfair Tax System

The reality increasingly felt by many households was that they were indeed paying more than their fair share of income tax; the difficulty lay in being able to prove it. In 1962 the Economic and Social Committee of the National Assembly set out to establish the effective distribution of the income tax burden across all socio-economic groups since 1950. They had attempted a similar exercise in the mid-1950s when they had tried to calculate the impact of all taxes on different socio-economic groups but had to abandon the project owing to its complexity. It quickly became apparent that even confining the study to the impact of income taxation was fraught with difficulty, largely due to the lack of data. The only source available was *Statistiques et études financières*, the annual publication of the Ministry of Finance. Given that this did not even give details of the number of wage earners in the public and private sectors or of the number of civil servants or of their wages and salaries, all that the committee could do was identify broad trends and calculate changes in the average tax burden over the years. Significantly though, it discovered the well-kept secret that the tax thresholds had not been adjusted between 1953 and 1959 to take account of inflation. This explained how national income had increased threefold between 1951 and 1961 but the revenue from the progressive surtax had increased eightfold. According to André Furst, the author of the 1964 report, the increase in receipts from the surtax was not due to rising incomes as successive governments had claimed, as much as to the deliberate policy of fiscal drag. Another conclusion drawn by Furst was that the 1959 reforms had greatly affected the relative amounts paid by the different socio-economic groups. Whereas the flat-rate proportional tax had accounted for two-thirds of the tax collected from the progressive surtax in 1950, the complementary tax that replaced it raised no more than 15.3 percent of the IRPP in 1959 and 8.68 percent in 1961. Other than that it was not possible, given the lack of statistical data, to prove which, if any, groups had been treated unequally by the tax system.[34]

Asked to comment on the Furst Report, Max Laxan, who had succeeded Robert Blot as General Inspector of Taxes in August 1961, insisted that the doubling of income tax receipts between 1950 and 1960 was the result of an increase in the working population of 800,000 and a rise in incomes rather than a greater tax burden placed on certain households. He challenged the Furst Report's conclusion that taxes at the individual level had soared in the 1950s. Yet when he produced detailed calculations of the income tax paid by different households in 1963 compared with 1950 the evidence suggested something different. What Laxan showed was that a married skilled worker with two children living on one income would have paid 0.6 percent of income in tax in 1950 and 1.9 percent in 1963, assuming that his or her income had increased over the period at the same rate as that of the equivalent civil service grade. (Our calculations show that a skilled worker was earning 1.5 percent more than the average wage.)[35] Someone in middle management with similar family circumstances and earning twice as much as a skilled worker would have paid 5.26 percent of income in tax in 1950 and 6.81 percent in 1963, while a more senior manager would have paid 7.8 percent tax in 1950 and 12.7 percent in 1963. Thus, it was the lowest paid who experienced the greatest proportional increase in income tax.

Asked to compare the tax burden in France with that of other European countries Laxan confirmed Blot's conclusions: French households paid less in income tax at all levels of income between 12,900 francs and 130,000 francs than West German, British, Dutch, Italian, and Swedish households. It was only at the lowest income level that Belgian households were in the same situation as the French in being exempt from any income tax. Agreeing with Blot that the degree of progressivity was much greater in France than in the other countries, he nevertheless argued that the differences had narrowed since 1950.[36]

Since Laxan's calculations were not made public, the demand for greater clarity about the distribution of the income tax burden continued. The Institut National des Études Économiques (INSEE) took up the challenge of finding out what households on different incomes and with various family structures actually paid in income tax. However, trying to do so by surveying a sample of 40,000 households on three occasions was fraught with difficulty since many people hesitated to divulge such sensitive information given the passions that the whole question of income taxes aroused. What the results of the surveys did show was that between 1959 and 1966 the income tax paid by a married man without children on an average wage had increased by more than the tax burden of similar households earning twice or three times as much and by much more than households with children.[37]

Given the lack of published data on the specific impact of the income tax system across a range of socio-economic groups, it was the benefits of the family quotient system for large, wealthy households, as well as the privileges given to the agricultural sector under the *forfait* system, which drew the greatest criticism from left-wing economists. Dismissing their arguments as hastily conceived and extremely difficult to implement the Tax Inspectorate maintained that to abolish the *forfait* system for assessing the tax liability of agriculture was fundamentally impractical since it exceeded the capability of the Tax Inspectorate to check all their returns if farmers were asked to submit them annually.[38] While agreeing that the advantages given to very high earners as a result of the family quotient system were "undoubtedly excessive" and bore no relation to the additional costs of raising a family, the problem could not be solved, it was argued, within the context of re-examining the income tax system. The only circumstance where any debate on ending the family quotient system could be envisaged was if it became an obligation to meet the terms of the EEC. However, it was recognized that since the attachment to the pronatalist agenda in France was as strong as the attachment to Europe, were France asked to choose between membership of the European Community and retaining the family quotient system, the choice would be very difficult indeed.[39]

In sharp contrast to any potential pressure from the EEC to change the family quotient system, criticisms of the tax system mounted by the domestic opposition in France were seen to be much easier to deal with. In discussing with Prime Minister Georges Pompidou what the best solution to mounting criticism of the income tax system was, Laxan was very relaxed: "There is no need to philosophize about taxation: public expenditure has to be covered. That's all there is to it."[40]

Referring to the popular notion that the older the tax the more likely it was to be tolerated, he told Pompidou that although income tax had been introduced in France during the First World War, it was still considered relatively new since many people had not started paying it until under the Fifth Republic. On the other hand, because income taxation in Britain dated back to the Napoleonic Wars, Britain was able to raise more from income taxes than France. While it was true that tax revenue had increased since 1958, Laxan pointed out that, based on the statistics compiled in the National Accounts, they had risen only from 21.9 percent of GDP to 22.3 percent. This slight increase was not because public expenditure had risen, but because the government was no longer running a budget deficit as it had done between 1952 and 1958. Justifying the current system, he said that in the 1950s the government had levied the most unjust tax of all in the form of inflation. It was also the case, he said, that when living standards were rising rapidly, income taxes would also rise, particularly under a progressive system, as demanded by the political Left. At the same time, revenue from indirect taxes would also go up as more would be spent on luxury goods on which the rate of VAT was higher than on necessities. That would explain why receipts from indirect taxation had risen by more than the national income. In his view it made no sense for the Left to complain about the weight of indirect taxes while complaining that more households were paying income tax. The real problem, in his view, was that the combined weight of central government taxation, local taxes, and social security contributions was probably too high as a proportion of GDP. Local taxes in particular had been rising at about 10 percent a year. Displaying a profound lack of sympathy with the financial hardship felt by many French households at the time, Laxan declared: "we should not be surprised if from time to time the tax burden on some people rises very quickly partly as a result of the increase in local taxes but also because of the very progressive nature of income taxes."[41]

When pressed further, Laxan went back over his figures and calculated that in 1958 income tax had been just 8 percent of total tax receipts. Over the following nine years it had doubled and the revenue raised from it, measured in constant francs, had quadrupled. Over the same period the number of households paying income tax had more than doubled, from 4.3 million in 1957 to more than 9 million in 1966. This represented two-thirds of all non-agricultural households. Due to deficiencies in the statistics it was not possible to calculate the number of households that paid the proportional tax but were not liable for the progressive tax. What was clear was that the number paying the proportional tax had fallen from 2.2 million in 1957 to 1.8 million in 1966. Many farmers, as he explained, were liable to pay the proportional tax but not the progressive tax since their incomes, as estimated under the *forfait* system, fell below the threshold. If the receipts from income tax were comparatively low in France, he insisted that this was due to the generous allowances, particularly the operation of the family quotient system.[42] But what Laxan had to admit was that he could not provide data to show how much households on different incomes had actually been paying in income tax over a period of time. All that he could offer were global figures of the total receipts from the IRPP as a proportion of the total income liable for this tax. This was 66.5 percent of 1957 incomes and 69 percent of 1964 incomes. From this he could calculate the average tax paid, but not its distribution across the social strata.[43]

The lack of interest displayed by the Tax Inspectorate in the effect of the tax system on the living standards of French households was echoed by the government and revealed how remote it was from poorer households and its disregard for equity in the tax system. Pompidou's reaction to the explosion of social and political discontent in 1968 and to de Gaulle quitting politics following his defeat in the 1969 referendum was to try to secure the vote of the self-employed middle class in his bid to succeed de Gaulle as president. The key, in his view, was to abolish the proportional tax altogether while ignoring the stipulation made in 1959 that the resulting fall in revenue should not be offset by increasing the tax burden of salaried and waged earners.[44] The proportion of households paying income tax continued to increase, especially as inflation accelerated after 1971. Although Valéry Giscard d'Estaing, Minister of Finance under President Pompidou, responded to mounting pressure for more information on the distribution of the income tax burden by setting up a Tax Council in 1971, its biannual reports failed to satisfy public opinion. A poll taken in 1975 showed that 65 percent believed that the French tax system itself was unfair.[45] By 1979 it had to admit that the way in which financial statistics were presented made it very difficult to use them. The Audit Court also criticized the way that tax revenue was presented since it failed to distinguish between the income tax of households, corporations, and local councils. A group of self-styled "new economists" spelled out the problem in a letter to the Minister for the Budget, Maurice Papon:

> Consent to taxation is the foundation of democracy. In the absence of clear and widely diffused information among voters and contributors democracy cannot really function. At the moment it is governments and civil servants who have a complete monopoly over this information and are therefore judge and jury.[46]

To be told by the Tax Council in its 570-page report in 1979 that, contrary to popular perception, the French people paid much less income tax than in those other countries—12.5 percent of total tax receipts compared with 54 percent in Denmark, 43 percent in Sweden, 30–38 percent in West Germany, Britain, and the United States—was cold comfort to people who had seen their tax burden rise each year. The Tax Council replied that if more French households now paid income tax or paid more in tax that was because real incomes had risen.[47] What the report failed to acknowledge in full was that such a comparison was invalid since the figures for income tax also covered social security payments in several of these countries.

It was the OECD that took up the challenge of producing comparative data on the effective rates of income tax and social security paid by households on average incomes both with and without children from the late 1970s onwards across member states. Since it did not try to provide any data for earlier periods or for households on other sources of incomes our research has tried to fill that gap. Given that the data were not collected systematically by governments or other organizations, we applied the

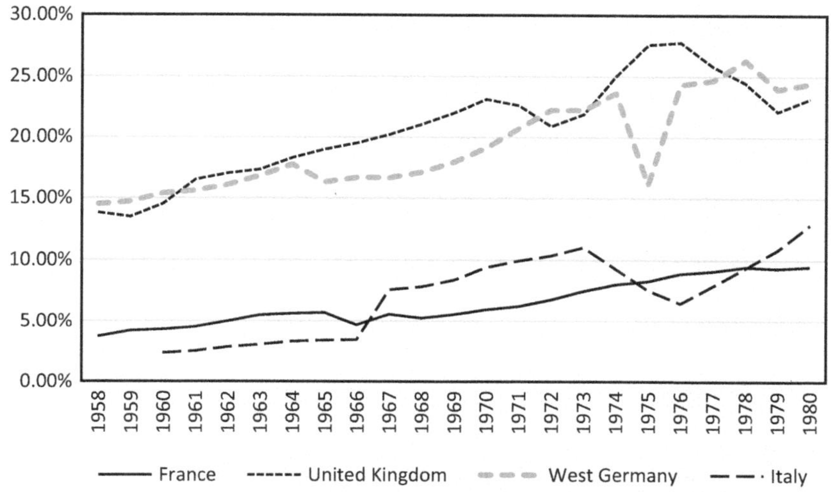

Fig. 2 Effective income tax rates paid by a single worker on average earnings in France, the United Kingdom, West Germany, and Italy. Source: Lynch and Weingarten, *EuroPTax*

published rules governing income tax to households across a range of incomes and family structures.[48] What we could not calculate was how much fraud there was in declaring income by those not in receipt of a wage or salary. What the results confirm is that French households did indeed pay less in income tax, and in income tax and social security combined, than their counterparts in other European countries. A single worker without dependent children paid much less income tax than someone in the United Kingdom or West Germany, but more than someone in Italy until the mid-1960s (see Fig. 2).

But if single workers on average income paid less income tax than those in other European countries, they paid comparatively more than a married middle manager with two children and earning twice as much (see Fig. 3). It was the perceived inequity of the French system itself that was the cause of concern among those who felt that they were being penalized by having to pay high consumption taxes as well as high income taxes. To increase the share of income taxes still further in order to reduce consumption taxes would not have addressed the problem in the income tax system itself.

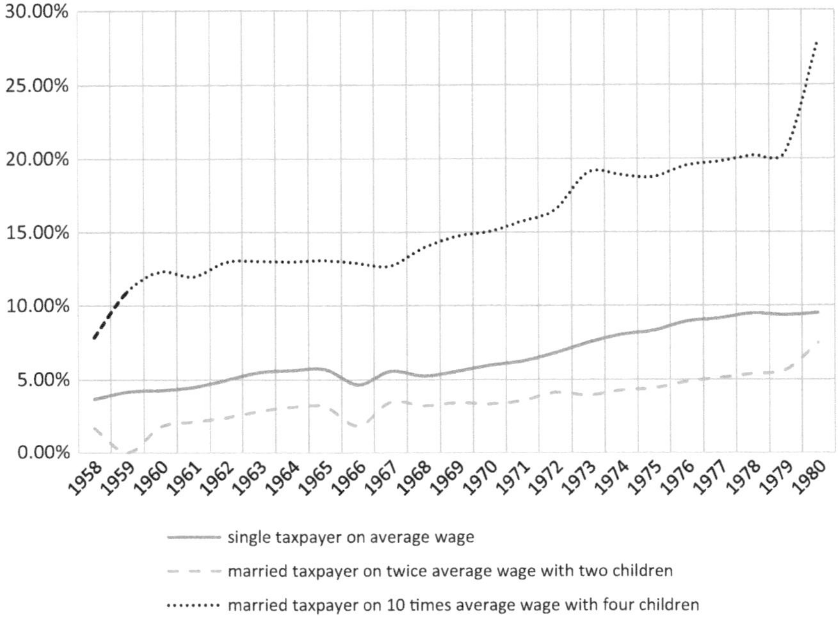

Fig. 3 Effective tax rates paid by different French households. Source: Lynch and Weingarten, *EuroPTax*

Conclusion

This research has demonstrated how the attempt to make the French tax system fairer and more progressive after the Second World War by increasing the weight of income taxes in total tax revenue was reversed under the presidential regime of the Fifth Republic. The acknowledgement built into the 1948 income tax system that workers whose wages were declared by their employer were at a disadvantage compared to the self-employed was largely removed under the tax reform of 1959. However, what ultimately reduced the yield from income taxes was the family quotient system introduced in 1945 to boost the French birth rate. This system gave considerable tax advantages to large, wealthy families at the expense of poorer families and single people, and was the single most regressive aspect of income tax policy. Unlike the fiscal privileges given to agricultural workers, it did not decline as the French economy developed. France has managed to retain this unique system despite being a member of the European

Union with its limited fiscal harmonization. The impact of the family quotient, and indeed of all the rules governing French taxation, was largely removed from public debate by the refusal of successive governments to publish details of the impact of income tax policies on different socio-economic groups. However, what our research has revealed has been the utter indifference of the French Tax Inspectorate to the hardship of poorer French households or the possible inequity of the income tax system or of the tax structure.

One reason that the proportion of households paying income tax increased during the postwar period was that the numbers of salaried workers as opposed to the self-employed grew. Between 1962 and 1969, their share of all those paying income tax rose from 63.7 percent to 70 percent (as a proportion of the total population they increased from 54.2 percent to 61.8 percent). In 1962, the self-employed represented 22.5 percent of all households paying income tax whereas by 1969 they comprised only 14.8 percent.[49] Another reason for the increase in numbers was due to the steep gradient of the progressive tax bands. Under the Fourth Republic, the policy of not adjusting these bands to take account of the rise in prices and wages made many more households liable for income taxes and increased the effective tax paid by existing taxpayers. Under both the Fourth and the Fifth Republics the tax imposed on lower-income single people rose faster than for other groups because of the operation of the family quotient system. Research on France supports Alex Hertel-Fernandez and Cathie Jo Martin's argument that employers and conservatives shaped the tax state of the Fifth Republic.[50] However, the structures laid down immediately after the Second World War, the family quotient system, and the method of funding social security were put in place by one of the most left-wing parliaments of modern times in France.[51]

Notes

1. Kato, *Regressive Taxation*, 94.
2. Piketty, *Hauts revenus*, 347.
3. There is a proposal to introduce PAYE in 2018. See also Isaac W. Martin in this volume.
4. Kato, *Regressive Taxation*, 94.
5. Lynch and Weingarten, *EuroPTax*.
6. Piketty, *Hauts revenus*.
7. Hansen and Snyder, *Fiscal Policy*, 158.

8. Schremmer, Taxation, 372; Mitchell, *Historical Statistics,* 21, 25.
9. Dutton, *French Welfare,* 212.
10. Archives du Ministère de l'Économie et des Finances (AEF), B-1457, Note sur le quotient familial et la limite d'exonération. September 18, 1966.
11. Dutton, *French Welfare,* 219.
12. In practice this was seldom the case and in 1990 a CSG was finally set up, based on both taxes and contributions. Plagnet, *L'impôt,* 169–94.
13. Delalande, *Batailles,* 370–7.
14. Piketty, "Hauts revenus," 347.
15. Baum, *French Economy,* 164; Lynch, *Tax for Europe,* 73–6.
16. Lynch, *France, 83, 94–5,* Margairaz, *L'état,* 111–415, Chapman, "Réformateurs," 323.
17. Plagnet, *L'impôt,* 170–1.
18. AEF, B-64459, Communication en conseil des ministres, March 8, 1982.
19. Baum, *French Economy,* 139.
20. Ibid., 143.
21. Pinay, *Un Français,* 59–75.
22. Chapman, "Réformateurs," 332.
23. AEF, B-1457, Étude présentée par M. André Furst, June 16, 1964.
24. AEF, B-52489 Note pour la commission d'étude, from R. Blot, April 26, 1961.
25. Nizet, *Fiscalité,* 90–1.
26. Delalande, *Batailles,* 386.
27. Ibid., 385.
28. Hansen and Snyder, *Fiscal Policy,* 152–3.
29. Nizet, *Fiscalité,* 17; Hansen and Snyder, *Fiscal Policy,* 153–4.
30. Nizet, *Fiscalité,* 176.
31. AEF, B-52489/1 Note pour la Commission d'étude from R. Blot, Directeur général des impôts, April 26, 1961.
32. Ibid.
33. AEF, B-1457 Article in Time magazine, May 10, 1963, 'Liberté, Égalité—Mais Vérité?
34. AEF B-1457, Étude présentée par M. André Furst, June 16, 1964.
35. Lynch and Weingarten, *EuroPTax* calculations for France.
36. AEF B-52489, Note from Laxan, Observations sommaires sur les conclusions du rapport de M. Furst relatives à l'évolution de l'impôt depuis 1951–1952.
37. AEF B-1457, Enquête sur les revenus des ménages, July 31, 1967.
38. AEF B-1457, note for the Prime Minister, October 10, 1966.
39. AEF B-1457, Memorandum from J-R Bernard.
40. AEF B-1457, note for the Prime Minister, "Il ne faut pas faire trop de philosophie avec la fiscalité: il y a des charges publiques, il faut les couvrir. Voilà tout." October 10, 1966.

41. Ibid.
42. Ibid.
43. Ibid.
44. Nizet, *Fiscalité*, 176.
45. AEF B-71335 Résultats d'un sondage de la SOFRES, March 1975.
46. AEF B-71335 Letter from Salin to Papon, "Le consentement à l'impôt est. le fondement même de la démocratie. Sans information claire et largement diffusée auprès des électeurs-contribuables la démocratie ne peut réellement fonctionner. Or le monopole de l'expertise en matière fiscale semble actuellement détenu par les hommes de l'État, gouvernants, élus et fonctionnaires, qui sont à la fois juge et partie." March 22, 1979.
47. AEF 620.5 REC.
48. Lynch and Weingarten, *EuroPTax*.
49. Spire, "L'inégalité," 164–87.
50. See Alex Hertel-Fernandez and Cathie Jo Martin in this volume.
51. Piketty, *Hauts revenus,* 285–6.

References

André, Christine, and Robert Delorme. 1983. *L'état et l'économie. Un essai d'explication de l'évolution des dépenses publiques en France, 1870–1980.* Paris: Seuil.

Archives du Ministère de L'Économie et des Finances (AEF), Savigny-le-Temple.

Ardant, Gabriel. 1972. *Histoire de l'impôt.* Paris: Fayard.

Baum, Warren C. 1958. *The French Economy and the State.* Princeton, NJ: Princeton University Press.

Bouvier, Jean, and Jacques Wolff, eds. 1973. *Deux siècles de fiscalité française, xix–xx. Histoire, économie politique.* Paris: Mouton.

Brownlee, W. Elliot, Eisaku Ide, and Yasunori Fukagai, eds. 2013. *The Political Economy of Transnational Tax Reform. The Shoup Mission to Japan in Historical Context.* Cambridge: Cambridge University Press.

Chapman, Herrick. 2006. Réformateurs et contestataires de l'impôt en France après la Seconde Guerre Mondiale. In *L'impôt en France aux XIXe et XXe siècles. Colloque des 2,3 et 4 mai 2001*, ed. Maurice Lévy-Leboyer, Michel Lescure, and Alain Plessis, 319–335. Paris: CHEFF.

Dard, Olivier. 2006. Économistes, jurists, technocrats et publicists face aux questions fiscales, de l'entre-deux-guerres aux années soixante. In *L'impôt en France aux XIXe et XXe siècles. Colloque des 2,3 et 4 mai 2001*, ed. Maurice Lévy-Leboyer, Michel Lescure, and Alain Plessis, 249–272. Paris: CHEFF.

Delalande, Nicolas. 2011. *Les Batailles de l'Impôt. Consentement et résistances de 1789 à nos jours.* Paris: Seuil.

Dutton, Paul V. 2002. *Origins of the French Welfare State. The Struggle for Social Reform in France, 1914–1947*. Cambridge: Cambridge University Press.

Hansen, Bent, and Wayne W. Snyder. 1969. *Fiscal Policy in Seven Countries 1955–1965*. Paris: OECD.

Jabbari, Eric. 2012. *Pierre Laroque and the Welfare State in Postwar France*. Oxford: Oxford University Press.

Kato, Junko. 2003. *Regressive Taxation and the Welfare State*. Cambridge: Cambridge University Press.

Le Cacheux, Jacques. 2008. *Les Français et l'impôt*. Paris: Odile Jacob/La Documentation française.

Lescure, Michel, Maurice Lévy-Leboyer, and Alain Plessis, eds. 2006. *L'impôt en France aux xix et xx siècles. Colloque des 2,3 et 4 mai 2001*. Paris: CHEFF.

Lévy-Leboyer, Maurice, Michel Lescure, and Alain Plessis, eds. 2006. *L'impôt en France aux X1Xe et XXe siècles. Colloque des 2,3 et 4 mai 2001*. Paris: CHEFF.

Lynch, Frances M.B. 1988. A Tax for Europe: The Introduction of Value Added Tax in France. *Journal of European Integration History* 4 (2): 67–87.

———. 1997. *France and the International Economy from Vichy to the Treaty of Rome*. London and New York: Routledge.

———. 2013. The Haig–Shoup Mission to France in the 1920s. In *The Political Economy of Transnational Tax Reform. The Shoup Mission to Japan in Historical Context*, ed. Elliot Brownlee, Eisaku Ide, and Yasunori Fukagai, 61–85. Cambridge: Cambridge University Press.

Lynch, F., and Weingarten, N. 2010. *EuroPTax. Who Pays for the State? The Evolution of Personal Taxation in Postwar Europe, 1958–2007* [data collection]. UK Data Service. SN: 6358, https://doi.org/10.5255/UKDA-SN-6358-1. Accessed 9 Feb 2018.

Margairaz, Michel. 1991. *L'État, les finances et l'économie: histoire d'une conversion. 1932–1952. 2 vols*. Paris: CHEFF.

Mitchell, B.R. 1978. *European Historical Statistics, 1750–1970*. New York: Columbia University Press.

Nizet, Jean-Yves. 1991. *Fiscalité, économie et politique. L'impôt en France 1945–1990*. Paris: Librairie générale de droit et de jurisprudence, E.J.A.

OECD. various years. *The Tax/Benefit Position of a Typical Worker in OECD Member Countries*. Paris: Organisation for Economic Co-operation and Development.

Piketty, Thomas. 2001. *Les hauts revenus en France au xx siècle. Inégalités et redistribution. 1901–1998*. Paris: Grasset.

———. 2014. *Capital in the Twenty-First Century*. Cambridge, MA: The Belknap Press of Harvard University Press.

Pinay, Antoine. 1984. *Un Français comme les autres. Entretiens avec Antoine Veil*. Paris: Belfond/Jean-Cyrille Godefroy.

Plagnet, Bernard. 2006. De l'impôt sur le revenu à la CSG. In *L'impôt en France aux XIX et XX siècles. Colloque des 2,3 et 4 mai 2001*, ed. Michel Lescure, Maurice Lévy-Leboyer, and Alain Plessis, 169–194. Paris: CHEFF.

Rueff, Jacques. 1972. Rapport sur la situation financière presenté à Monsieur le Ministre des Finances et des Affaires Économiques en exécution de sa décision du 30 septembre 1958. In *Combats pour l'ordre financier*, ed. Jacques Rueff, 171–248. Paris: Plon.

Schremmer, D.E. 1984. Taxation and Public Finance, Britain, France and Germany. In *The Cambridge Economic History of Europe*, ed. Peter Mathias and Sidney Pollard, vol. VIII, 315–494. Cambridge: Cambridge University Press.

Spire, Alexis. 2009. L'inégalité devant l'impôt. Différences sociales et ordre fiscal dans la France des Trente glorieuses. *Revue d'histoire moderne et contemporaine* 56 (2): 164–187.

Tax Policy in the United States: Was There a "Neo-Liberal" Revolution in the 1970s and 1980s?

W. Elliot Brownlee

This chapter examines the question of whether or not there was a "neo-liberal" revolution in tax policy in the United States during the 1970s and 1980s. Answering this question requires three tasks: a definition of "neo-liberalism"; an assessment of the extent to which tax and fiscal policies during the 1970s and 1980s, especially the policies promulgated by President Ronald Reagan and his administration, constituted a "neo-liberal" break from historic patterns; and an evaluation of the impact of those policies on the American political economy. That, in outline, is the structure of my chapter.[1]

What Is Meant by "Neo-Liberal" Tax Policy?

Answering the question of whether or not there was a "neo-liberal" revolution in the United States during the 1970s and 1980s requires first discussing the meaning of "neo-liberalism," especially in the American

W. E. Brownlee (✉)
University of California, Santa Barbara, Santa Barbara, CA, USA
e-mail: brownlee@history.ucsb.edu

G. Huerlimann et al. (eds.), *Worlds of Taxation*,
Palgrave Studies in the History of Finance,
https://doi.org/10.1007/978-3-319-90263-0_7

context. In doing so, we have the benefit of the impressive work of the numerous scholars who have explored the significance of "neo-liberalism" to the development of the state since World War II.[2]

Historical actors who declared themselves "neo-liberal" and scholars who have studied "neo-liberalism" sometimes have used the terms in different ways. By "neo-liberal," scholars generally have meant certain "free-market" policies that took hold during the 1970s and 1980s in the wake of slowing economic growth and accelerating inflation. They have often cited tax policies as constituting an important element of "neo-liberalism." Anthropologist David Harvey, to take one example, has cast a very broad net, identifying a variety of specific policies as neo-liberal. He described what he calls "the neoliberal state" as revising "the tax code to benefit returns on investment rather than income and wages, promotion of regressive elements in the tax code (such as sales taxes), the imposition of user fees … , and the provision of a vast array of subsidies and tax breaks to corporations." Harvey goes on to add to his list "the corporate welfare programmes" that "amount to a vast redirection of public moneys" and tax deductions that provide subsidies "to upper income homeowners."[3]

Some prominent members of the very first generation of self-conscious "neo-liberals" ranged even more widely over the terrain of tax policy, embracing powerfully progressive taxation as well if it served to restore, foster, or protect free-market conditions. A leading American example is Walter Lippmann, whose book *The Good Society* (1937) inspired French philosopher Louis Rougier to organize a conference in 1938 (the precursor to the Mont Pèlerin Society) under the rubric of "neo-liberalism." In the book, Lippmann called for tax reform that would "strike at the source of the big incomes which arise from the various kinds of monopoly, from exclusive rights in land and natural resources, from bad markets in which the ignorant and the helpless are at a disadvantage. Income arising from these inequalities of opportunity and legal status is unearned by the criterion of the exchange economy." Such income is not, he declared, "the wages of labor or management, the interest on capital, or the profits of enterprise, as determined in free and efficient markets, but tolls levied upon wages, interest, and profits by the subversion or the manipulation of the market price for goods and services." In addition, Lippmann called for tax reform "to divert excess savings from the hoards of the rich and to plough them back into the improvement of the quality of the people and of their estate." This redistribution was "required not only by the long view of the imponderable national interest, not only as an expedient to allay discontent, not only as a matter of social justice, but as a requisite for preserving the equilibrium of the exchange economy itself."

Like most other American members of the first generation of "neo-liberals," Lippmann sought to steer a middle course between collectivist initiatives of the New Deal and pristine nineteenth-century laissez faire. More generally, Lippmann's shift in 1937 from his earlier (1914) embrace of Theodore Roosevelt's New Nationalism in *Drift and Mastery* produced what Arthur Schlesinger Jr. correctly called "the most lucid statement of the tradition of the New Freedom" of Woodrow Wilson. In 1914 Lippmann had seen no need for an elaborate system of federal taxation to cope with the issues of inequality, monopoly power, and unearned income.[4] But in *The Good Society*, Lippmann outlined a tax program that was essentially that of Woodrow Wilson. Thus, Lippmann's tax program put him where Wilson had been: on the offensive, advancing the ideals of both liberalism and republicanism on the boundary of progressivism where it bordered social democracy.[5]

The leading American economist among the first generation of self-identified "neo-liberals" was the University of Chicago economist Henry C. Simons. At the same time as Lippmann, but in a more technically sophisticated way, Simons proposed a program of tax reform that also squared ethically with Wilsonian principles. Simons' central theme was the need to address the inequality that he saw as arising inevitably in a capitalist society. He viewed progressive income taxation as a necessary tool to address the concentration of wealth, and his most distinctive proposals were to treat all property transfers as realizations for taxation of capital gains and to tax capital gains at the same rate as other forms of income. This program would, he believed, cut off the relentless effort to transform taxable income into nontaxable gain and promote economic equality while advancing economic efficiency. During the 1940s, Simons, along with other self-identified neo-liberals, shifted their interests to attacking what they regarded as democratic-statism. But he continued to believe that the success of free enterprise depended on government structures, including tax policies, that would advance economic equality.[6]

The next generation of "neo-liberals," including Simons' student Milton Friedman, joined the intellectual fray during the 1940s. They retained, until the 1950s, an interest in anti-monopoly policies, but generally dropped an interest in tax reform that sought to promote both equality and competition. By the 1960s, these neo-liberals had abandoned as well a concern with monopoly (except perhaps where government was thought to cause it) and ceased identifying themselves as "neo-liberals." Friedman may have done so as early as 1951. He and the other members of what Daniel Stedman Jones calls "the second Chicago school" probably shed the term so to avoid confusion with New Deal liberals. In effect, they (Friedman et al.) acknowledged that they had abandoned Walter Lippmann's and Herbert Simon's "neo-liberalism"—a political and social philosophy that steered between nineteenth-century liberalism and twentieth-century democratic-statism. They did so in favor of what historian Angus Burgin accurately describes as "the triumphant return of laissez-faire." In their social policies, they were far more than pro-capital or pro-business. They engaged in sweeping attacks on government in general, regarded free markets as the most important source of social freedom, largely ignored inequality as a social and economic problem, and disregarded evidence regarding market failure and dysfunction. To describe the economists and others who championed these views during the 1960s and after as "neo-liberals" fails to do credit to the social theorists who devised the term. A new and different term—let me suggest "retro-liberals"—better captures the reality that the "neo-liberals" of the 1960s had returned to the liberalism of the nineteenth century and, in some instances, to one of the narrowest versions of that liberalism.[7]

Political Consensus and Tax Cutting, 1945–1971

The first tax measure undertaken during the administration of Ronald Reagan was the Economic Recovery Tax Act (ERTA) of 1981, which made substantial cuts in personal and corporate income taxation. The adoption of this legislation took place in the context of a policy consensus that had prevailed since the end of World War II. The 1981 cuts seemed dramatic but a central element of that the post-1945 political consensus was a broad bipartisan agreement that in peacetime the revenue bonanza from personal and corporate income taxation would be sufficiently large to provide frequent cuts in those taxes. The cuts were in the form of reduction of rates and the expansion of tax expenditures—special preferences offered under the tax code in the form of income exclusions, tax deductions, and tax credits. A closely related element in the prevailing consensus was that the cuts would provide tax benefits across the income spectrum but wealthy taxpayers and corporations would reap a disproportionate share. After World War II, and the consequent ebbing of wartime patriotism as a factor in income tax compliance, tax cutting played a central role in enhancing public acceptance of the new tax regime. Thus, well before 1981 and the enactment of ERTA, significant and sustained tax cutting had become a huge program funded by buoyant tax revenues. It had become well established as a fundamental component of the nation's fiscal consensus.

Ironically, perhaps, the structure of the US tax system, especially its highly progressive and mass-based character, was responsible for the scale and shape of the tax cutting as spending program. Its revenue elasticity in an era of high economic growth produced the revenues that funded the cuts, and the progressivity, coupled with the mass base of the income tax, created incentives for all taxpayers and a large fraction of the citizenry to seek tax cuts. The incentives were greatest for taxpayers with the largest incomes, and the pressures were especially great during episodes of inflation. During inflationary periods, increasing prices, absent indexing that was difficult politically and technically, pushed taxpayers into higher income brackets (the process known as "bracket creep") and imposed capital gains taxes on gains that resulted from inflation rather the growth in the real value of assets.

This ironic interplay of progressive taxation and tax protest had deep historical roots in inter-class tension over tax policy in the United States. Since the mid-nineteenth century, the political effort to reconcile an increasing concentration of income and wealth with democratic ideals and practice had produced volatile and intense debates over tax policy and profound shifts in tax regimes, particularly during major wars or periods of severe economic crisis.[8] The cumulative effect of the crises of the Great Depression and the two World Wars was to make the US tax system the most progressive among the large capitalist nations.[9] At the end of World War II, a new tax regime was in place, a product of both the New Deal and the mobilization for World War II. At the core of the tax regime created during World War II was a progressive and mass-based income tax that produced a revenue bonanza by exploiting the economic successes of the high growth era that accompanied and followed the war. But, at the same time, the successes of the progressive income tax stimulated a sustained reaction by class interests—those of large corporations and wealthy elites. Their power was the main driver in the expansion of tax cuts designed to reduce tax progressivity. But the combination of mass-based income tax and the process of "bracket creep" meant that high-income taxpayers had readily available allies within the middle class for cutting taxes. The reactionary force, as it played out over the last half of the twentieth century, produced a "long-swing" away from progressive taxation toward what became a "retro-liberal" fiscal regime during the early twenty-first century.[10]

Tax cutting at the federal level began immediately after the war in two major measures enacted in 1945 and 1948, during a period of both high economic growth and inflation. The cuts in 1945 repealed the wartime excess-profits tax, cut income taxes across the board for all taxpayers, and reduced wartime excise taxes. The rationales included both a supply-side argument for encouraging private investment and demand-side one for stimulating consumer demand.[11] In 1948 Congress made additional across-the-board cuts and introduced the income-splitting joint return for husbands and wives.[12] President Harry Truman was able to restrain the tax cutting somewhat, arguing publicly for the need to contain inflation and work down wartime debts. But in 1946 his threat of a tax increase had contributed to Republicans winning control of Congress for the first time in 13 years, and doing so with the most dramatic gains in their congressional power until 2014. As a consequence, in passing the Revenue Act of 1948 the Republican Congress had been able to override Truman's veto.

Enthusiasm for tax cutting waned for a time during the Korean War but the last wartime measure, the Revenue Act of 1951, included tax increases and a variety of cuts in the form of larger tax expenditures. These included expansion of mineral depletion allowances to 30 mineral groups, exemption of home-sale profits from capital gains taxation if reinvested in another home, deduction of certain medical expenses by the elderly, various exclusions and exemptions for veterans, and exclusions of income for citizens living abroad.[13]

After the Korean War, the Eisenhower administration's Treasury and the Joint Committee on Internal Revenue Taxation undertook the most elaborate analysis of the income tax since World War II. In 1954 the two entities proposed 25 major revisions, some of which would have broadened the base. At the end of the day, the Revenue Act of 1954 closed a few loopholes but expanded many others. The reform intent of the Treasury had served mainly to provide political cover for continued tax cutting on behalf of special pleading. The 1954 measure expanded employer contributions to employee health plans as income (which became one of the most expensive tax expenditures), the deductibility of interest on installment purchases, the deductibility of charitable donations, the exclusion of dividend income, the option of certain partnerships to be taxed as corporations, and expanded depreciation allowances. Most of the tax expenditures were of greatest value to wealthy individuals, who continued to pay the high marginal rates established during World War II.

As a consequence of the various tax cuts during the 1940s and 1950s, the effective rate of income taxation of the rich (defined as the richest 1% of households) fell to roughly 25%. Such rates were high by pre–World War II standards, but less than half of the peak rates of effective income taxation on the top 1% during the war.[14]

Interest in aggressive tax cutting intensified in the Democratic administrations of John F. Kennedy and Lyndon B. Johnson and the Republican administration of Richard M. Nixon. The two Democratic Presidents advocated a variety of selective tax cuts favoring the wealthy by both hawking long-term "supply-side" benefits, much as Andrew Mellon had done during the 1920s, and short-term Keynesian stimulation. In 1962 Congress enacted a corporate deduction that provided a credit of 7% of new investment against tax obligations and increased depreciation allowances, thus favoring capital income that was already treated well under the corporate income tax. At the same time, the Kennedy administration began considering an even larger set of tax cuts. The project came to fruition in 1964 when Congress responded to Johnson's call for a tax cut "to increase our national income and Federal revenues." The Revenue Act of 1964, enacting what became known as the Kennedy-Johnson tax cuts, slashed taxes in the face of large deficits. At the heart of the cuts were across-the-board cuts of 20–30% in income tax rates, reductions in capital gains taxes, and increases in depreciation allowances. The effect of the cuts in the rates of taxing personal incomes was somewhat progressive but the cuts in corporate taxes made the overall impact of the 1964 act regressive. The Council of Economic Advisers, led by economist Walter Heller, was committed to what was called "growthmanship" and actively supported the 1964 cuts. Most liberals in Congress regarded the 1964 tax cuts as a victory for Keynesian countercyclical stimulation of demand. But many also embraced a supply-side rationale for the cuts, particularly those that reduced the marginal rates on the rich. The trickle-down rhetoric echoed that of Andrew Mellon during the 1920s.[15]

The war in Vietnam delayed further tax cuts until August 1971, when the war was winding down and President Nixon launched a major program of economic stimulation. In doing so, he announced: "Now I am a Keynesian in economics." And, Nixon became the first President to express a belief in an extreme "supply-side" position, declaring that "as a result" of the cuts, "federal tax collections in the long run will increase."[16]

Nixon hoped the tax-cutting approach would set the table for his re-election campaign in 1972. He had blamed his defeat in the 1960 Presidential elections partly on fiscal decisions of the Eisenhower administration that had contributed to a recession and rising unemployment in 1960–1961. Nixon was determined to avoid those conditions in 1972. The resulting Revenue Act of 1971 allocated most of the cuts to the business sector, mainly through the codification of provisions that accelerated depreciation allowances; the authorization for the creation of "Domestic International Sales Corporations" (known as DISCs); and the re-enactment of the investment tax credit, which was set at an annual rate of 7% of investment expenses. (The credit had been enacted in 1962 but suspended in the Revenue Act of 1969.) The remainder of the cuts included increases in the minimum standard deduction and personal exemptions.[17]

The relentless tax cutting that began after World War II and continued into the 1960s undoubtedly contributed to the political success of the tax regime created during the war. The cutting won support from groups across American society that benefitted from the rate reductions and increases in tax expenditures. While all income groups received some of the largesse, the nation's poorest citizens received the smallest and the wealthiest the largest shares, partly because of the progressive structure of income taxation.[18] The overall effect was to reduce the progressivity that had been established during World War II. The erosion of the progressivity embedded in the tax system inherited from the New Deal and World War II began well before the 1970s.

The Crisis of the 1970s and Its Impact on Tax Policy

In the 1970s, during a crisis-ridden decade, two significant economic problems deepened the political base of support for tax cutting. One problem, a slowing of productivity growth, had actually begun during the late 1960s. The other was accelerating inflation, which resulted partly because of slower productivity but mainly because of oil crises in 1973 and 1979 (producing surges in oil prices) and the demise of the Bretton Woods international monetary system. In what became known as the "Great Inflation" the increase in the consumer price index peaked in 1980 at 13%.[19] An increasing rate of inflation had always added new energy to the continual search for new tax preferences and the exploiting of old ones as ways to offset bracket creep. For example, the huge inflation following World War I, between 1918 and 1920, led to irresistible pressure for new tax preferences, and much the same kind of thing had occurred, to a lesser extent, after World War II. The inflationary pressures of the 1970s were not as intense as those immediately after World War I, but they were more severe than those following World War II and they held sway for a longer period of time than either of the two postwar episodes of inflation.

The price increases meant large, unlegislated, and prolonged tax increases for most individual taxpayers. The effective rates of taxation paid by the rich edged up during the 1970s. The rates reached nearly 30%, or roughly those that had prevailed immediately before and after World War II.[20] But it was not just the rich and middle class who were affected. Many lower-income people, especially those with dependents, had to pay income tax for the first time as the value of their personal and dependent exemptions and the effective tax-exempt level of income eroded. By the early 1980s, the portion of the labor force paying taxes had increased to more than 75% from the 60% reached at the end of World War II.[21]

The "bracket creep" (actually often bracket leap) drove even greater efforts on the part of pressure groups to find loopholes, and the level of tax exclusions, exemptions, deductions, and credits soared. In 1974 Congress recognized the magnitude of the problem by including in the Congressional Budget Act of that year the annual publication of a "tax-expenditure budget," which Stanley Surrey, the Assistant Secretary of the Treasury from 1961 to 1969, had recommended in order to highlight the degradation of the income tax base. Later the bipartisan Congressional Budget Office estimated that in 1967 tax expenditures had cost the federal government nearly $37 billion, which was equal to 21% of federal expenditures. By 1984 the total cost had soared to $327 billion by 1984, equal to 35% of federal expenditures.[22]

During the 1970s, for the first time in the history of the American income tax, calls for rolling back the surging wave of tax preferences seemed to gain significant momentum.[23] In the 1976 Presidential campaign, Democratic candidate Jimmy Carter called the US tax system "a disgrace to the human race" and promised to eliminate tax expenditures and thereby broaden the base of taxation as part of a larger progressive economic agenda.[24] As such, he focused on those that favored the rich, hoping to make the tax system more progressive, more horizontally equitable, and more economically efficient. Whatever the details of his program might turn out to be when in office, he promised to avoid "a piecemeal approach to change."[25] During his first two years in office, he continued to advocate systematic reduction of tax expenditures and in January 1978 he proposed a program of sweeping tax reform which more or less followed the Treasury's proposals in a document, *Blueprints for Basic Tax Reform*, which the department had published in 1977, at the very end of the administration of President Gerald Ford. Nonetheless, Carter found himself entangled and paralyzed in working with Congress on piecemeal change. Carter never offered rate reduction at the top to sweeten base broadening for powerful economic interests, and his reform efforts stalled.[26]

The political problem that Carter could not solve was that the Democratic Party was badly divided over tax reform. Many Democrats as well as most Republicans in Congress favored a very different approach to the fiscal implications of stagflation—an approach that was philosophically at odds with Carter's. Their approach was to expand, rather than reduce, tax preferences in order to stimulate economic growth and provide tax relief in the face of inflation. And, in contrast to Carter, they sought to favor the rich.

The advocates of this approach, following in the tradition of Andrew Mellon, relied on "trickle-down" arguments for tax subsidies that would favor business investment. They argued that previously enacted tax preferences designed to reduce the cost of capital had stimulated productivity and growth, and called out, in particular, the putative results of the Kennedy-Johnson tax cuts of 1964. They also stressed that the combination of personal income and corporate taxation meant taxing some capital income twice—taxing the income after corporations earned it and then taxing it again after it was passed on to individuals as dividends. They went further, arguing the income tax penalizes savers by taxing twice income that is earned and saved while taxing only once income that is earned and spent. They called for tax breaks for capital income as compensation.[27]

For the most part, these were old rationalizations and familiar to many both inside and outside the economics profession. But they received new, energetic, vocal, and well-financed advocacy during the 1970s from the "retro-liberal" movement, whose origins I discussed at the beginning of this chapter. The leadership of this movement consisted of a diverse collection of people and organizations. They included economists who held extreme free-market views, entrepreneurs of think tanks like the Heritage Foundation and the Cato Institute, op-ed contributors and to the pages of the *Wall Street Journal*, and their supporters within the business community, including lobbying groups which proliferated and grew in strength during the 1970s. Among the economists in this informal group, the most prominent and influential was no doubt Milton Friedman, the leader of the "second Chicago school" of economics. Many economists promoted "supply-side" tax cuts to reduce the cost of capital and promote growth, but retro-liberal economists like Friedman proposed cuts within the context of a broad-gauged attack on government. They received support framing a broad retro-liberal attack on government from economists like James Buchanan of the University of Virginia (1956–1968), Virginia Tech (1969–1983), and George Mason University (1983–2013), who developed a libertarian critique of modern government within what he described as the theory of "public choice."[28]

At the same time, both Democrats in Congress and President Carter had difficulty countering the retro-liberal campaign with progressive programs and messages. No one found an effective way to dramatize the call for horizontal equity, and many Democratic leaders were no more interested in closing loopholes in the income tax than were the Republicans. Some, led by Senator Russell Long (D-Louisiana), chair of the Finance Committee, and Representative Al Ullman (D-Oregon), chair of the Ways and Means Committee, weakened Carter's position by proposing, in 1978, the adoption of a value-added tax (VAT), rather than reforming the income tax, as a means of both broadening the federal tax base and shoring up tax revenues. Adopting a VAT might have been an effective means of accomplishing these goals, but most liberal Democrats, along with Carter, disliked adding regressive sales taxes to the federal tax system, and business leaders, whose support Long and Ullman hoped to attract, opposed the VAT because they feared, probably correctly, that it would encourage the growth of government. The proposal for a VAT never came to a vote in Congress, and in 1980 Oregon voters, perhaps precisely because of their dislike of a VAT, failed to return Ullman to the Congress.

The most effective member of Congress in mobilizing a broad base of support for a combination of capital-favoring cuts and across-the-board cuts was Representative Jack Kemp (R-New York). In 1975, with the support of retro-liberal economists on his staff, Kemp invoked conventional Mellon-style supply-side arguments, enhanced by the claim that it was necessary to reduce the penalty that income taxation placed on earnings saved rather than consumed.[29] Over the next two years, Kemp and his staff refined the program in order to package wealth-favoring tax cutting in ways that he hoped would have broad popular appeal to voters, including Democrats. To that end, in 1977 Kemp expanded his proposed tax reform by including deep, across-the-board cuts in income taxes. He first proposed a 30% reduction across the board in one year. Then, in July, he joined with Senator William Roth (Republican-Delaware) to spread the cuts over three years—to cut across the board by 10% every year, for three years (these became known as the 10-10-10 tax cuts). They emphasized the benefits that would accrue to all voters but conveniently ignored the fact that a large portion of the tax cuts would benefit many wealthy families even though they had no "bracket creep" problem because they were firmly ensconced in the top income bracket.

In promoting the cuts Kemp and his colleagues added an argument that Mellon had used in only a limited way. The cuts, Kemp and his colleagues claimed, would actually reduce budget deficits and thus relieve the upward pressure on prices, including interest rates. This deficit reduction would occur, they argued, because big cuts in tax rates would invigorate American investors and workers to expand the tax base. Thus, Kemp et al. embraced what would become the most controversial proposition of the supply-side argument for tax cuts: The cuts would not just stimulate productivity; they would also reduce deficits.

The Kemp-Roth plan gained support even from some Democrats in Congress, including Senator Sam Nunn (D-Georgia). In 1978, Senator Nunn nearly succeeded in including a version (a 5% per year cut linked to spending restraints) in the Revenue Act then under consideration. Both houses endorsed the Nunn Amendment, but Carter used the threat of a veto to force Congress to drop the supply-side initiative. Ultimately, Carter signed the Revenue Act of 1978, stripped of the across-the-board cut. The final measure provided only minimal tax relief and simplification for individuals but offered significant cuts in capital gains and business taxes, including a reduction in the maximum capital gains rate from 39% to 28%.[30]

Thus, this measure stood firmly in the tradition of the tax cuts that had begun in 1945. In the future, with a less progressive President in the White House, little would stand in the way of expanding these cuts and enacting the kind of broad cuts that the federal government had made in the 1920s, in 1945, and again in 1964.

Ronald Reagan and the Economic Recovery Tax Act (ERTA) of 1981

While Jack Kemp had crafted his tax policy within Congress, Ronald Reagan engaged in a parallel effort in what became his campaign for the Presidency. Both Kemp and Reagan shared the goal of exploiting the inflationary situation to develop a tax program as the core of a populist economic message and a promise to expand tax benefits for the wealthy members of the traditional Republican base.

When Reagan had been Governor of California (1967–1975), he had been frustrated in his attacks on the size of government that had been staples of his political rise. He had been particularly disappointed by the 1973 failure of Proposition 1, a measure that would have amended the state constitution to limit state spending. He had campaigned extensively, with economist Milton Friedman in tow, for the measure. After his two terms as Governor, Reagan began campaigning for President, and used a weekly radio address to develop new approaches to limiting government and cutting taxes. In 1977, he endorsed first the indexing of income rates for inflation and then the 10-10-10 proposal of Jack Kemp's, including its supply-side rationale. Martin Anderson, a Hoover Institution Fellow and a central economic adviser during Reagan's Presidential campaign and first term as President, later claimed that Reagan and the supply-siders were actually moderate in their views, arguing only that tax cutting "would *not lose as much revenue as one might expect*" (emphasis in original). Anderson was correct for most supply-siders—especially among professional economists who leaned toward that view—but not all. On occasion, Reagan himself suggested that he held the most extreme view, which implied almost no loss in revenues, even in the initial years.[31]

For both Kemp and Reagan, the political wisdom of their anti-tax strategies was born out in 1978 by the smashing victory of Proposition 13 revolt by California taxpayers.[32] Reagan observed that victory and became certain that dismal economic conditions had created an opportunity to use tax issues in a popular revolt against the size of government. This approach was likely to be far more successful than California's Proposition 1 five years earlier. Reagan made tax reform the core of his economic program in his bid for the presidency in 1980, and he settled on Kemp's proposals as the core of his tax program. Under the leadership of Martin Anderson, Reagan's campaign organization began drafting a fully detailed piece of tax legislation.

The proposed legislation did not push beyond rate cutting to reform the federal tax system in a fundamental way. Most important, broadening the base of income taxation was a nonstarter for Reagan and his campaign. In July 1979, he declared that the term "tax expenditures" was "the new name government has for the share of our earnings it allows us to keep. You and I," he said, "call them deductions." "All told," Reagan concluded, "our rich ... Uncle Sam has an eye on about $170 billion that we think is ours."[33] Reagan's sympathy for tax expenditures meant that he lacked a principled position from which to oppose the efforts of corporate lobbyists to influence his tax program. However, some of Reagan's economic advisers resisted the lobbyists, fearing that corporate favoritism might diminish the popular appeal of across-the-board cuts. But in the summer of 1980, the lobbyists succeeded in inserting huge tax expenditure into the Reagan proposals. Their leader was Charls Walker. He represented industrial clients with enormous investments in plant and equipment. Reagan was less concerned than his advisers with the optics of Walker's support and was more enthusiastic himself about the prospect of expanding business support for his campaign. Consequently, the Republican platform committee approved Walker's proposal of a dramatic increase in the allowances to corporations and individuals for the depreciation of tangible assets. The platform plank became known as "10-5-3," which was shorthand for the three new depreciation lifetimes for structures (ten years), equipment (five years), and light vehicles (three years). To pay for 10-5-3, the platform committee abandoned the proposal to index the personal income tax rate for individuals, even though that reform would have provided a major tax cut to middle-class families.[34]

Pragmatism reigned within the Reagan campaign. Reagan and his political operatives played down the fact that their tax program now included traditional pro-capital Republican legislation. At the same time, they focused the public campaign on the enactment of the deep, across-the-board tax cut that would be easily understood. After the Republican convention, Reagan and his economic advisers worked intently to refine their tax cut proposal. The programmatic marriage between 10-10-10 and 10-5-3, however, did not go entirely smoothly. Charls Walker and Reagan's economic advisers, including Alan Greenspan, began to worry that the entire package might be too large, increasing budgetary deficits. Larger deficits, through the upward pressure on interest rates, could impede capital formation and, perhaps even worse from their standpoint, might prompt Congress to pare back the 10-5-3 cuts in the face of the popularity of 10-10-10. About three weeks after Reagan's nomination, in what became a famous meeting, Reagan resisted the pressure from Walker and Greenspan to scale back 10-10-10, and successfully protected the 10-10-10 formula and never proposed reducing the benefits of 10-5-3.[35] He wanted to cut everyone's taxes, regardless of whether or not they increased deficits, and he may actually have wanted higher initial deficits to restrain spending. He said as much in February 1981, in a national address. "Well," he said, "we can lecture our children about extravagance until we run out of voice and breath. OR we can cure their extravagance simply by reducing their allowance."[36]

As a political proposition, Reagan's tax populism was decidedly successful. The tax platform helped Reagan sweep to victory in 1980, and the passage of the Economic Recovery Tax Act of 1981, expedited by an outpouring of popular support for the President after a serious assassination attempt, became the first major legislative victory for the Reagan administration. In the process of enacting the legislation, the Congress significantly expanded the capital-favoring aspects of the administration's proposal and, at the same time, reduced the across-the-board benefits to taxpayers. A bipartisan bidding war decorated what became a "Christmas tree" bill with a spectacular array of tax shelters. To help pay for the larger benefits in the form of tax expenditures, Congress reduced the across-the-board cuts. The final legislation turned the 10-10-10 cuts into 5-10-10 and delayed indexing until 1985, moving many people back into higher tax brackets. Thus, Congress turned Reagan's campaign proposal into a measure even more closely resembling the Mellon tax cuts of the 1920s.

Was Reagan's Tax Program Revolutionary?

There are various ways in which the Economic Recovery Act of 1981 may have constituted or initiated a revolution in tax policy. But, in terms of the possible ways, any revolution was short-lived, at best. First, the capital-favoring cuts were of a piece with the entire stream of tax cutting since World War II. Second, the across-the-board cuts, which were the central element in Reagan's tax populism, were not breaks in principle from the inflation-adjusting cutting in income taxes that the federal government undertook following the periods of inflation during and after both World Wars. Third, while all the 1981 cuts, taken together, reduced income taxes, relative to gross domestic product (GDP), more than had the earlier big tax cuts, the 1981 cuts were followed immediately by three significant tax increases, not by a wave of further neo-liberal "Starve-the-Beast," anti-government tax cutting. The three measures were the loophole closing Tax Equity and Fiscal Responsibility Act of 1982 (TEFRA), the 1983 acceleration of Social Security taxes, and the Deficit Reduction Act of 1984 (DEFRA), which closed more loopholes. Taken together, these three tax measures restored most of the revenue that ERTA cut from the federal budget in 1981, making the revenue reductions no more consequential than the earlier post-inflation cuts. Even by the end of the Reagan administration, ERTA, in terms of its net fiscal effect, had turned out to be essentially a routine contributor to a much longer history of significant tax cutting. ERTA represented a continuation of the long-term swing of tax policy that began immediately after World War II. Following Reagan, two other Presidents, George H.W. Bush and Bill Clinton, continued the tax increases. George H.W. Bush followed in the Omnibus Budget Reconciliation Act (OBRA) of 1990, which raised the top marginal personal income tax rate from 28% to 31%. Clinton drove the adoption of OBRA 1993, which raised the top marginal rate again, to 39.6%. The string of tax increases that began in 1982 and continued over more than a decade amounted to the most significant string of peacetime tax increases in American history outside of the New Deal era.

Why did Reagan's efforts to cut taxes collapse so quickly, and so hard, after 1981? This is a puzzle because, in fact, various members of the Reagan administration, including Reagan himself, had reservations about the tax increases following the passage ERTA. The short answer as to why they had so little effect on the course of tax policy: is "deficits," and how they were regarded by the nation's most powerful economic elites. As early as 1981, bipartisan worries about defeats and their upward pressure on interest rates led to serious questioning of the wisdom of the tax cutting of 1981. Pressure from the business community and, most importantly, the financial community was most influential. The nation's investment bankers worried about the possibility that large deficits would crowd out private capital, and that high interest rates would threaten recession. Also, American exporters wanted to reduce interest rates and thereby reduce the attractiveness of American federal debt to Japanese investors whose dollar holdings enabled Japanese exporters to maintain the advantage of a low-priced yen. At the same time, leaders in both political parties, including the President, wanted to avoid cuts in Social Security (the "third rail of American politics"), Medicare, and national defense. Moreover, many veteran lawmakers in Congress, like Russell Long, the chair of Senate Finance Committee, had never fully embraced ERTA. They voted for it knowing that in the future they could comfortably support tax increases.

ERTA proved not to be revolutionary but another element of the Reagan tax program had the potential to become revolutionary—the Tax Reform Act of 1986. If the measure had succeeded, its effects would have been very different from those of retro-liberal tax reforms. It would have produced a base broadening that powerfully strengthened the base of the income tax and the financing of the federal government. The movement toward the 1986 act began with a retro-liberal proposal for converting the income tax into a tax on consumption and replacing the progressive tax structure with a single, low rate of tax. But the more important source of support was the growing outrage within the Treasury, key congressional leaders, and the general public over the soaring expansion of tax shelters and tax expenditures during the Great Inflation of the late 1970s and early 1980s. Ever since the inflation that had followed World War II, economic experts within the Treasury had pressed for base-broadening reform, but their program never gained any traction beyond the tax policy community. Finally, the combination of public outrage and vigorous leadership on the part of President Reagan presented these experts an opportunity for a major legislative victory. At the end of the Reagan administration, many observers believed that it might be possible to expand even further the base broadening. However, the administrations of George H.W. Bush and Bill Clinton failed to search for such opportunities and, in the next century, the George Bush administration actively reversed the base broadening as it forged a retro-liberal tax regime.[37]

In sum, by 1993, the remnants of ERTA's across-the-board cutting and capital-favoring tax expenditures were moderate adjustments for inflation in income taxation, and some business-oriented tax expenditures. All were similar in scope and impact to those that had come earlier during the period since World War II. There had been no revolution in tax policy. How much of an impact did Reagan have on these relatively moderate measures? It is worth remembering that even before Reagan's election there was considerable support in Congress for the kind of cuts enacted in 1981. If Jimmy Carter had won re-election in 1980, his administration, in the face of additional inflation, might have agreed to across-the-board cuts and base-broadening reforms. By the end of Carter's second term, the policy outcome might have turned out to be roughly the same, except perhaps without the policy gyrations of the Reagan administration.

Effects of the Reagan Tax Cuts on Inequality

The across-the-board reduction of income tax rates and the investment-favoring tax expenditures in ERTA may not have marked a revolution in tax policy from the standpoint of revenue reduction or increases in tax expenditures, but the legislation's cuts in the highest marginal rate, combined with the additional cut in that rate by the Tax Reform Act of 1986, may have had a major impact on the distribution of income and wealth. The cut in 1981 was from 77% to 50%—a cut of 27 percentage points that reduced the top rate by 35%. The cut in 1986 was even larger—from 50% to 28%, a cut of 22 percentage points that reduced the top rate by 44%. Both of these were the largest of either of the two earlier post–World War II cuts in the top rate. The two other cuts came in 1964—a cut from 91% to 77%, a cut of 14 percentage points that reduced the top rate by 14%, and in 1946—a cut from 94% to 86.45%, a cut of 7.55 percentage points that reduced the top rate by 8%. The Reagan cuts were more on the scale of the large cuts engineered by Andrew Mellon during the early 1920s. These cuts, in 1922 and 1923, reduced the top rate from 74% to 43.5%. The reduction by 29.5 percentage points reduced the top rate by 40%. This reduction was huge—but not as large as the overall cut of about two-thirds in the top rate in 1981 and 1986. Certainly, if all else had been equal, the reductions in the top rate in 1981 and 1986 would have increased the overall level of inequality substantially, just as did the cuts of the early 1920s. But other things were not equal.

Other elements in the tax legislation during the Reagan administration actually had offsetting effects, in the direction of reduced inequality. The lower rates reduced the value for the wealthy of the tax preferences than remained in the tax code after 1986, and they may have increased voluntary compliance with the tax code. More important, the loophole closing in 1982 through 1986, along with the expansion of the Earned Income Tax Credit (part of the 1986 legislation that provided major tax benefits for the working poor) and a set of increases in personal exemptions and standard deductions in 1986 (taking 6 million taxpayers off the rolls), had distinctly progressive effects. These provisions represented the success of a kind of rearguard action by Congressional Democrats, joined by some members of the Reagan administration, against the declining progressivity of the income taxation. As a consequence, the net effect of the tax policies of the Reagan administration was to leave the overall progressivity of the income tax essentially unchanged between 1981 and 1989. During the next decade, the tax increases of the administrations of George H.W. Bush and Bill Clinton moved that rate in a progressive direction.[38]

While the overall rate of progressivity did not change across the 1980s, the rate of taxing the top 1% of taxpayers did decline significantly. For this elite group, the effective tax rate (including all federal taxes and taking into account tax preferences as well as statutory rates) declined from slightly more than 35% in 1979 to under 30% in 1989.[39] In other words, the Reagan revisions of the highest marginal rates tended to increase the concentration of income and wealth at the very top of the income scale. However, as a consequence of the increases in the taxation of the highest income earners during the Bush and Clinton administrations, the most affluent 1% of taxpayers experienced the largest increases of any income group in their effective rates. In the 1990s, the average effective rate on the top 1% increased to slightly less than 35%, representing a reversal of their gains during the Reagan administration.[40]

For an even more select group, the top 0.1% of taxpayers, the fluctuations in the effective rate across the 1980s and 1990s were even greater. Thomas Piketty and Emanuel Saez found that their rate fell from about 50% in 1980 to about 30% in 1990 and then increased to about 40% by the end of the century. The increase would have been even greater but, as Leonard Burman has pointed out, a 1997 cut in the capital gains tax eased the increase for the highest income families.[41]

The combination of the cutting of the highest income tax rates during the 1980s and the late 1990s, coupled with the fluctuations in those rates, may have significant effects on the political and institutional behavior of the wealthiest Americans. Thomas Piketty has recently suggested an example of an important institutional response. He writes that the "very large decrease in the top marginal income tax rate in the English-speaking countries after 1980 ... seems to have totally transformed the way top executive pay is set, since top executives had much stronger incentives than in the past to seek large raises."[42] Changes in the tax code—especially the 1997 cut in capital gains taxation—may also have been important to the trends he identifies.

The most important effect of the political successes of both the wealthiest Americans, and the reversals they experienced, during the years of the Reagan, Bush, and Clinton administrations may well have intensified their efforts to shape the future course of tax legislation during late 1990s and the administrations of George W. Bush and Barack Obama. Large tax cuts in 2001 and 2003 decisively undid the effort of the framers of the Tax Reform Act of 1986 to equalize the rates of taxation on labor and capital income and roll back tax expenditures. The combination of these cuts, coupled with the large cuts of the top rates in 1986 rate cuts, most of which survived the Clinton administration, initiated a new tax and fiscal regime, which I have referred to as "retro-liberal."[43]

Effects of the Reagan Expenditure Policies on Inequality

Focusing on ERTA in particular, or tax policy in general, as the expression of Reagan's retro-liberalism, or neo-liberalism, risks neglecting a major fiscal thrust of the President's program. He wanted not only to cut taxes but also to contain or even roll back the scale of domestic government. Perhaps the dominant fiscal expression of a "Reagan Revolution" was on the expenditure side of the public ledger. This aspect of fiscal policy may have had a significant effect on the distribution of income and wealth, particularly through the weakening of the middle class.

Federal tax revenues were stable as a share of GDP during the 1980s, to some extent as a result of the strengthening of the income tax system by the Tax Reform Act of 1986. However, entitlement spending through the Social Security and Medicare systems was increasing. This meant that spending on the remainder of federal programs—the spending on discretionary programs in education, infrastructure development, job training, and welfare—was declining as a share of GDP. The Reagan administration encouraged this trend as a useful point of departure in rolling back the domestic programs that had been established during the New Deal and expanded through the 1970s. In 1981, especially with the 1981 OBRA, the administration was able to make real cuts in discretionary domestic spending and then slowed the growth of this spending, reducing its size as a percentage of GDP.[44]

Reagan's rhetorical attacks on the tax system contributed to this slowing of discretionary domestic spending. The attacks undermined tax consciousness and public confidence in the tax system. Throughout his post-1981 period of tax raising Reagan railed against big government in general and welfare spending in particular, reinforcing the public perception that their income taxes went primarily to fund wasteful social spending. As late as 1982 he repeated the racist "welfare queen" story he had told for the first time in 1976, exacerbating the racial divides that had long weakened many of the major initiatives in social policy undertaken by the federal government from the New Deal through Lyndon Johnson's Great Society.[45]

In yet another way, Reagan's rhetoric confused the public and interfered with the development of a healthy tax consciousness. In discussing its tax increases, Reagan never admitted he was, in fact, raising taxes. For example, he described the Social Security tax increases as simply acceleration of increases that had been previously scheduled while he largely ignored the benefit cuts. And, he described TEFRA and DEFRA as tax reforms rather than tax increases. By stressing the goal of deficit reduction rather than support of government programs, Reagan further contributed to undermining public support for taxing on behalf of social spending.

Arguably, the campaign of Reagan and his administration against discretionary social spending had greater long-term social effects than did the Reagan tax cuts. While the changes in the tax system during the 1980s were neutral overall in their effects on the overall distribution of income and wealth, the Reagan administration's anti-government campaign contributed significantly to the stagnation of social spending during the decade.

Reagan's immediate successors in the Presidency, George H.W. Bush and Bill Clinton, helped make the tax system more progressive but they did not ease the restraint on discretionary social spending that Reagan had initiated. In fact, they reinforced it. Neither Bush nor Clinton ever justified their tax increases in terms of increasing funding for domestic programs. George H.W. Bush was as fervent as Reagan in feeding negative images of welfare recipients, and Clinton never challenged those images in his program of welfare reform. To his credit, Clinton may have held the belief that controlling deficits through a tax increase would pave the way for subsequent expansion of domestic programs and even the enactment of some form of national health insurance. But he did not make that part of his public case for the tax increases in OBRA 1993. The only significant program of cash redistribution that Bush and Clinton expanded was the Earned Income Tax Credit (EITC). Republican leaders in Congress generally accepted the EITC because it created incentives for the working poor to get off traditional welfare and because it was funded within the tax system, enabling it to fly under the public's anti-government radar. The EITC's survival did not reflect popular tax consent.

Collectively, Reagan, Bush, and Clinton stabilized domestic spending as a share of GDP at approximately the 15% level. Thus, Bush and Clinton as well as Reagan pursued fiscal consolidation not only by raising taxes but also by reversing what had been a trend of increasing spending on civilian programs as a share of GDP. Meanwhile, demographic trends and the increasing relative cost of health care caused spending on the entitlement programs Social Security and Medicare to grow more rapidly than GDP. In response, Bush and Clinton, as well as Reagan, accepted spending cuts, as a share of GDP, in education, infrastructure, job training, and other discretionary programs. With the reductions in discretionary domestic spending Bush and Clinton may have offset entirely the progressive effects of the tax increases during their administrations. In fact, these reductions probably contributed more than any changes in the tax code to the growing concentration of income and wealth during the last two decades of the twentieth century. At the very least, the regressive distributive effects of cuts in discretionary spending reinforced the regressive effects of tax expenditures that favored the wealthy, and these regressive effects may well have been growing in size during the 1990s.[46] The result was an increase in poverty and the weakening of the middle class that rose to the level of a national crisis in the early twenty-first century.

The success of the organized retro-liberal movement undoubtedly helped undermine popular confidence in government, beginning in the 1970s and 1980s. As a consequence, political leaders, including liberals, became increasingly hesitant to discuss tax increases as a means of funding new programs. But retro-liberals were able to succeed only because of a fundamental weakness of the American welfare state that had become apparent during the progressive and New Deal eras. This weakness was its setting within a broker state. The American welfare state had always been fragmented rather than comprehensive in the scope of its benefits, and included the nation's wealthiest among its clients. The fragmentation of traditional welfare functions became reflected in programs such as cash benefits for relief of old age, unemployment, disability, and poverty; provision of services such as education and medical care; and innumerable tax preferences extended to the entire spectrum of taxpayers. This fragmentation in turn created opportunities for retro-liberal forces to pit the beneficiaries of various welfare programs against one another and meanwhile conceal their own benefits.[47] In short, the relative decline of discretionary domestic spending that began during the last two decades of the twentieth century, and resulting growth in inequality, resulted from long-standing weaknesses in the American welfare state as well as from the growing force of the organized retro-liberal movement during the Reagan years.

American Exceptionalism Redux

The structural weaknesses in American welfare provision, in turn, had their basis in a web of social and institutional realities with profound historic roots in the United States. The realities included the sustained significant surge in economic productivity and rising expectations that began in the nineteenth century and continued into the late 1960s.[48] The same period, however, was also marked by episodes of significant unemployment and increasing concentration of incomes. The most notable such episode was the Great Depression of the 1930s. The combination of productivity increases, rising expectations, and economic reversals for many Americans fueled political confrontations over distributional tax policy. These were sharpest during the 1930s and major mobilizations for war but reoccurred even after World War II. But productivity gains gradually strengthened popular support for tax policies that favored capital investment and tended to weaken the American labor movement, which failed to generate sustained support for building a comprehensive welfare state. The flagging of productivity in the 1970s and 1980s further increased the appeal of tax cuts that favored capital as a means of restoring economic health. Persistent nativism and racism reinforced such policies by creating opportunities for the largest and most powerful beneficiaries to undermine popular support for addressing the problems of structural poverty. It has become fashionable in recent decades to describe and dismiss such explanations of policy shifts as building on an "'American exceptionalism' thesis."[49] But such dismissal may neglect explanatory factors, embedded in institutional development, that are more fundamental to explaining policy and distributional trends than the circumstances immediately surrounding crisis-driven public policy choices. And, paying attention to factors often associated with American "exceptionalism" may, in fact, help create a framework that is more robust in explaining comparative international trends in fiscal policy and distribution.[50] For the American case, the long retro-liberal swing in American fiscal institutions that began after World War II was driven primarily by profound political and economic contradictions. Resolution of those tensions may well be required before the American polity is able to reverse the long swing toward retro-liberalism.

Notes

1. I have benefitted from many careful readings of this chapter, which began in draft for the workshop, "Taxation for and Against Redistribution since 1945: Trajectories and Comparative Outcomes," sponsored by the German Historical Institute in December 2014. I am especially grateful to the other contributors to this volume, and to the following: Nicholas Barreyre, Carl-Henry Geschwind, Roman Huret, Ajay Mehrotra, and Joseph Thorndike.

2. See, for example, Angus Burgin, *The Great Persuasion*; David Harvey, *A Brief History of Neoliberalism*; Roman Huret, *American Tax Resisters*, Daniel Stedman Jones, *Masters of the Universe*; Philip Mirowski and Dieter Plehwe, *The Road From Mont Pèlerin*; Kim Phillips-Fein, *Invisible Hands*; Raymond Plant, *The New-liberal State*; and Monica Prasad, *The Politics of Free Markets*.
3. David Harvey, *A Brief History of Neoliberalism*, 164–165.
4. Walter Lippmann, *The Good Society*, 225–226 and 230, and *Drift and Mastery*. On Lippmann's larger economic agenda in *The Good Society*, see Crauford D. Goodwin, *Walter Lippmann*, 233–245. For Arthur Schlesinger's assessment see his *The Politics of Upheaval*, 393.
5. W. Elliot Brownlee, "Wilson's Reform of Economic Structure."
6. See, most importantly, Henry C. Simons, *Personal Income Taxation*. For a superb analysis of the complexities of Simons' thought, see Daniel Shaviro, "The Forgotten Henry Simons."
7. W. Elliot Brownlee, *Federal Taxation in America: A History*, 176–177. The last time Friedman referred to "neo-liberalism" in print seems to have been in 1951, when he published "Neo-liberalism and its Prospects." On "the two Chicago schools," see Jones, *Masters of the Universe*, 89–100.
8. Decades ago I began my study of the political economy of American taxation by analyzing the hotly contested issues surrounding the adoption of the Wisconsin income tax, the first modern such tax in the United States, during the progressive era. See, for example, Brownlee, "Income Taxation and the Political Economy of Wisconsin," 299–324. About ten years later I suggested a more general framework to analyze that class-based volatility, emphasizing the "path-dependent" nature of the development of American tax institutions, particularly for the period between the 1890s and the end of World War II. See W. Elliot Brownlee, "Taxation for a Strong and Virtuous Republic," *Tax Notes*. In 1996 I argued that beginning in the late nineteenth century, the polarized construction of "tax issues would exacerbate class conflict for nearly a century." Brownlee, *Federal Taxation in America: A Short History*, 35. In her 2006 book, Monica Prasad took a somewhat similar approach in understanding the enactment of ERTA, suggesting the importance of progressive income taxation and adversarial politics in explaining its timing. See Prasad, *The Politics of Free Markets*, 3–4, 43–61, and 280–283. In contrast with my analysis, hers discounted the influence of class in shaping tax policy.
9. An OECD analysis of inequality suggests that over the two decades beginning in the mid-1980s the United States ranked nearly at the top of the 22 nations in progressive tax redistribution. See OECD, *Growing Unequal*, especially 111–115.

10. For my definition and survey of US tax regimes, see Brownlee, *Federal Taxation in America: A History*, and the previous two editions. In the 2016 edition I engaged in an effort to integrate my concepts of tax regime shifts and "long-swings."
11. "Supply-side" has taken on various meanings in the context of tax cuts or tax reform. In the broadest sense, which is its meaning here, it refers to changes in tax policy that seeks to make the production of goods and services more efficient rather than to stimulate demand for goods and serves by leaving more money in the hands of consumers. In the 1970s, the term "supply-side" took on a narrower and sometimes pejorative meaning, referring to tax cuts that proponents claimed would pay for themselves by stimulating demand, incomes, and finally tax revenues.
12. The economic benefits of the latter change were enjoyed mainly by relatively wealthy families. See Carolyn C. Jones, "Mass-Based Income Taxation: Creating a Taxpaying Culture, 1940–1952," 132–138; Edward J. McCaffery, *Taxing Women* 29–62; and Dennis J. Ventry, "The Treatment of Marriage under the U.S. Federal Income Tax."
13. On the early postwar tax cuts in the United States, see John F. Witte, *The Politics and Development of the Federal Income Tax*, 131–134; Steven A. Bank, Kirk J. Stark, and Joseph J. Thorndike, 12–125; and Joseph J. Thorndike, *Their Fair Share*, 265–272.
14. Brownlee, "Historical Perspective on U.S. Tax Policy Toward the Rich," 60–61.
15. On the Revenue Acts of 1962 and 1964, see Brownlee, *Federal Taxation in America: A History*, 166–167; Herbert Stein, *The Fiscal Revolution in America*, 385–453; and "The Fiscal Revolution in America, Part II," 194–201; John F. Witte, *The Politics and Development of the Federal Income Tax*, 155–165; Seiichiro Mozumi, "A Prelude to Fiscal Gridlock of the United States: Social Policy, Taxation and Policymaking of the Administration of John F. Kennedy." On the favorable taxation of capital income under the corporate income tax, see Steven A. Bank, *From Sword to Shield*, xxv. For the Lyndon Johnson quotation, see Public Papers of the Presidents of the United States, 9–10.
16. Nixon quoted by Stein, "The Fiscal Revolution: Part II," 228.
17. On the Revenue Act of 1971 see Witte, *The Politics and Development of the Federal Income Tax*, 176–179; Stein, "The Fiscal Revolution: Part II," 234–241; Steven A. Bank et al., *War and Taxes*, 139–141.
18. There is much important scholarship on the income tax preferences that have classic welfare, rather than a corporate welfare function. See, for example, Christopher Howard, *The Welfare State Nobody Knows* and Molly C. Michelmore, *Tax and Spend: The Welfare State, Tax Politics, and the Limits of American Liberalism*.

19. Consumer price index for urban wage earners, U.S. Bureau of Labor Statistics data in *Economic Report of the President*, 351.
20. Brownlee, "Historical Perspective on U.S. Tax Policy Toward the Rich," 61.
21. Brownlee, *Federal Taxation in America: A History*, 173. For a summary of the operation of postwar individual income tax, including the trends in progressiveness, see Jon Bakija and Eugene Steuerle, "Individual Income Tax since 1948," 451–475.
22. Leonard Burman and his colleagues have noted that non-business tax expenditures increased swiftly between 1976 and 1985, growing from 4.2% to 6.4% of GDP. Leonard E. Burman, Christopher Geissler, and Eric J. Toder, "How Big are Total Individual Income Tax Expenditures?," 79.
23. On the history of the base-broadening movement and the role of the Treasury, see Brownlee, *Federal Taxation in America: A History*, 168–172.
24. Jimmy Carter: "Our Nation's Past and Future."
25. Jimmy Carter, "A New Beginning."
26. On Carter's program for tax reform, see Brownlee, *Federal Taxation in America: A History*, 173–174; Mozumi, "Tax Reformers' Ideas, the Expenditure-Taxation Nexus, and Comprehensive Tax Reform in the United States, 1961–1986," Chap. 8, this volume, 196–200; W. Carl Biven, *Jimmy Carter's Economy*, 198–200; and Witte, *The Politics and Development of the Federal Income Tax*, 199–219. See, also, Department of the Treasury, *Blueprints for Basic Tax Reform*.
27. Brownlee, *Federal Taxation in America: A History*, 174–175.
28. Ibid., 175. Recently, the historian Nancy MacLean has written a powerful analysis of the career of James Buchanan, effectively highlighting the importance of that career, which histories of retro-liberalism have often neglected. See MacLean, *Democracy in Chains*. On the "second Chicago school" of economics, see p. 158, above.
29. On the development of the Kemp proposals, see Paul Craig Roberts, *The Supply-Side Revolution*, 1–33 and 69–88.
30. Brownlee, *Federal Taxation in America: A History*, 180; Michael B. Berkman, *The State Roots of National Politics*, 48–49 and 53–56; and Witte, *The Politics and Development of the Federal Income Tax*, 204–217.
31. Brownlee, *Federal Taxation in America: A History*, 177–178. On Reagan and Friedman's friendship and cooperation during the Prop 1 campaign, see Milton Friedman and Rose Friedman, *Two Lucky People*, 172–173. On Reagan's endorsement of Kemp's supply-side argument, see Ronald Reagan, "Taxes, October 18, 1977." For Martin Anderson's explanation of supply-side theory, see his Anderson, *Revolution*, 152.
32. There is now a fine collection of studies of the movement for Proposition 13. See, for example, Isaac Martin, *The Permanent Tax Revolt* and Huret, *American Tax Resisters*, 229–232.

33. Ronald Reagan, "Tax Loopholes, May 1975" and "Tax Expenditures, July 27, 1979."
34. On the development of the "10-5-3" proposal; the mobilization of the business community behind it; the negotiations over the formation of a coalition between the Reagan transition team and organized business; and the crucial role of Charls Walker, who became the chair of President Reagan's tax transition team, see Brownlee, *Federal Taxation in America: A History*, 183–184; Cathie J. Martin, *Shifting the Burden*, 47 and 116–123; Cathie J. Martin, "American Business and the Taxing State: Alliances for Growth in the Postwar Period," 383–386; and Jeffrey H. Birnbaum and Alan S. Murray, *Showdown at Gucci Gulch*,16–18. Monica Prasad places greater emphasis on the tensions between advocates of "10-10-10" and the architects of "10-5-3." See Prasad, "The Popular Origins of Neoliberalism in the Reagan Tax Cut of 1981," 351–383.
35. Charls Walker quoted by Martin Feldstein, ed., *American Economic Policy of the 1980s*, 224–225.
36. Ronald Reagan, "Economic Speech—Address to the Nation, February 5, 1981," 490. David Stockman, Reagan's director of the Office of Budget and Management, denied that Reagan and the administration had a "Starve the Beast" strategy, but he may not have fully understood Reagan's intentions or have known how much weight others gave to this approach at least as a secondary consideration. David Stockman, *Triumph of Politics*, 267–268. See also his comments quoted by Feldstein, ed., *American Economic Policy of the 1980s*, 287.
37. On the long-standing interest of the Treasury in broadening the base of income taxation, see Brownlee, *Federal Taxation in America: A History*, 168–172. For a summary and analysis of the enactment of the Tax Reform Act of 1986, see W. Elliot Brownlee and C. Eugene Steuerle, "Taxation," 168–173.
38. Brownlee and Steuerle, "Taxation," 173–174.
39. It should be emphasized that this measure includes social security taxes, incorporating the increase in the regressive payroll taxes during the 1980s.
40. See Brownlee and Steuerle, "Taxation," 181 n. 64; C. Eugene Steuerle, *Contemporary U.S. Tax Policy*, 50–51; and Burman, "Taxes and Inequality," 571–572.
41. Thomas Piketty and Emmanuel Saez, "How Progressive is the U.S. Federal Tax System?," 16; Burman, "Taxes and Inequality," 572.
42. Thomas Piketty, *Capital in the Twenty-First Century*, 335.
43. Brownlee, *Federal Taxation in America: A History*, 264–266.
44. For a useful analysis of Reagan's budgeting for discretionary domestic programs, see Dennis S. Ippolito, *Deficits, Debts, and the New Politics of Tax Policy*, 143–146.

45. For the Reagan story, see Lou Cannon, *President Reagan*, 518. On Reagan's racial attitudes, rhetoric, and policies, see Cannon, *President Reagan*, 516–525 and Jeremy D. Mayer, "Reagan and Race: Prophet of Color Blindness, Baiter of the Backlash," 70–89.
46. In 2008 Leonard Burman and his colleagues found that "overall, tax expenditures for individual taxpayers ... disproportionately benefit those with higher incomes." And, they found that while non-business tax expenditures had declined during the late 1980s as a consequence of the Tax Reform Act of 1986, by 2001 they had increased as a share of GDP to about the same level as in 1985. Burman et al., "How Big Are Total Individual Income Tax Expenditures?," 79–80.
47. For analytical surveys of the fragmentation of traditional welfare services, including the contribution of liberals to the process, see Michelmore, *Tax and Spend* and Howard, *The Welfare State Nobody Knows*. For the related suggestion that high progressive taxation contributed to this fragmentation, in part by privileging "the development of a private system of welfare," see Monica Prasad, *The Land of Too Much*, 153–171.
48. For the best survey of the long-term patterns of productivity change see Robert J. Gordon, *The Rise and Fall of American Growth*.
49. See, for example, Prasad, *The Politics of Free Markets*, 3.
50. For suggestions along these lines, see W. Elliot Brownlee and Eisaku Ide, "Fiscal Policy in Japan and the United States since 1973: Economic Crises, Taxation, and Weak Tax Consent."

References

Anderson, Martin. 1988. *Revolution*. San Diego: Harcourt Brace Jovanovich.

Bank, Steven A. 2010. *From Sword to Shield: The Transformation of the Corporate Income Tax, 1861–Present*. Oxford: Oxford University Press.

Bank, Steven A., Kirk J. Stark, and Joseph J. Thorndike. 2008. *War and Taxes*. Washington, DC: The Urban Institute Press.

Berkman, Michael B. 1993. *The State Roots of National Politics: Congress and the Tax Agenda, 1978–1986*. Pittsburgh: University of Pittsburgh Press.

Birnbaum, Jeffrey H., and Alan S. Murray. 1987. *Showdown at Gucci Gulch: Lawmakers, Lobbyists, and the Unlikely Triumph of Tax Reform*. New York: Random House.

Biven, W. Carl. 2002. *Jimmy Carter's Economy: Policy in an Age of Limits*. Chapel Hill: University of North Carolina Press.

Brownlee, W. Elliot. 1976. Income Taxation and the Political Economy of Wisconsin, 1890–1930. *Wisconsin Magazine of History* 59: 299–324.

———. 1989. Taxation for a Strong and Virtuous Republic. *Tax Notes* 45 (15): 1613–1621.

———. 1996. *Federal Taxation in America: A Short History*. 1st ed. Cambridge and Washington, DC: Cambridge University Press and Woodrow Wilson Press.
———. 2000. Historical Perspective on U.S. Tax Policy Toward the Rich. In *Does Atlas Shrug? The Economic Consequences of Taxing the Rich*, ed. Joel B. Slemrod, 29–73. New York and Cambridge: Russell Sage Foundation and Harvard University Press.
———. 2008. Wilson's Reform of Economic Structure: Progressive Liberalism and the Corporation. In *Reconsidering Woodrow Wilson: Progressivism, Internationalism, War, and Peace*, ed. John Milton Cooper Jr., 57–89. Washington, DC and Baltimore, MD: Woodrow Wilson Center Press and The Johns Hopkins University Press.
———. 2016. *Federal Taxation in America: A History*. Cambridge: Cambridge University Press.
Brownlee, W. Elliot, and C. Eugene Steuerle. 2003. Taxation. In *The Reagan Presidency: Pragmatic Conservatism and Its Legacies*, ed. W. Elliot Brownlee and Hugh Davis Graham, 155–181. Lawrence, KS: University Press of Kansas.
Brownlee, W. Elliot, and Eisaku Ide. 2017. Fiscal Policy in Japan and the United States Since 1973: Economic Crises, Taxation, and Weak Tax Consent. In *Leviathan After the Boom: Public Finance in Western Capitalist Countries Since the 1970s*, ed. Marc Buggeln, Martin Daunton, and Alexander Nützenadel, 57–82. Cambridge: Cambridge University Press.
Burgin, Angus. 2012. *The Great Persuasion: Reinventing Free Markets Since the Depression*. Cambridge: Harvard University Press.
Burman, Leonard E. 2013. Taxes and Inequality. *Tax Law Review* 66: 571–572.
Burman, Leonard, Christopher Geissler, and Eric J. Toder. 2008. How Big Are Total Individual Income Tax Expenditures, and Who Benefits from Them? *American Economic Review: Papers and Proceedings* 98 (2): 79–83.
Cannon, Lou. 1991. *President Reagan: The Role of a Lifetime*. New York: Simon & Schuster.
Carter, Jimmy. 1976a. A New Beginning: Presentation by Jimmy Carter to the Platform Committee of the Democratic Party. Copy in Walter F. Mondale Papers, Minnesota Historical Society. http://www2.mnhs.org/library/findaids/00697/pdfa/00697-00150-5.pdf
———. 1976b. 'Our Nation's Past and Future': Address Accepting the Presidential Nomination at the Democratic National Convention in New York City. Online by Gerhard Peters and John T. Woolley, *The American Presidency Project*. http://www.presidency.ucsb.edu/ws/?pid=25953
Economic Report of the President: 1991. 1991. Washington, DC: U.S. Government Printing Office.
Feldstein, Martin, ed. 1994. *American Economic Policy of the 1980s*. Chicago: University of Chicago Press.
Friedman, Milton. 1951. Neo-Liberalism and Its Prospects. *Farmand* 17: 89–93.

Friedman, Milton, and Rose Friedman. 1998. *Two Lucky People: Memoirs*. Chicago: University of Chicago Press.
Goodwin, Crauford D. 2014. *Walter Lippmann: Public Economist*. Cambridge: Harvard University Press.
Gordon, Robert J. 2016. *The Rise and Fall of American Growth: The U.S. Standard of Living since the Civil War*. Princeton: Princeton University Press.
Harvey, David. 2005. *A Brief History of Neoliberalism*. Oxford: Oxford University Press.
Howard, Christopher. 2007. *The Welfare State Nobody Knows: Debunking Myths About U.S. Social Policy*. Princeton: Princeton University Press.
Huret, Roman. 2014. *American Tax Resisters*. Cambridge: Harvard University Press.
Ippolito, Dennis S. 2012. *Deficits, Debt, and the New Politics of Tax Policy*. Cambridge: Cambridge University Press.
Jon, Bakija, and Eugene Steuerle. 1991. Individual Income Tax Since 1948. *National Tax Journal* 44: 451–475.
Jones, Carolyn C. 1996. Mass-Based Income Taxation: Creating a Taxpaying Culture, 1940–1952. In *Funding the American State, 1941–1995: The Rise and Fall of the Era of Easy Finance*, ed. W. Elliot Brownlee, 107–147. Washington, DC and Cambridge: The Wilson Center Press and Cambridge University Press.
Jones, Daniel Stedman. 2012. *Masters of the Universe: Hayek, Friedman, and the Birth of Neoliberal Politics*. Princeton: Princeton University Press.
Lippmann, Walter. 1937. *The Good Society*. Boston: Little, Brown.
———. 1986. *Drift and Mastery*. Madison: University of Wisconsin (republication of the 1914 edition).
MacLean, Nancy. 2017. *Democracy in Chains: The Deep History of the Radical Right's Stealth Plan for America*. New York: Viking.
Martin, Cathie Jo. 1991. *Shifting the Burden: The Struggle Over Growth and Corporate Taxation*. Chicago: University of Chicago Press.
———. 1996. American Business and the Taxing State: Alliances for Growth in the Postwar Period. In *Funding the American State, 1941–1995: The Rise and Fall of the Era of Easy Finance*, ed. W. Elliot Brownlee, 353–406. Washington, DC and Cambridge: The Wilson Center Press and Cambridge University Press.
Martin, Isaac. 2008. *The Permanent Tax Revolt: How the Property Tax Transformed American Politics*. Stanford: Stanford University Press.
Mayer, Jeremy D. 2007. Reagan and Race: Prophet of Color Blindness, Baiter of the Backlash. In *Deconstructing Reagan: Conservative Mythology and America's Fortieth President*, ed. Kyle Longley, Jeremy D. Mayer, Michael Schaller, and John W. Sloan, 70–89. Armonk, NY: M.E. Sharpe.
McCaffery, Edward J. 1997. *Taxing Women*. Chicago: University of Chicago Press.
Michelmore, Molly C. 2012. *Tax and Spend: The Welfare State, Tax Politics, and the Limits of American Liberalism*. Philadelphia: University of Pennsylvania Press.

Mirowski, Philip, and Dieter Plehwe, eds. 2009. *The Road From Mont Pèlerin: The Making of the Neoliberal Thought Collective*. Cambridge: Harvard University Press.

Mozumi, Seiichiro. 2014. *A Prelude to Fiscal Gridlock of the United States: Social Policy, Taxation and Policymaking of the Administration of John F. Kennedy*. PhD dissertation, Keio University.

OECD. 2008. *Growing Unequal?: Income Distribution and Poverty in OECD Countries*. OECD Publishing. http://www.oecd-ilibrary.org/social-issues-migration-health/growing-unequal_9789264044197-en

Phillips-Fein, Kim. 2009. *Invisible Hands: The Businessmen's Crusade against the New Deal*. New York: W.W. Norton.

Piketty, Thomas. 2013. *Capital in the Twenty-First Century*. Cambridge: Harvard University Press.

Piketty, Thomas, and Emmanuel Saez. 2007. How Progressive is the U.S. Federal Tax System? A Historical and International Perspective. *Journal of Economic Perspectives* 21 (7): 1–24.

Plant, Raymond. 2010. *The New-Liberal State*. Oxford: Oxford University Press.

Prasad, Monica. 2006. *The Politics of Free Markets: The Rise of Neoliberal Economic Policies in Britain, France, Germany, and the United States*. Chicago: University of Chicago.

———. 2012a. The Popular Origins of Neoliberalism in the Reagan Tax Cut of 1981. *Journal of Policy History* 24 (3): 351–383.

———. 2012b. *The Land of Too Much: American Abundance and the Paradox of Poverty*. Cambridge: Harvard University Press.

Public Papers of the Presidents of the United States. 1965. *Lyndon B. Johnson, 1963–1964, Book 1*. Washington, DC: U.S. Government Printing Office.

Reagan, Ronald. 2001a. Tax Loopholes, May 1975. In *Reagan, In His Own Hand: The Writings of Ronald Reagan that Reveal his Revolutionary Vision for America*, ed. Kiron K. Skinner, Annelise Anderson, and Martin Anderson, 268–270. New York: The Free Press.

———. 2001b. Taxes, October 18, 1977. In *Reagan, In His Own Hand: The Writings of Ronald Reagan that Reveal his Revolutionary Vision for America*, ed. Kiron K. Skinner, Annelise Anderson, and Martin Anderson, 274–277. New York: The Free Press.

———. 2001c. Tax Expenditures, July 27, 1979. In *Reagan, In His Own Hand: The Writings of Ronald Reagan that Reveal His Revolutionary Vision for America*, ed. Kiron K. Skinner, Annelise Anderson, and Martin Anderson, 283–284. New York: The Free Press.

———. 2001d. Economic Speech—Address to the Nation, February 5, 1981. In *Reagan, In His Own Hand: The Writings of Ronald Reagan that Reveal His Revolutionary Vision for America*, ed. Kiron K. Skinner, Annelise Anderson, and Martin Anderson, 487–492. New York: The Free Press.

Roberts, Paul Craig. 1984. *The Supply-Side Revolution: An Insider's Account of Policymaking in Washington*. Cambridge, MA: Harvard University Press.
Schlesinger, Arthur M., Jr. 1960. *The Politics of Upheaval*. Boston: Houghton Mifflin.
Shaviro, Daniel. 2013–2014. The Forgotten Henry Simons. *Florida State University Law Review* 41 (1): 1–38.
Simons, Henry C. 1938. *Personal Income Taxation: The Definition of Income as a Problem of Fiscal Policy*. Chicago: University of Chicago Press.
Stein, Herbert. 1969. *The Fiscal Revolution in America*. Chicago: University of Chicago Press.
———. 1996. The Fiscal Revolution in America, Part II. In *Funding the American State, 1941–1995: The Rise and Fall of the Era of Easy Finance*, ed. W. Elliot Brownlee, 194–286. Washington, DC and Cambridge: The Wilson Center Press and Cambridge University Press.
Steuerle, C. Eugene. 2004. *Contemporary U.S. Tax Policy*. Washington, DC: The Urban Institute Press.
Stockman, David. 1986. *Triumph of Politics: How the Reagan Revolution Failed*. New York: Harper & Row.
Thorndike, Joseph J. 2013. *Their Fair Share: Taxing the Rich in the Age of FDR*. Washington, DC: The Urban Institute Press.
U.S. Department of the Treasury. 1977. *Blueprints for Basic Tax Reform*. January 17. https://www.treasury.gov/resource-center/tax-policy/Documents/Report-Blueprints-1977.pdf
Ventry, Dennis J. 2001. The Treatment of Marriage Under the U.S. Federal Income Tax, 1913–2000. Ph.D. Dissertation, University of California, Santa Barbara.
Witte, John F. 1985. *The Politics and the Development of the Federal Income Tax*. Madison: University of Wisconsin Press.

Tax Reformers' Ideas, the Expenditure-Taxation Nexus, and Comprehensive Tax Reform in the United States, 1961–1986

Seiichiro Mozumi

Introduction

Since the 1930s, the US Treasury and tax experts have attempted to accomplish a "one package," comprehensive tax reform program. The aim has been to create a simpler, fairer, and more equitable federal income tax regime with the power to raise revenue.[1] It was Robert Murray Haig who first introduced this idea; later, it was taken up and developed by Henry C. Simons, Carl Shoup, and Stanley S. Surrey, as well as the Treasury.[2] Although attempts at tax reform failed in the early 1960s and the 1970s, they finally succeeded in 1986. Tax cuts and tax expenditures, which were frequently resorted to since the 1960s, had undermined not only the ability to raise revenue, but also the fairness and equity of the federal income tax system. This chapter discusses three episodes of federal tax reform—tax reforms introduced in 1964, 1978, and 1986—to demonstrate the process in and for which tax-cutting measures became influential and the

S. Mozumi (✉)
Department of Economics, Yokohama National University, Yokohama, Japan
e-mail: mozumi-seiichiro-jc@ynu.ac.jp

G. Huerlimann et al. (eds.), *Worlds of Taxation*,
Palgrave Studies in the History of Finance,
https://doi.org/10.1007/978-3-319-90263-0_8

significance of this process in federal tax policy. It also examines how and why the Reagan administration succeeded in enacting base-broadening reform in 1986.

Comprehensive Tax Reformers and John Maynard Keynes, 1920s–1950s

The idea of "one-package," comprehensive tax reform, emphasizing fairness, simplicity, equity, and the power to raise revenue, began with public finance scholars such as Edwin R. A. Seligman and Robert Murray Haig in the early twentieth century.[3] To justify the ability of the federal government to tax income, Haig defined income as "the increase or accretion in one's power to satisfy his wants in a given period in so far as that power consists of (a) money itself, or, (b) anything susceptible of valuation in terms of money. More simply stated … Income is *the money value of the net accretion to one's economic power between two points of time.*"[4] According to Haig, it was "very undesirable from the point of view of economics and equity that the judicial definition of income should develop along narrow lines by the process of definitely eliminating from the concept certain items as not being income."[5]

In 1938, Henry C. Simons, an economist of the Chicago School, following the concept that Haig had advocated, defined income as "the algebraic sum of the individual's consumption expense and accumulation during the accounting period." For Simons, progressive individual income taxes that distributed the tax burden among taxpayers equitably were the only appropriate means of financing government expenditures and mitigating poverty and inequality without creating inequity in political power.[6] In the 1940s, Simons insisted that drastic tax reform based on his definition was one of most significant components of liberty and equity.[7] In his view, such a tax reform would increase enough revenue to finance expenditures without revenue gain or loss, and achieve greater equity and fairness, neutrality, simplification, and greater taxpayer compliance.[8] Learning of Haig's and Simons's concepts while studying at Columbia University Law School and in the course of his employment at the Treasury and the University of California, Berkeley, one tax law scholar, Stanley S. Surrey, significantly influenced the Treasury's crafting of tax reform after World War II.[9]

Having been appointed a law professor in the Harvard Law School faculty in 1951, Surrey convened a number of conferences attended by economists and tax lawyers to discuss the federal tax structure and administration.[10]

Surrey also advised members of the House Committee on Ways and Means (CWM) on tax reform proposals in the late 1950s.[11] Throughout these activities, he emphasized the requirement that comprehensive tax reform should promote fairness, simplicity, horizontal and vertical equity, and progressivity. He believed that the federal tax system should allow for more equity in the tax burden according to the type and level of income, and should smooth the rate structure without sacrificing progressivity and tax revenues.[12] He also believed that preferential treatment for certain types of income created an unduly narrow tax base, excessively high marginal rates, low effective rates, and an unfair tax burden across different types of income. Furthermore, he argued that reducing the rate of tax and eliminating upper-bracket differentials would improve the tax system without loss of revenue. With respect to the significant differentials between the lower and middle brackets, he believed that their elimination would be far easier in the context of a general overhaul of revenue, involving compensating rate cuts, dividing the first bracket, or increasing in personal exemptions.[13]

Surrey's thoughts on taxation were similar to John Maynard Keynes's and his American contemporaries, Alvin H. Hansen and Abba Lerner. In 1936, Keynes argued in *General Theory of Employment, Interest and Money* that low consumption under advanced capitalism would widen the gap between aggregate income and aggregate consumption, which in turn would reduce the incentive to invest while increasing savings. To close this gap, Keynes argued that fiscal policy should be used to distribute incomes more equally. With respect to tax policy, he suggested for the possibility of income tax reform aimed at redistributing income equally by combining capital levies to raise funds for government programs with reducing taxes on income and consumption.[14] In *How to Pay for the War*, Keynes sought to avoid inflation and the exhaustion of resources; to raise funds for government expenditure in order to prevent deflation and unemployment in the first recession that might follow World War II; and to prevent the aggravation of income and consumption inequality among the working class, capitalists, and the wealthy. To accomplish these goals, Keynes advocated boosting progressivity sharply through the exemption minimum and increasing taxes mainly on the middle- and high-income classes, along with a general capital levy.[15] By the 1950s, Keynes's ideas had been disseminated throughout the United States thanks to his American contemporaries.[16] They—in line with Keynes—favored not only progressive but also equitable income taxation in order to finance expanding fiscal demand and balance the budget when the national economy approached full employment.

Defeat of Comprehensive Tax Reform in 1964

In the late 1950s, the Treasury, in cooperation with the CWM, began to complete the projects begun under the administrations of Harry S. Truman and Dwight E. Eisenhower before 1954—that is, reforming the defects in the federal income tax system constructed during World War II. The income tax system at that time included lower personal exemptions, a steep and high rate structure, and a narrower tax base that favored unearned income and the relatively high-income classes.[17] Representative Wilbur D. Mills (Democrat—Arkansas), an accomplished and politically talented member of the CWM, made significant contributions to this movement. Through his involvement in several congressional committees in the 1950s, Mills concluded that a single tax reform package should combine base-broadening measures and rate reductions. He expected that this would achieve a fairer, simpler, and more equitable and progressive income tax system, one that would raise total revenue, keep the federal budget more or less in balance in the long term, and create an atmosphere of equal opportunities to achieve steady economic growth and expansion.[18]

Once Mills had been appointed the chairman of the CWM in 1958, the Committee, in cooperation with the Treasury, held hearings to discuss the specific measures of such tax reform from November 16 to December 18 in 1959.[19] In a series of hearings, the CWM led by Mills and the Treasury succeeded in informing tax experts, economists, and members of Congress of the need for comprehensive tax reform. After John F. Kennedy took office on January 20, 1961, the Treasury, led by Surrey, now Assistant Secretary for Tax Policy, and the newly appointed Director of the Office of Tax Analysis (OTA) Harvey E. Brazer, began crafting a comprehensive tax reform based on the discussions between the CWM and the Treasury that had taken place in the late 1950s.[20] In 1961, the Treasury drafted a "coherent package" of tax reform combining base-broadening reforms with rate reductions, to provide a broader and more uniform tax base with an appropriate rate structure to boost economic growth and achieve a more equitable tax structure and a simpler tax law without net revenue losses.[21]

While discussions were in progress, Walter Heller, James Tobin, and Kermit Gordon, members of the Council of Economic Advisers (CEA), attempted to persuade Kennedy of the importance of deliberate deficit financing. The CEA viewed the most important economic problem as the gap between actual output and full-employment output.[22] They estimated that the federal tax system could increase revenue by $7–8 billion annually under normal economic conditions. In a slack economy, however, "fiscal drag," as Heller called it, would frustrate any chance of expansion. In response, the CEA turned to the concept of a "full-employment budget surplus" to suggest that any such "fiscal drag" should be offset by "fiscal dividends" through tax cuts or increases in government expenditure.[23] However, yet more expenditure programs were met with considerable resistance.[24] As part of an address Kennedy planned for April 1961, Heller urged Kennedy to emphasize that economic output was far below its potential, that the consumption-stimulating deficit would be inadequate without a tax cut, that congressional reluctance and administrative foot-dragging would bring under control any increases in government spending, and that an economy stimulated by tax cuts would increase federal revenues.[25]

Economic and political conditions at the time were gradually making it difficult to realize the administration's original tax reform program. From the early days, criticism was voiced among Republicans and businesses because, in their opinion, appointments to regulatory agencies were unsatisfactory and at the same time it occurred a serious conflict over the rising price of steel. The decline in the rate of economic growth and falling stock prices in 1962 left businesses, investors, and analysts worrying that a recession was imminent.[26] Heller then attempted to persuade Kennedy to push for tax cuts rather than comprehensive tax reform. He recommended that the administration should present their reform program as a net tax cut, in a two-stage approach: permanent tax rates cuts and other tax-cutting measures would take effect first, followed a year later by base-broadening reforms to get round predictable opposition.[27] Business interests, as well as economists outside the administration, including Richard Musgrave and Gerhard Colm, supported the CEA.[28] Tax cuts now became a measure that appealed to the Kennedy administration while making secondary the tax reform principles Surrey had emphasized: a coherent, almost revenue-neutral base-broadening tax reform boosting vertical and horizontal equity. The White House expected that it would adhere to the Democratic tradition while circumventing conflict with business interests.[29]

The Treasury and Mills opposed this approach. The Treasury wished to stem the growing wave of doubt abroad concerning where the domestic economy and balance of payments were heading due to the loss of revenue and a sizable budget deficit.[30] Mills and the Treasury also viewed that the economic trend had shown some improvement in July 1962 after a slowdown in the spring.[31] They were also concerned that enacting rate reductions separately would result in much larger revenue losses than were necessary before the feedback effect of the tax cuts would start.[32] In addition, although Mills saw the existing tax rate structure as an impediment to economic growth and higher employment, he argued that rate reductions in individual and corporate taxes should be accompanied by base-broadening measures in order to avoid loss of confidence in the government's fiscal responsibility and maximize the possibility of getting the program adopted in Congress. Mills maintained that neither the proposed tax cuts nor the separation of the rate cuts from tax reform were desirable, and foresaw that the House would reject them. As a result, in August 1962, the CWM concluded that no tax cuts were needed at that time. The members argued that an excessively bleak and self-serving picture had been painted by businesses, and that the administration had overemphasized implementing tax cuts.[33]

The CEA, the Treasury, and Kennedy worked toward a compromise. On November 19, 1962, Special Assistant Secretary of the Treasury Robert Wallace wrote that it was necessary for the Treasury to consider a compromise. Pressures continued for the two-stage approach on the one hand, and congressional resistance to a large deficit persisted on the other. As a compromise, he suggested the two-stage approach, and the Treasury agreed with his suggestion. The Treasury finally decided to propose that the bulk of the tax cuts along with the simplest reforms be presented for early action. The rest of the cuts and the more controversial reforms could be considered later.[34] Mills concurred. The Treasury and Mills resultantly abandoned their ideal bill. However, they did believe the two-package approach would make the eventual adoption of tax reform far more likely.

The tax reform program, when proposed in January 1963, did not take a coherent, revenue-neutral form. It comprised a huge tax cut according to a two-stage approach. The administration's proposal emphasized not only the purpose of stimulating consumption and investment but also structural reform measures to boost progressivity, fairness, simplicity, and horizontal and vertical equity.[35] However, businesses, Republicans, and many newspapers nevertheless fervently attacked the proposed structural reform measures. Their opposition mainly focused on the restraint of itemized deduction, the repeal of dividend credit and exclusion, and the restraint of preferential treatment for capital gains. These criticisms against the reform measures were based on their idea that this tax reform program unfairly imposed excessive tax burden on higher-income classes, investors, and homeowners.[36] In the face of such opposition, Mills, who had been one of the foremost proponents of comprehensive tax reform, now became a tax-cut proponent.[37] In the Senate Finance Committee (SFC), Chairman Harry Byrd (Democrat—Virginia) strongly opposed the reform, especially the limits it would impose on preferential treatment for capital gains taxation. Consequently, most loophole-closing provisions were abandoned or emasculated by the CWM and the SFC. The tax reform program was finally passed into law in 1964 and became the largest ever tax cut until 1981, with huge rate cuts in the individual and corporate income taxes but almost no reform measures. It became known as the "Kennedy–Johnson tax cut."[38]

The defeat of comprehensive tax reform left two legacies to federal tax and fiscal policy. First, as Herbert Stein once concluded, through "domesticated Keynesianism," the "full-employment budget" concept—tax and expenditure policies should produce a balanced budget if the economy was operating at full employment—seemed established once the tax-cut bill became law.[39] The ideas of comprehensive tax reform proponents were more similar to Keynes, Hansen, and Lerner in their beliefs than those of "tax-cut" proponents today referred to as "Keynesians." However, the tax-cut argument finally prevailed. Kennedy's economic advisers repeatedly applauded the tax cut as having immediately contributed to economic expansion and resulting in increasing tax revenues.[40] Heller argued that prosperity produced by the "domesticated Keynesian" fiscal policy would enlarge individuals' economic freedom, create jobs, and mitigate poverty.[41] Then, ignoring Keynes's idea of an equitable progressive income tax system, the victorious CEA and other economists promoted the popularity of the Kennedy-Johnson tax cut as part of "the completion of the Keynesian revolution." In doing so, domesticated Keynesians separated the two halves of the expenditure-taxation nexus, which meant that any decision regarding taxation in the budgetary process would be made in isolation from decisions about expenditure.[42]

Second, the 1964 tax cut meant that any comprehensive tax reform should contain rate reductions and be proposed as a net tax reduction. The Treasury, Surrey, and Mills had never argued that comprehensive tax reform should be a tax reduction program before Kennedy proposed his tax reform in 1963. However, Mills acted inconsistently and changed his stance during the legislative process. Bearing in mind the legislative process and result of the Kennedy-Johnson tax cut, Mills thereafter argued that every comprehensive tax reform program should in effect be a tax reduction program in order to pass it through Congress.[43]

The Momentum Toward Comprehensive Tax Reform up to the Mid-1970s

Domesticated Keynesianism dominated the mainstream of federal tax policy through the enactment of the Revenue Act 1964. When it turned out the Treasury would very likely be defeated, however, they began another attempt to reverse the gradual erosion of the tax base created through the inclusion of special preferences and privileges for certain groups of taxpayers.[44] Surrey and the new director of the OTA, Gerard M. Brannon, for the most part directed it within the Treasury.[45] In order to accomplish this goal, in 1965, they formulated the concept of "tax expenditures" to assess tax preferences in the same way as government expenditures were. Brannon suggested that this concept would help assess whether or not a certain government expenditure or tax preference was more appropriate.[46]

Following Brannon, Surrey determined to adopt the viewpoint that any tax preferences designed to further a specific and desirable social goal should be tested against whether or not these preferences would enable the goals to be achieved more efficiently, directly, and fairly than through government direct expenditure programs.[47] It was clearly Surrey's view that taxes forgone to benefit or induce a particular activity, such as preferential treatments for capital gains, dividend credits, and exclusion, were the equivalent of "monies spent." In contrast, for education, pollution, personnel training, and research and development programs, Surrey favored a non-tax approach.[48] In the late 1960s, the Treasury, led by Surrey and Brannon, continued to research the "tax expenditure" concept, and drafted another tax reform program based on the concept during the presidency of Lyndon B. Johnson. They held that it would provide the federal tax system with the ability to generate revenue for constructive government programs for those most in need and for Great Society programs in as fair, equitable, and simple ways as possible.[49]

Although Johnson did not recommend the tax reform program, the administration of Richard M. Nixon inherited the effort of the Johnson administration. The tax reform program he recommended on April 21, 1969, consisted of the measures Surrey and Brannon had envisioned during the Johnson presidency. On December 30, 1969, Nixon signed the Tax Reform Act of 1969 into law. The act achieved structural reform measures, including repeal of the investment credit and a slight increase in the capital gains tax rate. These measures would amount to \$6.6 billion a year when fully effective. In the meantime, it contained tax cuts of \$9.1 billion that would result in an annual loss of $2.5 billion, although the Nixon administration was faced with expanding budget deficits and rising prices.[50] Nixon stressed that most of his major reform proposals were adopted, and that they would make the federal income tax system simpler, fairer, and more equitable. However, he added: "The tax reforms, on the whole, are good," but "the effect on the budget and on the cost of living is bad" in the face of the increasing budget deficits and inflationary pressure.[51]

By 1968, the consensus on the "full-employment budget" concept that appeared to have been established by the 1964 tax cut had broken down. However, the efforts of the Johnson presidency regarding tax reform could not restore the expenditure-taxation nexus that domesticated Keynesianism had broken by the 1964 tax cut. As a result, most policy-makers were now unwilling to subordinate their desires for specific tax and expenditure programs to any aggregate goals and a balanced budget. By the end of the Nixon presidency, any idea of government finance for society was no longer a force within government and Congress, and almost everyone was now opposed to raising taxes.[52]

Although there was no significant tax legislation, momentum toward comprehensive tax reform stepped up a gear in the mid-1970s. In 1973, Nixon recommended a carefully balanced tax reform program aimed at simplifying the tax system and discouraging tax shelters for higher-income taxpayers. This attempt had once been doomed, but in 1975, Gerald Ford could no longer avoid the issue—reducing the tax burden while broadening the tax base to boost fairness, equity, and simplicity—faced as he was with the need to defeat stagflation and bracket creep. Ford successfully achieved two tax-cut programs in 1975. These programs reduced tax rates in the first four brackets, increased standard deduction and investment credits, and introduced the Earned Income Tax Credit (EITC). Successively, Ford recommended his tax reform program that was based on an expansion of the Nixon proposal offered in 1973. The bill passed through Congress as the Tax Reform Act of 1976 on October 4, 1976. The act introduced 30 loophole-closing measures, which primarily affected higher-income taxpayers, and 20 revenue-reducing reforms. In total, the act accounted for $27.3 billion tax cut over next two fiscal years. However, it made the federal tax system more complex and did little for capital formation, investment, and the middle-income classes who were suffering the effects of inflation and the rapid escalation of state and local taxes. This result set the tone for the next five years of tax politics.[53]

The Defeat of Tax Reform in 1978

In the face of Ford's two tax reforms, Democratic presidential candidate Jimmy Carter adopted a strong campaign commitment to reform the federal tax system, which he called a "disgrace to the human race" and "a welfare program for the rich." He criticized the federal tax system for being regressive, shifting the total tax burden to the average wage earner. He called for lowering taxes on the lower- and middle-income classes and replacing it by moving more of the tax burden to the wealthy and corporations. In his view, the nation was ready for the comprehensive tax reform. His plan was to eliminate hundreds of tax loopholes and greatly reduce tax rates. Stressing the importance of vertical equity over horizontal equity, Carter sought a simpler, more equitable and progressive federal tax system. In addition, he expressed a desire to complete tax reform without any significant loss of revenue.[54] All this was based on *Blueprints for Basic Tax Reform*, which the Treasury had published at the end of the Ford administration, on January 17, 1977.[55]

Soon after Carter took office, the Treasury, led by the Secretary, Michael Blumenthal, along with Assistant Secretary for Tax Policy, Lawrence Woodworth, began publicly discussing the tax reform provisions under consideration.[56] Within the administration, several members of the White House Domestic Policy Staff (DPS) were working toward devising the administration's tax reform program. Executive Director of the DPS, Stuart Eizenstat, and one of the members, Robert Ginsberg, led the group. The administration also created an advisory group labeled the Economic Policy Group (EPG), which consisted of Carter's first Director of the Office of Management and Budget (OMB), Bert Lance, the chairman of the CEA, Charles Schultze, and Blumenthal.[57] As part of the economic stimulus package, they recommended the Treasury and the DPS that the administration's tax reform program should contain tax-cut elements. Moreover, in Congress, the CWM, led by Al Ullman (Democrat—Oregon), and the SFC, chaired by Russell Long (Democrat—Louisiana), also considered the provisions that the tax reform should include.

Carter's aides recommended that the administration should base its tax reform program primarily on its own intentions. In early 1977 the Carter administration discussed the outline of its reform program with Ullman and Long but discovered that they favored keeping many tax preferences. However, the administration, especially Blumenthal and Eizenstat, did not agree as they feared that their approach might produce revenue losses, as well as an inequitable effect on taxpayers and on the complexity of federal tax system.[58] Thus, they urged Carter to stick to his original goal and press for congressional action with as little change as possible.[59] In light of what Congress was demanding, several members inside the White House staff, such as Lance, thought that the work of planning the tax reform program should be coordinated with the interests of each agency within the administration. Lance warned Carter that past experience indicated that the operating agencies of the executive branch would be enemies of tax reform because each of them would view loopholes as essential to their programs and constituents.[60] Furthermore, Eizenstat and Ginsberg recommended that Carter should involve his principal economic advisers, such as the CEA and the EPG, from the outset in helping the Treasury block out the general areas of tax reform to be considered.[61]

The first Treasury tax reform plan, mainly designed by Woodworth and the Treasury, contained reform of personal deductions and business tax preferences, capital gains taxes, rate reduction, taxation of foreign income, and capital formation.[62] However, Eizenstat and Ginsberg believed that these provisions were detrimental to the administration's goal for two reasons. First, in their opinion, the Treasury had made a number of ad hoc political judgments as to which reform measures would be acceptable to Congress, such as substituting a general credit for the existing $750 personal exemption, and remaining travel and entertainment expense deductions and other tax shelters. Second, Eizenstat and Ginsberg were concerned about the estimated cost the Treasury's reform proposals would create. The Treasury plan included the reduction of the rate schedule from 14–70 percent to 13–50 percent and the integration of corporate and individual income taxes.[63] Eizenstat and Ginsberg concluded that the tax reform package based on the Treasury's recommendation would be extremely costly, and tilted largely in favor of tax reductions for the wealthy and business.

Based on this evaluation, Eizenstat and Ginsberg revised their own tax reform proposal, emphasizing that tax reform should be comprehensive and eliminate tax expenditures that were principally tilted to favor higher-income taxpayers and enabled them to avoid paying their fair share. They added to the Treasury plan elimination of the capital gains preference and preferential treatment for dividends and interest, tax shelters, and business expense deductions such as those for first class travel and "three-martini lunches," and foreign deferral provisions. However, their proposal deviated from Carter's almost-revenue-neutral requirement. Eizenstat and Ginsberg thought that to meet it would be extremely difficult because an average taxpayer would probably not view the tax reform effort favorably if it did not reduce his or her taxes. They also believed that Congress was likely to reduce taxes in the future to offset the effects of bracket creep. Eizenstat and Ginsberg estimated that their program would give the average taxpayer a good-sized ($200–$300) tax reduction. They believed that such kinds of tax reduction would be essential to the success of their tax reform effort while keeping the revenue loss within bounds by reducing the existing tax expenditures.[64]

Changes to the budgetary, economic, and political realities prompted Carter's aides to modify the tax proposal. The most significant event was that Congress watered down the administration's economic stimulus program proposed on January 31, 1977. The program included tax cuts incorporating $50 tax rebate and business tax reduction such as an increased investment credit and a wage credit. On May 16, however, Congress attenuated the stimulating effect by eliminating the rebate and tax credits for business from the original proposal. Shortly after Carter took office, the administration had engaged in the intensive attempt to persuade Japan and West Germany into acting as international economic leaders in order to stimulate their domestic demand in order to increase their imports. Domestic economic expansion through the tax cut was to be the incentive for them to accept this requirement. However, Japan and West Germany evaluated that the resultant tax cut had less stimulating effects than the tax cut originally proposed. Then the Carter administration was situated to make the pressure on Japan and West Germany weaker than the administration actually wanted.[65] In the face of these conditions, Schultze recommended the administration become aggressive in proposing the larger revenue losses of the tax reform program.[66]

Although it deviated from his original revenue-neutral requirement, Carter finally accepted Schultze's recommendation, in addition to the recommendation of Eizenstat and Ginsberg. Carter thus required the Treasury to revise their tax reform program as reducing more tax revenues than the original proposal, along with the intention of the DPS and the CEA in several ways. Carter first recommended greater tax reductions for middle-income taxpayers. Second, he recommended the Treasury maintain the average taxes paid by individuals in the $50,000 and over brackets at about their present levels. To meet this recommendation, Carter requested they should identify more tax preferences they could eliminate. He focused on reducing the use of tax expenditures especially benefiting upper-income taxpayers while lowering the rate schedule for those who did not use them.[67] The Treasury agreed with Carter's requests, and completed their drafting in July 1977.[68] Checking the revised Treasury program, the CEA urged Carter to add more tax-cutting measures that would mainly target businesses. It based its recommendation on the slow pace of economic expansion in the third quarter of 1977.[69] Although Carter initially disagreed owing to his desire not to fuel inflation, he finally accepted the CEA's recommendation.[70]

The Carter administration launched the comprehensive tax reform program on January 21, 1978. The proposal echoed the tax reform elements that Surrey and domesticated Keynesians had suggested in the early 1960s. The bill contained tax-cut provisions aimed at providing relief for the lower- and middle-income classes, as well as reform measures to close loopholes such as the "three-martini lunches" that the upper-income classes and businesses enjoyed. The proposed tax reform included several measures to stimulate investment, including sizable rate cuts of individual and corporate income taxes. The reform program provided a $25 billion net tax reduction, a larger amount than the Treasury had expected ($20 billion). When he recommended the reform program, Carter chose to downplay the tax-cut aspect, emphasizing instead opposition to existing tax loopholes favoring business and to any liberalization in the capital gains tax. The reform proposal emphasized the goals of simplification, equity (vertical rather than horizontal), progressivity, and the stimulation of capital formation.[71]

The coalition, consisting of unified Republicans and Democrats in the CWM, sharply scaled down base-broadening measures. In the committee's panel, Barber Conable (Republican—New York) summarized the feelings of the coalition: "The proposals have a lot of appeal in terms of simplification and structure, provided we don't stick it in the ear of the middle class ... I'll support doing away with them as long as it isn't a redistribution gimmick." On April 20, 1978, Ullman went to the White House, with Daniel Rostenkowski (Democrat—Illinois) and Joseph Waggonner, Jr. (Democrat—Louisiana), to tell Carter that the tax reform proposal was in serious jeopardy. They warned Carter, "scale down the proposals or face a substantial defeat." As a result, the CWM bill dropped most of the administration's base-broadening reforms while retaining the personal exemption at a higher level and gearing more marginal rate reductions to the middle class. It also increased the capital gains exclusion, cut the maximum effective rate on capital gains, and indexed capital gains to inflation. Since the coalition was concerned about deficits, the bill provided a smaller tax cut ($16.1 billion) than Carter had requested.

The SFC proved to be even more generous, voting to expand many existing tax breaks and adding numerous new loopholes targeted at farmers, teachers, Alaskan natives, railroads, record manufacturers, and so on. The final Senate bill was estimated to reduce income taxes by $29.1 billion. This result tilted the tax-cut effect toward upper-income taxpayers. Carter almost vetoed the bill because he felt he had been double-crossed and the final bill contained more tax loopholes than the existing federal tax code did. However, the CEA persuaded Carter that a veto of the bill might have brought greater fiscal restraint, more unemployment, and mild inflation in 1979. They repeatedly described how badly the economy needed a tax cut.[72] Eventually, Carter signed the tax bill on November 6, but with no statements of approval. The final bill bore almost no resemblance to what Carter had proposed.[73]

The 1978 tax reform ended a tax reform movement that had continued from the 1940s. Although the Carter administration attempted to keep the spirit of tax reformers alive, they proposed the tax reform as a tax cut to tackle stagflation. In the end, they failed in achieving almost all base-broadening measures because of opposition in Congress. The final bill reduced tax rates and the number of brackets, and added more tax preferences than Carter had recommended. The 1978 tax reform did not at all resolve the issues of the federal tax system the Ford administration had left, except reducing the tax burden borne by middle-income taxpayers. The Carter administration did not, and could not, claim victory.

The defeat of Carter's tax reform proposal also signaled a new era in tax policy, the triumph of a broad coalition of business lobbyists who united under the rubric of "capital formation." They argued that the best remedy for the faltering economy was to create new tax breaks for businesses and investors. They championed a provision in the 1978 reform that enhanced the preferential treatment of capital gains income, bringing the top tax rate on gains down from 35 percent to 28 percent. However, the capital-formation coalition maintained that the tax break would stimulate investment and promote economic growth. As a result, "tax reform was clearly out; capital formation was in." The influence of special interests in Congress had reached unprecedented heights.[74]

An Exceptional Victory in 1986

The Economic Recovery Tax Act (ERTA) of 1981, Ronald Reagan's first tax reform, was emblematic of the influence of special interests in Congress and the requirements of capital formation. ERTA largely cut both individual and business income taxes more than Reagan had recommended, and it increased the number of tax loopholes. Despite these measures, the outcome they anticipated was not achieved. As a consequence of the deepening recession and substantial increases in defense expenditures, each successive projection of the budget deficit increased after it was legislated.[75] Thus, in September 1981, while tackling mandatory entitlement spending, the Reagan administration initiated a new proposal for several tax increases. Eventually, the administration succeeded in enacting the Tax Equity and Fiscal Responsibility Act 1982 (TEFRA), along with several tax reform measures, as a part of the Deficit Reduction Act 1984 (DEFRA). These acts closed tax loopholes, some of which had been created by ERTA.[76]

While the Reagan administration had worked on these base-broadening reforms, Democrats and Republicans in Congress forced it to discuss the possibility of recommending a base-broadening tax reform. Based on the idea of a "flat tax," in 1982, a member of the SFC, Senator Bill Bradley (Democrat—New Jersey), inspired by Surrey's earlier reform program, and Congressman Richard Gephardt (Democrat—Missouri) introduced a base-broadening tax reform proposal with a top individual income tax rate of 30 percent. White House political officials were concerned at that time that the Democrats would take the lead on tax reform and make it a major issue in the 1984 election campaign. In this context, Reagan initially suggested a plan to simplify the tax code and make it fairer for all taxpayers in his 1983 State of the Union address in a low-key.[77] In response to the address, the Secretary of the Treasury, Donald Regan, and his staff paid serious attention to the adoption of a lower, flatter tax rates, and significant broadening of the income base by eliminating the tax privileges enjoyed by the few during 1983.[78]

Considering the federal deficit and rate structure, the Treasury began drawing up a base-broadening tax reform program. It first determined that the major guideline was the "revenue-neutral" principle. Second, the Treasury identified the three major issues on which they would focus: broadening the individual tax base, simplifying the taxpaying process by eliminating costly and widely used tax expenditures, and taking the poor off the tax rolls. Furthermore, the Treasury determined to extract additional revenues from corporate income tax in part to finance rate cuts in individual income tax. The corporate income tax increase would combine rate reductions with eliminating or restricting business tax preferences, including some of those introduced by ERTA. To ensure that the reform program would be politically acceptable, the Treasury adopted the individual income rate structure of 15-25-35, which Regan favored, and a corporate rate reduction to 33 percent, down from 46 percent. By the time the 1984 election came round, on the basis of these elements, Treasury staff had completed and submitted to Secretary Regan a reform proposal, "Treasury I." It would balance taxable against economic income as fully as possible by means of a broad-based tax with lower, less graduated rates.

After Treasury I was published, interest groups loudly protested while it also picked up broad support from Republicans and Democrats, both conservative and liberal press, and think tanks. At this point, the tax reform became a political issue. After swapping jobs with the White House chief of staff, James A. Baker, in January 1985, Regan repeatedly met with interest groups to find out what kind of tax preferences they wanted the administration to retain. Using the information gained in this way, the Treasury amended Treasury I, which now became "Treasury II." Treasury II kept the principles of Treasury I while including an element needed to win Presidential support—a further reduction in the top tax rate.[79]

On May 28, 1985, Reagan finally announced his tax proposals for "the sake of fairness, simplicity, and growth." The proposal replaced 14 tax rate brackets ranging from 11 percent to 50 percent with a simple three-bracket system of 15, 25, and 35 percent. While raising the personal exemption, reducing the tax rate on capital gains, and maintaining other tax preferences "central to American values," the proposal simplified the complex federal tax system by closing loopholes that benefited a privileged minority. To promote business formation, it reduced the maximum corporate tax rate from 46 percent to 33 percent while cutting back tax preferences for some businesses such as the investment tax credit. "Restoring confidence in the federal tax system means restoring and respecting the principle of fairness for all," Reagan stated. "There is one group of losers in the tax plan—those individuals and corporations who did not pay their fair share or … any share." In the address, however, Reagan most emphasized the effect of reducing the tax burden on all taxpayers. He also maintained that the proposal would radically reform the structure of the federal tax system in ways of making it both easier to invest and more equitable horizontally.[80]

Most of the House Democrats and Republicans were hostile toward the tax reform. In the CWM, almost all members favored tax preferences that benefited individual taxpayers and were intended to stimulate productivity and subsidize US firms.[81] In response, Rostenkowski decided to retain and expand existing tax preferences in favor of supportive members and key constituencies to build a bipartisan coalition. In addition, he applied an additional fourth higher tax rate to achieve the commitment to revenue neutrality.[82] Based on Rostenkowski's recommendations, the CWM completed its crafting of the "tax overhaul bill," and approved it on December 3. The bill provided larger average reductions for all income classes under $75,000 than the Reagan proposal did. It also retained or expanded the popular middle-class deductions, including deductions for state and local taxes and employee fringe benefits. To help pay for these benefits, it would raise more taxes from corporations through higher corporate tax rates of 36 percent and substantial cuts in tax preferences for banks, heavy industry manufacturers, natural resource industries, and defense contractors than those proposed in Reagan's proposal.[83] On the House floor, however, the unenthusiastic Representatives almost succeeded in killing the bill on December 11 by 202 to 223 votes. To help win support, the House added to the CWM bill a provision for a 100 percent deduction of state and local taxes, a credit of up to $100 a year in contributions to congressional candidates in each taxpayer's home state, and a number of special tax breaks for selected projects. The House passed the bill on December 17, 1985, by a huge majority of 426 to 99.[84]

Before discussions in the SFC began, panel members of the Senate recommended that the SFC craft a bill that would raise the same amount of revenue as the current law did while retaining a number of tax breaks that had been removed from the House bill.[85] In the face of political reality, Robert Packwood (Republican—Oregon), the chairman of the SFC, released a tax-overhaul plan on March 13, 1986. The Packwood proposal contained individual income tax cuts that equaled those Reagan was hoping for. To accommodate members of the SFC and the Senate, it retained numerous tax advantages for everything from the timber and oil industries to employer-provided fringe benefits.[86] After only three weeks of mark-up sessions, the panel approved a wave of amendments that would basically retain or expand current tax breaks for special interests. By April 18, as a result of a series of defeats on the loophole-closing measures, the reform bill faced a $29 billion loss of revenue and the prospect of a much larger shortfall. In response, Packwood suspended the committee's mark-up.[87]

In a series of closed meetings, SFC members agreed to stop trying to preserve or expand tax benefits enjoyed by their own constituents and supporters. They also agreed to revise all amendments to make the bill revenue neutral again. The revised SFC proposal would reduce the individual tax rate structure to two brackets of 15 percent and 27 percent while increasing the benefits of the EITC. Capital gains would be taxed at the same rate as ordinary income. The top corporate tax rate would be reduced from 46 percent to 33 percent. Furthermore, the proposal would also provide more generous deductions for depreciation while additionally abolishing many tax preferences, including deductions and exemptions for interests on consumer purchases, as well as loans and tax shelter investments.[88] It would yield a $103 billion shift in taxes from individuals to businesses over the next five years, compared to a $144 billion shift provided by the House-passed bill. The revised bill would as a result lead to a $21.2 billion loss of revenue because of the revenue shift. The SFC approved the revised bill on May 7.[89] On June 24, the Senate passed the bill agreed upon almost unanimously (97–3).[90]

The House-Senate conference could no longer enact the tax reform bill that reduced the overall level of tax revenues in the face of massive deficits and the need to cut the budget deficit to comply with the Gramm-Rudman-Hollings law of 1985 (GRH). After a one-month discussion that progressed slowly in the face of loud congressional criticism, the House-Senate conference resolved the differences between each bill—the rate structure, top tax rates, and the restoration or elimination of tax breaks—and agreed on a final version of the bill on August 16. It reduced the individual tax rate to 15 percent and 28 percent, and the top corporate rate from 46 percent to 34 percent. In addition, it restricted state and local taxes bonds and tax shelter investments, and repealed special exclusion for capital gains. Furthermore, the final bill slashed corporate tax preferences, including the deduction of bad debt reserves for banks and the write-offs of oil and gas drillers. In total, the final bill reduced the taxes paid by individuals by $121.7 billion over six years (1986–1991), while increasing corporate taxes by $120.4 billion.[91] On October 22, Reagan signed the final version, as written in the House-Senate conference committee, into law as the Tax Reform Act of 1986.

As Elliot Brownlee concluded, the 1986 Act accomplished the most dramatic reform of the federal tax system since World War II. A bipartisan group of political entrepreneurs had successfully championed an approach to tax reform never previously achieved: broadening the income tax base and creating a more horizontally equitable tax system by eliminating and restricting tax preferences. The 1986 reform also succeeded in increasing capital gains taxes for higher-income taxpayers for the first time since World War II. Many individuals, corporations, and industries lost tax preferences that were greater than their gains from the reduction of the top tax rates. Among businesses, the biggest winners were investment bankers, high-technology industries, service industries, and some multinational firms. Moreover, the 1986 reform took millions of poorer Americans off the tax rolls by increasing personal exemptions, standard deductions, and the EITC.[92]

Giving a tax cut—cutting tax rates while retaining or expanding other tax expenditures—to millions of Americans significantly contributed to the exceptional success of the Reagan administration in 1986. Reagan provided tax reform with the image that it would involve tax reductions beneficial to the public, and in particular to corporations. Reagan and Regan believed in the importance of bringing down marginal tax rates to "sell" the tax reform to taxpayers as it would reduce the burden of almost all taxpayers and promote economic efficiency. As Ronald Pearlman, who served at the Treasury as Assistant Secretary for Tax Policy, explained, "Once the politicians saw this [tax reform proposal] they said, 'Aha! This is the way we're going to sell tax reform. It's a tax reduction for individuals.' "[93] Political entrepreneurs, especially Rostenkowski and Packwood, eventually succeeded in passing each committee's bill in exchange for other tax breaks and bringing down tax rates. This exchange enabled the Reagan administration to achieve the base-broadening tax reform.

What the Treasury and political entrepreneurs assumed when they did the exchange was not finance for the government, but the restriction of the GRH, the revenue-neutral principle, and interest politics. The 1986 act largely sacrificed a progressive rate structure by drastically reducing the tax rates and the number of brackets. This was the result of the attempts of the Treasury and political entrepreneurs to convince the opponents to base-broadening measures they wanted to accomplish. Only on the assumption of the revenue-neutral principle and the GRH could they make this compromise in the face of the largest budget deficit in history. At that time, while attempting to meet the requirement of the GRH and the "revenue-neutrality," they did not consider the tax reform as restoring the financing ability of the federal tax system for federal government programs, such as entitlement programs. The 1986 tax reform not only abandoned the points that Simons, Keynes, and Surrey had emphasized—progressivity and vertical equity;

it left the expenditure-taxation nexus broken. Reagan, the Treasury, and Congress only accomplished the 1986 tax reform by ignoring Simons's suggestion: equitable progressive taxation to finance government programs to ease poverty and inequality.

Concluding Remarks

From the 1964 tax cut to the 1986 tax reform, tax-cutting measures—cutting tax rates and expanding tax preferences—had become strongly influential in the legislative process of federal tax policy. The Kennedy administration had presented its tax reform in the form of a huge tax cut as a way to stimulate the economy. The tax reform proposal in 1978 was also proposed as a tax cut under the banner of "capital formation," while containing measures to restrict tax preferences that benefited upper-income taxpayers and businesses. Nevertheless, Democratic and Republican leaders in Congress favored tax preferences for the higher-income brackets, and it was their approach that prevailed. In the case of the 1986 tax reform, the Treasury and the White House revised Treasury I into Treasury II by incorporating the tax preferences in which they found interest and which members of Congress favored through negotiation. In the legislative process, Rostenkowski and Packwood attempted to convince opponents to each bill by expanding existing tax preferences and reducing tax rates in exchange for shifting the tax burden on corporations. By adjusting benefits and the tax burden among taxpayers through rate cuts and expanding tax expenditures while restricting or eliminating other tax preferences, the Reagan administration succeeded in accomplishing its comprehensive tax reform.

The "revenue-neutrality" of tax reform was another key to accomplishing comprehensive tax reform. In 1963, Kennedy emphasized the tax-cutting aspect of his tax reform proposal to stimulate consumer demand and investment rather than structural reforms to improve the fairness and the equity of the federal tax system horizontally and vertically. As a result, Congress in 1964 abolished most loophole-closing measures in response to the fervent opposition from business, Republicans, and conservative Democrats. Carter similarly recommended his tax reform plan as a tax reduction to stimulate consumer demand and business investment in 1978. In 1986, Reagan, the Treasury, and leaders of two tax-writing committees took for granted the revenue-neutral principle when they discussed each tax reform plan in the face of the most massive federal deficit in history and the GRH. Under the restriction of the principle, Rostenkowski and Packwood succeeded in convincing opponents of the value of loophole-closing measures in Congress by invoking tax justice rooted in horizontal equity in exchange for the economic efficiency that would result from lowering tax rates and expanding the existing tax preferences the opponents favored.

The Reagan administration succeeded in enacting the base-broadening tax reform by ignoring several points that Simons and Surrey had stressed. Tax reformers before the 1964 tax cut had emphasized vertical and horizontal equity and progressivity of the federal income tax system as a way to finance the government and redistribution. The 1964 reform became the first example that tax-cut proponents could advocate that a tax cut or rate cuts would stimulate consumption and investment, and thereby raise more tax revenue. In 1978, Carter also stressed the stimulating effect of tax-cutting measures, while advocating the reduction of tax expenditures which had been used in the early 1970s. However, his attempt failed. In contrast, while ignoring the importance of vertical equity and progressivity, along with the need to raise revenue, the Reagan administration emphasized that their base-broadening reform would boost the economy and horizontal equity. In this way, the Reagan administration succeeded in receiving support from Republicans and Democrats alike by combining rate cuts and base-broadening measures. By achieving the 1986 success, the Reagan administration banished the importance of the effect of tax reform to boost vertical equity, progressivity, and the financing ability of the federal income tax system from the discussion of comprehensive tax reform, while emphasizing the boosting effect of horizontal equity and economic efficiency.

Notes

1. Thorndike, *Their Fair Share.*
2. Brownlee, "Tax Regimes," 37–104.
3. The idea of German Historical School strongly influenced Seligman's fiscal thought. See Mehrotra, *Making the Modern American Fiscal State*, 96–118.
4. Haig, "Concept of Income," 7.
5. Ibid., 27.
6. Simons, *Personal Income Taxation*, v–vii, 205–220.
7. Simons, *Economic Policy*, 57, 65–68.
8. Simons, *Federal Tax Reform*, 4–32.

9. For Surrey's background, see, for example, Eyal-Cohen, "Preventive Tax Policy," 877–880; and Griswold, "A True Public Servant."
10. See, for example, Stanley S. Surrey, "The Relationship of Revenue Administration to Fiscal Policy with reference to Underdevelopment Countries," November 15, 1956, Historical Special Collection (HSC), Harvard Law School Library (HLSL), Stanley S. Surrey Papers (SSSP), Box 35, File No. 26-3: Tax Administration Conference.
11. See, for example, Stanley S. Surrey to Wilbur D. Mills, "Memorandum re General Tax Revision Activities of House Committee on Ways and Means, 1959–1961," December 24, 1958, HSC, HLSL, SSSP, Box 14, File No. 40-5: Hon. Wilbur D. Mills, 1956–1959.
12. Andrews, "A Source of Inspiration," 332.
13. Stanley S. Surrey, "Summary Statement of Stanley S. Surrey for Hearings on Broadening the Tax Base, House Committee on Ways and Means November 16, 1959, The Federal Income Tax Base for Individuals," undated, HSC, HLSL, SSSP, Box 39, File No. 28-1: Ways and Means Committee, 1957–1960.
14. Keynes, *The Collected Writings*, 94–95, 372–373.
15. Keynes, *How to Pay for the War*, 34–51.
16. Lerner, *The Economics*; Hansen, *Fiscal Policy*.
17. As for the tax regime structured during World War II, see Brownlee, "Tax Regimes," 88–96; Jones, "Class Tax to Mass Tax." For details of the federal tax system structured by tax reform programs until 1954, see Joint Economic Committee, *The Federal Revenue System*.
18. See, for example, Cassels, "This Man." For Mills's background and his contribution to federal tax policy, see Zelizer, *Taxing America*.
19. "Program of Panel Discussion in General Revenue Revision, 1959," September 8, 1959, National Archives College Park (NACP), Record Group (RG) 56, Office of Tax Policy: Subject Files (OTPSF), Box 68, File Folder No. 55: Tax Legislative Program for 1959–1960, Mills Subcommittee, 1959–1962.
20. Harvey E. Brazer, born in Montreal, received a BC from McGill University (1943). After World War II, he received an MA (1947) and PhD (1951) at Columbia University. He taught economics at Rutgers (1947–48) and finance at Lehigh (1948–50) and Wayne State universities until 1957, when he joined the faculty of University of Michigan as an associate professor. He served in the Treasury as a deputy assistant secretary and director of the OTA in the Kennedy administration from 1961 to 1963. See Faculty History Project, "Harvey E. Brazer."
21. Stanley S. Surrey, "Preliminary Statement of Tax Reform Program for 1962," April 22, 1961, JFKL, WWHPP, Box 22, File: Tax Cut 4/61-11/61.

22. "Full-employment output" is the notion of output assumed when an economy is at full employment. The CEA defined the criterion of full employment as a 4 percent unemployment rate.
23. The "full-employment budget surplus" is the difference between the balance of the actual budget and of the full-employment budget, which is assumed when an economy is at full employment.
24. Heller, *New Dimensions*, 60, 113.
25. Walter W. Heller to James Tobin and Kermit Gordon, "Eventual Memo to the President on Tax Cuts," February 20, 1961, John F. Kennedy Library (JFKL), Walter W. Heller Personal Papers (WWHPP), Box 21, File: Tax Cut 11/24/60-3/29/61.
26. Schlesinger, Jr., *A Thousand Days*, Chap. 23.
27. Walter W. Heller to John F. Kennedy, "Where We Stand on Budget and Tax Policy Decisions," June 9, 1962, JFKL, WWHPP, Box 22, File: Tax Cut 6/62-7/62.
28. Richard Musgrave, "Fiscal Policy Outlook," June 28, 1962, JFKL, WWHPP, Box 22, File: Tax Cut 6/62-7/62; Gerhard Colm to Walter W. Heller, July 11, 1962, JFKL, WWHPP, Box 22, File: Tax Cut 6/62-7/62; Walter W. Heller to John F. Kennedy, "Business Economists on the Economic Outlook and Tax Policy," July 12, 1962, JFKL, WWHPP, Box 22, File: Tax Cut 6/62-7/62.
29. Arthur M. Schlesinger, Jr. to John F. Kennedy, "Tax Cut," July 17, 1962, JFKL, WWHPP, Box 22, File: Tax Cut 6/62-7/62.
30. C. Douglas Dillon, "The Current Economic Situation and Proposals to Meet it," June 6, 1962, JFKL, WWHPP, Box 22, File: Tax Cut 6/62-7/62. This is a blind report.
31. "Kennedy Bars Tax Cuts Now, Citing Upturn," *The New York Times*, August 14, 1962.
32. Warren Smith to Walter W. Heller, "Financing of a Deficit Resulting from a Tax Cut," August 7, 1962, JFKL, WWHPP, Box 22, File: Tax Cut 8/62.
33. Lee Preston to Walter W. Heller, "Dillon Testimony before Ways and Means Committee," August 7, 1962, JFKL, WWHPP, Box 22, File: Tax Cut 8/62.
34. Robert A. Wallace, "Possible Compromise on Tax Package," November 19, 1962, JFKL, Record of Department of Treasury Microfilm Print Outs, Roll 40, Folder 2 of 2, File: Assistant Secretary of the Treasury (Robert A. Wallace), Troika, September–December 1962.
35. Kennedy, *Public Papers, 1963*, 73–92.
36. Porter, "5 Per Cent Tax Deduction."
37. Stein, *The Fiscal Revolution*, 449–450.
38. Treasury Department, *Annual Report, 1964*, 36. Richard Goode demonstrates the result and effect that the tax reform of 1964 had on the individual income tax system. See Goode, *The Individual Income Tax*, 236.

39. Stein, *The Fiscal Revolution*.
40. Walter W. Heller to Lyndon B. Johnson, "Economic Impact of the Tax Cut," June 2, 1964, JFKL, WWHPP, Box 23, File: Tax 6/63.
41. Heller, *New Dimensions*, 1–13.
42. Buchanan and Wagner, *Democracy in Deficit*, 21–22, 77–105, 156.
43. Wilbur D. Mills, "Remarks before the American Institute of Certified Public Accountants, Washington, D.C.," October 16, 1968, The Hendrix College Archives (HCA), Wilbur D. Mills Papers Collections (WDMPC), Box 644, File 3.
44. "Remarks of the Honorable Henry H. Fowler, Under Secretary of the Treasury, at the Fourteenth Annual Midyear Conference of the Tax Executives Institute, Mayflower Hotel, Washington, DC, Monday, March 2, 1964, 7:30 pm, EST: A Turning Point in Tax Policy," March 3, 1964, NACP, RG 56, OTPSF, Box 69, Folder No. 96: Tax Policy (1964–1965).
45. Gerard M. Brannon was born in Manila, Philippines, on June 28, 1922. He received an AB in 1943 and an MA from Georgetown University. After receiving the MA, he began his career in Washington with the staff of the Joint Committee on Taxation. He received his PhD from Harvard University in 1950. After obtaining his doctorate, he taught economics at the University of Notre Dame before returning to Washington to join the staff of the CWM. Brannon moved to the Treasury in 1963, serving as director of the OTA. He retired from the Treasury in 1972 and returned to Georgetown University as chairman of the Economics Department. See "Gerard M. Brannon," *The Washington Post*, March 5, 2015.
46. Gerard M. Brannon, "Statement of Treasury Policy on Tax Credits," March 30, 1964, NACP, RG 56, OTPSF, Box 69, Folder No. 96: Tax Policy (1964–1965).
47. "Remarks by the Honorable Stanley S. Surrey Assistant Secretary of the Treasury before the Tax Executive Institute Shoreham Hotel, Washington, DC 6:30 pm EST, Sunday, March 7, 1965: The Function of Tax Policy," undated, NACP, RG 56, OTPSF, Box 69, Folder No. 96: Tax Policy, 1964–1965.
48. Treasury Department, "Remarks by the Honorable Stanley S. Surrey, Assistant Secretary of the Treasury at the Financial Analysts Federation Conference, Washington Hilton Hotel, Washington, DC, Tuesday, October 5, 1965, 12:30 pm EDT: The Role of Tax Policy in the Great Society," undated, NACP, RG 56, OTPSF, Box 69, Folder No. 96: Tax Policy, 1964–1965.
49. Mozumi, "Tax Policy."
50. Congressional Quarterly, *Congressional Quarterly Almanac, 1969*, 589.
51. Nixon, "Statement on Signing the Tax Reform Act of 1969."

52. Stein, "The Fiscal Revolution in America, Part II," 201–209.
53. Witte, *The Politics and Development*, 179–198.
54. Birnbaum and Murray, *Showdown*, 15.
55. Department of the Treasury, *Blueprints for Basic Tax Reform*, January 17, 1977.
56. Lawrence Woodworth was born on March 2, 1918, in Loudenville, OH. He received an AB from Ohio Northern University in 1940 and an MS in government from the University of Denver in 1942. From 1942 to 1943, he worked as a tax analyst on local government for the Civic Research Institute in Kansas City, MO. He worked for the Tax Foundation in New York City in 1943–1944, and he became a member of the staff of the Joint Committee on Taxation in 1944. In 1960, he received his PhD in economics and public administration from New York University, and became the chief of staff for the Joint Committee on Internal Revenue Taxation in 1964. Woodworth died on December 7, 1977. See Carter, "Department of the Treasury."
57. Biven, *Jimmy Carter's Economy*, 40–45. Lance's deputy, James McIntyre, later replaced him.
58. Stuart Eizenstat to Richard Hutcheson, "Congressman Ullman's Employment Tax Credit Proposal," January 31, 1977, Folder: 2/5/77 [1], Container 5, Office of the Staff Secretary Files (OSSF), Presidential Files (PF), Jimmy Carter Library (JCL).
59. Mark Siegel to Jimmy Carter, "Ullman's Tax Proposal," January 31, 1977, Folder: 2/5/77 [1], Container 5, OSSF, PF, JCL.
60. Bert Lance to Jimmy Carter, February 10, 1977, Folder: 2/15/77 [1], Box 7, OSSF, PF, JCL.
61. Stuart Eizenstat and Robert Ginsburg to Jimmy Carter, "Secretary Blumenthal's Memorandum Re Organizing for Tax Reform," February 11, 1977, Folder: 1/20/77-5/31/77, Box FI-28, FI 10, WHCF, SFE, JCL.
62. W. Michael Blumenthal to Jimmy Carter, "Possible Tax Reform Program," undated, Folder: 5/19/77 [2], Container 21, OSSF, PF, JCL.
63. US income tax system has long had a problem regarding the tax treatment of corporate income, the so-called double taxation—corporate income can be taxed twice, first by the corporate income tax and again when the income is received by shareholders. Tax scholars, the Treasury, and successive administrations have considered mitigating double taxation by integrating the corporate and individual income tax system, providing tax relief at the individual level for dividends, and capital gains, on which corporate income tax has already been paid. See, for example, Slemrod and Bakija, *Taxing Ourselves*, 270–273.

64. Robert Ginsberg and Stuart Eizenstat to Jimmy Carter, "Tax Reform Meeting," May 16, 1977, Folder: 5/18/77, Container 21, OSSF, PF, JCL.
65. Shimada and Mozumi, "Construction State."
66. Charles Schultze to Jimmy Carter, "Taxes as a Percent of GDP," June 3, 1977, Folder: 6/4/77 [1], Container 24, OSSF, PF, JCL.
67. Jimmy Carter to W. Michael Blumenthal and Lawrence Woodworth, "Tax Reform," June 29, 1977, Folder: 6/29/77, Container 26, OSSF, PF, JCL.
68. W. Michael Blumenthal to Jimmy Carter, "Tax Reform," July 15, 1977, Folder: 7/15/77 [1], Container 31, OSSF, PF, JCL.
69. Biven, *Jimmy Carter's Economy*, 199.
70. Hargrove and Morley, *The President*, 495.
71. Heineman, Jr., and Hessler, *Memorandum for the President*, 259.
72. Hargrove and Morley, *The President*, 495.
73. Congressional Quarterly, Inc., *Congressional Quarterly Almanac, 1978*, 218–226.
74. Birnbaum and Murray, *Showdown*, 16.
75. Between 1980 and 1984, the federal deficit rose from 2.8 percent to 5 percent of GDP, implying that more than half the deficit was there when Carter left office. See Feldstein, "American Economic Policy in the 1980s," 47–48.
76. Brownlee, *Federal Taxation*, 182–190.
77. Darman, *Who's in Control?*, 118–119.
78. Regan, *For the Record*, 196–207.
79. Brownlee, *Federal Taxation*, 196–197
80. Reagan, "Address to the Nation on Tax Reform."
81. Conlan, Wrightson, and Beam, *Taxing Choices*, 86–88.
82. Fessler, "Panel Votes," 2102.
83. Fessler, "Ways and Means," 2484.
84. Fessler, "House Reverses Self," 2705–2711.
85. Fessler, "Search for Senate Tax Plan," 492.
86. Fessler, "Markups to Begin March 19," 591–594.
87. Fessler, "Finance Panel Suspends," 840–842.
88. Shanahan, "Finance Panel OKs," 1007–1013.
89. Shanahan, "'Christmas Presents'," 1377–1379.
90. Shanahan, "Tax Conferees," 1677–1679.
91. Shanahan, "'Congress Expected to OK," 1947–1951.
92. Brownlee, *Federal Taxation*, 204–209.
93. Conlan, Wrightson, and Beam, *Taxing Choices*, 45–80.

References

Andrews, William D. 1984. A Source of Inspiration. *Harvard Law Review* 98 (2): 332–334.

Birnbaum, Jeffrey H., and Alan S. Murray. 1987. *Showdown at Gucci Gulch: Lawmakers, Lobbyists, and the Unlikely Triumph of Tax Reform*. New York: Random House.

Biven, W. Carl. 2002. *Jimmy Carter's Economy: Policy in an Age of Limits*. Chapel Hill, NC: The University of North Carolina Press.

Brownlee, W. Elliot. 1996. Tax Regimes, National Crisis, and State-building in America. In *Funding the Modern American State, 1941–1995: The Rise and Fall of the Era of Easy Finance*, ed. W. Elliot Brownlee, 37–104. New York: The Woodrow Wilson Center Press and Cambridge University Press.

———. 2016. *Federal Taxation in America: A History*. New York: Cambridge University Press.

Buchanan, James M., and Richard E. Wagner. 1977. *Democracy in Deficit: The Political Legacy of Lord Keynes*. New York: Academic Press.

Carter, Jimmy. 1977. Department of the Treasury—Nomination of Laurence N. Woodworth to be an Assistant Secretary. February 17. Gerhard Peters and John T. Woolley. *The American Presidency Project*. www.presidency.ucsb.edu/ws/?pid=6599. Accessed 1 June 2017.

Cassels, Louis. 1956. This Man Shapes Your Tax Bill. *Nation's Business*, March.

Congressional Quarterly. 1970/1979. *Congressional Quarterly Almanac, 1969/1978*. Washington, DC: Congressional Quarterly.

Conlan, Timothy J., Margaret T. Wrightson, and David R. Beam. 1990. *Taxing Choices: The Politics of Tax Reform*. Washington, DC: Congressional Quarterly.

Darman, Richard. 1996. *Who's in Control? Polar Politics and the Sensible Center*. New York: Simon & Schuster.

Eyal-Cohen, Mirit. 2008. Preventive Tax Policy: Chief Justice Roger J. Traynor's Tax Philosophy. *Hastings Law Journal* 59 (4): 877–910.

Faculty History Project. Harvey E. Brazer. www.um2017.org/faculty-history/faculty/harvey-e-brazer. Accessed 26 Dec 2016.

Feldstein, Martin. 1994. American Economic Policy in the 1980s: A Personal View. In *American Economic Policy in the 1980s*, ed. Martin Feldstein, 1–81. Chicago, IL: The University of Chicago Press.

Fessler, Pamela. 1985a. Panel Votes Breaks for Banks, Charitable Gifts. *Congressional Quarterly Weekly Report*, October 19, 2102–2103.

———. 1985b. Ways and Means Finishes Tax Code Overhaul. *Congressional Quarterly Weekly Report*, November 30, 2483–2485.

———. 1985c. House Reverses Self, Passes Major Tax Overhaul. *Congressional Quarterly Weekly Report*, December 21, 2705–2711.

———. 1986a. Finance Markup Completion Target is May 1: Roth Presses New Business Tax, as Reagan Repeats Opposition. *Congressional Quarterly Weekly Report*, January 25, 135–139.

———. 1986b. Search for Senate Tax Plan Proceeds. *Congressional Quarterly Weekly Report*, March 1, 492.

———. 1986c. Markups to Begin March 19: Packwood Draft Cuts Rates, Retains Selected Tax Breaks. *Congressional Quarterly Weekly Report*, March 15, 591–594.

———. 1986d. Finance Panel Suspends Markup of Tax Bill. *Congressional Quarterly Weekly Report*, April 19, 840–842.

Fullerton, Don, Charls E. Walker, and Russell B. Long. 1994. Tax Policy. In *American Economic Policy in the 1980s*, ed. Martin Feldstein, 165–233. Chicago, IL: The University of Chicago Press.

Goode, Richard. 1964. *The Individual Income Tax*. 1st ed. Washington, DC: The Brookings Institution.

Griswold, Erwin N. 1984. A True Public Servant. *Harvard Law Review* 98 (2): 329–331.

Haig, Robert M. 1921. The Concept of Income—Economic and Legal Aspects. In *The Federal Income Tax*, ed. Robert M. Haig, 1–28. New York: Columbia University Press.

Hansen, Alvin H. 1941. *Fiscal Policy and Business Cycles*. New York: W. W. Norton.

Hargrove, Erwin C., and Samuel A. Morley. 1984. *The President and the Council of Economic Advisers: Interviews with CEA Chairmen*. Boulder, CO: Westview Press.

Heineman, Ben W., Jr., and Curtis A. Hessler. 1980. *Memorandum for the President: A Strategic Approach to Domestic Affairs in the 1980s*. New York: Random House.

Heller, Walter W. 1966. *New Dimensions of Political Economy*. New York: W. W. Norton.

Joint Economic Committee. 1961. *The Federal Revenue System: Facts and Problems, 1961*. Washington, DC: US Government Printing Office.

Jones, Carolyn C. 1989. Class Tax to Mass Tax: The Role of Propaganda in the Expansion of the Income Tax during World War II. *Buffalo Law Review* 37 (3): 685–737.

Kaufman, Burton I., and Scott Kaufman. 2006. *The Presidency of James Earl Carter Jr*. 2nd edn., revised. Lawrence, KS: University Press of Kansas.

Kennedy, John F. 1964. *Public Papers of the Presidents of the United States, John F. Kennedy: Containing the Public Messages, Speeches, and Statements of the President, January 20 to November 22, 1963*. Washington, DC: US Government Printing Office.

Keynes, John M. 1940. *How to Pay for the War*. London: Macmillan.

———. 1973. *The Collected Writings of John Maynard Keynes, Volume 7: The General Theory of Employment, Interest and Money*. Cambridge: Cambridge University Press.

Lerner, Abba P. 1947. *The Economics of Control: Principles of Welfare Economics*. New York: Macmillan.

Mehrotra, Ajay K. 2013. *Making the Modern American Fiscal State: Law, Politics, and the Rise of Progressive Taxation, 1877–1929*. New York: Cambridge University Press.

Mozumi, Seiichiro. Tax Policy for Great Society Programs: Tax Expenditure and the Failure of Comprehensive Tax Reform in the United States in 1969. Keio-IES Discussion Paper Series, DP2017-009.

Nixon, Richard M. 1969. Statement on Signing the Tax Reform Act of 1969, December 30. In *The American Presidency Project*, ed. Gerhard Peters and John T. Woolley. www.presidency.ucsb.edu/ws/index.php?pid=2388.

Porter, Frank. 1963. 5 Per Cent Tax Deduction. *The Washington Post, Times Herald*, February 14, A6.

Reagan, Ronald. 1985. Address to the Nation on Tax Reform, May 28. In *The American Presidency Project*, ed. Gerhard Peters and John T. Woolley. www.presidency.ucsb.edu/ws/index.php?pid=38697&st=&st1=. Accessed 26 Dec 2016.

———. 2001. Taxes, October 18, 1977. In *Reagan, In His Own Hand*, ed. Kiron K. Skinner, Annelise Anderson, and Martin Anderson, 274–277. New York: The Free Press.

Regan, Donald T. 1988. *For the Record: From Wall Street to Washington*. San Diego, CA: Harcourt Brace Jovanovich.

Schlesinger, Arthur M., Jr. 1965. *A Thousand Days*. Boston, MA: Houghton Mifflin.

Shanahan, Eileen. 1986a. Finance Panel OKs Radical Tax Overhaul. *Congressional Quarterly Weekly Report*, May 10, 1007–1013.

———. 1986b. 'Christmas Presents' Beginning to Pile Up: Panel's Tax Bill Largely Intact as Senate Nears Final Passage. *Congressional Quarterly Weekly Report*, June 21, 1377–1379.

———. 1986c. Tax Conferees Decide to Tackle Big Issues First. *Congressional Quarterly Weekly Report*, July 26, 1677–1679.

———. 1986d. Congress Expected to OK Tax Overhaul Bill. *Congressional Quarterly Weekly Report*, August 23, 1947–1951.

Shimada, Takaharu, and Seiichiro Mozumi. 2014. Construction State and International Politics: The Relations and Choices of Japan, the United States, and Germany Over 'Locomotive Strategy'. In *Modern History of Japan's Public Finance I (NIHON ZAISEI NO GENDAISHI I)*, ed. Eisaku Ide, 277–299. Tokyo: Yuhikaku (in Japanese).

Simons, Henry C. 1938. *Personal Income Taxation: The Definition of Income as a Problem of Fiscal Policy*. Chicago, IL: The University of Chicago Press.
———. 1948. *Economic Policy for a Free Society*. Chicago, IL: The University of Chicago Press.
———. 1950. *Federal Tax Reform*. Chicago, IL: The University of Chicago Press.
Slemrod, Joel, and Jon Bakija. 2008. *Taxing Ourselves*. 4th ed. Cambridge, MA: The MIT Press.
Stein, Herbert. 1969. *The Fiscal Revolution in America*. Chicago, IL: The University of Chicago Press.
———. 1996. The Fiscal Revolution in America, Part II. In *Funding the Modern American State, 1941–1995: The Rise and Fall of the Era of Easy Finance*, ed. W. Elliot Brownlee, 194–286. New York: Woodrow Wilson Center Press and Cambridge University Press.
Thorndike, Joseph J. 2013. *Their Fair Share: Taxing the Rich in the Age of FDR*. Washington, DC: The Urban Institute Press.
Treasury Department. 1965. *Annual Report of the Secretary of the Treasury on the State of the Finances for the Fiscal Year Ended June 30, 1964*. Washington, DC: Government Printing Office.
Witte, John F. 1985. *The Politics and Development of the Federal Income Tax*. Madison, WI: The University of Wisconsin Press.
Zelizer, Julian E. 1998. *Taxing America: Wilbur D. Mills, Congress and the State, 1945–1975*. New York: Cambridge University Press.

The Rise and Fall of the Industrious State: Why Did Japan's Welfare State Differ from European-Style Models?

Eisaku Ide

Introduction

This study discusses the history of how Japan's welfare state, which is dependent on public works and tax-cutting policy, has been formed. The major goal is to understand how and why that welfare state differed from the West-European style of welfare state.

During the 1950s and 1960s, in developed nations, including those in Western Europe, the expansion of social welfare systems was affected by the social advancement of women and the intensification of labor movements. Consequently, in-kind benefits, including interpersonal social services, have increased along with cash benefits such as public pensions. Meanwhile, in Japan, welfare services have been provided by housewives, local communities, and major enterprises rather than by the government.[1] In addition, Japan's welfare state has been heavily dependent on public

E. Ide (✉)
Keio University, Tokyo, Japan
e-mail: ask_ide@econ.keio.ac.jp

G. Huerlimann et al. (eds.), *Worlds of Taxation*,
Palgrave Studies in the History of Finance,
https://doi.org/10.1007/978-3-319-90263-0_9

investment.[2] While Japan, along with the United States, stood the lowest among the developed nations in the ratio of social services to gross domestic product (GDP), the ratio of public investment to GDP reached 6% at the time of its peak in the 1990s. This figure was between one-and-a-half and two times larger than that in other developed nations. This public investment, which forms the core of the economic policy and the redistribution policy of the Japanese welfare system, took the form of public works projects. Hence, the Japanese-style welfare state has often been referred to as the "Construction State."[3]

As will be discussed later in this chapter, the fact that public works projects played an important role in equalizing income disparity did not necessarily mean that Japan was indifferent to social security issues. In 1961, the government established universal health insurance and a universal public pension scheme, indicating that Japan was not far behind other nations, including those of Western Europe, in terms of its welfare system. Furthermore, in 1973, when the oil crisis occurred, Prime Minister Kakuei Tanaka and his cabinet carried out large-scale improvements in the public pension scheme, introduced indexation, and made medical care for the elderly free. Subsequently, the social security expenditures in the general account of the national budget ballooned.

One of the major problems with the interpretation of the Japanese welfare state as the "Construction State" was that this view neglected significant cuts in personal income taxation during the high economic growth era from 1956 to 1972.[4] During Japan's economic "miracle," large-scale individual income tax cuts were enacted at the same time as the expansion of public works projects. The Prime Minister at the time, Hayato Ikeda, dubbed these the "*Bukka Chosei Genzei* (CPI adjustment tax cuts)" because they were used to restrain the percentage of income going to taxes, which had been surging due to inflation and the progressive income tax. During this period, almost every year the government raised one or more of the major income tax deductions. Meanwhile, wages grew at a rapid pace. This growth, combined with the reduction in income taxes, gave Japan one of the highest saving rates in the world, even among developed countries.[5] In this way, compared with European countries, the fiscal scale of the government became smaller, and the foundation of Japan's welfare state, under which individuals must assume responsibility for child-raising, education, and retirement, had been formed.

This chapter, by shifting from the concept of the "Construction State" to the "Industrious State," will explore more deeply the reasons why Japan took the road to establishing its characteristic welfare state—one that was heavily dependent on public works and tax cuts—and why Japan did not take the road to establishing a West-European style welfare state, which remained a possibility in 1970s. With such questions in mind, this paper will discuss the political rationale of the Japanese system and in the last section consider what limitations are likely to befall such systems.

Industrious State: Its Historical Basis and the Conservative Policy Thoughts of Prime Minister Hayato Ikeda

Customs and attitudes that value "kinro," a Japanese term meaning "industrious labor and hard work," had a major influence on the development of the welfare state in Japan. Such ideas exist in some form in virtually all societies. But after World War II it was a rare nation that formed a welfare state founded on the concept of a strong "work ethic" such as that embodied in the Japanese constitution as a citizen's obligation.

During the eighteenth and nineteenth centuries, the popular ethics of work and thrift took root in Japan.[6] During the Edo period, under the *murauke* system, which was village-based governance and taxation, it was mandatory to pay taxes at the village level rather than individually. That meant that anyone who refused to work or abandoned their fields increased the public tax burden on those who did work, leading directly to instability in clan finances and loss of revenue. It was for this reason that the public ethic involving hard work, thrift, and supporting those in need found broad acceptance among leaders and the medium- and high-income strata of society. At the same time, the *biko-chochiku* (famine stores) system that took root during the eighteenth century required holding stocks of grain as preparation against famines and crop failures. However, economic support for the needy became a huge burden which tormented the medium- and high-income strata in farm villages. Viewed in this context, the ethics associated with the impetus to help others had less to do with a spirit of goodwill than the self-serving interest of economic elites to reduce an economic burden. The subsequent birth of the modern state during the Meiji era prompted the abolition of the *murauke* system and the introduction of a system of individual taxation. At the same time, translations of Western literature stressing the importance of hard work and savings circulated widely. Perhaps most influential was Samuel Smiles' *Self-Help* (1859) which became a best-seller in Japan after its translation in 1871.

During World War II, the "virtue of kinro (industrious labor)" was used as a slogan to mobilize citizens for production.[7] The "*Kinro Shintaisei Kakuritsu Yoko* (Framework for Establishing a New System for Labor)" adopted by the Cabinet in November 1940 held that work was "both the responsibility and the honor of His Majesty's subjects." According to Hakuichi Kachi, a government bureaucrat of the Ministry of Health and Welfare, during the war labor was characterized as a service to the state, an honor, and something that instills happiness rather than a utilitarian, commoditized sense of labor, as in the West.[8]

In the post-war era "kinro" persisted both as a notion suggesting the ideal Japanese and as a written "character" etched into the word "labor." The platform of the Japan Social Democratic Party issued in November 1945 began by noting that "our party is a union of the "kinro-kaiso (working classes)." The platform of the Japan Communist Party, published during the following month, also used the term of "kinro," invoking it repeatedly in short sentences. Subsequently, the Japanese constitution, which went into force in May 1947, set forth in Article 27 the principle that "all people shall have the right and the obligation to work."[9]

The Liberal Democratic Party (LDP), which came to represent the mainstream of post-war politics, was no exception to the post-war embrace of "kinro." In its platform at the time of its formation, the LDP declared its commitment to "the stability and safety of the nation's citizens, and the perfection of the welfare state." The Nobusuke Kishi administration (1957–1960) succeeded in passing legislation for universal health insurance and universal pensions, and the Hayato Ikeda administration (1960–1964) established the framework of the Japanese welfare state. Concerned about the lack of capital formation faced by Japan after the war, Prime Minister Ikeda wrote: "In government finances, companies, and household budgets, there may be a psychology of ignoring waste and not being concerned about it. But one must remember that capital formation, as it turns out, happens as each individual citizen industrious labors and saves."[10]

Two of Ikeda's economic policies received particular emphasis, namely, tax cuts "for the industrious labors" and public works designed to "improve the efficiency of industrious labor and raise productivity." Against the background of punitive taxation imposed during the war, politicians on the left rolled out a vigorous anti-tax campaign after the war.[11] By comparing his tax plans with the self-assessed income tax under which tax evasion had often transpired as a "regular" practice, Ikeda sought the support of workers who felt a heavy tax burden due to tax withholding. He claimed that his tax program would return to workers the fruits of their labor. However, because more than half of the taxes withheld were in urban areas such as Tokyo, Osaka, and Aichi (the area around Nagoya), the income tax cuts would distribute benefits in favor of mid-tier urbanites. Based on the need for political equilibrium, the government then formulated the Comprehensive National Development Plan, which was designed to expand the store of social capital and create opportunities for work.

A popular ethic symbolized by industrious labor and thrift has continued to exert a strong influence on the nature of the welfare state, which was centered on lower taxes and public works. Even after the oil crisis, those dependent on taxes paid by others or on social insurance were considered depraved.[12] As shown in Fig. 1, social insurance that benefitted the

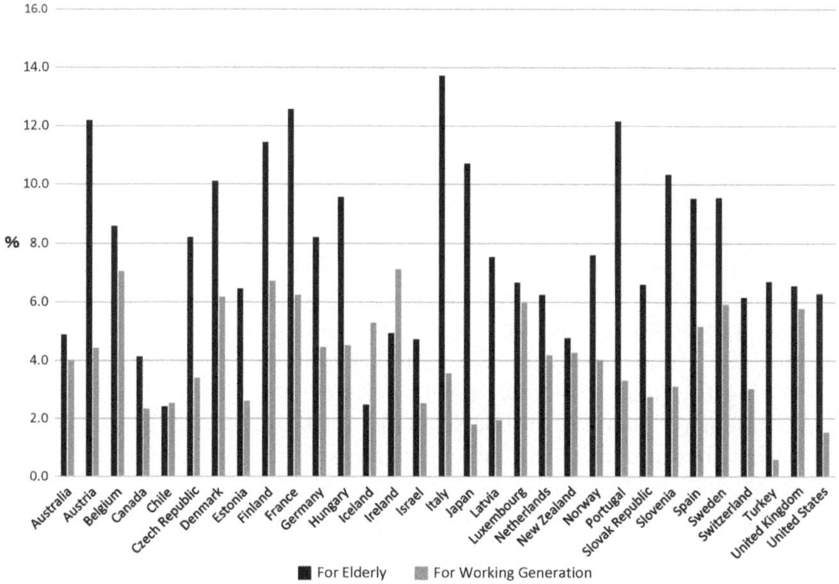

Fig. 1 Social expenditures of GDP for elderly and working generation. Source: OECD stat. "For Elderly" means "Old Age" expenditures in OECD stat of GDP and "For Working Generation" means "Family" "Housing" "Unemployment" "Active Labor Market Programs" of GDP

working generation in Japan remained extremely modest. Japan's saving rate had been going up, supported by the virtues of work and thrift. However, this high savings rate was coupled with limited social insurance. Together, they represented the two-sided coin of "self-responsibility" that characterized the Industrious State.

Necessity of Public Works and Tax Reduction During the High Economic Growth Era

Public works projects and tax reduction under the Industrious State created a profit-sharing system which had broad and powerful social ramifications. Public works projects included the public investments necessary for industrial and social infrastructure, such as roads, ports and harbors, railroads, and water/sewage. In Japan and other nations, public works have been at times mainly instruments of Keynesian full (or high) employment policy. However, Japanese public works have historically played a central role in government policies whose purposes extend far beyond the countercyclical management of demand.

In the aftermath of World War II, public works played a key role in transitioning industry from military to peacetime production in Japan. The industries concentrated in military production during World War II suffered a devastating blow from the end of the war and the ensuing relinquishment of military power. During the period of US occupation of Japan, the government tried to reconvert industry into ordinary peacetime production by increasing the public works-related budget.[13] While heavy industry, which had grown dramatically during wartime, served as a source of economic growth in post-war Japan, the government's public works provided strong support for a fundamental transformation of industrial structure.[14]

During the high economic growth period that followed, the Japanese government restructured public works in ways that would be consistent with the government's economic programs. These programs included, most notably, the Income-Doubling Plan (1960) and the Comprehensive National Development Plan (1962). The former sought to double national income from by 1970 specified well-balanced development among regions. In parallel to this change, agricultural policy also shifted from what had been the stimulation of food production during the occupation era to restructuring agriculture around independent and stable farm managers. Public works projects and technological improvements in the construction and manufacturing industries facilitated increasing productivity of agriculture by increasing arable land and accelerating the mechanization of farming. As can be seen in Fig. 2, this reduced agricultural working hours dramatically. This change made many farmers redundant and, in response, they sought more profitable employment opportunities outside agriculture. This pressure required the government to provide more jobs through public works. Public works increased both agricultural income and the debt required to purchase the modern machinery and equipment, and also increased the surplus of farmers. These increases then generated further strong political demands for public works.[15]

Thus, public works projects became indispensable in bolstering the rural economy, and in providing stronger support for the ruling party, the LDP, from rural communities.[16] The fact that public works laid the ground for the regional economy also meant that the LDP had a lucrative new pork barrel to offer to the rural electorate. At the same time, especially since the first half of the 1970s, the swift growth of public works projects encouraged the establishment of a kind of profit sharing in which Diet members became special-interest lawmakers. These lawmakers, the special interests, and government ministries formed powerful triangles of influence. The ministries involved included not only the Ministry of Construction and the Ministry of Transport, which had primary responsibility for social capital improvement, but also the Ministry of Education, the Ministry of Health, Labor, and Welfare, and the Ministry of Agriculture, Forestry and Fisheries.

Fig. 2 Rate of developed paddy fields and agricultural working hours. Source: http://www.maff.go.jp/j/wpaper/w_maff/h27/h27_h/trend/part1/chap2/attach/xls/c2_2_00-1.xls

The latter ministries received significant budget allocations of their own and exercised influence over the distribution of capital spending. The budgeting of resources for all these ministries, which established pork barrels for the benefit of the local electorate, fueled the "*Zokugiin Seiji* (special-interest politics)" at the core of the Industrious State.[17]

Tax cutting, which out carried out through the 1960s and the first half of the 1970s, was also an important component of the profit-sharing system within the Industrious State. During this period, Prime Minister Ikeda recognized the tax burden of the lower income and middle class as a serious political issue.[18] In 1935, taxpayers with more than 5 million yen in income paid 55.3% of total personal income tax revenue, but in 1956 this number fell dramatically to 3.8% as the burden of the income tax shifted to less wealthy taxpayers.[19] In 1961 Ikeda took the lead in reducing this burden by introducing a spousal deduction and, based on a report of a tax commission in that year, adopted a policy of keeping the ratio of taxes to national income less than 20%.[20]

Rapid economic growth, the progressive income taxation, and a rate of corporate produced a revenue bonanza that offset much of the effect of the tax cuts.[21] Nonetheless, the government was able to use a huge portion of its new fiscal capacity, not for increasing social expenditures but for delivering tax-cut benefits to the lower income and middle class every year.[22] In turn, the increases in lower income and middle-class savings served as a financial resource for vigorous capital investment and indirectly stimulated private-sector-led economic growth. This result was the virtuous circle in which the high growth generated more revenues for further tax cuts and thus prepared the basis for more dynamic growth.

The related accumulation of national savings also enabled the Japanese government to increase its fiscal leverage through its Fiscal Investment and Loan Program (FILP). This program was created so that the government could use public money from national postal savings and public insurance to make low interest loans to public banks, other corporations, and local governments. The government used these funds to encourage public works projects while at the same time avoiding tax increases and increases in the size of the government.[23] Prime Minister Ikeda clearly recognized the interrelationships among tax reduction, the work of FILP, and the promotion of economic growth. He declared "I would improve the way of traditional fiscal investment based on tax revenue, and on the contrary, I would make private capital accumulation increase more through the reduction of tax burden, and utilize this resource to FILP for further private capital accumulation."[24]

The above profit sharing through public works and cuts in personal income taxation proved to be efficient, at least from the government's standpoint. The government reinforced its emphasis on the concept of industrious work and self-responsibility, and the government avoided heavy dependence of the public on transfer expenditures such as cash benefits and the provision of human services.[25] Expanding public works and reducing personal income tax were thus feasible but did not require any drastic revision of the economic system or a great increase in civil servants. Indirectly guaranteeing the income not only of the middle class but also of lower income class through public works and tax cuts enabled workers to afford the purchase of educational or welfare services from the private sector. These policies, along with the universal national pension and medical care systems, assisted in the social integration of lower-income groups.[26] The result was the creation of a workfare state in which the emphasis was on securing income through labor and decreasing the number of people who were dependent on public assistance. At the same time, these policies helped keep government small. In fact, as is shown in Fig. 3, in 2015

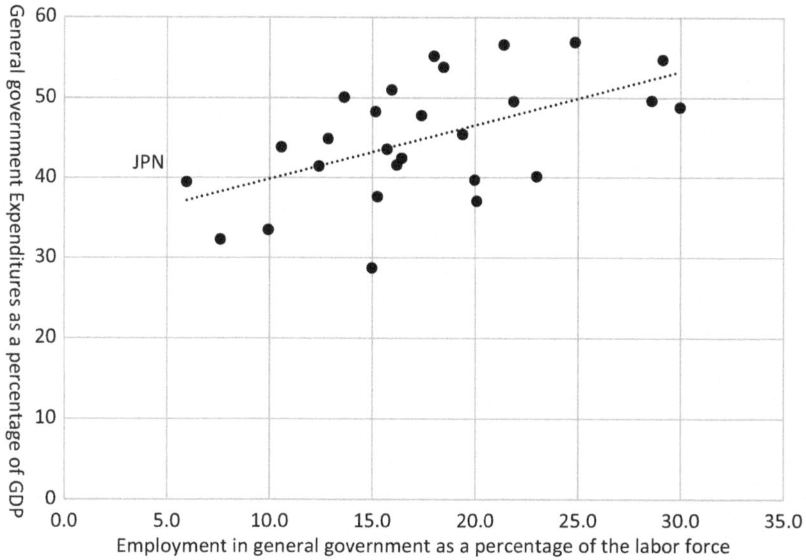

Fig. 3 Government expenditures and employment in government in OECD countries in 2015. Source: https://data.oecd.org/gga/general-government-spending.htm, https://doi.org/10.1787/888933532048

Japan, among all the developed nations, had the smallest government as measured by the ratio of civil servants to all workers and public spending relative to GDP. This was the result of the public works projects, the repeated reductions of personal income taxation, and the underlying legacy of the ideals of virtuous self-help and industrious labor.[27]

The Rise of Progressive Governors and Mayors, and LDP Strategy

During the late 1960s and early 1970s, rapid economic growth prompted an exodus of workers from the countryside into the cities, generating new fiscal demands and boosting the influence of politically progressive groups, which included employees of large companies and public servants.[28] Many municipalities around main metropolitan centers such as Tokyo, Osaka, and Kanagawa became centers of progressive activism, alarming the LDP. Also concerning were threats to sustained growth such as the bankruptcy of Sanyo Special Steel, Ltd. and the management crisis at Yamaichi Securities in 1965. All of this disruption prompted the LDP to push proactive fiscal policies and thereby preempt the calls of progressive groups for the issuance of government bonds.

In the general election held in 1972, the LDP suffered a devastating setback. In 1973, in response to this result, the administration of Kakuei Tanaka (1972–1974) inaugurated several reforms, including the exemption of seniors from medical expenses, the creation of the "50,000 yen pension" scheme, the adoption of pension price-indexing, and the establishment of a system for covering high-cost medical treatments. Because of these reforms, the year 1973 became known as the "*Fukushi Gannen* (first welfare year)." Subsequently, as is shown in Fig. 4, growth in social insurance and other social security-related spending surged, exceeding public works spending in the general account by the middle of the 1970s.

In tandem with this, the LDP vigorously organized groups which backed Diet members within the cities and promoted policies that advanced interests of small and medium enterprises.[29] With regard to the latter strategy, the LDP followed the example of progressive municipalities which had previously adopted a financial system providing unsecured loans. In addition, the LDP implemented tax exemptions favoring small and medium enterprises. The LDP hoped that the tax cuts would weaken support for the progressive commercial and industrial organizations. That

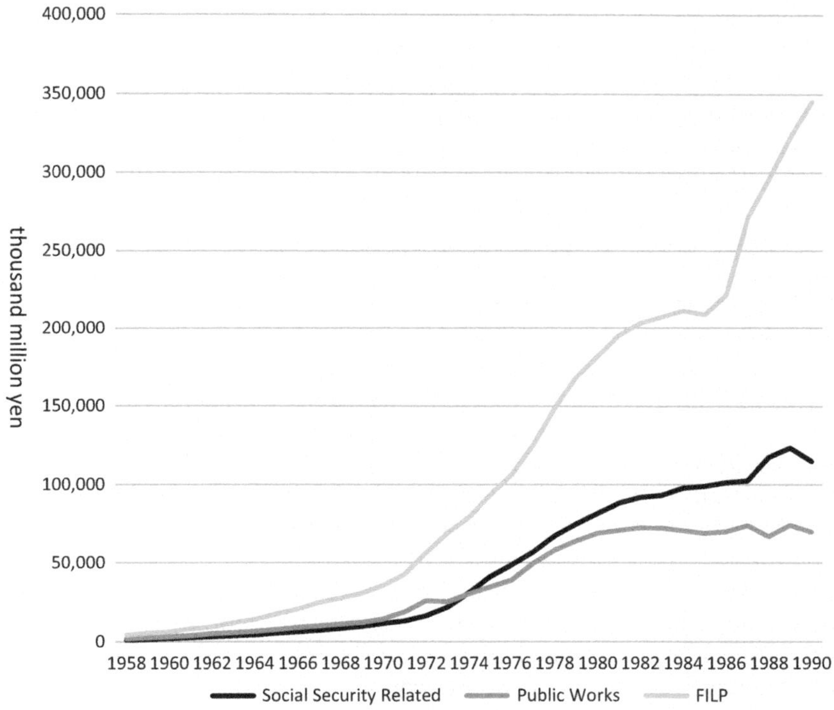

Fig. 4 Spending on public works and social security in general account and FILP. Source: Chapter 5 "Public Finance," Historical Statistics of Japan

is exactly what happened. Support grew for the LDP among the metropolitan middle class and among very small to medium-sized enterprises, and the membership of progressive organizations steadily eroded.

While Tanaka paid close attention to political opposition in urban areas, his increases in social security-related spending for them were modest, and quite the contrary, he did not intend to reduce profit sharing to the rural areas. The LDP's traditional support base was firmly rooted in the rural areas, so his most important objective was to revitalize the economy of the countryside. In the process of accomplishing this, he hoped to reduce the migration of people from the countryside to the cities. This, in turn, would both reduce the costs of meeting the demands of urban progressive groups and slow the growth of progressive cities.[30] As such, Tanaka launched and implemented a full-scale plan to restructure the Japanese archipelago to create jobs in the countryside. He undertook this rural program by relying heavily on FILP. Figure 4 shows the trends in social security spending and public works expenditures for the 1970s. As stated before, within the general account growth in social security spending surpassed that for public works beginning in the "first welfare year." However, public investment through the FILP far surpassed both of these. This growth accelerated after 1973.

Tanaka's response to the progressive threat also included the so-called two trillion-yen tax cut, which he included in the fiscal year (FY) 1974 budget. In actuality, the "two trillion-yen tax cut" was about 1.5 trillion yen, and it was bundled with an increase in corporate taxes. Nonetheless, this was the largest tax cut in post-war history, and it greatly reduced the burden of the income tax on the mid-tier urban population. The tax cut was not just for small business. It is worth noting that Takeo Fukuda, who was the Finance Minister at the time, strongly opposed the cut, citing skyrocketing prices after the oil crisis as his reason. But the major tax agencies wanted the cut and they, as well as Tanaka, overwhelmed Fukuda's opposition.

Tanaka's policies had profound effects. Before the Industrious State took hold in rural Japan, the exodus of surplus labor force was particularly extensive because in rural Japan, especially in areas where monoculture rice farming prevailed, the firstborn typically inherited the house and other assets and continued to work on the farm while the second- and third-born children did not have that right. The creation of jobs via public works projects and the spending by FILP changed the story, allowing children to live close to their farmer parents. The strengthening of agricultural cooperatives by the LDP also contributed to the demand for rural jobs by strengthening agricultural incomes.[31] As a consequence of these rural strategies, population migration into urban centers tapered off during the first half of the 1970s. Meanwhile, the LDP's use of the general account and the LDP's tax cuts expanded welfare for the middle-class living in the cities. LDP leaders gained support among urban workers and small and medium business owners, and the governors and mayors that formed the progressive camp were forced out of the cities.[32]

In late 1976, however, Finance Minister Takeo Fukuda became the Prime Minister (1976–1978) and undertook a significant shift in policy, expanding public works projects and abstaining from tax cuts, despite the fact that economic growth was still sufficient to fund tax cuts. Two reasons account for this shift.

One of the reasons had to do with the complicated system of issuing government bonds in Japan. The major tax reduction by the Tanaka administration, coupled with the second oil crisis, caused a serious revenue fall of general account funds, forcing the government to consider resuming the issue of "deficit-financing bonds."[33] But the framework provided by Public Finance Law prohibited issuing deficit-financing bonds. Consequently, the government had to enact a special law in order to engage in deficit finance. Under this amendment, initiated by Ministry of Finance (MOF), "construction bonds" could be issued to build social infrastructure. MOF believed that these bonds would be effective deficit finance and would prove to be more acceptable to public than deficit-financing bonds. In addition, MOF believed expanded public works would stimulate economic expansion more effectively than further tax cuts.[34]

The second reason was that Japan was coming under heavy external pressure to increase its domestic demand.[35] In January 1977, US President Jimmy Carter, who had been complaining about German and Japanese auto imports, dispatched Walter Mondale, his vice president, to persuade that government to take steps to produce a real GDP growth of 6.7%.[36] The Japanese government adopted this target at the London Summit in 1977, and, at the 1978 Bonn Summit, made a pledge to the international community to achieve 7% real GDP growth. The Fukuda cabinet, which at the time was grappling with a low domestic approval rating, decided that it needed to show "that Fukuda is making the world his stage," in other words, taking on the burden of leading the world economy, in order to revive public support.[37]

Fulfilling this promise proved to be a difficult task because the Japanese economy was still in a slump following the oil crisis[38] The government first stuffed the supplementary budget for FY 1977 with public works spending, and then implemented extraordinarily bold measures in FY 1975. First, public works spending grew by an astounding 34.5% from the previous FY, while FILP grew by 18.7%. Second, the government completely froze non-public works spending (applying the so-called zero ceiling) to secure the resources for the public works budget. Finally, the government took the emergency step of accelerating the collection of some corporate taxes.

Public works projects expanded sharply despite the tattered financial condition of the nation's economy. But this situation could not last long because almost 32% of the revenue for the general account depended on issuance of public debt. In 1978, the administration of Masayoshi Ohira (1978–1980) shifted course and focused on fiscal austerity. In an effort to reign in social security expenditures, Ohira advocated the "*Nihon-gata Fukushi Shakai* (Japanese-style welfare society)," or a welfare society that emphasized individual self-preservation, mutual dependence, and solidarity among families and neighbors. State welfare spending was seen as being unproductive. Ohira and the LDP attempted to win support for slowing the growth in budget expenditures by eliciting attacks on social security from conservative supporters of the party. Ohira explained that his party could shrink government by relying more heavily on the household labor of full-time housewives.[39] Ohira also attempted to introduce a general consumption tax. If he had enacted this tax, Japanese fiscal history and the nature of the Industrious State would have changed fundamentally. But before the 1979 general elections, this initiative succumbed to opposition within the LDP and the strong political pressure from small and medium businesses.[40]

Upon Ohira's sudden death in 1980, Zenko Suzuki assumed the mantle of prime minister (1980–1982) and in 1981 he attempted to set a course for revitalizing the country's finances by implementing a huge increase in corporate taxes.[41] Suzuki wanted to reduce budget deficits but saw no possibility for raising income taxes or adopting a general consumption tax. As one finance bureaucrat reflected, getting the public to accept an increase in the income tax would be extremely difficult in a country that has cut taxes every year between 1961 and 1974.[42] And, Suzuki encountered the same kind of opposition to the consumption tax that the Ohira had faced. But Suzuki's push to increase corporate taxes in 1981, and again the following year, met a cascade of vociferous criticism from the business world, which felt unfairly targeted. Finally, the government was forced to remove the corporate tax from the list of possible candidates for a tax increase.

The Suzuki cabinet, its options for increasing taxes having run out, was left only with the path of "fiscal consolidation without tax increase." This meant mainly cutting spending through administrative reform. The business world supported this so-called *Daini Rincho Rosen* (political line of the second special administrative investigation) in order to lighten the business tax burden. While it cut taxes, in 1980s the Suzuki cabinet increased funding through FILP, which was separate from the general account and subject to less public scrutiny. Despite curbs on public works spending, after Suzuki the government continued to pour money into the countryside through FILP. In fact, in the late 1980s, the government expanded FILP to urban areas where tax cutting had forced a halt in profit sharing. Under the strict budget constraint, Suzuki cabinet abolished the exemption of seniors from medical expenses, and shifted the top policy priority from tax cuts to public works using FILP because it would impose less of a fiscal burden on the general account. Thus, the Industrious State of Japan took root and Japan's fiscal system started down a different path than the so-called European-style welfare state.[43]

The Position of the Ministry of Finance in the 1970s

Under the provisions of the Japanese constitution, the MOF acquired a powerful influence on the budgetary making process. Comparisons of the Industrious State with the welfare systems of other nations should take account of the influence of MOF. This section asks: How did this cabinet agency use its power in response to the economic and political trends during the 1970s?[44]

Shigeya Yoshise, who had been Vice Minister of Finance in 1977 and 1978, described the Japanese political economy of the 1970s as shaped by "a process in which the government and businesses alike ate away at what was accumulated during the era of high economic growth." He emphasized the resulting deficits and described their causes as follows: (1) the inertia of spending during the high growth period; (2) a sharp decline in businesses' capital expenditures; and (3) an overly strong yen in the early 1970s. In the face of these forces, MOF, when it realized that the economy was losing steam, allowed the same level of spending during the 70s as that of the high growth era, as it became clear that the economy was losing steam.[45]

Prime Minister Tanaka began stimulating spending in 1973. Despite showing some resistance, MOF leaders generally fell in line with his policies. Jiro Yoshikuni, vice minister during the FY 1973 budget drafting process, recalled that "Mr. Tanaka had just formulated the plan for remodeling the Japanese archipelago, and the general public was concerned about a decline in exports due to the rise in the yen. These combined to create a tremendous push for an expanded budget ... the MOF was worried as well, but eventually they we were pulled along by the momentum of the budget formulation process."[46] Thus, there were at least some within the ministry who viewed the aggressive spending with unease. However, they deferred to Hideyuki Aizawa, who was close to Tanaka politically and served as chief of the Budget Bureau during his administration before taking over the post of vice minister after Yoshikuni. Aizawa continued to fully support the policy of fiscal stimulation, asserting that "it was not a mistake given the state that the Japanese economy was in at the time."[47]

This was also the period in which the balance of power between the bureaucrats and the politicians began to shift. Fumio Takagi, who was a Director-General of Tax Bureau and had supported Tanaka's "two trillion yen" tax cut, was promoted to vice minister, while Osamu Hashiguchi, who was a Director-General of Budget Bureau and opposed Tanaka's will, was relegated to the National Land Agency.[48] For MOF bureaucrats, ignoring or challenging the prime minister and LDP policy was becoming increasingly difficult.

Nonetheless, fierce criticism within the MOF re-emerged over the surge in public works spending in the 1978 budget. Masataka Okura, who was then Vice Minister, recalled that the critics within the MOF argued that the country's finances would be crippled if the government tried to achieve 7% real GDP growth through spending alone, and declared that such a ridiculous promise should never be made again.[49] But Prime Minister Fukuda and the chief of the Economic Planning Agency Kiichi Miyazawa forced MOF to submit to their judgment. Fukuda and Miyazawa succeeded because of external pressure for expanded domestic demand in Japan, and because both of these men themselves came from MOF and still had powerful influence over promotion decisions.[50]

Throughout the 1970s, MOF had no option except to yield to the LDP's demands for expanded public works projects. However, MOF did not take the situation lying down, as demonstrated by its strongest resistance effort, which was against the imposition of a zero ceiling on administrative spending in the FY 1978 budget. In October 1978, the Budget Bureau director Nagaoka Minoru gathered his underlings and issued the following manifesto: "With no exception, our only option is to thoroughly scrap and rebuild. And if a tax increase is taken away from us, we can only conduct a budget assessment that strips everything to the bone and uses only what's available."[51]

This counterattack by the MOF succeeded in shifting public works spending to FILP, accompanied by deep cuts to all other parts of the budget. Thus, MOF supported the path of limited social security as envisioned by the Ohira administration's "Japanese-style welfare society." MOF's passion for restoring the health of the nation's finances intertwined with several other factors—the radical shift in the balance of power between the MOF and politicians, the political decline of progressive groups seen in the latter half of the 1970s the unique social qualities of welfare provided by the traditional Japanese society sector (and full-time housewives), and the conservative thinking that emphasized these traits. This powerful constellation of factors provided a strong tailwind to the continuation of the Industrious State.

Conclusion: Where Is the Industrious State Headed Now?

The bubble economy from 1987 to 1990 dramatically improved Japan's fiscal condition, and after the collapse of the bubble economy, the government continued with tax cuts and the expansion of public works projects—the two central policy elements of the Industrious State. However, in the 1990s, the Japanese economy proved unable to bounce back again to earlier levels of economic growth, which gave rise to extraordinary levels of government debt.

The dominant factor behind the accumulation of government debt was deflation. During the bubble, Japanese financial institutions had lent to companies against real estate as collateral. When the bubble collapsed, it drove down land prices and decreased the value of real estate. The companies which had borrowed were required to put up additional collateral. Unable to deal with sagging profits, stagnating stock prices, and this need to come up with additional collateral, Japanese firms pulled back on their capital investment and began to pay back their loans. This was the so-called balance sheet recession. For their part, financial institutions, which were required by the Bank for International Settlements to increase their capital ratio in 1993, reduced corporate lending.[52] To raise funds to pay back the banks and to carry out capital investment while making up for the decreased levels of corporate lending, companies began to lower employee wages.

Signs of the shift to deflation had been visible around 1994 and peaked roughly at the time of the Asian Financial Crisis in 1997. But 1998 was still a troubled year in which part-time employment increased, disposable income declined, and the savings rate dropped, all at the same time. The decrease in wages and decline in income levels affected consumption negatively, which in turn led to a drop in corporate profits. Companies were also ravaged by price competition with the developing economies. This further depressed product prices and wages.

With the collapse of the bubble, the government tried to raise growth rates by adopting the classic economic policies of the Industrious State—drastic cuts in personal and corporate income tax cuts and increases in public investment. The Japanese economy, however, bedeviled by the balance sheet recession and caught in a massive deflationary spiral, refused to return to its former growth rate. Even with the repeated income tax cuts and public spending, there was no increase in incomes or in GDP growth rates. Public borrowing was the only thing that went up, and it did so rapidly.[53]

In the first decade of the next century, during the administration of Prime Minister Junichiro Koizumi (2001–2006), the government turned its course sharply toward fiscal austerity. With the support of the booming Chinese economy and growth in exports, the Japanese economy enjoyed its longest period of growth since the war. Unfortunately, the growth in exports was predicated partially on a decline in wages, and wage share and household income continued to decline. Combined with cuts in fiscal outlays, especially public works, and the controlled growth of social insurance, income disparities grew more severe. In the 2009 Lower House election the LDP suffered a stinging defeat, with the Democratic Party of Japan (DPJ), which had run on a manifesto of "fix the income disparities" and "people, not concrete," taking the reins of government.

The DPJ sought to move toward a European-style welfare state by increasing child allowances and eliminating income caps, making public high schools free, and greatly expanding college scholarships. This was a moment when the Industrious State could have changed dramatically, and perhaps become something very different. Unfortunately, the party, which had campaigned on the promise of raising 16.8 trillion yen by cutting wasteful expenditures, failed to raise the money. In order to meet its promises, the party decided to increase the consumption tax, which had not been in its platform. March 2011 saw the tragic occurrence of the Tohoku Earthquake. MOF panicked over the increase in spending and thus developed a plan to use 80% of the revenue from consumption tax raised from 5% to 10% for fiscal consolidation, which was accepted by the government.[54] However, the electorate pushed back strongly against the broken campaign promise and an increase in taxes with few perceived benefits. Consequently, the DPJ fell from power in 2012.

Returning to power, the LDP implemented a set of economic policies known as "Abenomics," taken from the name of Prime Minister Abe Shinzo. These policies set government back on the path of growth supported by massive monetary easing and the expansion of public works—in other words, the path of the Industrious State. Following these policy shifts would come the Olympic Boom, with Tokyo being awarded the 2020 Summer Olympics. During the four-year period from 2013 through 2016 under the Abe administration, however, the average real GDP growth rate was a paltry 1.2% compared with 9.3% during the period of the miracle (FY 1956–1972), 4.3% from the oil crisis to the bubble (FY 1973–1990), and 0.9% for the period after the bursting of the bubble (FY 1991–2016).[55] This record clearly illustrates the limited benefits of returning to the Industrious State.

Comparing 2017 with 1997, household income went down 18%, or 14% if considering only working households, with the number of households making less than 4 million yen making up 47% of the total.[56] Part-time employment nearly doubled from 16.4% in 1985 to 37.5% in 2016. In addition, while the Industrious State continued to follow a fiscal model of preparing for future instability in life by means of self-responsibility and savings, the savings rate dropped to nearly zero in 2017. As a result, because of the lack of the economic ability to save money and take self-responsibility, a large number of the Japanese people are suffering from the inability to meet their needs for child-rearing, education, illness, and retirement by themselves.[57]

The growth in income disparity has become significant. In terms of the GINI coefficient, Japan now has the sixteenth largest value of the 37 countries surveyed. Its ranking in terms of relative poverty is at a high of 6 countries out of 36. Looking at the income disparity between the top and bottom 20%, Japan ranks 11 out of 35 countries.[58] There is no longer any sign of the egalitarian country that Japan was once known to be.

The limits of the Industrious State, in which individuals take responsibility for designing their lives supported by work, thrift, and savings, have become crystal clear. The Abe government has shifted its emphasis over time from "growth" to "distribution," eventually moving to dissolve the Lower House while stating the reason as the implementation of the twice-delayed increase of the consumption tax in 2017 to 10% and a change in how the revenue would be used. Proposing to use a part of the resources from the tax increase to make pre-school education free, the LDP scored a resounding victory in the Lower House election. Has the death knell sounded at last for the Industrious State? Or, will the implementation of a major tax increase be delayed yet again, and the gyrations in fiscal policy repeat themselves? Historically speaking, Japan finds itself in a crucial phase.

Notes

1. Naohiko Jinno, "Nihon-gata Hukushi Kokka Zaisei no Tokushitu;" Mari Osawa, *Gendai Nihon no Seikatu Hosho System.*
2. See, for example, Margarita Estevez-Abe, *Welfare and Capitalism in Postwar Japan*; Gene Park, *Spending without Taxation*; Sven Steinmo, *The Evolution of Modern States.*
3. Eisaku Ide, "Tochi noZentai-zo to shite no Doken Kokka (The Construction State as the Whole Picture of Governance);" Toshiya Kitayama, "Doken Kokka Nihon to Shihonshugi no Shoruikei;" Thomas Feldhoff "Japan's Construction Lobby Activities;" Gavan McCormack, "Growth, Construction, and the Environment."
4. On the tax history of postwar Japan, see W. Elliot Brownlee and Eisaku Ide, "Fiscal Policy in Japan and the United States since 1973: Economic Crises, Taxation, and Weak Tax Consent:" Eisaku Ide and Sven Steinmo, "End of the Strong State? The Evolution of Japanese Tax Policy."
5. See Charles Yuji Horioka, "A Survey of Household Saving Behavior in Japan."
6. About the description of local community in Japan in the eighteenth and nineteenth century, see Yusaku Matsuzawa, *Cho-son Gappei kara Umareta Nihon-Kindai*; *Meiji ChihoJichi Taisei no Kigen*; Yoshihiro Yamasaki, *Kinsei Koki no Ryoshu Shihai to Chiiki Shakai.*
7. Eisaku Ide and Yusaku Matsuzawa, "Bundan Shakai no Gen-hukei."
8. Hakuichi Kachi, "Obei Denrai no Jinsei-kan to Kokoku Kinro-kan no Dokuji-sei."
9. It is important to pay attention to the fact that this "obligation to work" meant, in Japanese, not just the "obligation to work," but the "obligation to industrious labor." "The Constitutional Problems Investigation Committee" (Kenpomondai chosa iinkai), chaired by Joji Matsumoto, made the following significant comment about the obligation to work: "Labor is not something where you work for the state; it is the notion that if you don't work you can't eat and, therefore, we must guarantee the right to survive to those who do work." This statement represented the view, which was common among Japan's educated classes, that the right to survival was something to be guaranteed to those who fulfilled their "obligation to work." See Hirohumi Takase, "Arubeki kokumin no Saiteigi to shiteno Kinro no Gimu."
10. Hayato Ikeda, *Kinko Zaisei*, 164.
11. Ryo Muramatsu, "Senryo-ki Nihon ni okeru Zeimu Gyosei to Shotoku-zei Genzei."
12. In 1953, Prime Minister Masayoshi Ohira said that "It would certainly be heaven if you could eat even if you played, or avoid responsibility for getting

sick, but the vitality of our nation and the feeling of personal responsibility would be lost" (http://www.ohira.or.jp/cd/book/zai/za_08.pdf). In 1978, when he sought to become the governor of the LDP, he said "I want to work toward building a fair and vigorous Japanese-style welfare society, incorporating appropriate levels of public welfare while fully protecting the Japanese spirit of autonomy and self-help, close interpersonal relationships, and the system of mutual help" (http://www.ohira.or.jp/cd/book/zc/zc_48.pdf).

13. Kazuo Shibagaki, "Sangyo Kozo no Henkaku," 86–87.
14. Yoshio Hayashi, Zaisei-ron, 34–35.
15. Kazuhiko Kase, "Nouson to Chiiki no Henbo," 238–239.
16. While around 1950, the percentage of those supporting the conservative party in farming communities was less than 30% on average, by 1970 it had reached approximately 60%. Kent Calder, *Jiminto Choki Seiken no Kenkyu*, 197.
17. Regarding the special-interest politics, see Takashi Inoguchi and Tomoaki Iwai, *Zokugiin no Kenkyu.*
18. Ikeda, *Kinko Zaisei*, 62–63.
19. Hiromitsu Ishi, *Gendai Zeisei Kaikaku-shi*, 198.
20. Ishi, *Gendai Zeisei Kaikaku-shi*, 176.
21. On the history of the corporate income tax reform in postwar Japan, see Satoshi Sekiguchi, "Corporate Income Tax in Postwar Japan and the Shoup Recommendations."
22. Takatsugu Akaishi called this "tax-cutting culture." See Takatsugu Akaishi, "The Shoup Recommendations and Japan's Tax-Cutting Culture."
23. For the details of FILP, see Park, *Spending without Taxation.*
24. Ikeda, *Kinko Zaisei*, 93.
25. Ikeda thought that during the occupation era economic reforms designed to enhance the social welfare had gone too far, given the weakness of the economy. Moreover, he criticized popular attitudes that favored expanding entitlements without requiring personal effort on the part of their recipients. Ikeda, *Kinko Zaisei*, 46.
26. However, workers without a home or a regular job were excluded from the social security system. This triggered frequent riots by workers. Shouji Arakawa, *Yutakasa e no Katsubou*, 143–147.
27. For an important comparison of Japan's welfare state with those of other industrial nations, see the influential work of political scientist Margarita Esétvez-Abe, *Welfare and Capitalism in Postwar Japan.* Her stress on the importance of Japan's "functional equivalent programs" is suggestive, but it is not clear why and how such programs function equivalently. This paper aims to examine such questions by focusing on the historical development of key fiscal institutions.

28. For example, according to "the polling data on urban life" in 1970, city dwellers considered environment disruption and traffic accident problematic and expressed their intention to accept a greater tax burden in order to reduce these problems. See https://survey.gov-online.go.jp/s44/S45-01-44-15.html.
29. Kazushi Tamano, *Tokyo no Local Community*, last chapter; Calder, *Jiminto Choki Seiken no Kenkyu*, 292.
30. Kakuei Tanaka' program, "The Plan for Remodeling the Japanese Archipelago," emphasized the importance of strengthening local economies. Shigezo Hayasaka, *Tanaka Kakuei Kaiso-roku*, Chap. 3.
31. Kase, "Nouson to Chiiki no Henbo," 233–234, 240–242.
32. On the local progressive movements in the 1960s and 1970s, see Junichi Hasegawa, "The Rise and Fall of the Progressive Governors and Mayors of the Local Governments in Japan;" Naoki Kawakita, "The Establishment of the Kuroda Local Government;" Chuji Sakamoto, "Sengo Nihon ni okeru Chio Jichi Zaisei no Kaiko;" Kurt Steiner, Ellis S. Krauss, and Scott C. Flanagan, *Political Opposition and Local Politics in Japan.*
33. Tax revenue had decreased by 3.9 trillion yen and, in response, in FY 1975 the government created a supplementary budget that included issuance of 2.3 million yen of debt-finance bonds. *Oral records by Michio Takeuchi (October 30, 1979, Ministry of Finance, Policy Research Institute)*, 19. This was the first major increase resurgence of debt-financing bonds since a supplementary budget in FY 1965.
34. Susumu Sato and Hiroshi Miuajima, *Sengo Zeisei-shi*, 283–284. Minoru Nagaoka, who was a Director-General of the Budget Bureau of Ministry of Finance during the 1977–78 budgetary process, noted that excessive investment in plant and equipment shortly before the oil crisis had caused a structural recession and that, at the same time, domestic demand was inadequate. *Oral records by Minoru Nagaoka (December 1, 1983, Ministry of Finance, Policy Research Institute)*, 4–5.
35. W. Carl Biven, *Jimmy Carter's Economy*, Chap. 5; Eisaku Ide, *Keizai no Jidai no Shuen*, Chap. 1.
36. According to the recollections of Hirosuke Dan, the person in charge of this negotiation, Japan was required to turn its trade surplus into a deficit and to expand the import of products. He also mentioned that this requirement bordered on inappropriate interference in Japanese domestic affairs. *Oral records by Hirosuke Dan (February 6, 1980, Ministry of Finance, Policy Research Institute)*, 31–32.
37. Thanks to this public relations strategy, the Fukuda cabinet succeeded in restoring its approval rates. Masaru Mabuchi, *Okura-sho Tousei no Seiji Keizaigaku*, 288–290. It is worth noting the pressures to expand domestic demand and expand public works were not entirely external. Some policymakers were worried about a strong yen and its discouragement of exports.

38. Shortly before Fukuda became Prime Minister, he said he regarded 3% real GDP growth as reasonable. *Oral records by Shigeya Yoshise (July 25, 1980, Ministry of Finance, Policy Research Institute)*, 38.
39. See, for example, Masatsugu Amou, "Nihongata Fukushi Shakai to Kigyou Chusin Shakai no Keisei;" Liberal Democratic Party, *Nihon-gata Hukushi Shakai*; Naomi Maruo, *Nihon-gata Hukushi Shakai.*
40. Junko Kato, *Zeisei Kaikaku to Kanryo-sei*, 129–138; Masaru Mizuno, *Zeisei Kaisei Gojyu-nen*, 242–247.
41. Excluding the occupation period, this was the largest post-war tax increase.
42. Mizuno, Zeisei Kaisei Gojyu-nen, 177–178, 276–278.
43. The reliance of the government on the borrowing of private savings to increase expenditures during the formation of the Japanese-style welfare state had a significant effect in shaping public opinion regarding fiscal policy. The extended practice of building roads and public facilities without increasing taxes conditioned the public to assume that only the reduction of expenditures would suffice to fix the budget deficit.
44. For a discussion of the constitutional basis for MOF's influence, see W. Elliot Brownlee and Eisaku Ide, "Fiscal Policy in Japan and the United States since 1973: Economic Crises, Taxation, and Weak Tax Consent," 67–68.
45. *Oral records by Yoshise*, 33–37.
46. *Oral records by Jiro Yoshikuni*, (*August 22, 1979, Ministry of Finance, Policy Research Institute*), 45.
47. Hiroshi Ando, *Sekinin to Genkai, Jyo-kan*, 132–134.
48. Most of the directors of the Budget Bureau in the post-war period later became Vice Minister of Finance. Only four individuals who had experience as director of the Budget Bureau never became Vice Minister, and three of the four were either ejected from public office altogether or ensnared in corruption scandals. Hashiguchi's misfortune was a rare occurrence within a bureaucracy that operated under strict political discipline. Mabuchi, *Okurasho Tosei no Seiji Keizaigaku*, 257.
49. *Oral records by Masataka Okura, (November 28, 1983, Ministry of Finance, Policy Research Institute)*, 10.
50. Vice Minister of Finance Okura strongly objected to the idea of expanding domestic demand while implementing emergency import measures to improve the current account balance. However, he was told by Miyazawa that "Prime Minister Fukuda and I have told you to do it, so it doesn't matter what you say." Okura felt he had no choice except to follow orders. *Oral records by Okura*, 11.
51. *Oral records by Nagaoka*, 24.
52. The minimum equity ratio, which is calculated as equity divided by total assets, was set at 8% for companies that wished to conduct international

operations. Financial institutions cut back drastically on their corporate lending in order to shrink the denominator, which is total assets.

53. Outstanding public debt as a share of GDP increased from 66.9% in 1990 to 131.5% in 1999 and this reached to 238.1% in 2015. Government Finance Statistics, IMF.
54. This was a two-phase tax increase, with the rate going to 8% in 2014 and 10% in 2015. As described below, the Abe administration, while carrying out the rise to 8%, twice delayed the rise to 10%.
55. The consumption tax increase that went into effect in April 2014 pushed the GDP growth rate for that fiscal year down to −0.3%. However, growth in the previous fiscal year had been 2.6% as people consumed in advance of the tax increase.
56. The percentage of households with an income under 4 million yen in 2017 is about the same as it was during the 1980s.
57. About 30% of households comprising at least two persons and 50% of single-person households responded that they had no savings.
58. See OECD Income Distribution Database.

References

Akaishi, Takatsugu. 2013. The Shoup Recommendations and Japan's Tax-Cutting Culture. In *The Political Economy of Transnational Tax Reform: The Shoup Mission to Japan in Historical Context*, ed. W. Elliot Brownlee, Eisaku Ide, and Yasunori Fukagai, 306–335. New York: Cambridge University Press.

Amou, Masatsugu. 2011. Nihongata Fukushi Shakai to Kigyo Chusin Shakai no Keisei [Formation of Japanese-style Welfare Society and Corporation-centered Society]. In *Kokyo suru Shakai: "Jiritsu to Chouwa" no Seiji Keizaigaku [Creating a Harmonious Society: Political Economy of Social Configuration]*, ed. Eisaku Ide, Toshiko Kikuchi, and Masaki Handa, 149–181. Tokyo: Nakahishiya Shuppan.

Ando, Hiroshi. 1987. *Sekinin to Genkai*, Vol.1 [Responsibility and Limitation]. Tokyo: Kinyu Zaisei Jijyo Kenkyukai.

Arakawa, Shouji. 2009. *Yutakasa heno Katsubo [Thirst for Abundance]*. Tokyo: Shogakkan.

Biven, W. Carl. 2002. *Jimmy Carter's Economy: Policy in An Age of Limits*. Chapel Hill, NC: The University of North Carolina Press.

Brownlee, W. Elliot, and Eisaku Ide. 2017. Fiscal Policy in Japan and the United States Since 1973: Economic Crises, Taxation, and Weak Tax Consent. In *The Political Economy of Public Finance: Taxation, State Spending and Debt Since the 1970s*, ed. Marc Buggeln, Martin Daunton, and Alexander Nützenadel, 57–82. Cambridge: Cambridge University Press.

Calder, Kent E. 1989. *Jiminto Choki Seiken no Kenkyu: Kiki to Hojyo-kin [Crisis and Compensation; Public Policy and Political Stability in Japan, 1949–1986].* Tokyo: Bungei Syunjyu.

Estevez-Abe, Margarita. 2008. *Welfare and Capitalism in Postwar Japan.* New York: Cambridge University Press.

Feldhoff, Thomas. 2002. Japan's Construction Lobby Activities: Systemic Stability and Sustainable Regional Development. *Asien* 84: 34–42.

Hasegawa, Junichi. 2011. Kakushin Jichitai no Sosei to Suitai [The Rise and Fall of the Progressive Governors and Mayors of the Local Governments in Japan]. *Keio Journal of Economics* 104 (3): 483–505.

Hayasaka, Shigezo. 2016. *Tanaka Kakuei Kaiso-roku [Memoir of Kakuei Tanaka].* Tokyo: Shuei-sha.

Hayashi, Yoshio. 1963. *Zaiseiron [Public Finance].* Tokyo: Chikuma Shobo.

Horioka, Charles Yuji. 2007. *A Survey of Household Saving Behavior in Japan.* Discussion Paper No. 684, Institute of Social and Economic Research, Osaka University.

Ide, Eisaku. 2014. Tochi no Zentai-zo to shite no Doken Kokka [The Construction State as the Whole Picture of the Governnance]. In *Nihon Zaisei no Gendai-shi dai Ikkan Doken Kokka no Jidai 1960–1985[Modern History of Japan's Public Finance, Vol.1, Era of Construction State 1960–1985]*, ed. Eisaku Ide, 1–24. Tokyo: Yuhikaku.

———. 2015. *Keizai no Jidai no Shuen [The End of the Ethos of the Marketplace].* Tokyo: Iwanami Shoten.

Ide, Eisaku, and Yusaku Matsuzawa. 2016. Bundan Shakai no Gen-hukei: Kemono no Yo to shote no Nihon [Original Landscape of the Divided Society: Japan as the "World of the Beasts"]. In *Bundan Shakai Nihon: Naze Watashi-tachi ha Hikisakareru noka [Divided Society Japan: Why Are We Divided?]*, ed. Eisaku Ide and Yusaku Matsuzawa, 2–15. Tokyo: Iwanami Shoten.

Ide, Eisaku, and Sven Steinmo. 2009. End of the Strong State? The Evolution of Japanese Tax Policy. In *New Fiscal Sociology: Taxation in Comparative and Historical Perspective*, ed. Isaac Martin, Monica Prasad, and Ajay Mehrotra, 119–137. New York: Cambridge University Press.

Ikeda, Hayato. 1999. *Kinko Zaisei [The Balanced Finance].* Tokyo: Chuo Koron Shin-sha.

Inoguchi, Takashi, and Tomoaki Iwai. 1987. *Zokugiin no Kenkyu [Study on the Special-Interest Legislators].* Tokyo: Nihon Keizai Shinbunsha.

Ishi, Hiromitsu. 2008. *Gendai Zeisei Kaikaku-shi: Shusen kara Bubble Hokai made [Modern History of Tax Reform: From the End of the War to the Collapse of Bubble].* Toyo Keizai Shinpou-sha.

Jinno, Naohiko. 1992. Nihon-gata Hukushi Kokka Zaisei no Tokushitu [Characteristics of Public Finance of Japanese-style Welfare State]. In *Hukushi Kokka Zaisei no Kokusai Hikaku [International Comparison of Public Finance*

of Welfare State], ed. Takehisa Hayashi and Eiichi Kato, 217–238. Tokyo: Tokyo Daigaku Shuppan-kai.
Kachi, Hakuichi. 1944. Obei Denrai no Jinsei-kan to Kokoku Kinro-kan no Dokuji-sei [Life Philosophy from Western Countries and Originality of Attitude toward Japan's Industrious Labor]. *Naigai Roudo Shuho* 589: 3–15.
Kase, Kazutoshi. 2005. Noson to Chiiki no Henbo [Transfiguration in Agricultural Community and Region]. In *Nihonshi Kouza 10: Sengo Nihon-ron [The Course in Japan's History: Postwar Japanology]*, ed. Rekisi-gaku Kenkyu-kai and Nihon-shi Kenkyu-kai, 227–251. Tokyo: Tokyo Daigaku Shuppan-kai.
Kato, Junko. 1997. *Zeisei Kaikaku to Kanryo-sei [Bureaucrats, Politicians and Tax Reform]*. Tokyo: Tokyo Daigaku Shuppan-kai.
Kawakita, Naoki. 2011. Kakushin Jichitai no Seijigaku-teki Kenkyu: Kuroda Kakushin Husei no Tanjyo [The Establishment of the Kuroda Local Government]. *Kokusai Koukyo Seisaku Kenkyu* 16 (1): 195–210.
Kitayama, Toshiya. 2003. Doken Kokka Nihon to Shihon-shugi no Shoruikei [Typology of the Construction State Japan and Capitalism]. *Leviathan* 32: 123–146.
Liberal Democratic Party. 1979. Nihon-gata Hukushi Shakai [Japanese-style Welfare Society]. In *Jiyu Minshu-to Kouhou Iinkai Shuppann-kyoku.*
Mabuchi, Masaru. 1994. *Okurasho Tosei no Seiji Keizaigaku [Political Economy of Treasury Control]*. Tokyo: Chuo Koron-sha.
Maruo, Naomi. 1984. *Nihon-gata Hukushi Shakai [Japanese-style Welfare Society]*. Nihon Houso Shuppan Kyokai.
Matsuzawa, Yusaku. 2009. *Meiji Chiho Jichi Taisei no Kigen: Kinnsei Shakai no Kiki to Seido Henyo [Origin of Local Autonomy Regime: Crisis of the Early Modern Society and Institutional Transformation]*. Tokyo: Tokyo Daigaku Shuppan-kai.
———. 2013. *Cho-son Gappei kara Umareta Nihon-Kindai: Meiji no Keiken [Japan's Modern Times Viewed from the Merger of Towns and Villages: Experiences in Meiji Era]*. Tokyo: Kodan-sha.
McCormack, Gavan. 1995. Growth, Construction, and the Environment: Japan's Construction State. *Japanese Studies Bulletin* 15 (1): 26–35.
Mizuno, Masaru. 2006. *Zeisei Kaisei Gojyunen: Kaiko to Tenbo [Fifty Years of Tax Reform: Retrospect and Vision]*. Tokyo: Okura Zaimu Kyokai.
Muramatsu, Ryo. 2011. Senryo-ki Nihon ni okeru Zeimu Gyosei to Shotoku-zei Genzei: Sengo Genzei Seisaku no Kaishi [Tax Administration and Income Tax Cuts During the American Occupation of Japan: Initiation of the Postwar Tax Cut Policy]. *Keio Journal of Economics* 104 (2): 55–98.
Osawa, Mari. 2007. *Gendai Nihon no Seikatsu Hosho System: Zahyo to Yukue [Livlihood Security System in Modern Japan: Coordinate and Future]*. Tokyo: Iwanami Shoten.
Park, Gene. 2011. *Spending Without Taxation: FILP and the Politics of the Public Finance in Japan*. Stanford, CA: Stanford University Press.

Sakamoto, Chuji. 1999. Sengo Nihon ni okeru Chio Jichi Zaisei no Kaiko:Iwayuru 「Kakushin Jichitai」 no Yakuwari ni tsuite [Retrospect of Finance of Local Autonomy in Postwar Japan: Regarding the 'Progressive Local Government']. *Okayama Daigaku Keizai Gakkai Zasshi* 30 (4): 389–412.

Sato, Susumu, and Hiroshi Miuajima. 1979. *Sengo Zeisei-shi [Tax History in Postwar Japan]*. Tokyo: Zeimu Keiri Kyokai.

Sekiguchi, Satoshi. 2013. Corporate Income Tax in Postwar Japan and the Shoup Recommendations. In *The Political Economy of Transnational Tax Reform: The Shoup Mission to Japan in Historical Context*, ed. W. Elliot Brownlee, Eisaku Ide, and Yasunori Fukagai, 365–396. New York: Cambridge University Press.

Shibagaki, Kazuo. 1975. Sangyo Kozo no Henkaku [Transformation of the Industrial Structure]. In *Sengo Kaikaku 8: Kaikaku go no Nihon Keizai [Reforms in the Postwar Period Vol.8: Japan's Economy after the Reforms]*, ed. Institute of Social Science, 63–107. Tokyo: The University of Tokyo.

Steiner, Kurt, Ellis S. Krauss, and Scott C. Flanagan. 1981. *Political Opposition and Local Politics in Japan*. Princeton, NJ: Princeton University Press.

Steinmo, Sven. 2010. *The Evolution of Modern States: Sweden, Japan and the United States*. Cambridge: Cambridge University Press.

Takase, Hirohumi. 2011. Arubeki kokumin no Saiteigi to shiteno Kinro no Gimu [An Historical Essay on the Obligations in the Constitution of Japan: Redefining the Idealized Standards of the Japanese People]. *Review of Asian and Pacific Studies* 36: 101–119.

Tamano, Kazushi. 2005. *Tokyo no Local Community: Aru Machi no Monogatari [Local Community of Tokyo: A Story of a Certain Town]*. Tokyo: Tokyo Daigaku Shuppankai.

Yamasaki, Yoshihiro. 2007. *Kinsei Koki no Ryoshu Shihai to Chiiki Shakai: "Hyakusho Naritachi" to Chukan-so [Dominance of Lords in the Late Modern and Local Society: "Formation of Farmer Status" and Middle Class]*. Osaka: Seibun-do Shuppan.

A Reverse-Functioning System: Japan's Social Security System and Tax Progression in the Early Twenty-First Century

Mari Osawa

Introduction

The safety net in Japan's social security system is breaking down. Not only do its functions require reinforcement, but the model itself needs to be overhauled. This problem has been recognized by prime minister-appointed panels since 2008. However, the annual reports 'Basic Policies for the Economic and Fiscal Management and Reform' ('Basic Policies 2014'), approved by Shinzo Abe's Cabinet in every June since 2013, consecutively show weak political will to achieve this, as argued later in this chapter. In response, this chapter draws attention to the fact that, more than simply being dysfunctional or deteriorating, Japan's tax and social security schemes are 'reverse-functioning'. That is, contrary to solving the problems they are supposed to be addressing, the systems are making them worse because valuable resources are used inappropriately, and not simply beyond the point of inefficiency, but against their intended

M. Osawa (✉)
Institute of Social Science, University of Tokyo, Tokyo, Japan
e-mail: marosawa@sb4.so-net.ne.jp

G. Huerlimann et al. (eds.), *Worlds of Taxation*,
Palgrave Studies in the History of Finance,
https://doi.org/10.1007/978-3-319-90263-0_10

purposes. The policy implication of this is to radically question the current administration's approach.

The reverse-functioning of Japan's security system was the theme of a book I published in late 2013.[1] Section 'Exclusion and Poverty Effects of Japan's Social Security System' below draws on the main points of this earlier analysis while keeping in mind the situation that had become clear by the end of 2017. Section 'Changes in the Tax and Social Security Burden and Level of Progressivity Over Time' comprehensively examines the features of Japan's tax and social security schemes and progressivity, using data from the Organisation for Economic Cooperation and Development (OECD), which leads to the conclusions in Section 'Conclusion and Outlook'. Section '"A Common Stream" and Abe's "Basic Policies"' briefly reviews the history of how government panels have acknowledged the functions of social security.

'A Common Stream' and Abe's 'Basic Policies'

The problems in Japan's security system—its deteriorating functions and the need to update them—were officially recognized by a prime minister-appointed panel and expressed in a 2008 report by the National Council on Social Security (*Shakaihosho Kokumin Kaigi*), which had been established by the Yasuo Fukuda Cabinet. This continued with the Relief Society Meeting (*Anshin Shakai Jitsugen Kaigi*), established by the Taro Aso Cabinet in 2009, and was brought into sharper focus by the Expert Panel on Social Security Reform, established in autumn 2010 by the Democratic Party of Japan (DPJ) administration.[2]

Acknowledgement of Japan's social security problems was not limited to individual committees. The report of the National Council on Social Security System Reform (*Shakaihosho Seido Kaikaku Kokumin Kaigi*), submitted to Prime Minister Abe in August 2013, stated that since the publication of 2008 report of the National Council on Social Security, 'a common stream [of awareness] has existed that transcends the two changes in administration'.[3] Turning to the direction in which the reforms should go, the same 2013 report called for a shift from 'the 1970s model' to a 'twenty-first century (2025) Japanese model'. According to the report, the 1970s model is a 'livelihood security model' premised on a family composed of a breadwinner husband in regular and lifetime employment, a full-time homemaker wife, and their children. The model seeks to secure a livelihood with 'employment' for the working generation and with 'social security' for the elderly. In contrast, the twenty-first-century model seeks to provide benefits to all generations without anyone falling through the cracks in the system. Instead of 'contribution by age', the cost burden should be shifted to 'contribution by ability to pay'.[4] Why was this thought to be necessary? In the 1970s model, a livelihood was to be secured for the working generation through the male breadwinner's stable employment. At the same time, social security for the elderly was supported by benefits, funded by taxes and social insurance contributions, and services based on care provided domestically by daughters-in-law. According to the National Council's 2013 report, the workings of this model declined with the emergence of changing socioeconomic conditions, namely, the difficulty of intergenerational support due to the rapid ageing of the population, loss of support from families as the number of dual-income households increased, loss of community support due to urbanization and population loss and debasement of the functions of livelihood security provided by companies as a result of economic globalization and sluggish growth.[5] This official interpretation hits the mark. I have called the 1970s model an outdated 'male breadwinner model' and have demanded that it be abandoned since at least the early 2000s.[6] At the same time, it seems important to look into the very functions of Japan's social security system because more than simply degrading or becoming dysfunctional, the country's tax and social security schemes have been reverse-functioning.

In fact, this problem was recognized by the National Council on Social Security in its interim report of June 2008, which focused on an important aspect of the problem. It stated that because the expansion of social insurance to include non-regular workers was not implemented, the division of the labor market and increase in the number of non-regular workers reinforced.[7] This went beyond a simplistic view that the range of beneficiaries covered by the 1970s model narrowed due to changes in the labor market; the system had become dysfunctional. This recognition could have enabled the National Council to realize that the 1970s model[8] is reverse-functioning, because the model itself magnifies such changes, however, the National Council failed to grasp this. An 'amplification' effect was mentioned only in the context of some scholarly discussions of the shortcomings in the social security scheme.[9]

In contrast to this 'common [awareness] stream' described by the National Council in 2013, the Abe Cabinet's 'Basic Policies 2014' is drastically different in tone, even if it is not a policy paper specifically on social security reform. The need for 'strengthening the functions of social security' is mentioned only once, and then simply as a stock phrase.[10] 'Basic Policies 2014' does not even refer to the National Council's 2013 report. Rather, it treats social security reform as simply a 'major expenditure item' to be prioritized and streamlined in its Chap. 3, on the 'Virtuous Cycle of Economic Revitalization and Fiscal Consolidation'.[11]

Nevertheless, this 'Basic Policies 2014', unlike 'Basic policies' in other years, does not ignore the socioeconomic changes, such as Japan's rapidly ageing society and its shrinking population. Under the heading 'Achievements to date of Abenomics and challenges facing the Japanese economy', 'Basic Policies 2014' describes four major issues, one of which reads: 'Overcoming the rapidly declining and ageing population'. The chapter on Abenomics (based on the 'three arrows' of monetary easing, fiscal stimulus and structural reform) celebrates the current government's achievements in real GDP growth, discussed in Section 'Conclusion and Outlook', in ending deflation and creating employment, and in improving wages, examined in Section 'Exclusion and Poverty Effects of Japan's Social Security System'. 'Basic Policies 2014' states that to further advance a growth strategy that 'puts [Japan's] economy on a stable and sustained growth track', the tide of 'Japan's rapidly declining and ageing population' has to be turned. It also announces the need to review 'institutions and systems in all areas' to 'create an environment where people can work, get married, and raise children as they wish and thus change their mindset', and to 'drastically increase resource allocation to support children'.[12] In short, 'Basic Policies 2014' seeks to develop measures to counteract Japan's low birthrate in order to promote economic growth. What is lacking is an awareness that in Japanese society an issue more urgent than the difficulty of getting married or raising children is the growing number of cases where even obtaining and maintaining a livelihood can be hard.[13] This chapter argues that a principal reason for the growing hardships consists in the reverse-functioning of Japan's tax and social security schemes as part of the country's livelihood security system. By the concept of 'livelihood security system' I mean the framework in which laws and governmental policies, such as the tax and social security schemes and labor policies, on the one hand, and private institutions and practices, such as businesses, families and not-for-profit organizations, on the other, cooperate (or fail to do so) to continually meet the basic necessities for life.[14]

Underlining the tax and social security schemes is not to treat its impact as greater than that of changes in individuals' awareness and behaviors or than the impact of the product and labor markets. With global economic competition, governments, businesses and labor unions tend to revolve passively round the effects of the market. On the other hand, even though they are not independent of people's awareness or market conditions, tax and social security schemes are established by the government and so can be revised. If the assumption that the tax and welfare systems are reverse-functioning is true, a cogent policy conclusion should consist in putting this right.

Exclusion and Poverty Effects of Japan's Social Security System

This section describes two major aspects of the reverse-functioning of Japan's livelihood security system. The first is due to its design: the social insurance system is turning into a scheme that excludes individuals and certain groups. The second finding is that income redistribution through the tax and social security schemes exacerbates poverty in a great number of cases.

Why, how and whom does the Japanese social insurance system exclude? Social insurance is designed as an unequal, vertically divided scheme in so far as the social insurance system to which a person subscribes differs depending on whether she or he is an employee, and not self-employed or unemployed. For employees, the system further depends on hours worked and the size of the company. Similar divisions are also found in continental Western Europe. Unequal means that contributions and benefits differ depending on the system to which one subscribes. A well-paid, regular employee in a leading corporation makes a relatively small contribution yet receives generous benefits.[15] The size of a company not only makes a difference to the employee's contributions and benefits but also affects the employer's cost burden. Data from the General Survey on Working Conditions (*Shuro Joken Sogo Chosa*) show labor costs and employer's monthly social security contributions for an 'ordinary worker' by company size, where the bigger the company is in terms of the size of its labor force, the smaller are rates of contribution to their labor costs, though a large company pays a higher absolute amount as fringe benefits because large companies spend more for non-statutory welfare benefits. Social security contributions for an ordinary worker as a percentage of labor costs tend to be smaller for bigger companies because the standard remuneration (cash earnings) from which the insurance premium is deducted has a maximum limit, and wages above this limit, paid mostly in bigger companies, are not subject to premium payments.

Tracking the changes in the average statutory contribution per month from 1998 to 2015 based on five rounds of survey, we see that from 1998 to 2002, despite the insurance premium rate being constant, average cash earnings (nearly equal to standard remuneration) fell by about 40,000 yen, and that the statutory contribution fell by nearly 5000 yen. Then, the insurance premium rate increased, but average cash earnings kept falling until 2015 by 30,000 yen from 2002, for employers' statutory contributions in 2015 rose by only about 825 yen from 1998.[16]

This survey treats almost all part-time workers as 'ordinary workers', and the increase in the number of part-timers as a percentage of the workforce was the major reason of the decline in average incomes in Japan since 1997, more than wage cuts for full-time regular employees.[17] From 2005 to 2015, even though the insurance premium rate rose, the amount of statutory contributions did not increased much. This is the outcome of cash earnings falling, mainly due to the increase in part-time (i.e., less than 30 hours worked a week) employees, for whom employee social insurance does not apply. The system of uneven, vertically divided enrolment acts as an incentive to employers to greatly increase the percentage of part-timers and non-regular employees on their payroll.

Non-regular workers as a percentage of total employees did not rise for both men and women in the latter half of the 2000s. After the collapse of the US investment bank Lehman Brothers, companies terminated the employment contracts of many non-regular workers, and so the rate of non-regular workers fell briefly. However, according to data from the Labor Force Survey, the number of non-regular employees rose for both men and women from 2012 to 2017. This trend was accompanied by a decline in the actual number of regular employees in 2013 and 2014, and a slow increase since then.

Using data from the Ministry of Health, Labor and Welfare's Monthly Labor Survey (Maitsuki Kinro Toukei Chosa), let us track the changes in real monthly wages over time (with the 2010 average indexed at 100) for 'ordinary workers' which include a large number of part-time workers. This index had been falling under the Aso administration (September 2008–September 2009), before Lehman's collapse, but rebounded to almost 100 under the DPJ administration (September 2009–December 2012). Under the Abe administration, however, it fell sharply, and has stagnated at about 95 since summer 2014. This is consistent with the rapid rise in the percentage of non-regular employees and is expected to impact the rate of insured persons in employees' pension.[18]

Employers' tendency to tighten their contributions is more apparent in the Employees' Pension Scheme (Kosei Nenkin Seido) than in Health Insurance (Kenko Hoken Seido: Kenpo). Companies keep their contributions to a minimum not only legally by employing part-time workers, but in many cases illegally by not duly contributing to employees' pensions. It has come to light that, since summer 2008, many businesses have failed to apply employees' pension scheme to their labor force or reduced the classifications of their standard remunerations in order to evade the burden of contributions. In short, the problem of falsifying pension records has been exposed. Companies evading contributions are mostly small enterprises rather than large companies as the burden on small companies is relatively heavy and the fear of bankruptcy due to social insurance premiums is a real concern.

Investigation of the pension problem reveals that social insurance officers more than tacitly approved of these illicit practices, but 'systemically' participated in them in order to avoid driving the companies into bankruptcy due to the burden of social insurance premiums. The officers also participated because evasion reduced the 'denominator' (the insurance premium mandated to be paid), thus raising the rate of 'numerator' (insurance premium actually paid) and producing good performances for their offices.[19] As long as Japan's unequal, vertically divided system stays in place and small companies, which have little room for maneuver, and social insurance officers are pressured to increase the payment rate, illegal practices will continue.

The social insurance system itself is changing into a means of exclusion. This is shown by the change in the percentage of insured workers. Since 1986, when the current system was adopted, the number of insured men in Employees' Pension (Kosei Nenkin) as a percentage of the total number of employees grew overall (with fluctuations) from about 65 percent to a little over 70 percent. In the case of insured women, however, the percentage fell from about 54 percent to just under 50 percent in the early 2000s. Even though that later rose slightly, it did not recover to the level achieved in around 1990.[20] Women form the majority of those who are excluded from employees' social insurance system.

Even if an employee is excluded, he or she can try to maintain their health insurance card and receive an old age pension by paying into the National Health Insurance (*Kokumin Kenko Hoken: Kokuho*), and the National

Pension (*Kokumin Nenkin*) schemes in which he or she is a Category 1 insured person. However, because these schemes impose a flat rate premium (or a portion of a flat rate premium) as they were originally designed for the self-employed and their families, and because employers do not contribute, the burden is heavier on low-income earners.[21] The rate of insurance premium payments to the National Health Insurance scheme thus fell between the early 1990s and 2009, when a major reform was introduced, and the effective rate of insurance premium payments by the Category 1 insured of the National Pension has fallen since the mid-1990s.[22]

In summary, revenue from personal income taxation and corporate taxation has declined since 1990 (although it rose slightly from 2003 to 2008, and again since 2010 due to minor tax reforms) because in addition to slack income growth due to economic stagnation, the tax burden of high-income earners and companies was repeatedly cut.[23] Meanwhile, the social security burden as a percentage of GDP has consistently risen, and approached the total amount of direct tax revenue in 2010. Japan's social security burden as a percentage of GDP reached and surpassed Sweden's level in 2010. However, employers in Sweden pay a greater percentage of social insurance premiums, while employers and employees pay half and half in Japan and Germany. The split between employers and employees is critical, as employers' social insurance burden cannot be shifted entirely to wages. If we consider only employees' social insurance burden, Japan's follows Germany's.

The second aspect of reverse-functioning can be seen in Japan's high poverty rate among OECD members on the one hand, and its low poverty reduction rate through the government's income redistribution on the other.[24] By poverty I mean relative poverty as defined by the OECD, according to which equivalent income that is household income adjusted by the number of household members is less than 50 percent of the median income. The poverty reduction rate is calculated by dividing the difference between the poverty rate at the market income level and the disposable income level by the market income-based poverty rate. It shows the extent to which direct tax and social security contributions and cash benefits from social security reduce poverty.

The meaning of the market income-based poverty rate is threefold. First, although a statistical construct, it indicates the extent to which poverty can be curbed by measures other than state-directed income redistribution, such as privately or publicly provided earning opportunities and remittances. That is, the market income-based poverty rate can serve to measure the effects of the functional equivalents of income redistribution. Second, the rate reflects the impact of in-kind benefits from social security (services) such as health care and childcare/nursing for supporting earning activities. Third, the market income-based poverty rate reflects the nature and size of income redistribution because if people can rely on pensions, unemployment benefits and income compensation during maternity leave, they do not need to earn market income. In this situation, the market income-based poverty rate rises. Esping-Andersen and Myles, therefore, argue that welfare states produce large populations, such as pensioners or people on parental leave, whose market income is zero.[25]

Low disposable income-based poverty is the result of a high poverty reduction rate on an originally high market income-based poverty rate. It should be able to show the extent to which poverty can be avoided without depending on market income (or commodification), thanks to income redistribution. The extent to which poverty can be eradicated without dependence on market income thanks to income redistribution by the government overlaps Esping-Andersen's explanation of the concept of 'decommodification' 'to denote the degree to which social policy makes individuals (and families) independent of the market for income and consumption'.[26] In other words, both market income-based and disposable income-based poverty rates and the poverty reduction rate can serve as an approximation of decommodification.[27]

Around 2012, major OECD countries with a high disposable income-based poverty rate (poverty rate hereafter) in the overall population were the US (17.4 percent), Japan (16.1 percent), Korea (14.6 percent) and Australia (13.8 percent). The rate was also high in Southern Europe. Scandinavia and Central and Eastern Europe, on the other hand, had low disposable income-based poverty rates, ranging from 5 percent to 8 percent. Continental Western European countries such as France and Germany also had low rates, at less than 10 percent.[28]

Countries with relatively low poverty rates tend to have high poverty reduction rates (with the exception of Switzerland). The countries that curb poverty in this way have a high level of social expenditure as a share of GDP. And, as the OECD social expenditure database reveals, the size of Japan's social expenditure was a little above the OECD average in 2012, and for cash benefits it is concentrated in pensions for the elderly and survivors. Scandinavian countries such as Denmark and Sweden, on the other hand, devote a considerable portion (5–8 percent) of their GDP to non-medical social service benefits.[29]

Reviewing the trend in Sweden and Denmark based on OECD.Stat, we see that in both countries non-medical social service benefits as a share of GDP steadily rose from the 1980s. Because cash benefits as a percentage of GDP did not rise, this indicates that the weight of public social expenditure shifted from cash to services. Primary non-medical social services consist of family support (i.e., preschool education, daycare and elderly care) and active labor market measures. These services are investments in the next generation and, at the same time, support the earning activities of the working-age population. In both countries, the market income-based poverty rate fell in the early 2000s compared with 1995, which is consistent with the shift in emphasis to service benefits for social expenditure. Accompanying this, their poverty reduction rates due to income redistribution fell slightly.

Unlike Sweden and Denmark, Japan's market income-based poverty rate was high in 2012, though it was low from the 1980s to the 1990s. In other words, functionally equivalent measures and social service benefits cannot usually substitute for the function of income redistribution, except in Switzerland. Furthermore, because Japan's poverty reduction rate through income redistribution is low, its disposable income-based poverty rate is high. But in the case of the working-age population, poverty reduction rate is not only low, but can even turn negative as Aya Abe shows for households with children.[30] Furthermore, the OECD's 2009 *Employment Outlook* provides highly suggestive data on poverty reduction rates among the working-age population from a gender perspective. For the 28 OECD countries in 2005, the report examined poverty reduction rates of households in which all adults worked and households in which only one of the couple worked. The results reveal that, in Japan, households in which all adult members worked have an astounding poverty reduction rate of minus 7.9 percent.[31] Instead of reducing poverty, income redistribution through taxes and transfers has the opposite effect of increasing the number of poor dual-income households and working single parents.

This result for the mid-2000s is supported by research based on more recent panel data. Kohei Komamura and colleagues' analysis of the Japan Household Panel Survey reveals that, in 2009, non-regular employees and the self-employed (business owners and family workers) are at high risk of falling into poverty despite being employed, and that women's poverty rate was higher than men's because the proportion of regular female employees is much lower than that of male employees. Furthermore, this analysis reveals that, for workers, the relative poverty rate is higher at the disposable income level than at the market income level. This negative effect is the result of the social insurance burden.[32] In the following section, the interplay between the social security and the tax systems that produce this double effect of exclusion and poverty increase are critically examined.

Changes in the Tax and Social Security Burden and Level of Progressivity Over Time

What, then, characterizes Japan's tax and social security schemes, and how have they changed in recent years? As Komamura and colleagues' analysis demonstrates, the negative state of the poverty reduction rate calls for an examination of the burden of contributing to the tax and social security systems.

In the *Taxing Wages* column in OECD.Stat, the amounts and rates of average wages, personal income tax (including local taxes) and the net burden as a result of the tax burden plus employee's social security contributions less social security cash benefits for regular employees[33] in various types of household since 2000 are listed. For the most recent year (currently 2016), it shows the amounts and rates for three household types earning 50–250 percent of the average wage at 1 percent increments. Generally, if the burden from income tax and social security is heavier for high-income earners and social security cash benefits are concentrated among low-income earners, the net burden progressivity is stronger. The OECD's Taxing Wages adopts average-rate progression as a measure to show and examine trends regarding progressivity by family type, including single persons, single parents, one-earner couples and dual-earner couples.[34]

The Net Burden on Single-Parent/Two-Child Households

Figure 1 examines the rates of the net burden of tax and social security on single-parent/two-child households vis-à-vis gross wage income (average burden rate) for several countries, including Japan, from 2000 to 2016. Table 1 shows the breakdown of those rates in 2016. I focus on single-parent households because they generally run a higher risk of falling into poverty than other household types and because among households with a working single parent, the poverty rate in Japan was estimated to be the highest among the OECD nations.[35]

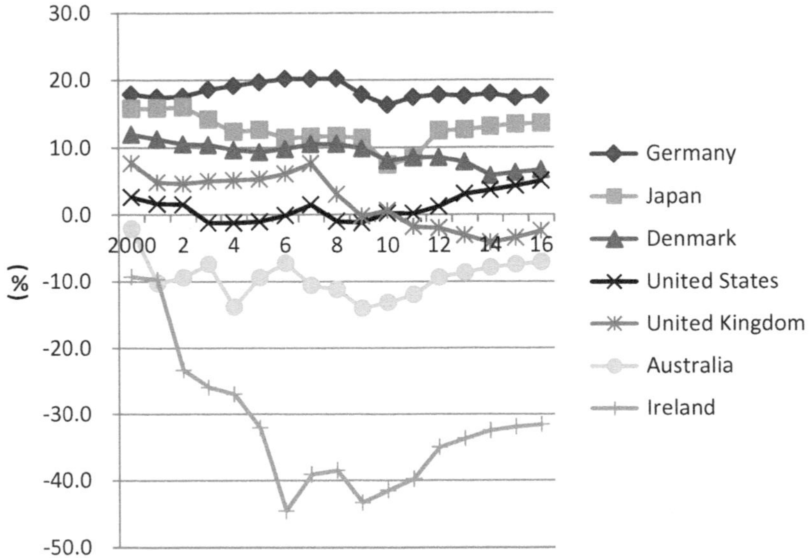

Fig. 1 Net burden of single parents with two children, 2000–2016. Source: OECD.Stat taxing wages data. Notes: Net burden refers to income tax plus the employer's contribution to social insurance premiums minus social security cash benefits. This figure shows the ratio (percent) of net burden to gross wage income set at 67 percent of average wage

In time series data of Taxing Wages, the gross wage income of single parents is set at 67 percent of the average wage. This in Japan in 2016 was considerably high at 3,424,103 yen.[36] What we learn from Fig. 1 is that Japan is at the higher end when it comes to the rate of net burden on single parents. With the exception of 2010 and 2011, it was in excess of 10 percent, and at 13.5 percent in 2016 ranked seventh highest among the 34 OECD member states. By contrast, as Figs. 2 and 3 suggest, Japan's net burden for other households such as couples is on the low side.

Returning to Fig. 1 and Table 1, in Ireland, Australia, the UK and the US, the net burden is sometimes negative, particularly in the case of Ireland, because the burden is exceeded due to social security cash benefits or tax deductions with benefits and so on. Third, there was a clear drop in the net burden rate, even in Japan, from 11.3 percent in 2009 to 7.4 percent in 2010, with Japan ranking 14th among the 34 OECD member states. For single parents from 2009 to 2010, there was no decline in the

Table 1 Net burden on single-parent/two-child households, 2016

	Tax allowance / credits (c = refundable)*	*Income tax (a)*	*Social security contributions employees (b) (and employers)*	*Cash transfers from general government c*	*Net burden (a + b–c)*
Germany	a < c*	−2.8%	20.4% (19.3%)		17.6%
Japan		6.2%	14.4% (15.1%)	7.1%	13.5%
Korea	c < a	0.0%	8.4% (10.4%)		8.4%
Denmark	a < c	32.3%	0% (1.2%)	25.6%	6.6%
US	c* < a	−2.6%	7.7% (8.8%)		5.0%
UK	c* < a	−3.2%	8.1% (9.2%)	7.3%	−2.4%
Australia	c* only	18.8%	0% (6.0%)	25.9%	−7.1%
Ireland	c only	2.5%	4.0% (10.8%)	38.0%	−31.5%

Source: OECD *Taxing Wages 2017*: Part III data

Note: Percent of net burden to gross wage income set at 67 percent of average gross wage. Tax allowance for dependent children under 15 was abolished in 2011 in Japan

income tax levied, and the social security burden grew, while cash benefits for children increased from 120,000 yen in 2009 to 312,000 yen in 2010.[37] Thus, the clear drop in the net burden rate from 2009 to 2010 is undoubtedly the impact of child allowance, which was introduced by the DPJ administration.

Owing to the demands of the Liberal Democratic Party (LDP) and Komeito, who were in opposition but comprised the majority in the Upper House, from FY2012 child allowance was cut (294,000 yen in 2011, 240,000 yen from 2012), and the tax exemption of 760,000 yen for a child under the age of 16 was abolished (from national taxes from January 2011, from local taxes from June 2012).[38] In one sweep, the burden increased to 12.7 percent in 2012, a rate higher than Sweden's (not shown in Fig. 1).[39]

Next, we examine changes in net burden rates for two-child households in Japan and Denmark (Fig. 2). Compared to average wages, the household income of a single-parent/two-child household is set at 67 percent as mentioned earlier, for a single-earner couple/two-child household 100 percent, and for a dual-earner/two-child household 100 percent for the one of the couple, and for the other 33 percent (dual-earner A) or 67 percent (dual-earner B).

Of interest in Fig. 2 is that it is clear that the vertical distance between each of the four curves is narrower in Japan than in Denmark. This means that even with different family sizes and numbers of earners, the differences

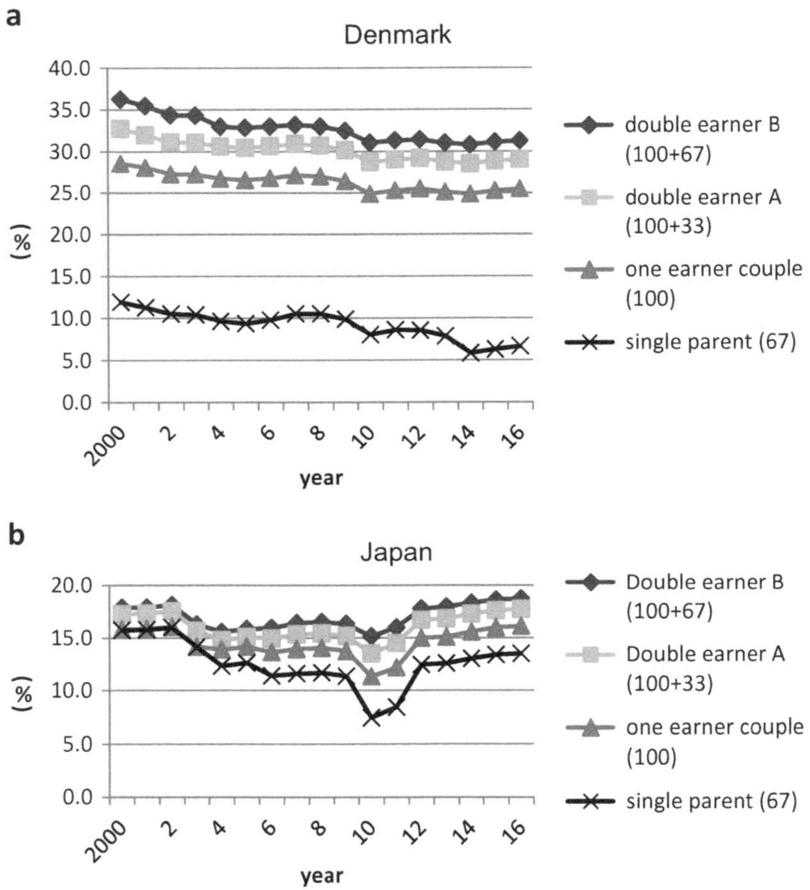

Fig. 2 Trends of net burden rates for two-child household, in Japan and Denmark, 2000–2016. Source: OECD.Stat Taxing wages data. Note: Vertical axis: Ratio of net burden to gross wage income

between the net burden rates of these households, whose average incomes are 33 percent apart, are small. Second, while the net burden rate is decreasing in Denmark, the vertical distance between each curve is maintained. In Japan, the vertical distance between each curve slowly widened during the first decade of the twenty-first century, followed by a clear drop in the net burden from 2009 to 2010. Here, the smaller the household income, the bigger the drop, creating greater vertical distances shown in Fig. 2. After this, the burden for low-income earners grew considerably, narrowing these vertical distances.

Recent Progressivity

We now turn to recent progressivity. In general, progressivity is high among the Anglo-Saxon nations but not among those of continental Western Europe and Scandinavia. The Southern European countries, Japan and South Korea are in the group showing the weakest progressivity among the OECD nations in terms of the tax and social security systems for each household type.[40]

Figure 3 shows the ratios for net burden to gross wage income in 2016. Gross wage income shown as a ratio to average wages is used as the horizontal axis to create a graph of the average burden per income level and show local progressivity through the trends in and among the various income levels. Households with two children in Japan, Germany, Ireland and Denmark are divided into those with single parents and one-earner married couples to show the net burden on gross wage income for 50–250 percent of the average wage. The grade of the curve shows local progressivity (average burden rate progressivity). The width scale of the vertical as well as horizontal axes is even and does not exaggerate the gradients for any specific country.

What can be gathered from this is that Japan's curve is extremely gentle, showing weak progressivity, while in the other three countries there is strong progressivity (a steep gradient) until income approaches average wages. This steep gradient is not due to taxation alone, but also to the effect of social security cash benefits. Second, in Ireland, the net burden (receipt in the case of low-income earners) for both single parents and one-earner married couples is almost equal up to the average wage level, and in Denmark, the net burden for single parents is significantly lower than for one-earner married couples throughout the income range.

Third, in Japan and Germany, the net burden on single parents is heavier than one-earner married couples throughout the income range. In the case of Germany this is because of the availability of tax-splitting by which the couple's incomes are combined then halved, and income tax is levied on each amount. In Japan's case, this is through a spousal deduction applied to both national and local taxes.[41] Under both the Japanese and German systems, a non-earning wife is regarded as reducing the husband's

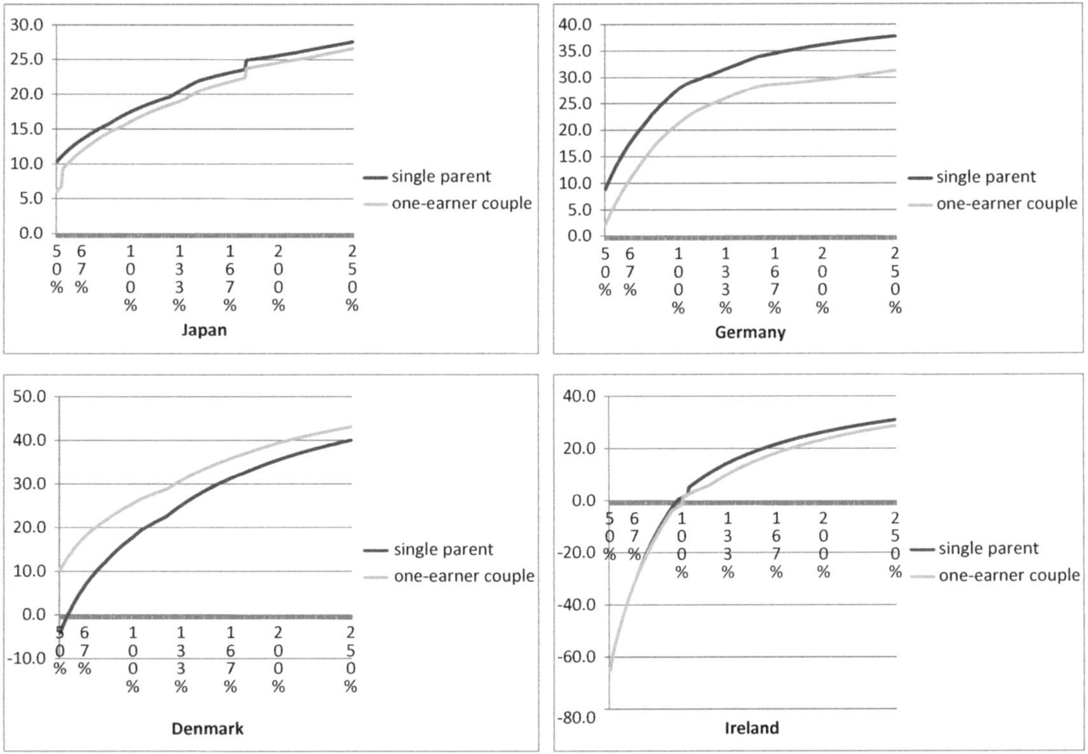

Fig. 3 2016 Net burden rates for two-child (single parent, one-earner couple) households. Source: OECD.Stat: Taxing wages data. Note: Vertical axis: Ratio of net burden to gross wage income. Horizontal axis: Gross wage income in percent of average wage

tax-paying capacity, and her reduction of expenses through housework and childcare (attributed wages) is not recognized. Compared to Ireland and Denmark, the systems in Germany and Japan are favorable to male breadwinners (households with full-time homemakers).

Conclusion and Outlook

As touched on in Section 'Changes in the Tax and Social Security Burden and Level of Progressivity Over Time', the Anglo-Saxon countries have progressive tax and social security schemes in general but, with the exception of Ireland, their poverty reduction rates have been low. As a result, poverty rates among the total population on the disposable income level for these countries are not low (and high in the US). This is arguably related to the fact that their social expenditure is low (Ireland is not an exception here).

While progressivity in Scandinavia and continental Western Europe, including France, is not high, these countries have high poverty reduction rates thanks to high levels of social expenditure, and their poverty rates are generally low. Of these countries, Scandinavian countries such as Denmark and Sweden tend to attach more weight to services such as preschool provision and active labor market policies. These countries can be said to practice methods of supporting child-raising and employment through policy measures that establish environments conducive to commodifying labor under decent working conditions and preventing poverty, while maintaining decommodification in Esping-Andersen's original sense.

In contrast, the size of Japan's social expenditure was slightly below the OECD average until 2009. The overall progressivity of its tax and social security schemes is found in the lowest group for each type of household. The regressive social security burden is great, and for households with children and households in which all adults are working, income redistribution has an extremely weak effect on reducing poverty. There are patterns where income redistribution is feeble or the poverty reduction rate is negative because limited funds for income redistribution are not efficiently allocated. In these conditions, those who work while having and raising children are penalized by the tax and social security systems. For a society already anxious about its falling population, especially in the workforce, it is reverse-functioning to a grotesque degree.

This chapter suggests not only the causes of reverse-functioning but also evaluates policy methods for eliminating it. In Section 'Changes in the Tax and Social Security Burden and Level of Progressivity Over Time'

I compared the changes in the net burden rate of income taxation and social security contributions less social security cash benefits over time for single-parent households. In the 2000s, cash benefits for children in Japan slowly grew. Thanks to the introduction of child allowance in 2010, the net burden on single parents for income taxation and social security contributions fell to 7.4 percent, and the progressivity of the system increased. As a means of using finite funds for income redistribution, child allowance can be considered to be efficient. The lack of a limit based on the parents' income for this allowance has been criticized by opposition parties such as LDP, Komeito, and the mass media as a 'pork barrel (baramaki)'.[42] However, this has to be examined in light of the changes in the net burden and their progressivity. Due to the shift to new child allowances and the abolition of tax breaks for families with children under 16, the net burden for single-parent households in 2012 rose to 12.7 percent, 4 percent higher than in the previous year, thereby lowering progressivity. According to the Summary Report of the Comprehensive Survey of Living Conditions 2013, released by the Ministry of Health, Labor and Welfare in July 2014, Japan's overall poverty rate in 2012 reached 16.1 percent, the worst level in the country's recent history. Especially of note were the poverty rate among children at 16.3 percent, which exceeded the rate of the whole population for the first time, and the poverty rate of single-parent households at 54.6 percent, which rose nearly 4 percent from the previous survey in 2009.[43] The rapid rise is consistent with trends in single-parent households' net burden and progressivity of tax and social security system examined in this chapter.

Now, even though employment and wages have not improved since Prime Minister Abe assumed office in late December 2012, has the GDP grown, as the administration had trumpeted? According to data from the GDP statistics of the Cabinet Office, growth in real GDP (seasonally adjusted quarter-over-quarter comparison) was off to a quick start during the first quarter after the inauguration of the administration. However, it quickly lost momentum, and the annual real growth rates from 2013 to 2016 were 2 percent, 0.3 percent, 1.4 percent and 0.9 percent, respectively. Quarterly real growth rates in 2017 were 0.7 percent, 0.5 percent, 0.5 percent and 0.1 percent.[44]

Although Abe had decided to implement the consumption tax hike from 5 percent to 8 percent in November 2013 after seemingly strong GDP growth, he had to postpone in November 2014 the second consumption tax hike from 8 percent to 10 percent, originally scheduled to take effect in October 2015, to April 2017, and again to October 2019 (the latter was announced in June 2016). The systematic deterioration of GDP cannot be explained as a result of the consumption tax hike in April 2014. Delaying the second consumption tax hike, therefore, is no guarantee that the economy will improve. Moreover, accompanying this postponement, the budgets since FY 2015 were anything but policies to 'drastically increase resource allocation to support children' as 'Basic Policies 2014' had declared and as has been critically analyzed earlier in this chapter.

What I wish to emphasize with regard to the direction taken by the Abe administration is that reverse-functioning carries the seed of hope if we manage to improve the total effect of the livelihood security system, even before the consumption tax is raised again and the tax and social security burden increases. It is critical that the government takes responsibility for redressing the current trend. If the Abe administration truly seeks to create 'a society where people can work, get married, and raise children as they wish' and sever the intergenerational link to poverty (Cabinet Guidelines to Combat the Poverty of Children 2013), it is critical that it squarely faces the plight of young people and single parents, and begins by removing reverse-functioning from the country's tax and social security scheme.

Notes

1. Osawa, *Livelihood Security*.
2. This panel was chaired by Taro Miyamoto and vice-chaired by Kohei Komamura. I was an ad hoc member.
3. National Council on Social Security System Reform, *Report*, 2. Translation of this and the following quotes from Japanese sources by the author.
4. National Council on Social Security System Reform, *Report*, 7, 9.
5. National Council on Social Security System Reform, *Report*, 7–8.
6. See Osawa, *Social Security*, and Osawa, *Livelihood Security*.
7. National Council on Social Security, *Interim Report*, 5.
8. National Council on Social Security in 2008 did not use the term '1970s model'.
9. Osawa, *Social Security*, 160–161.
10. Cabinet Decision, *Basic Policies 2014*, 23.
11. Cabinet Decision, *Basic Policies 2014*.
12. Cabinet Decision, *Basic Policies 2014*, 5, 10.
13. In *Basic Policies 2014*, the term 'poverty' appears only in 'the poverty of children', and 'the needy' appears in the context of strengthening incentives for becoming self-reliant and finding employment (Cabinet Decision, *Basic Policies 2014*, 9, 26).

14. The basic concept of the livelihood security system was developed in 2005 in Osawa, 'Japan's Livelihood Security System in Reverse Functioning.' The political scientist Taro Miyamoto described welfare politics as 'politics concerning livelihood security' (Miyamoto, *Welfare Politics*, 2–3). The use of the term 'livelihood security model' by the National Council on Social Security System Reform seems to reflect Miyamoto's influence who was one of its members.
15. Osawa, *Social Security*, 48–49.
16. Osawa, *Social Security*: 77–78; Osawa, *Livelihood Security*: 191–192; Ministry of Health, Labor and Welfare. *Press Release (Hodo Happyo)*, 28 February 2017.
17. Osawa, *Social Security*: 136; Osawa, *Livelihood Security*: 298.
18. As a result of the revision of the social security system passed in August 2012, social insurance coverage was expanded to part-time workers from October 2016. This was expected to increase coverage by about 250,000 persons.
19. Osawa, *Social Security*, 151–153; Osawa, *Livelihood Security*, 312–313.
20. Osawa, *Livelihood Security*, 193.
21. Osawa, 'Japan's Postwar Model of Economic Development has Rendered Japanese Society Vulnerable to Crises and Disasters', 28–29; Osawa *Livelihood Security*, 195, 197, 199, 319.
22. Ministry of Health, Labor and Welfare, *Press Release*, 30 June, 2017; Nihon Keizai Shinbun, 30 June 2017.
23. Osawa, *Livelihood Security*, 242–243.
24. Osawa, *Social Security*, 122; Osawa, *Livelihood Security*, 270–273, 375–378, 380.
25. Esping-Andersen and Myles, 'Economic Inequality and the Welfare State', 640.
26. Esping-Andersen, 'Hybrid or Unique?', 182.
27. Even though there are issues with its operationalization, I believe that the concept of decommodification itself is valid.
28. OECD.Stat.
29. OECD, *Update*, 4.
30. Abe, 'Current State of Poverty and its Factors;' Osawa, *Livelihood Security*, 212–214; Abe, *Child Poverty 2*.
31. OECD, Employment Outlook 2009, Figure 3.9.
32. Komamura et al., 'The impact of social transfer on relative poverty rates', 94.
33. The self-employed, unemployed and pensioners are not included; nor does it reflect the situation of employees with short working hours, who are not covered by employees' social insurance schemes.
34. Average-rate progression is one indicator for measuring the progressivity of certain aspects of the burden; it is also known as structural or local progressivity. There is also effective or global progressivity. Local progressivity

is defined according to the following equation with T0 as the tax burden (or tax wedge) for income Y0 and T1 as the tax burden (or tax wedge) for income Y1 (but Y1 > Y0): (T1/Y1–T0/Y0)/(Y1–Y0). If the value is positive, it is progressive, if zero, it is proportional, and if negative, it is regressive (OECD, *Taxing Wages 2013*, 33).

35. OECD, *Employment Outlook 2009*, Figure 3.6; OECD, Family Database, CO2.2.
36. OECD, *Taxing Wages 2017*: 366. Its equivalent disposable income is 1,709,783 yen. According to the 2013 Comprehensive Survey of Living Conditions, the median value for equivalent disposable income (nominal) in 2012 was 2,440,000 yen. Among households with single parents of working age, almost 75 percent had equivalent disposable income of less than 1,700,000 yen (Ministry of Health, Labour and Welfare, *Summary Report*, 18–19).
37. OECD, *Taxing Wages 2010*, 320; OECD, *Taxing Wages 2011*, 374.
38. See Akemi Kita for a detailed comparison of the current and previous child allowances (Kita, 'The child allowance system and gender as the focal point for social policy').
39. OECD, *Taxing Wages 2012*, 370; OECD *Taxing Wages 2013*, 370; OECD *Taxing Wages 2014*, 366.
40. OECD, *Taxing Wages 2013*, Special Feature; OECD *Taxing Wages 2014*, Special Feature.
41. OECD, *Taxing Wages 2017*, Part III.
42. See Fumihiko Yamada, 'Child Allowance: From a Journalist's Perspective'.
43. Ministry of Health, Labor and Welfare, *Summary Report*, 17.
44. Based on the GDP Statistics of the Cabinet Office of Japan at http://www.esri.cao.go.jp/en/sna/data/sokuhou/files/2018/qe181/gdemenuea.html. Accessed on June 3, 2018.

References

In English

Esping-Andersen, Gøsta. 1997. Hybrid or Unique?: The Japanese Welfare State between Europe and America. *Journal of European Social Policy* 7 (3): 179–189.

Esping-Andersen, Gøsta, and John Myles. 2011. Economic Inequality and the Welfare State. In *The Oxford Handbook of Economic Inequality*, ed. Brian Nolan, Wiemer Salverda, and Timothy M. Smeeding, 639–664. Oxford: Oxford University Press.

OECD. 2009. *Employment Outlook, Tackling the Jobs Crisis*, OECD.

———. 2010. *Taxing Wages 2008–2009*, OECD.

———. 2011. *Taxing Wages 2009–2010*, OECD.
———. 2012. *Taxing Wages 2011*, OECD.
———. 2013. *Taxing Wages 2013*, OECD.
———. 2014a. *Taxing Wages 2014*, OECD.
———. 2014b. *Social Expenditure Update*, November.
———. 2015. *Taxing Wages 2013–2014*, OECD.
———. 2016. *Taxing Wages 2014–2015*, OECD.
———. 2017. *Taxing Wages 2015–2016*, OECD.
OECD, Family Database. http://www.oecd.org/els/family/database.htm. Accessed 11 Feb 2018.
Osawa, Mari. 2011. *Social Security in Contemporary Japan, a Comparative Analysis*. London and New York: Routledge/University of Tokyo Series.
———. 2013a. Japan's Postwar Model of Economic Development Has Rendered Japanese Society Vulnerable to Crises and Disasters. *GEMC Journal (Tohoku University Global COE on Gender Equality and Multicultural Conviviality in the Age of Globalization)* 8: 22–40.

In Japanese

Abe, Aya. 2006. Current State of Poverty and Its Factors (*Hinkon no Genjo to sono Yoin*). In *Income Distribution in Japan (Nihon no Sokoku Bunpai)*, ed. Takashi Ohio, Eiji Tajika, and Tetsuo Fukawa, 111–137. Tokyo: Tokyo Daigaku Shuppankai.
———. 2014. *Child Poverty 2 (Kodomo no Hinkon 2)*. Tokyo: Iwanami Shoten.
Cabinet Decision. 2014. Basic Policies for the Economic and Fiscal Management and Reform (Keizai-zaisei Unei to Kaikaku no Kihon Hoshin).
Kita, Akemi. 2014. The Child Allowance System and Gender as the Focal Point for Social Policy (*Shakai Seisaku no kessetsuten to shiteno Jido Teate Seido to Jenda*). *Social Policy (Shakai Seisaku)* 5 (3): 38–61.
Komamura, Kohei, Atsuhiro Yamada, Masahito Shikata, and Soichiro Tanaka. 2010. The Impact of Social Transfer on Relative Poverty Rates (*Shakai Iten ga Sotaiteki Hinkon ni Ataeru Eikyo*). In *The Dynamism of Poverty (Hinkon no Dinamizumu)*, ed. Higuchi, Yoshio, Tamaki Miyauchi, C. R. McKenzie and Panel Data Research Centre at Keio University, 81–101. Tokyo: Keio Gijuku Daigaku Shuppankai.
Ministry of Health. 2017a. Labor and Welfare. *Press Release* (Hodo Happyo), February 28.
———. 2017b. Labor and Welfare. *Press Release* (Hodo Happyo), June 30.
Ministry of Health, Labor and Welfare. *Summary Report of the 2013 Comprehensive Survey of Living Conditions (Heisei 25 nen Kokumin Seikatsu Kiso Chosa no Gaikyo)*. http://www.mhlw.go.jp/toukei/saikin/hw/k-tyosa/k-tyosa13/index.html. Accessed 1 Jan 2017.

Miyamono, Taro. 2008. *Welfare Politics (Fukushi Seiji)*. Tokyo: Yuhikaku.
National Council on Social Security (*Shakaihosho Kokumin Kaigi*). 2008. *Interim Report* (*Chukan Hokoku*).
National Council on Social Security System Reform (*Shakaihosho Seido Kaikaku Kokumin Kaigi*). 2013. *Report of the National Council on Social Security System Reform* (*Shakaihosho Seido Kaikaku Kokumin Kaigi Hokokusho*).
Nihon Keizai Shinbun. 2017, June 30. https://www.nikkei.com/article/DGXLASFS30H2X_Q7A630C1EA4000/. Accessed 11 Feb 2018.
Osawa, Mari. 2005. Japan's Livelihood Security System in Reverse Functioning (*Gyaku- Kino suru Nihon no Seikatsuhosho shisutemu*). *Japanese Journal of International Society for Gender Studies (Kokusai Jenda Gakkaishi)* 3: 35–61.
———. 2013b. *Governance of Livelihood Security (Seikatsuhosho no Gabanansu)*. Tokyo: Yuhikaku.
Yamada, Fumihiko. 2018. Child Allowance: From a Journalist's Perspective. *Monthly Journal of the Economic Policy Institute for Quality Life (Seikatsu Keizai Seisaku)*, 252.

A Fair Case for Tax Relief: Swiss Tax Policy, 1940s to 1960s

Gisela Huerlimann

Despite its position as a politically and militarily neutral country, Switzerland had, like other nations, significantly expanded its tax base during World War II. In 1950, the Swiss tax and welfare policy looked very different than it had only a few decades before. Income and wealth taxes were now levied at all three state levels, by the communes, the cantons, and by the federal state. This multiplicity of tax authorities operated as a willfully complicated entanglement of levying authorities, revenue participation, and subsidies. This enmeshment should prevent a subversion of the federalist division of power on the one hand. On the other hand, direct democracy facilitated abundant veto points against the perpetuation of a mass tax system in times of peace and prosperity. Accordingly, the level of income, wealth—and consumption—taxation became a site of contestation from the late 1940s until the mid-1960s. The following contribution analyzes how the perception of an unfair tax burden and the subsequent call for tax relief transcended party lines, and how this intersected with federalism, welfare policy, and economic wisdom.[1]

G. Huerlimann (✉)
ETH Zurich Institute of History, Zürich, Switzerland
e-mail: huerlimann@history.gess.ethz.ch

G. Huerlimann et al. (eds.), *Worlds of Taxation*,
Palgrave Studies in the History of Finance,
https://doi.org/10.1007/978-3-319-90263-0_11

The Great Expansion: Tax and Welfare Development Since World War I

Since 1948, the same year that the British National Health Service (NHS) had been launched, Swiss residents benefited from a national old age and survivors' insurance plan (AHV). The majority of the then 25 cantons[2] had modern tax systems in place, which by now not only covered assets but also income. Most importantly, the federal state also levied taxes on income, profits, and wealth. At the end of the tumultuous period of wars and crises, the federal state had four new taxes at its disposal, excluding a rather short-lived luxury tax: a tax on income and company earnings, a turnover tax, a withholding tax, and stamp duties.[3] Only a generation and a half earlier, this would have been unthinkable for many. Until 1915, the federal state had been financed primarily through customs duties. Remaining revenues mainly flowed from the postal service and liquor excise as well as from interest payments and fees. Before World War I, left leaning politicians and the occasional liberal had called in vain for the levy of a federal income tax in order to finance social insurance programs. The vast majority of parliamentarians, business leaders, and cantonal representatives objected, insisting, first, on the traditional federal division of powers. Simply put, direct taxes were the purview of the cantons, and indirect taxes those of the federal government. Second, this opposition was fundamentally skeptical of the establishment and expansion of a federal welfare state, arguing against it with federalist, corporatist, and liberal economic arguments. The war brought an end to this political deadlock. Following the example of other states, Switzerland imposed a national war tax and an excess profits tax in 1916–1917.[4] The war tax equated to an income tax with an integrated surtax on assets. As their names suggest, these new taxes were intended as extraordinary and temporary measures.

At the end of the war, Parliament legislated the continuation of the tax to cover debts incurred by defense spending. It remained in force until 1932, when the Great Depression brought new hardships. The war tax was reconceived as a crisis tax and collected from 1934 to 1940. World War II prompted a further continuation of the tax, this time under the name "federal defense tax" and with a tax base that included an ever-expanding circle of the population. Additionally, in 1940 and 1945, the federal state levied a one-time wealth tax, as well as, again, an excess profits tax. Beyond these measures, the federal government also instituted a turnover tax in order to cover its increased expenditures.

The interconnections between federal and cantonal taxation were manifested in the role that the cantons played in levying the "defense tax" (federal income tax) on behalf of the federal state. While the cantons were financially compensated for their cooperation, they also had to open their own tax ledgers to federal scrutiny. In 1943, this led to the introduction of the federal withholding tax on interest income from private assets, which was transferred directly from the banks and other financial service providers to the government. This new tax made the role of the federal government as the dominant regulator and controller obvious as it was intended to root out the problem of tax fraud, which was rampant in many cantons. Next to punishing tax dodging by the means of a deduction at source, the new scheme rewarded honest self-assessment since declaring one's assets on a cantonal tax return would trigger a refund of the withholding tax. Above all, the withholding tax allowed the federal government to tap a new a revenue source and to create a useful indicator for the evaluation of tax evasion levels. From the perspective of the financial industry, the new tax was a lesser evil when compared to possibly more intrusive measures against tax evasion. Similarly, it had accepted stamp duties in 1917.[5]

By 1950, the four new types of tax generated a total of 61 percent of federal fiscal revenues, as shown in Table 1. The remainder flowed mainly from customs revenues (29 percent), duties on tobacco and beer, and the military service exemption tax.[6] The most politically controversial—and most important—taxes, the defense tax and the turnover tax, supplied the treasury with well over half of its receipts. Focusing on the federal level, these two taxes brought in over 70 percent of all tax revenues (Table 1).[7]

Compared with the development of cantonal and municipal tax revenues, federal tax revenues exploded up to the 1950s.[8] The "thunder of world history," which the fiscal sociologist Joseph Schumpeter had discerned in state budgets at the end of World War I, could hardly have been expressed more powerfully.[9] In 1950, federal taxes accounted for more than half of total Swiss tax revenues, compared to just over a quarter in 1915.[10]

At first glance, this situation appears as a complete reversal of federal-cantonal fiscal relations, and thus as an echo of the fiscal displacement and centralization effects identified by Peacock and Wiseman for Great Britain.[11] This displacement must also be understood as part of a politically willed process, which increased the financial entanglements between

Table 1 Relative importance of different federal taxes and tax groups for the Swiss federal treasury, 1950

Type of tax/duty	*Percent of federal tax revenue*	*Percent of federal fiscal revenue (2)*	*Percent of overall federal revenue (3)*
New federal taxes (1)	87	61	30
Income and wealth taxes	37	26	22
Turnover tax	35	25	21
Last two groups together	72	51	43
Customs duties	–	29	24

(1) Defense tax and defense sacrifice (wealth tax), turnover tax, withholding tax, stamp duties

(2) Revenue from taxes, customs duties, the military service exemption tax and from duties on tobacco and beer

(3) (2) plus revenue from federal enterprises, federal assets, charges, fines, income from sales, rent, and so on

Data: Historical Statistics of Switzerland Online (HSSO), Table U.10a: Fiscal and non-fiscal federal revenue, and federal taxes and duties, 1913–1950; Table U.5: Federal Financial Statements and Federal Debt, 1913–1986 (all data in million CHF)

the various levels of government so as to pave the way for new redistribution mechanisms. The cantons were awarded 30 percent of defense tax revenues as a compensation for their cooperation in the levying process as well as for the federal intrusion into the once cantonal domain of direct taxation.[12] In addition, the cantons benefited from a growing share of federal revenue through the receipt of federal subsidies.[13] Besides, the federal social security system added to shifting the welfare burden toward the federal state. As a result of the impressive growth of federal taxes in particular, the overall Swiss tax quota—the share of tax revenue on all government levels in comparison to the gross domestic product—had almost tripled since 1915, amounting to over 13 percent in 1950. By 1960, however, this ratio fell below 13 percent, and over the next ten years, it only marginally increased to nearly 15 percent (see Table 2).

The reasons for this tax growth limitation were, first, the very nature of the political deal on the continuation of the federal income tax, and second, the prevailing understanding of tax justice, which expressed itself in a widespread displeasure with the growing tax burden. In the context of post-war boom and inflation, the perceived unfairness of the effects of fiscal drag became a forceful argument for tax relief.

Table 2 Evolution of Swiss tax quota, 1915–1970

Years	*1915*	*1950*	*1960*	*1970*
Overall tax revenue mCHF	245	3094	5700	16,222
GDP, nominal mCHF	5223	23,192	45,434	111,309
Tax quota in %	*4.7*	*13.3*	*12.5*	*14.6*

Data: Historical Statistics of Switzerland Online (HSSO), Table U.15: Tax revenue of the federal, the cantonal and the communal governments 1900, 1910, 1915, 1920, 1925, and 1930–1989; Table Q.16a: gross domestic product (expenditure approach) in real 1929 prices and nominal, 1890–1948; Q.16b: GDP (expenditure approach) in real 1990 prices and nominal, 1945–2005 (all data in million CHF)

Federal Taxation Creates Abundant Veto Opportunities and a Twofold Social Contract

The new federal taxes were as distinctive to the extraordinary times of war and crisis as were the very procedures that created them. The legal context of the period between 1915 and 1945 was marked by emergency and crisis law and deviated from standard democratic procedure.[14] During World War II, the Federal Parliament awarded special powers to the Federal Council (federal government), allowing it to both legislate and execute their decisions with the necessary funds. In 1949, this emergency regime was finally abolished, thus allowing political parties in Parliament and business interests again to openly argue over the continued existence and size of the federal taxes. Political decision-making returned to the standard peacetime arrangement: Parliament and the government submitted their constitutional amendments and laws to the voters who decided on them in a referendum. For those bills that did not require a mandatory referendum, any party or interest group could collect a sufficient number of signatures to force a referendum vote. Under this system, significant veto points were incorporated into Switzerland's legislative process. Unsuccessful parliamentary factions and/or organized interest groups outside of Parliament orchestrated resistance against rising taxation, through the aforementioned referendal power or through popular initiatives. These participatory procedures of direct democracy generated considerable political pressure, bringing about major parliamentary and governmental concessions.

The defense and the turnover taxes, which had to be transferred from emergency law to the ordinary law of peacetime, were particularly susceptible to such veto opportunities, since their introduction had changed the existing social contract. First, the relationship between the federal state and its citizens had become more immediate through taxation, and second, the new taxes had forced a realignment of the federalist agreement between the cantons and the federal state. At both levels of this "fiscal-social contract"[15]—the state/individual and the federal state/cantonal—the fair distribution of tax burdens, revenues, and adequate compensation for discrepancies needed to be negotiated. Between 1941 and 1948 not only had the rate of the federal income tax risen, but the number of citizens subject to it had also increased by more than half, capturing nearly 30 percent of the resident population.[16] This vertical and horizontal expansion abetted a discourse that denounced the magnitude of the tax burden as inequitable and called for the restoration of justice through tax relief. The political left significantly participated in the fairness-through-tax relief endeavor.

A Sense of (In-)justice: Arguments for Lowering the Tax Burden

As the burden of war shrunk, the burden of taxes and duties became intolerable in the eyes of workers' advocates. With overlapping conflicts created by the defense tax and its impact on cantonal taxes, as well as the regressive turnover tax and the contributions for the social insurance schemes, Social Democrats in various Swiss cantons began to campaign for tax breaks that would benefit low to middle income households. In 1944, the Social Democrats in the canton of Aargau launched a popular initiative to "relieve the tax burden on workers," having failed with a similar proposition in the cantonal parliament. Their proposals, which included an increase of the tax exemption limit as well as other relief measures, would have resulted in the exemption of one-third of all Aargau taxpayers.[17] Social-democratic politician Arthur Schmid justified the initiative by contrasting the theory of progressive taxation with the socially detrimental reality of rising taxes and duties, even for social security. Schmid denounced, for example, the wage replacement scheme for soldiers, which had been introduced in World War II and was based on linear payroll contributions, as a type of "tax collection in its rawest form." The turnover tax was to him, of course, "very crude and unfair." But Schmid, who held a doctorate in law, also expressed reservations about the income tax—traditionally extoled by progressive liberals and by socialists: "The income tax is generally praised as a better and more modern form of tax." In Swiss practice, however, mainly "asset-holders had an interest" in introducing it, as Schmid made clear.[18] His judgment was based on the fact that until the 1930s, many Swiss cantons had predominately taxed assets, instead of earned income.[19] The systemic move toward income taxation extended tax liability to ever-greater swaths of society.

Added to this was the compulsory wage statement, which wage-earning taxpayers were required to enclose with their federal tax returns. The intrusiveness of wage slips engendered an unequal treatment of the salaried class compared to the self-employed, farmers, and freelancers, who had no similar reporting duty and whose self-assessment was not relativized in the same way.[20] In 1945, the canton of Aargau introduced a cantonal wage statement obligation. Arthur Schmid attempted to respond to such tax injustices by tabling a bill in the cantonal parliament, which called for tax relief for the employed. The Aargau government initially downplayed the problem, but by 1948 it was clear that the new law had significantly increased the tax burden on all groups except farmers. Once again, Social Democrats and the unions used popular initiatives to lead the charge for tax reductions, which was eventually successful through a 1949 cantonal tax reform.[21]

In the canton of Zurich, the left also called for tax relief for working-class families and pensioners in the 1940s, arguing for greater tax deductions, an increased exemption limit, and lower tax rates. Christian-Socialist politicians and members of the centrist Independent Party, who represented consumer interests, made similar demands. Liberal politicians with close ties to the business community vociferously opposed such reforms, which would have unburdened around 40 percent of all taxpayers at the expense of the higher income groups, as they argued.[22] The liberals painted the gloomy picture of a disastrous drain of high-income earners and corporations if small- and medium-income tax breaks were funded through an even more progressive tax rate. And they argued that tax revenues, returned as welfare benefits and health expenditures, already benefited precisely those social classes that the left wanted to unburden to exempt.[23] In the 1950s, as the booming economy supplied sparkling state budgets, the call for tax relief grew louder—including from within the liberal camp. Several cantons and cities lowered their taxes, some doing so by means of higher tax deductions, especially for low-income households and those with numerous children.[24]

The Difficult Case for a Peace-Time Federal Income Tax

The call for tax relief would soon spread to the federal level and help to substantiate traditional arguments for curbing federal taxation. The right-wing tax resistance had started with a political bias, as the Federal Finance and Customs Department (the finance ministry) was headed by Social Democrats from 1944 to 1953. But once instilled with the tax relief gospel, the bourgeois tax resisters even continued when one from their own camp became Head of the Department.

Ernst Nobs, a member of the Zurich cantonal government and Zurich's mayor, had undergone a thorough political transformation from his role as a promoter of the Swiss general strike in 1918 to become the first Social Democrat to be elected into the Federal Council in 1943. The executive body of the Swiss federal government was now composed of three liberals (or Free Democrats), two members of the Catholic-Conservative Party, one representative of the Peasants, Artisans and Bourgeois Party,[25] and one Social Democrat. Nobs, who had inherited the Finance and Customs Department from his liberal predecessor, failed in 1950 to bring the wartime tax regulations in line with constitutional provisions. Opposition, especially from conservatives who rejected any continuation of the defense tax, was simply too strong. The task was left to Nob's successor Max Weber, a professor of finance, who was the second Social Democrat to join the Federal Council and to head the finance ministry. In their 1953 bill, Weber and the federal government proposed a marginal tax rate of 15 percent (previously capped at less than 10 percent) for the income tax and the continuation of the built-in federal wealth tax, next to the perpetuation of the turnover tax. Although a parliamentary majority had supported the federal decree, influential business organizations such as the Swiss Bankers Association, the Swiss Federation of Commerce and Industry and the Swiss Association for Small and Medium Enterprises vehemently argued against the allegedly socialist "Lex Weber" in the subsequent referendum vote (Fig. 1).[26]

In December 1953, voters followed their advice and rejected the federal decree. In response, Max Weber resigned from government. In 1954, under the now liberal Head of the Finance and Customs Department Hans Streuli, Parliament approved a transitional arrangement for the legal continuation of the federal income and turnover taxes, until a new federal decree would be designed. This provisional agreement was

Fig. 1 "Barrel without bottom?—Tax bill: No". Postcard for the popular referendum vote on the Federal Decree on the Constitutional Reorganization of the Federal Financial Regime, December 6, 1953, designed by Peter Birkhaeuser, Swiss Social Archives Zurich, F Ka-0001-493

tolerated by business organizations. In return, the government kept its promise to lower the luxury tax.[27] The major parties agreed on a political "ceasefire" which meant that they would allow the liberal finance minister and his experts to prepare a new bill in due course. But if tax cuts guaranteed political success at cantonal level, why not try the same at the federal level?

Popular and Populist: The 1955 Race for Tax Relief

In spring 1955, the tax policy "ceasefire" became fragile. With federal elections approaching and an emerging surplus of 361 million Swiss francs in the federal financial statements, the liberal MP François Perréard, who was also Head of the Geneva Finance Department and a Board of Directors member at Credit Suisse, kicked things off in March 1955.[28] Federal tax revenues were more than sufficient to cover government spending, including an armaments program that was intensified in the context of the Korean War, he argued. Since the strong economy would cause tax revenues to naturally increase, tax relief was legitimate and feasible. Perréard's first proposed measure, the abolition of the supplementary wealth tax to the federal income tax, was a clear nod to the wealthy. Only secondarily did he demand an increase in tax deductions for the benefit of all taxpayers. Less affluent income groups would also benefit from an extended list of goods exempt from the turnover tax.[29] This order of priorities was straightforward, but, from a strategic point of view, somewhat tactless.

A programmatic essay in the leading Swiss business-friendly newspaper *Neue Zürcher Zeitung* (NZZ) demonstrated a more skillful approach.[30] The essay argued that a combination of economic development and currency devaluation had brought about an unjustified "inflation gain" for the state. This was due to a mechanism that the author described as a "self-propelled, continuous rotation of the tax screw." In a system of progressive taxation, an individual's growing nominal income pushed him or her into a higher tax bracket, triggering an additional tax burden, even if the real income did not increase due to inflation. Through this quasi-cybernetic mechanism, the original tax progression scales had become "completely distorted."[31] The NZZ article lumped together annual incomes between 13,000 and 80,000 Swiss francs and concluded that "this significant income bracket" would have to "pay, in part, considerably more in defense tax" as a result of inflation. The table accompanying the article, demonstrated, though, that the additional burden due to inflation only grew for incomes above 32,000 Swiss francs by more than 1 percent.[32] In 1954, a male white-collar employee earned, on average, barely more than 12,000.[33] Portraying income groups that earned between 6 and 7 times more as the "middle-class" was not only exceedingly generous, but served a political purpose. The author linked his analysis to an unequivocal claim: the 1954 transitional federal financial regime was not untouchable. In fact, the federal authorities had a "moral duty," by means of "tax rebates," to forgo any "revenue bonus" that had arisen out of the "unintended" effect of inflation on progressive taxation.[34] With the budget surplus, the looming election, Perréard's clumsy bill, and the NZZ's more sophisticated argumentation, all the necessary tesserae were assembled for the complicated mosaic of reform. The needed action was ultimately provided by the Lucerne branch of the liberal Free Democrats and their popular initiative.

Entitled "For Federal Tax Reduction," this liberal initiative called for immediate and substantial rebates and exemptions in the federal income and turnover taxes up until 1964. The initiative sought a reduction of the income tax by about a third which would entail a complete exemption for low-income individuals.[35] The Lucerne Liberals justified their initiative with the need for an "elimination of the tax burden caused by inflation," borrowing the language of the NZZ article.[36] In addition to reducing the income tax and increasing exemptions on the turnover tax, the initiative sought the abolition of the supplementary tax on wealth, citing the interests of savers and pensioners. While the federal government argued in neo-Keynesian terms that during boom years the state needed to build up budget reserves and skim off excessive purchasing power, the liberal initiative transposed such macroeconomic arguments onto the micro-economic level: precisely in times of economic boom, companies and individual household should benefit from tax relief so as to use that surplus to make provisions for the bad times ahead.[37]

For some right-wing and pro-business politicians, however, this initiative was poorly timed, at least at first sight. Conservatives were annoyed by this liberal election trick. They were particularly irritated by the prospect of a "representation without taxation," wherein, as a result of populist politics, hundreds of thousands of citizens would stop paying income taxes but continue, as voters, to decide on tax policy and the use of state funds. This group would no longer be interested in preventing a perpetuation of the federal income tax. Rather, the tax-exempt and tax-relieved voters would hold sway over the wealthy and entrepreneurial classes who already bore more than their fair share.[38] In Parliament, though, the liberal popular initiative triggered a wave of imitation.[39] The three major bourgeois factions joined forces to demand an immediate tax relief. The small communist-leaning Party of Labor was amused by the sudden redistributive zeal of its bourgeois opponents. The Communists, as traditional opponents of regressive consumption taxes, had long demanded that the list of goods exempt from the turnover tax be expanded.[40]

The Social Democrats, on the other hand, were at least as blindsided by this initiative as the right-wing anti-statists since they faced a serious dilemma. For the left, the federal income tax undoubtedly was a fair tax because its rate structure was more progressive than many cantonal schemes and because it provided financing for important national infrastructure and welfare expenditures. But if a liberal party promised such generous tax breaks even for those social classes that the Social Democrats claimed to represent, a counterproposal was imperative. Max Weber was the right man for the job. After stepping down from his position in the federal government, Weber had returned to Parliament, where he served as elder statesman and chief financial strategist for the social-democratic parliamentary group. In a programmatic magazine article from 1955, Weber demonstrated how "a just and fair tax reduction" should look like.[41] First, tax relief needed to have a time limit, so as not to restrict the federal budget for years to come. Second, a social-democratic tax reduction had to privilege the lower income brackets. As such, Weber's proposal progressively reduced tax rebates for annual incomes beyond 20,000 Swiss francs.[42] Above all, Weber insisted in retaining the supplementary wealth tax, albeit with some reductions. The lefts' proposal for tax cuts reduced the revenue loss in comparison to the Liberal tax reduction plan, but increased it on the turnover tax, where Weber proposed an even longer list of tax-exempt goods, which he justified as an attempt to curtail the rising cost of living. Once the Social Democrats submitted their plan, there was hardly anyone left in Parliament who did not participate in the competition for tax relief. The liberal finance minister commented on the various tax-cutting demands, with some irony: "What a misery, these vile taxes."[43]

In the summer of 1955, more and more liberal cantonal parties and eventually also the national parent Free Democrat Party began to support the initiative of the Lucerne Liberals. Signature sheets were distributed all across the country, causing no small distress to the Social Democrats. In their party newspapers, they warned their members against the liberal initiative "Do not sign!",[44] or "Workers and employees, do not be fooled!"[45] Since it was an "initiative for millionaires," members were told that "any worker, employee, farmer, or tradesman who was not a high earner must not sign the liberal referendum," but should support a "fair tax reduction by signing the initiative of the Social Democrats", which would be communicated shortly.[46] In September, the social-democratic initiative was launched. It carried the remarkably general title: "For the Reduction of the Federal Defense Tax and the Turnover Tax." Compared to the liberal initiative, the social-democratic plan was more redistributive, and set up tax cuts to decrease as incomes rose, the way Max Weber had outlined it. This political calculus was a success: After only three months, the party submitted its initiative with a record-high number of signatures.[47] In the federal election, held in late October 1955, the Social Democrats won the most seats in the "lower" parliamentary chamber, the National Council, becoming the strongest parliamentary group once again.[48] Pressured by Parliament and public opinion, the Federal Council tabled a tax relief bill in early November 1955, which included a 10 percent discount on both the income tax and the turnover tax; in the case of the income tax, the discount on the first 500 francs in taxes increased progressively up to 40 percent.[49] Parliament passed the bill after the liberal majority had managed to increase the 10 percent discount to 25 percent for incomes up to the middle-class, and to apply it to businesses as well.[50] The initiative of the Lucerne Liberals had produced a maximum impact. And it had successfully enshrined into tax policy the "fiscal science" argument, that inflation caused an unfair additional tax burden.

A Path Taken: Stabilization and Limitation

With this, the stage was also set for the continued negotiations surrounding the regular anchoring of the federal financial regime, which had only been prolonged in its wartime state of exception. The 1955 decision for immediate tax relief prefigured the outcome of debates on the constitutional amendment concerning the two principal federal taxes. The Federal Council already renounced the supplementary wealth tax in its Message to Parliament, proposed a marginal tax rate at 10 percent, and envisaged higher tax deductions for families and other social purposes than originally planned. After fierce wrangling in Parliament, an income tax rebate of 25 percent on tax amounts up to 2000 francs prevailed, while the marginal tax rate for the highest portions of income was lowered to 8 percent. A majority of the parliamentarians were uninterested in permanently anchoring the authority for raising the federal income and turnover tax in the constitution, and even halved the longevity of the federal financial regime from 12 to merely 6 years.[51]

These decisions limited the collection and redistribution potential of the federal income tax to such an extent that the liberal finance minister Hans Streuli angrily referred to it as a "rich man's bill" and denounced a "plundering of the federal government." Disappointed Social Democrats maintained this critical assessment in their no campaign before the referendum vote.[52] Nevertheless, in May 1958, a majority of voters approved the decree on the federal financial regime, which was to apply from 1959 until 1964.[53]

What could have been a historic shift in federal fiscal policy became in reality a mere stopgap for the federal government as discussions about the financial regime after 1965 began already by the end of 1960. In the interest of counter-cyclical economic and fiscal policy, the government initially planned to cancel the tax rebates and thus to marginally increase tax rates. It also hoped to anchor the income and turnover tax permanently in the federal constitution.[54] Pretty quickly, however, the Federal Finance Department had to backpedal and instead defend the status quo. Given the development of federal revenues, this turn of events was hardly surprising. Switzerland had been the "only country that had dared to reduce its budget revenues through tax cuts," André Guinand, a Free Democratic MP from Geneva, proudly stated in 1960, with a view to the healthy 1959 surplus.[55] Federal financial statements continued to be stronger than projected, thus validating the liberal viewpoint. When parliamentary commissions and organized interest groups began to discuss the future financial regime in spring 1961, they were under the spell of a stunning 715 million francs surplus in the 1960 financial statement. And during the ensuing parliamentary debate in 1963, a 433 million surplus colored expectations accordingly (Fig. 2).

In 1960, revenue from import duties had accounted for about 30 percent of total federal fiscal receipts and slightly exceeded the revenue from the turnover tax (28.9 percent).[56] In their preliminary budget forecasts, the federal administration tried to show that spending would exceed revenue in the long and that the coming free trade policy within the European Free Trade Association would reduce income from customs duties dramatically. These arguments held little sway, though. Pressured by all major parliamentary factions, the federal government gave in to demands for tax cuts. When called to the polls in December 1963, a large majority voted in support of a federal financial regime that provided renewed tax relief and continued the existing logic of political stabilization through limiting federal taxation authority on the income and turnover tax in substance and time.[57] The mechanism, which in 1955 had been clumsily described as a "self-propelled, continuous, rotation of the tax screw," now proved particularly convincing, as it had received the technical term "fiscal drag".

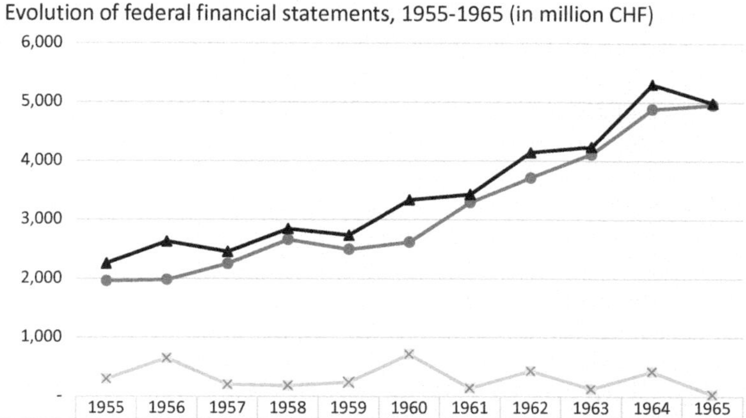

	1955	1956	1957	1958	1959	1960	1961	1962	1963	1964	1965
expenses	1,961	1,981	2,254	2,659	2,496	2,619	3,291	3,710	4,114	4,885	4,957
revenue	2,258	2,628	2,456	2,842	2,736	3,334	3,430	4,143	4,241	5,305	4,989
financial result	297	647	202	183	240	715	139	433	127	420	32

expenses revenue financial result

Fig. 2 Evolution of federal financial statements, 1955–1965. Data: Federal Finance Administration: Financial statements federal, cantonal and local governments, 1938–2007

Fiscal Drag, or the Heat from Inflation

In the twenty-first century, the concept of fiscal drag, referred to as "cold tax progression" (*kalte Progression*) in the German speaking countries and as *progression à froid* in French-speaking Switzerland, is well established.[58] The Federal Tax Administration (FTA) locates the debates on fiscal drag in the stagflation period of the 1970s.[59] This account overlooks, however, the earlier role of the fiscal drag argument. The newspaper *Neue Zürcher Zeitung* (NZZ) had painstakingly described the phenomenon as early as 1955, quickly inscribing the fight against "cold progression" into the liberal agenda.[60] In 1958, the newspaper determined that the interaction of currency devaluation and tax progression had "in recent years entered the vocabulary of tax policy under the terminology of 'cold progression'."[61] The term soon joined everyday politics as an advertisement of the City of Zurich Free Democrats in the NZZ in December 1962 shows: Under the subject line "Cold or hot?," the Zurich Liberals campaigned for a reduction of the City of Zurich tax rate, the church tax, and the federal income tax, justifying their claim with fiscal drag, a topic the "newspaper reader has frequently come across in recent times." The wordplay in the title not only referred to the meaning of "cold" for unintended tax progression versus a "hot" or politically intended measure, but also lent itself for a catchy comparison: In a "cold war," no shots were fired. In contrast, a cold progression was "just as painful as the hot one, as we have to pay either way—cold or hot."[62] By referencing the Cold War, the ad had brought the global political situation into the cozy Swiss living room. And like the Cold War, fiscal drag was subject to international debates and disputes.

In the United States, interest in "more aggressive" forms of tax cuts grew in the 1960s, as Elliot Brownlee has shown.[63] The Kennedy-Johnson tax cuts were also a response to the capital flight by US corporations to "tax havens such as Switzerland," as President John F. Kennedy stated in his April 1961 Special Message to the Congress on Taxation.[64] The US government's tax reform policy intended to combine carrots and sticks, so as to appear both politically credible and fiscally informed. The Kennedy administration aimed for a more restrictive approach to those tax privileges that transnational companies took advantage of through existing double-taxation treaties (DTAs). Switzerland had to revise its DTAs with the United States and with several European countries during the 1960s.[65] At the same time, Kennedy's Economic Reports to the US Congress also make plain how much the discourse on tax relief developed around the notion of fiscal drag. The January 1962 Economic Report mentioned a "full employment surplus," referring to the fiscal effect produced by the combination of employment, economic growth, and consistent tax rates.[66] The January 1963 report made an aggressive plea for a tax cut, inspired by both Keynesian ("personal and business purchasing power") and supply-side ("financial incentives for greater risk-taking and personal effort") ideas, which argued for the elimination of the "heavy drag our fiscal system now exerts."[67] That the tax system was capable of burdening the economy with "excessive drag" was soon common knowledge.[68]

In the Swiss case, such inverted Keynesian arguments were less important than those founded on the notion of (un)fair taxation. Nonetheless, also the Swiss debate took place against an economic background characterized by high growth rates as well as rising inflation. In the years 1960–1963, nominal growth amounted to between 10 and 12.5 percent, while real growth was between 5 and 8.4 percent.[69] This situation fueled a fear of economic "overheating," which in the eyes of many contemporaries was also linked to the large number of foreign workers who had arrived in Switzerland since the 1950s.[70] This dynamic of increased immigration numbers and rising prices fostered a discourse of "*Ueberfremdung*" denouncing an excess of immigration and of foreign influence, which corresponded to the perceived "overheating" (in German: *Ueberhitzung*) of the economy and its impact on the average Swiss household.[71] Talking of a "cold" progression suited this overheated moment, as did the demands for tax relief. However, the reasons for the rising inflation also lay with monetary policy. The return of Western European currencies to free convertibility triggered a massive demand for Swiss francs from 1960 onwards. In order not to strain the Bretton Woods system of stable exchange rates, the Swiss National Bank bought increasing sums of foreign currency. The resulting growth in the domestic money supply had to be reduced again by means of sterilized interventions and increased capital exports.[72] But these measures were insufficient to halt the rising rate of inflation, which averaged an annual 5 percent during the period 1962–1971.[73] Already in its 1961 Federal Financial Statement, the Federal Council hinted at an "unusually" high inflation rate of 3.5 percent.[74]

Such statements provided ready arguments to all those who peddled tax relief as the antidote to fiscal drag. The challenge consisted in distinguishing between a "real fiscal drag" and "nominal fiscal drag." In the latter case, wage inflation pushed taxpayers into higher tax brackets, while price inflation negated any corresponding purchasing power gains.[75] Nonetheless, in the 1962/63 debates on federal taxes, political actors regularly mixed in "real" tax rate increases with the nefarious effects of fiscal drag. This, though, was not just a politically calculated analytical imprecision by mainly bourgeois parliamentarians. Even the federal administration struggled to realize an adequate assessment of boom, income increases, inflation, and tax progression. In May 1962, the Federal Office of Industry, Trade and Employment (BIGA) examined the burden of direct federal, cantonal, and municipal taxes on the wages of male, married, and childless workers and white-collar employees from October 1939 to October 1961 in the ten largest Swiss cities.[76] Between fall 1939 and 1961, average workers' wages had risen by 188.4 percent nominally and by 54.5 percent in real terms. The average salary increases for white-collar employees were 154.5 and 36.3 percent, respectively.[77] Within the system of progressive tax brackets, these increases resulted in a higher overall tax burden. While a working-class couple in 1939 had to submit only 2.6 percent of their gross earnings to the state in the form of taxes, the relative tax amount increased to 4.8 percent by 1961. For employees, the values were 4.9 percent in 1939 and 7.3 percent in 1961. In between these poles,

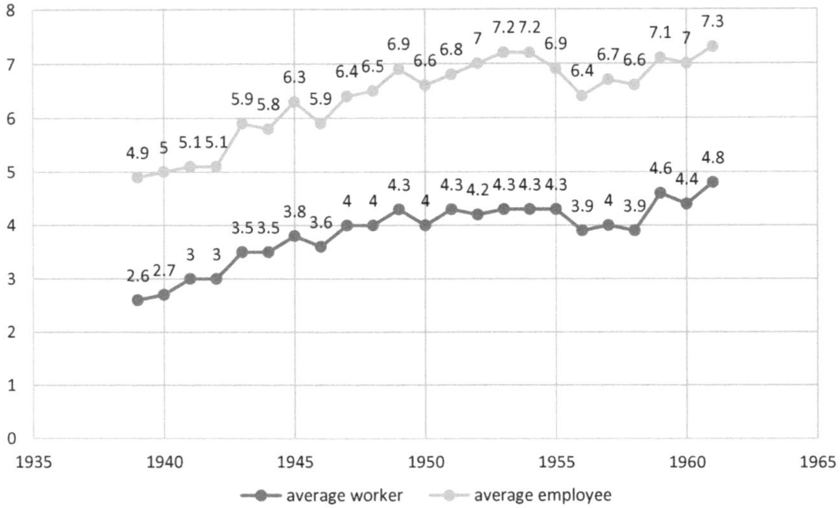

Fig. 3 Evolution of tax burden: workers and employees, 1939–1961. Average tax burden für married men without children in the 10 largest Swiss cities. Data: Bundesamt für Industrie, Gewerbe und Arbeit [BIGA]. "Steuerbelastung des Arbeitseinkommens der Arbeiter und Angestellten 1939–1961." In *Die Volkswirtschaft* 35:5 (May 1962), 231

however, no linear trend is apparent. In 1949, the tax burden on workers' incomes was at its first peak—as a result of both war-related taxation and the catching-up of wage income. Between 1953 and 1955, the tax burden increased to the same level, while for employees it even moved above the earlier peak (Fig. 3).

The data suggest that, between 1955 and 1958, tax relief measures began to have an effect. But then the tax burden began to increase again. The BIGA authors estimated the influence of inflation on the tax burden, for the whole period, at 10 percent for workers and about 15 percent for white-collar employees.[78] While BIGA statisticians described the increased tax liabilities as a natural consequence of "growing into" higher tax brackets, liberal stakeholders emphasized the share of fiscal—and thus avoidable—drag in this increase.

Wage and inflation data were also used by the Union Bank of Switzerland (UBS) in its 1962 article "The Creeping Tax Inflation," which analyzed the growth of the tax burden, between January 1961 and May 1962, from all levels of government, for income classes between 20,000 and 50,000 Swiss francs. The figures suggested a stark development, especially for the "lowest" income group. A childless household earning a net income of 20,000 francs in 1961 could count on an income increase of 6.2 percent in 1962. In the city of Zurich, the tax bill would increase by 11.1 percent; in Basel by 12.2 percent, and a hefty 17.6 percent with the federal government.[79] For UBS, this was the evidence for an "inflation-caused fiscal drag," which needed to be "corrected" by means of tax relief. The bank compared the Swiss and the US case for tax cuts. The Kennedy administration wanted to restore the "weakened confidence of the business world" with lower taxes. Whereas in Switzerland, tax reduction was needed to restore "the originally desired tax burden and its distribution" distorted by inflation.[80] UBS neglected to mention who moved into those income spheres: Only 5.5 percent of Swiss taxpayers earned a taxable income of 20,000 francs or more; the other 94.5 percent—1.2 million people—earned less.[81] The "progression spiral" affected the commercial interests of the Swiss banks in three ways: First, by increasing state revenues, tax progression reduced the state dependence on bank loans. Second, UBS blamed fiscal drag for ultimately harming the currency due to the increase in money supply. Third, higher taxes curbed the individual propensity to save which explained UBS' reference to groups with above-average incomes.[82]

The Government's Dilemma and Unintended Complicity

With its calculations, the bank nurtured existing demands for immediate income tax relief. The Federal Tax Administration (FTA) was sensitized to the financial industry's inclination for political intervention. In May 1962, the Federal Council had published a report, authored by the FTA, on the extent of Swiss tax evasion and tax fraud and on possible measures to counter-act it. The FTA had estimated the amount of undeclared assets by means of withholding tax revenues, and it had dared to analyze the Swiss bank secrecy as an institution that encouraged tax evasion and whose abolition might be a measure to "get to the root of the problem".[83] Such methods and observations caused a major backlash from the representatives of the banking sector, who put massive pressure on the government not to implement the proposed measures against tax evasion and who orchestrated a massive campaign in the media to discredit the government report.[84]

The atmosphere between the FTA and the big banks was thus rather tense, and FTA officers tried to refute UBS's interpretations on inflation and progression. FTA's vice director Pierre Grosheintz wrote a letter to the UBS, while Walter Stäuber, who had co-authored the tax fraud report, tried to downplay UBS' calculations in the parliamentary commission and in the newspapers. Until 1962 there had been no evidence of any significant fiscal drag, Stäuber claimed, by resorting to the trick of describing the evolution of tax liabilities and the share of fiscal drag in francs instead of percentages.[85] This looked fairly harmless. But if the additional tax amount was converted again into an increase in percentage, the fiscal drag effect became apparent.[86] That was not the only problem with Stäubers' approach. The FTA officer had wanted to refute the case for *immediate* tax relief. For the period of the renewed financial regime beginning in 1965, though, Stäuber conceded the potential for a reduction. The strategy of relieving lower and middle incomes pursued since 1955 was, however, exhausted because it implied another, highly controversial, intensification of the tax progression for higher incomes. To avoid this dilemma, Stäuber suggested a uniform "elongation" of the tax rate along the various tax brackets. This procedure would both satisfy the call for tax relief and ease the incline of rate progression.[87]

The FTA's appeal that Parliament should refrain from immediate tax relief remained futile, while the proposed "elongation" of tax rates opened a Pandora's box. Just over a week after Stäuber's NZZ article, the liberal national councilor Hermann Häberlin called for the "elimination of fiscal drag in the defense tax" through a generous tax rate elongation.[88] And when, in autumn 1962, the Council of States, the "upper" parliamentary chamber, took up deliberations on the continuation of the financial regime, it was firmly under the "unpleasant spell of fiscal drag," as one Zurich parliamentarian described it.[89] Federal Councilor Hans Peter Tschudi tried to pierce the veil by repeating that it was above all the substantial wage growth that had led to an increase in the tax burden and thus to a "real fiscal drag". But it was too late.[90] With a large bouquet of demands for tax rebates, rate elongation and higher tax deductions, right-wing and left-wing parliamentarians voted for tax relief in both chambers of Parliament. Similar to 1955, these demands were seconded by a popular initiative. Ironically, the right-wing groups who had launched it, where those who in 1955 had been outraged by the then Liberal proposal.[91] Rather blithely, the initiators blended their appeal for relief from the effects of fiscal drag with the demand for a generalized tax cut by means of an overall 20 percent tax rebate. Initially, the large business associations distanced themselves from this initiative, but over the course of 1963 they began to support similar demands in Parliament.

The federal government tried at first to separate the debate on immediate relief measures from the discussion on the continuation of the financial regime, but failed. The two agendas became intertwined when liberal politicians began to describe their bills for immediate tax relief as "transitional".[92] In the debate on the financial regime for the years 1965 to 1974, both the left- and right-wing concluded that the federal income and turnover tax should not, as proposed by the Federal Council in May 1962, continue unaltered. Be it that the federal treasury could afford it or be it the tax burden had assumed an unfair size: tax relief was needed.

Within this discussion, three different notions of justice stood in competition to each other: first, the idea of *social justice* through redistribution from top to bottom as proposed by Social Democrats and Christian-Socialist trade unionists. The second view, held by the administration and the government, was committed to a perspective of *equity*, which accepted the need to compensate for fiscal drag, but wanted a reduced relief for higher incomes. Right-wing parliamentarians represented a third conception—*absolute equality*—in their demands for equal tax rebates. The conservative National Councilor Rainer Weibel formulated a kind of package deal: He winked at the left by assuring that the parliamentary commission had taken into account some of their proposals "because we also want to create a *socially minded* bill." But that was not enough, because "we *also want a fair bill.*" Unfairness resulted, if taxes were reduced "unilaterally at the bottom." Instead, one should "also engage in a small equalization to the top," because "even the higher taxpayer is a human being."[93] In addition, the chances for a successful vote increased, if everyone was offered something. It was worthwhile to offer taxpayers "a dozen million more in tax cuts" if in return the federal state could secure "many hundreds of millions" more in annual tax revenues.[94]

Despite the haggling over details, the atmosphere was relaxed compared to 1958. Even in the eyes of the social-democratic spokesman Mathias Eggenberger, Parliament was dealing with "relatively moderate reduction plans."[95] Almost sociologically, Eggenberger analyzed "a certain objectification and depoliticization," which he interpreted "as the fruit of the economic boom and, thanks to it, of the federal state's excellent financial position."[96] There was little reason for a tax dispute with the economy booming, wages rising, and fiscal revenues bubbling. Ultimately, the policy outcome was a combination of the far-reaching tax relief demands of the liberal parliamentarians and the proposals by the social-democratic and trade unionist parliamentarians for relief of the lower income classes. In the autumn of 1963, both the Free Democrats and the Social Democrats were among the winners in the federal elections. Together, they had ensured that the two most important federal taxes—the income and turnover taxes—could be levied until 1974.

Conclusion: Compromise and Entanglement Galore

The left had long struggled for a federal income tax, which they had gained under conditions of war and crisis, but at the price of accepting a regressive turnover tax. For conservatives and right-wing liberals, the reverse was true. Accordingly, since the early 1950s, the two taxes were considered "Siamese twins" that could not be separated without harm.[97] Here, an "inspection effect" is visible: the insight that larger expenses and tax revenues become indispensable once they are allocated to social welfare, redistribution, and infrastructure projects.[98] In the Swiss case, the cantons became part of this redistributive entanglement, as participants in federal tax revenues and as recipients of federal subsidies. Part of Swiss historiography perceives the 1958 financial regime as unilateral victory of anti-redistributive forces. These authors also emphasize the class-based nature of federalist arguments and the Swiss links to the transnational neoliberal agenda.[99] These insights are important. However, proposals from Social Democrats and/or from parties representing workers and consumer interests also played a role in cantonal tax relief efforts that spilled over to the federal level. The 1955 federal tax reliefs created a path dependency that ultimately led to the 1958 agreement, which was confirmed again in 1963. The essence of the deal was: Yes to maintaining a federal income tax—and the federal turnover tax—but these taxes must be limited in their material and temporal scope. The disinclination of the liberal side toward a growing federal income tax, combined with the advocacy of the left on behalf of graduated reductions in the tax burden on workers and employees, produced an alliance for tax relief. Fiscal drag played an increasingly important role. Its discursive popularization was an attempt to respond to real economic changes, but also reflected developments in contemporary finance under the influence of the neoclassical-Keynesian synthesis.[100]

In the late 1960s, the limitation paradigm would give way to a lively debate on the (un-)fairness of tax competition, on the harmonization of cantonal tax systems, and on surtaxes on the rich. The general enthusiasm for reforms in politics and society as well as the onset of the currency and later economic and crisis oriented the momentum toward a revocation of tax privileges and tax relief. In the late 1970s, fiscal policy goals and arguments underwent yet another transformation. But the fundamentals remained unchanged: Since the late 1950s, it has been necessary to maintain a relative balance, not only between the federal income tax and the turnover tax that was replaced by a value added tax in 1994. The political compromise also demanded a balanced use of tax monies for welfare spending and subsidies. A further balancing, and redistribution, is intended with the fiscal equalization system among the Swiss cantons and between them and the federal state. And Swiss voters are still regularly called upon to allow the federal state to maintain its major revenue sources. The last time they renewed the financial regime was in March 2018, and the next time will be in 2035.[101]

Notes

1. I would like to thank Julia Sittmann and Elliot Brownlee for their help in editing this text. Of course, all remaining mistakes are entirely mine.
2. In 1979, that number increased to 26 cantons.
3. Swiss Federal Council, “Botschaft über Neuordnung,” 572. In 1982, the “federal defense tax” was renamed “direct federal tax”.
4. See Oechslin, *Bundessteuersystem*, 78–82.
5. The Federal Law on Stamp Duties dated from October 4, 1917. In the early 1960s, the banking industry began to lobby for an abolition of stamp duties, see Loepfe, *Aufstieg*, 155. In 2018, this demand was still pending.
6. Historical Statistics, table U.10a.
7. Ibid.
8. Growth of tax revenues 1915–1950 in nominal values, multiplication by x: federal tax revenues x 26, cantonal x 9, municipal x 7; data: Historical Statistics, table U.15.
9. Schumpeter, *Steuerstaat*, 332.
10. 1950: 54 percent; 1915: 26 percent; calculated from: Historical Statistics, table U.15.
11. Peacock and Wiseman, *Public Expenditure.*
12. Additionally, the cantons also received a cut of the federal stamp duties.
13. See Swiss Federal Council, “Botschaft über Neuordnung,” 600.

14. Kley, *Verfassungsgeschichte*, 382–385.
15. See for the contractual dimension of taxation: Martin, Mehrotra and Prasad, "Thunder of History," 14.
16. In 1947/48, 1,306,000 individuals listed as tax payers. Source: "Wenn eine Partei ihr Gesicht verliert." The resident population of Switzerland in 1948 amounted to 4,549,100.
17. Bieri, *Aargauische Steuern*, 275 and 284.
18. Schmid, "Steuerentlastung der Arbeitenden," 329.
19. The Swiss preference for property taxes was also referred to as the "Swiss system," see Bickel, "Vermögenssteuern," 52. Nevertheless, the canton of Basel (Basel City) had already introduced a progressive income tax in 1840. See Keller, *Visionen*, 47–57.
20. Schmid, "Steuerentlastung der Arbeitenden."
21. Bieri, *Aargauische Steuern*, 289–301.
22. See "Freisinnige Kreispartei 2."
23. Schlaepfer, "Die Revision des zürcherischen Steuergesetzes," "Ein Gesetz über die Ermässigung der Zürcher Staats- und Gemeindesteuern."
24. Eidgenössische Steuerverwaltung, *Steuerbelastung*, 5.
25. In French: Parti des paysans, artisans et bourgeois (PAB), today the Swiss People's Party.
26. Longchamp, *Politique financière fédérale*, 632–666.
27. Ibid., 672–683.
28. Federal Financial Statement 1954, 4–5.
29. Proceedings of the Debates in the National Council of March 23, 1955, 423 (Postulate Perréard, first parliamentary mention of his postulate) and June 21, 1955, (Postulate Perréard, 246–247, parliamentary debate).
30. "Die Entwicklung der Wehrsteuerbelastung." The author was in all likelihood Franz Aschinger, a Free Democratic Party member.
31. Ibid.
32. Ibid. The table is entitled: "Arbeitseinkommen 1941 bzw. Entsprechendes Realeinkommen 1954." For an annual income of CHF 80,000, the additional burden of inflation was 2.75 percent.
33. Based on an average monthly income of CHF 998. See Ritzmann-Blickenstorfer, *Historische Statistik*, 464.
34. "Die Entwicklung der Wehrsteuerbelastung."
35. For single households, a taxable income below CHF 6000; for married households, below CHF 7500. Cited in Swiss Federal Council, "Volksbegehren für den Steuerabbau im Bund," 1242–1247.
36. Ibid.
37. Archives for Contemporary History at ETH Zurich (AfZ), "Vom Reden zum Handeln," April 25, 1955.
38. See correspondence and meeting minutes in AfZ, Redressement National from 1955.

39. "Die Initiative als Initialzündung," *Bund*, June 26, 1955
40. Proceedings of the Debates in the National Council of June 21, 1955 (Marino Bodenmann, 261–263).
41. Weber, "Ein neuer Kampf um die Bundesfinanzen", 119.
42. Ibid., 121. Average annual income in the tax period 1955/56 amounted to CHF 13,800; see Lardi, *Personelle Einkommensverteilung*, 72.
43. Proceedings of the Debates in the National Council of June 21, 1955 (Hans Streuli, 265).
44. "Nicht unterzeichnen!"
45. "Arbeiter und Angestellte, nicht auf den Leim kriechen!"
46. "Die Initiative für die Millionäre."
47. Popular initative "Für den Abbau der Wehrsteuer und der Warenumsatzsteuer," submitted on December 14, 1955. 182,222 signatures were collected, see Swiss Federal Council, "Bericht über das Volksbegehren (vom 10. Januar 1956)." The liberal initiative had received 142,290 signatures, see Swiss Federal Council. "Bericht über das Volksbegehren (vom 25. November 1955)." In fall 1955, 1,425,421 individuals (only men) had the right to vote.
48. Federal Statistical Office, Distribution of mandates in the National Council, and: idem, Party strength in elections for the National Council (year 1955). The Swiss National Council equals the U.S. House of Representatives.
49. Swiss Federal Council, "Ermässigung der Wehrsteuer und der Warenumsatzsteuer," 971–972 and 975.
50. See the debates and decisions in Proceedings of the Debates in the Council of State [Ständerat] of December 16, 1955, and in Proceedings of the Debates in the National Council of December 20, 1955. The defense tax reductions benefited incomes up to CHF 60,000.
51. For details of the process of 1958, see Longchamp, *Politique financière fédérale.*
52. Streuli was cited with his exclamation, in German: "Vorlage des reichen Mannes," by the newspaper *Die Tat*, September 11, 1957. The social-democratic poster for the no campaign integrated his statement. See "Vorlage des reichen Mannes."
53. The Federal Decree on the Constitutional Reorganization of the Federal Finance Regime was adopted in the popular referendum vote on May 11, 1985.
54. See the discussions within the Federal Finance and Customs Department as documented in Swiss Federal Archives, Berne, BAR E6100B-01#1980/49#213*47.
55. Proceedings of the Debates in the National Council of June 29, 1960 (André Guinand, 648).

56. Federal Financial Statement 1960, 56–57; Federal Finance Administration, Federal fiscal revenue 1960–2000: shares of taxes and tax groups, table J.B.1.
57. Referendum vote on the Federal Decree concerning the Prolongation of the Federal Finance Regime, December 8, 1963. The yes-majority stood at 77.6 percent.
58. Scherf, *Öffentliche Finanzen*, 298.
59. Schweizerische Steuerkonferenz, *Die Kalte Progression*, 1.
60. "Entwicklung der Wehrsteuerbelastung;" "Steuerabbau-Initiative."
61. "Beseitigung der 'kalten Progression'."
62. Freisinnige Partei der Stadt Zuerich, "Kalt oder heiss?," B30.
63. Brownlee, *Federal Taxation in America*, 166.
64. Kennedy, "Special Message to the Congress on Taxation."
65. For a detailed account see Hürlimann, "Gesellschafts- und Bundesvertrag," 98–101.
66. Contrary to statements by Lee, "The effect of fiscal drag," 181, neither the 1962 Economic Report, nor the attached report of the Council of Economic Advisers include the term "fiscal drag." See Economic Report 1962.
67. Economic Report 1963, XV; Prachowny, *Kennedy-Johnson Tax Cut*; see also the contributions by Seiichiro Mozumi and W. Elliot Brownlee in this volume.
68. See Heller, *New Dimensions*, 65, and Ratner, *Taxation and Democracy*, 530–531.
69. Historical Statistics, tables Q.15 and Q.16b.
70. On Swiss immigration policies see, amongst many, Piguet, *L'immigration en Suisse*; Hürlimann and Jey Aratnam, "Aporien der Demokratie."
71. On the links between economic and immigrant related labor market policies see Prader, *Stabilisierungspolitik*, 229. For the history of the term "Ueberfremdung" see Kury, *Über Fremde reden*.
72. Loepfe, *Der Aufstieg*, 124–125.
73. I here follow Ronca, *Von der Krisenangst*, 27–28, and Bernholz, "Die Nationalbank," 156–158. Overall, inflation increased by 26 percent between 1960 and 1967, putting Switzerland roughly on par with France and the United Kingdom; the United States, Germany and Belgium had lower inflation rates, see Loepfe, *Der Aufstieg*, 152–153.
74. Federal Financial Statement 1961, 1–2.
75. This distinction is found, for example, in Heinemann, "After the death of inflation".
76. Bundesamt für Industrie, Gewerbe und Arbeit (BIGA), "Steuerbelastung des Arbeitseinkommens," 231–232.
77. Ibid., 232.

78. Ibid., 232 (chart).
79. Schweizerische Bankgesellschaft, "Die schleichende Steuerinflation," 1–3, chart on 2.
80. Ibid., 2.
81. These numbers were mentioned by finance minister Roger Bonvin in a letter from March 3, 1963, to the conservative politician Leo Schüermann. See Archives for Contemporary History at ETH Zurich, AfZ IB Vorort, file 71.2.2. BIGA data show an average worker's net salary of CHF 8539, and an average net salary of white collar employees of CHF 12,001, see BIGA, "Steuerbelastung des Arbeitseinkommens," 232.
82. Schweizerische Bankgesellschaft, "Die schleichende Steuerinflation," 1–2.
83. Swiss Federal Council, "Bericht Steuerdefraudation," 1078.
84. Telegram of the Swiss Bankers Association's presidency to the Federal Council, June 5, 1962 and various notes and letters following their meeting in June 1962. See Hürlimann, *Gesellschafts- und Bundesvertrag*, 96–98.
85. See Swiss Federal Archives, BAR E6100B-01#1980/49#213*47 and BAR E6300B#1973/93#A 17.1*30.
86. Stäuber, "Die kalte Progression," 5.
87. Ibid., 5–6.
88. Proceedings Proceedings National Council, September 19, 1962 (Postulate Häberlin, 29).
89. Proceedings Council of State, October 3, 1962 (Rudolf Meier, 280).
90. Ibid. (Hans Peter Tschudi, 288).
91. "Volksinitiative für Wehrsteuerabbau 1963/64."
92. Proceedings Council of State, March 6, 1963 (Albert Gemperli, 46).
93. Proceedings Council of State, March 14, 1963 (Rainer Weibel, 117, 119).
94. Ibid.
95. Ibid. (Mathias Eggenberger, 60).
96. Ibid.
97. The term was probably coined by then Federal Councilor Max Weber and was thereafter generally used. See Proceedings Council of State, March 18, 1953 (Max Weber, 119).
98. Peacock and Wiseman, *Public Expenditure*.
99. Guex, *L'argent de l'état*; Longchamp, *Politique financière fédérale*, 56, 63–64, with reference to contemporary neoliberalism, and the comments by Friedrich Hayek on progressive taxation during his visit to the University of Zurich in 1952, see Hayek, "Die Ungerechtigkeit".
100. Kaplow, "An Optimal Tax System;" Tobin and Weidenbaum, *Two Revolutions in Economic Policy*, 5; Samuelson, *Economics*.
101. "Federal Decree on the 2021 New Financial Regime," popular referendum vote on March 4, 2018.

References

Archival and Statistical Sources, Government Documents, Newspapers and Magazines

"Arbeiter und Angestellte, nicht auf den Leim kriechen!" 1955. *AZ Schaffhausen*, August 13.

"Die Beseitigung der 'kalten Progression' in der Bundesfinanzvorlage". 1958. *Neue Zürcher Zeitung*, April 30, p. 11.

"Die Entwicklung der Wehrsteuerbelastung. Ein ungerechtfertigter Zuschlag". 1955. *Neue Zürcher Zeitung*, March 18, p. A5.

"Die Initiative als Initialzündung. Zur Steuerabbaudebatte im Nationalrat". 1955. *Bund*, June 26.

"Die Initiative für die Millionäre". 1955. *Berner Tagwacht*, August 16.

"Ein Gesetz über die Ermässigung der Zürcher Staats- und Gemeindesteuern". 1948. *Neue Zürcher Zeitung*, July 23, p. A13.

"Fass ohne Boden? Steuervorlage Nein". Poster for the Popular Referendum Vote of December 6, 1953, Designed by Peter Birkhaeuser. *Swiss Social Archives Zurich*, Sozarch-F Ka-0001-493.

"Federal Decree on the 2021 New Financial Regime." https://www.admin.ch/gov/en/start/documentation/votes/20180304/neue-finanzordnung-2021.html. Accessed 26 Jan 2018.

"Federal Decree on the Constitutional Reorganization of the Federal Financial Regime [Arrêté fédéral du 31.01.1958 instituant de nouvelles dispositions constitutionnelles sur le régime financier de la Confédération]." https://www.bk.admin.ch/ch/f/pore/va/19580511/index.html. Accessed 18 Jan 2018.

"Federal Popular Initiative 'Für den Abbau der Wehrsteuer und der Warenumsatzsteuer'." https://www.admin.ch/ch/d/pore/vi/vis73t.html. Accessed 15 Jan 2018.

"Federal Popular Initiative 'Für den Steuerabbau im Bund'." https://www.admin.ch/ch/d//pore/vi/vis72t.html. Accessed 15 Jan 2018.

"Freisinnige Kreispartei 2". 1943. *Neue Zürcher Zeitung*, September 24, p. A2.

"Nicht unterzeichnen!" 1955. *Volksrecht*, August 5.

"Steuerabbau-Initiative und Wehrsteuertarif." 1955. *Neue Zürcher Zeitung*, June 13, p. 13.

"Volksinitiative für Wehrsteuerabbau 1963/64". 1963. *Der Steuerbatzen*, February.

"Vorlage des reichen Mannes". 1957. *Die Tat*, September 11.

"Wenn eine Partei ihr Gesicht verliert. Vorläufige Bemerkungen zur freisinnigen Steuer-Initiative". 1955. *Vaterland*, May 3.

Archives for Contemporary History at ETH Zurich (AfZ). 1955. AfZ IB Redressement National, File 67, Letters and Notes Concerning Federal Tax Policy.

———.1963. AfZ IB Vorort, file 71.2.2 Bundesfinanzprogramm und Steuerreform 1965–1974: Letter from Roger Bonvin to Leo Schürmann, March 3.

———. 1955. AfZ IB wf I, file 11.3.2.2.1 Steuerabbau-Initiative (Luzerner Initiative, FDP), 1955–1958: SPK, "Vom Reden zum Handeln. Die Steuerdiskussion führt zu einer Initiative", Bern, April 25.

Economic Report of the President: 1962. 1962. Washington DC: United States Government Printing Office.

Economic Report of the President: 1963. 1963. Washington DC: United States Government Printing Office.

Federal Finance Administration, Statistical Team, Federal fiscal revenue 1960–2000: Shares of Taxes and Tax Groups, Table J.B.1. Compiled for G. Hürlimann [Not Published].

Federal Financial Statements [Staatsrechnungen der Schweizerischen Eidgenossenschaft]. 1954 (Published on April 5, 1955), 1960 (Published on April 14, 1961), 1961 (Published on April 13, 1962). https://www.amtsdruckschriften.bar.admin.ch.

Federal Statistical Office, Distribution of Mandates in the National Council, Table je-d-17.02.02.02.01.03. https://www.bfs.admin.ch/bfs/fr/home/statistiques/politique/elections/conseil-national/repartitions-mandats.assetdetail.217214.html. Accessed 14 Feb 2018.

Federal Statistical Office, Party Strength in Elections for the National Council, Table je-f-17.02.02.03.01. https://www.bfs.admin.ch/bfs/fr/home/statistiques/politique/elections/conseil-national/force-partis.assetdetail.217195.html. Accessed 14 Feb 2018.

Freisinnige Partei der Stadt Zürich. 1962. Kalt oder heiss? *Neue Zürcher Zeitung*, December 10, p. B30.

Historical Statistics of Switzerland online (HSSO), tables Q.15, Q.16a, Q.16b, U.5, U.10a, U.15. https://hsso.ch/. Accessed 14 Feb 2018.

Kennedy, John F. 1961. 136 – Special Message to the Congress on Taxation, April 20. Online by Gerhard Peters and John T. Woolley, The American Presidency Project. http://www.presidency.ucsb.edu/ws/?pid=8074.

Proceedings of the Debates in the Council of State [Ständerat]. December 16, 1955, 270–271. October 3, 1962 (Rudolf Meier, 280; Hans Peter Tschudi, 288). http://www.amtsdruckschriften.bar.admin.ch

Proceedings of the Debates in the National Council [Nationalrat]. March 18, 1953 (Max Weber, 119). March 23, 1955, 423 (Postulate Perréard, entry). June 21, 1955, (Postulate Perréard, 246–247; Marino Bodenmann, 261–263; Hans Streuli, 265). December 20, 1955, 596–603. June 29, 1960, 637–724 (André Guinand, 648). September 19, 1962 (Postulate Häberlin, 29: entry). March 6, 1963 (Albert Gemperli, 46). March 14, 1963 (Rainer Weibel, 117, 119; Mathias Eggenberger, 60). http://www.amtsdruckschriften.bar.admin.ch.

Schlaepfer, Hans Ulrich. 1950. Die Revision des zürcherischen Steuergesetzes. *Neue Zürcher Zeitung*, September 17, p. B7.

Schmid, Arthur. 1944. Für die Steuerentlastung der Arbeitenden. Zu einer Aktion der aargauischen Sozialdemokraten. *Rote Revue* 23 (10): 328–332.

Stäuber, Walter. 1962. Die kalte Progression und die eidgenössische Wehrsteuer. *Neue Zürcher Zeitung*, September 11, p. 5.

Swiss Federal Archives, Bern. BAR E6300B#1973/93#A 17.1*30. The file contains a draft letter by Pierre Grosheintz for UBS, August 29, 1962.

———. BAR E6100B-01#1980/49#213*47. The file also contains: Walter Stäuber, "Die Entwicklung der Wehrsteuerbelastung 1941–1964" (Eidg. Steuerverwaltung, 22.10.1962); Proceedings of the Council of State Commission on the Federal Financial Regime, August 20–21, 1962.

Swiss Federal Council [Schweizerischer Bundesrat], Bericht zur Motion Eggenberger betr. wirksamere Bekämpfung der Steuerdefraudation (vom 25.5.1962). In *Bundesblatt* I:23 (June 7, 1962), 1057–1117.

Swiss Federal Council. Bericht über das Volksbegehren für den Steuerabbau im Bund (vom 25. November 1955). In *Bundesblatt* II:48 (December 1, 1955), 1242–1247.

———. Bericht über das Volksbegehren für den Abbau der Wehrsteuer und der Warenumsatzsteuer (vom 10. Januar 1956). In *Bundesblatt*, I:2 (January 12, 1956), 182–222.

———. Botschaft über die Ermässigung der Wehrsteuer und der Warenumsatzsteuer (vom 1. November 1955). In *Bundesblatt* II:45 (November 10, 1955), 964–977.

———. Botschaft über die verfassungsmässige Neuordnung des Finanzhaushalts des Bundes (vom 7.2.1957). In *Bundesblatt* I:9 (February 28, 1957), 505–630.

Weber, Max. 1955. Ein neuer Kampf um die Bundesfinanzen. *Rote Revue* 34 (5–6): 113–123.

Other Literature

Bernholz, Peter. 2007. Die Nationalbank 1945–1982: Von der Devisenbann-Wirtschaft zur Geldmengensteuerung bei flexiblen Wechselkursen. In *Die Schweizerische Nationalbank 1907–2007*, ed. Schweizerische Nationalbank, 119–213. Zürich: Verlag Neue Zürcher Zeitung.

Bickel, Wilhelm. 1962. Die Vermögenssteuern in der Schweiz. In *Impôts sur la fortune y inclus droits de succession et 'Debt Management' (Congrès de Zurich, septembre 1960, XVIe session)*, ed. Institut internationale de finances publiques, 48–70. Bruxelles: Bruylant.

Bieri, Markus. 1972. *Geschichte der Aargauischen Steuern von 1803–1968, insbesondere der direkten Staatssteuer*. Aarau: Keller.

Brownlee, W. Elliot. 2016. *Federal Taxation in America. A History*. 3rd ed. New York: Cambridge University Press.

Bundesamt für Industrie, Gewerbe und Arbeit [BIGA]. 1962. Steuerbelastung des Arbeitseinkommens der Arbeiter und Angestellten 1939–1961. *Die Volkswirtschaft* 35 (5): 231–232.

Eidgenössische Steuerverwaltung. 1955. *Steuerbelastung in der Schweiz/Charge fiscale en Suisse 1954, (Statistische Quellenwerke der Schweiz, 267).* Bern: Eidg. Statistisches Amt.

Guex, Sébastien. 1998. *L'argent de l'état. Parcours des finances publiques au XXe siècle.* Lausanne: Réalités sociales.

Hayek, Friedrich. 1952. Die Ungerechtigkeit der Steuerprogression. *Schweizerische Monatshefte* 32 (8): 508–517.

Heinemann, Friedrich. 2001. After the Death of Inflation: Will Fiscal Drag Survive? *Fiscal Studies* 22 (4): 527–546.

Heller, Walter. 1966. *New Dimensions of Political Economy.* Harvard: Harvard University Press.

Hürlimann, Gisela. 2016. Der moderne Gesellschafts- und Bundesvertrag. Steuerpolitik im Kontext von sozioökonomischem Wandel und föderalistischer Staatlichkeit. In *Staatlichkeit in der Schweiz. Regieren und Verwalten vor der neoliberalen Wende*, ed. Lucien Criblez, Christina Rothen, and Thomas Ruoss, 85–114. Zürich: Chronos.

Hürlimann, Gisela, and Ganga Jey Aratnam. 2004. Die Aporien der Demokratie. Politische Partizipation, Integration und die 'Ausländerfrage' 1960 bis heute. In *Die Erfindung der Demokratie in der Schweiz/L'invention de le démocratie en Suisse, (Studien und Quellen 30)*, ed. Schweizerisches Bundesarchiv, 109–143. Zürich: Chronos.

Kaplow, Louis. 2011. An Optimal Tax System. *Fiscal Studies* 32 (3): 415–435.

Keller, Christian. 2017. *Visionen, Volkshetze, Betrügereien. Der Weg zum modernen Steuerstaat am Beispiel der Kantone Basel-Stadt und Basel-Landschaft (1833–1928).* Zürich: Chronos.

Kley, Andreas. 2013. *Verfassungsgeschichte der Neuzeit. Grossbritannien, die USA, Frankreich, Deutschland und die Schweiz.* 3rd ed. Bern: Stämpfli.

Kury, Patrick. 2003. *Über Fremde reden. Überfremdungsdiskurs und Ausgrenzung in der Schweiz 1900–1945.* Zürich: Chronos.

Lardi, Peter. 1970. *Empirische Untersuchungen zur personellen Einkommensverteilung in der Schweiz.* Basel: Institut für angewandte Wirtschaftsforschung.

Lee, Sung-Kyu. 2012. The Effect of Fiscal Drag on Tax Revenue and Tax Burden. In *Institutional Economics and National Competitiveness*, ed. Young Back Choi, 179–199. London: Routledge.

Loepfe, Willi. 2011. *Der Aufstieg des schweizerischen Finanzplatzes in der Nachkriegszeit, 1945 bis 1975.* Weinfelden: Wolfau Druck.

Longchamp, Olivier. 2014. *La Politique financière fédérale (1945–1968).* Lausanne: Editions Antipodes.

Martin, Isaac W., Ajay K. Mehrotra, and Monica Prasad. 2009. The Thunder of History. The Origins and Development of the New Fiscal Sociology. In *The New Fiscal Sociology. Taxation in Comparative and Historical Perspective*, 1–27. New York: Cambridge University Press.

Oechslin, Hanspeter. 1967. *Die Entwicklung des Bundessteuersystems der Schweiz von 1848 bis 1966*. Einsiedeln: Etzel Druck.

Peacock, Alan T., and Jack Wiseman. 1967. *The Growth of Public Expenditure in the United Kingdom*. London: George Allen and Unwin.

Piguet, Etienne. 2009. *L'immigration en Suisse. Soixante ans d'entrouverture*. 2nd ed. Lausanne: Presses polytechniques et universitaires romandes.

Prachowny, Martin J. 2000. *The Kennedy-Johnson Tax Cut: A Revisionist History*. Northampton, MA: Edward Elgar.

Prader, Gaudenz. 1981. *50 Jahre schweizerische Stabilisierungspolitik. Lernprozesse in Theorie und Politik am Beispiel der Finanz- und Beschäftigungspolitik des Bundes*. Zürich: Schulthess.

Ratner, Sidney. 1967. *Taxation and Democracy in America*. New York: Wiley.

Ritzmann-Blickenstorfer, Heinz, ed. 1996. *Historische Statistik der Schweiz*. Zürich: Chronos.

Ronca, Marion. 2012. *Von der Krisenangst zu langfristiger Planung. Konjunkturbeobachtung und Wachstumsbewusstsein in der Schweiz 1945–1968*. Master-Thesis. University of Zürich.

Samuelson, Paul A. 1948. *Economics: An Introductory Analysis*. New York: McGraw Hill.

Scherf, Wolfgang. 2011. *Öffentliche Finanzen. Einführung in die Finanzwissenschaft*. 2nd rev. ed. UVK: Konstanz.

Schumpeter, Josef. 1976. Die Krise des Steuerstaats [1918]. In *Rudolf Goldscheid, Joseph Schumpeter. Die Finanzkrise des Steuerstaats. Beiträge zur politischen Ökonomie der Staatsfinanzen*, ed. Rudolf Hickel, 329–378. Frankfurt a.M.: Suhrkamp.

Schweizerische Bankgesellschaft [Union Bank of Switzerland]. 1962. Die schleichende Steuerinflation. In *SBG Wirtschafts-Notizen*, July/August, pp. 1–3.

Schweizerische Steuerkonferenz, ed. 2015. *Die kalte Progression* (Stand der Gesetzgebung: 1 January), (E Steuerbegriffe). Bern: Dokumentation und Steuerinformation ESTV.

Tobin, James, and Murray Weidenbaum. 1988. *Two Revolutions in Economic Policy: The First Economic Reports of Presidents Kennedy and Reagan*. Cambridge, MA: MIT-Press.

Unfairness, Inequality, and Tax Evasion: An Analysis of the Distribution of the Tax Burden in Greece, 1955–1989

Zoi Pittaki

Introduction

One of the main characteristics of Greece's taxation system is its lack of progressivity. This chapter focuses on the period 1955–1989 and suggests that the system's lack of progressivity added to its perceived unfairness and the public's dissatisfaction. I argue that the Greeks' low "tax conscience" is to a large extent a result of these issues, and seems to have contributed to widespread tax evasion which undermines the country's taxation system.[1]

During the mid- to late 1950s, when the second wave of globalization began,[2] the Greek taxation system was reformed. Right-wing governments attempted to set it within a wider framework of restructuring the economy at a time when, in the early days of the Cold War, economic development was considered to be a way to avert the spread of socialism.[3] These reforms were important by simplifying the process of filing a tax

Z. Pittaki (✉)
University of Glasgow, Glasgow, Scotland
e-mail: Zoi.Pittaki@glasgow.ac.uk

G. Huerlimann et al. (eds.), *Worlds of Taxation*,
Palgrave Studies in the History of Finance,
https://doi.org/10.1007/978-3-319-90263-0_12

return for both businesses and individual taxpayers, increasing how much tax revenue was collected, modernizing the tax service, and reducing tax inspectors' tendency to be inconsistent in their working practice.

The various governments of the period also declared their willingness to increase the progressivity and fairness of the tax system. However, in spite of legislation introduced in the mid-1950s, taxation in Greece never became truly progressive. This seems to be due to the lack of similar legislation in later decades, as well as some of the system's characteristics. One was tax rebates, which provided significant tax relief to the higher-income sector but not to the middle and lower strata. Another characteristic was that most tax revenue came from indirect taxation. Overall, it would not be an exaggeration to describe tax reform in Greece as a story of unrealized ambitions as there was always a gulf between legislative aims and their poorly implemented reality.

The chapter is set out as follows: first, I examine the tax reforms introduced by the state in the immediate postwar period. Next, the distribution of the tax burden throughout the postwar years is analyzed, with most of the data covering the period up to the late 1980s,[4] showing that distribution changed significantly throughout the period. Specifically, whereas until the mid-1970s industrialists and businesses paid more taxes than any other group, from 1975 onwards salaried employees started paying more than industrialists, businesses, and self-employed professionals. More broadly, we find that the low- and middle-income sectors bore a disproportionately large share of the tax burden.

The resulting lack of progressivity and a series of other characteristics increased the tax system's perceived unfairness and detracted from its legitimacy. I argue here that these issues contributed to widespread tax evasion.

Indirect and Direct Taxation: More Than Fairness Issues

Throughout the postwar period the tax system was largely based on indirect taxes,[5] as it had been since the late nineteenth century. This has been attributed to various reasons. According to Giouras, it was owing to the inability of tax inspectors to assess the tax accruing from business income and the income of the wealthier classes. It is also possible that indirect tax on consumption was preferred as it was concealed when compared to direct taxes.[6] In the period covered by this chapter, various kinds of indirect tax were in force, for example, excise duties such as the tax on spirits, the tobacco tax, and the public entertainment tax. There was also a purchase tax, a stamp duty, and a turnover tax.[7] The last of these, along with other indirect taxes, was replaced by the value-added tax (VAT) in 1987.[8]

The fact that direct taxes as a source of revenue were much less significant had implications for the tax system's fairness because direct taxes are generally more progressive than indirect ones.[9] Precisely because of their progressivity, direct taxes contribute to the fairer distribution of the tax burden, and are thus considered an effective tool for the redistribution of income.[10] Theory also suggests that direct taxes should increase as a country's economic development improves. This hypothesis is supported by data for other countries, but is not in the case in Greece.[11] It is also telling that until 1965, when the country was experiencing its fastest growth, the share of income taxes in total tax revenues consistently fell.[12]

All this[13] suggests that the increase in economic development experienced in the postwar period was not reflected in the tax system. For this reason, currently, the tax system has many characteristics found elsewhere in countries that are in the initial stages of economic development. It has, for example, a small profit taxation to total tax revenue ratio. Furthermore, social groups and professions in a strong negotiating position are taxed on more favorable terms than others.[14]

Post-Second World War Reforms: Unburdening Businesses and Farmers

The mid-1950s saw the introduction of legislation that unified the taxation of income. This is considered "the most important post-war tax law," one that marked "the tax future of Greece for the decades that followed."[15] Specifically, at the Federation of Greek Industrialists (FGI) annual meeting in 1955, the Minister of Coordination described the enactment of law 3323/1955 concerning individual taxation as a means to reduce the complexities of the tax system.[16] The new legislation replaced law 1640,[17] which was based on French corporate tax law.[18] Criticism of this law was premised on its structural weaknesses, such as the complexity and number of tax returns—up to seven—that had to be filed each year by taxpayers and the "institutional disadvantages resulting from the defective tax auditing procedures."[19] Against this backdrop, the legislation introduced in 1955 was presented as a means to simplify the whole procedure of filing a tax return, and also a way to increase tax fairness thanks to the rates for high-income thresholds it introduced.[20] In their 1964 monograph on the Greek tax system, economists George Break and Ralph Turvey described income taxation as follows:

> The tax scale is expressed as a scale plus a surcharge, the revenue from the latter being assigned to OGA. Since this surcharge is itself subsequently deductible, tax rates are not effectively as high as at first sight be thought. The marginal rate starts at 3% and does not get much beyond 60% for the very rich. But in addition to the graduated tax there is a flat 3% on unearned income imposed for reasons of equity.[21]

Overall, the new legislation found mixed favor among politicians. Some called it a coup d'état; however, most MPs hailed it as a "revolution."[22] Among those who supported it was Theodoros Sarantis, member of the right-wing ruling party, National Rally, who, in a parliamentary debate, noted that under unified taxation and with the aggregation of income from all sources, the process of submitting a tax return would be much less time-consuming, not only for taxpayers but also for the tax office, thereby increasing the efficiency of the latter: "[E]ach taxpayer will have to submit only one tax return and go through only one taxing procedure … anyone can understand how much this will free tax officers from a pointless preoccupation, [allowing them] to devote themselves in going after tax evaders."[23]

The new law also increased tax revenue as a share of gross domestic product (GDP)[24] and was accompanied by further modernization of the tax system. Such measures were aimed particularly at improving the organization of the tax administration and combating tax evasion. Nevertheless, the legislation was criticized. One newspaper article stated that the law had been introduced after the "briefest and most inadequate debate."[25] The same point was raised in a 1957 article in the *Bulletin of Tax Legislation*, where it was noted that the law was published two months into the beginning of fiscal year 1955/56, following an established practice according to which "by a strange coincidence - not to say tactic -all major tax laws in … [the] country are published late, as a rule, after the beginning of the economic year …"[26] Furthermore, critics noted that the 1955 legislation increased the tax burden on the middle-income sector, which was the "backbone" of the country's "civil regime."[27] At the same time, according to Michalis Stasinopoulos, member of the Council of State in the 1950s, the legislation exempted many low-income earners from taxation: "It is characteristic ... that while [with the previous law] the tax returns filed per year were almost 760,000, those that were filed during the first year of enactment of the new law, [taking also into consideration] those that were filed after an audit took place, were only 246,000."[28]

The reforms also covered corporation tax. At the 1955 FGI meeting, the Minister of Coordination announced that another law would soon be presented. Its aim would be the "consolidation of the terms under which firms are taxed." This was law 3843 regarding corporation tax,[29] which was passed in late September 1958.[30] It was a legislative decree and was amended in 1959 by a few minor additions and changes.[31] The law comprised 21 articles.[32]

Unlike the 1955 law on personal income tax, tax on corporate income was set at a flat rate of 35 percent.[33] Yet, as was the case with personal income, the tax was imposed on a business's income (e.g., the income of construction companies, trading companies, leased land, securities, and agricultural businesses, as well as employee and self-employed income).[34] The fact that income was taxed on an aggregate basis had significant positive implications; it meant that if a company made a loss from one source, its total taxable income would be reduced. A further implication was that instead of filing seven tax returns each year, companies would now file only one, covering their total income from all sources.[35] The legal entities that were subject to this law were: domestic corporations, public, municipal, and administrative district for-profit companies, cooperatives, foreign companies operating in Greece, and every other type of for-profit overseas organization.[36] Specific types of income of the state organizations, public, municipal, and administrative district for-profit organizations, as well as the income of churches and charitable organizations, were not included in this law, and were thus exempt from corporation tax.[37]

Another significant characteristic of law 3843 is that it provided tax exemptions for profits that would fund investment projects.[38] Similar tax incentives were introduced during the 1950s and 1960s. For example, law 3213 provided "[e]xemption from taxes, dues and other charges ... of the portion of capital stock in excess of 5 million drachmas for new corporations capitalized at over 15 million drachmas or for existing corporations increasing their capitalization to more than 15 million drachmas." It also allowed "freezing, for a period of up to 15 years from start-ups, of all taxes ... in effect at the time of approving an application to invest."[39] Law 3765 provided that, under specific criteria, mergers and conversions of sole ownerships and partnerships into corporations would be exempt from capital gains tax, property transfer taxes, stamp duty on revenues, and all types of third party taxes.[40]

According to Break and Turvey, the most important tax incentives in the period were introduced by law 4002, which granted tax exemptions for productive investment made by large industrial and craft enterprises until the end of 1964.[41] The exemption covered "Investment expenditure ... from undistributed profits which, in the case of partnerships, limited liability companies, etc., means net profits less the proprietors' withdrawals. The amount deducted may not exceed 50% of the undistributed profits in Attica, 60% in the provinces and 90% in the islands."[42] The law also provided a 50 percent deduction of the taxable profits of mining enterprises, as well as quarry enterprises exporting at least 50 percent of their production, to cover expenses related to investment in new productive facilities, irrespective of location.

More broadly, the incentives allowed firms to "recover the original cost of their new investments relatively quickly" and greatly reduced the taxes they paid.[43] By 1962, under law 4002, Greek corporations were claiming deductions amounting to DRS 91 million, equal to 15 percent of their total taxable profits.[44] Whereas in 1959 tax allowances provided by laws 4002 and 3213, and 2176/1952 concerning provincial firms and firms located on the Greek islands rather than the mainland,[45] were equal to 12 percent of the total taxable profits of domestic corporations, three years later their absolute size was four times greater, amounting to 28 percent of these corporations' total taxable profits, as Table 1 suggests.

Table 1 Ratio of total special allowances* to taxable profits of domestic corporations

1959	*1960*	*1961*	*1962*
12%	16%	22%	28%

Source: Break and Turvey, p. 199

*Allowances under laws 4002, 3213, and 2176

Generally, the tax incentives were important not only in terms of number but also by reducing the tax burden. According to Break and Turvey, in the 1960s there were so many tax incentives that "opportunities for [their] further expansion [were] extremely limited."[46]

However, implementation of these incentives was not without problems and these reduced the effectiveness of the reform. It has been stressed that in most cases the incentives involved "undue bureaucratic procedures,"[47] which to a large extent complicated the structure of the tax system. For example, according to the first national accounting congress (1957), the country was suffering from "[the] unquestionably serious problem of the application of tax justice," which functioned under a "labyrinthine" regime.[48] Also, as various studies indicate, the tax incentives were much less effective for the whole economy. Nikolaos Moscholios noted that whereas at one level the tax incentives seemed sufficient to increase industrial investment in new projects or used to extend existing projects, closer examination indicated that their usefulness depended on other factors that were usually more important. These included creating a social and economic environment that would "give a sense of certainty or high probability that the business will survive."[49] An environment like this could not be achieved with tax incentives, but required a stable tax system, one that guaranteed economic stability and a fair income distribution.[50] It was noted that although tax incentives were expected to contribute significantly to the country's industrialization, over time they had been much less effective than anticipated.[51]

Importantly for the present analysis, people believed that businesses were being unfairly privileged by the tax system. As a result, tax incentives and exemptions passed by the state to promote investment increased the tax system's perceived unfairness. In fact, Greece had a regressive tax system, which meant that some sectors were favored at the expense of others. An example here was the preferential tax regime for farmers. Legislative order 3323 concerning personal income taxation set a "very high tax-free threshold, which virtually exempted agricultural income from any kind of taxation," according to Dertilis,[52] who notes that the percentage of agricultural income in the state's total tax revenue amounted to less than 1 percent until the 1990s.[53] Also, there were tax rebates that provided significant tax relief for high-income earners but minor or no relief for medium and low earners.[54] From 1960 to 1998 per capita tax exemptions and rebates given to industrialists, traders, and self-employed professionals increased far faster than those given to pensioners and waged or salaried employees.[55]

Another example of preferential tax treatment concerns taxes in favor of third parties, a category of taxes that were usually levied on transactions and characterized by Break and Turvey as "[one] of the most distinctive features of the Greek tax system."[56] Taxes in favor of third parties were first introduced in the 1920s and are still a feature of the tax system. They take the form of taxes, duties, and other levies. Revenue from these is obtained directly or through payments via the state budget from various organizations, professional classes, or lobby groups in a strong negotiating position, "of a political, economic or trade union nature."[57] There were 1500 such bodies in 1951[58] and 1800 taxes in favor of third parties in 1967.[59] Currently, they number between 350 and almost 1000.[60]

Apart from making the distribution of the tax burden even more unequal, taxes in favor of third parties made the tax system less transparent and predictably added to the perceived unfairness on the part of taxpayers who paid them.[61] The fact that the finances of the recipient bodies were usually not taken into account in the state's budget,[62] along with the lack of any control in terms of the way the bodies used these funds,[63] has been described as a body blow to the relationship between taxpayers and the state.

The Distribution of the Tax Burden: A Tale of Significant Changes

Although at a "somewhat slower pace"[64] than other European or Organisation for Economic Co-operation and Development (OECD) countries, after the Second World War Greece witnessed a gradual increase in its total tax revenues. Specifically, the rate over total GDP increased from 15.9 percent in 1948 to 34.3 percent in 1995.[65]

As Tatsos[66] indicates, whereas in 1960 salaried employees and pensioners contributed 28 percent of the total tax burden, in 1998 their contribution had increased to 58.4 percent. This probably reflected a corresponding change in the population composition: according to census data, in 1961 salaried employees and pensioners comprised 17.21 percent of the population, this had soared to 45.8 percent of the population by 2001.[67] Until 1975 industrialists and traders bore a larger part of the tax burden than salaried employees. Self-employed professionals also paid less tax than salaried employees. Yet the difference between the latter two groups was more or less stable. From 1975 onwards, however, salaried employees started paying more taxes than industrialists, traders, and the self-employed.[68] Tatsos notes that it is important to examine whether these changes reflected a real increase in the tax burden of salaried people after 1975 or other factors, such as an increase in their number.[69] Nevertheless, in his analysis Tatsos's main focus is on fiscal drag, the inevitable increase in the tax burden due to inflation "even when taxpayers' real income remains stable or is even reduced."[70] According to Tatsos fiscal drag had an impact on the distribution of the tax burden, but, focusing particularly on 1980–95, he suggests that all professional classes were hit by inflation, not only salaried employees.[71] However, the data he presents, in conjunction with occupation data from the 1961 and 1981 censuses, indicate that salaried employees bore a disproportionately large part of the tax burden. For example, in the 1980s, when farmers paid around 0.2 percent of the total tax burden, they comprised approximately 10 percent of the population.[72] Twenty years earlier, when they accounted for 23.3 percent of the population, they still paid less than 1 percent of total taxes. Also, for socio-demographic reasons, between 1960s and 1980s the pensioner population increased almost fivefold,[73] and their contribution to the total tax burden more than doubled. This increase was similar to that of salaried employees, whose number had seen a much more modest increase. Specifically, they comprised 14.4 percent of the population in 1961 and 17.7 percent in 1981.

It is difficult to reach a clear understanding of the distribution of the tax burden because the allocation of income in the various income brackets, the only available data, comes from personal income tax returns, which are considered to be inaccurate. It is also difficult to ascertain the level of taxes imposed on each income bracket, owing to the tax shifting that took place and, of course, tax evasion. However, some studies indicate that from 1964 to 1984 the distribution of the tax burden was regressive, as in the three top income brackets the burden was significantly lower than in the bottom three.[74]

Such an unequal distribution[75] led to economic inequalities as "the tax system made income distribution more unequal than it was before the application of taxation."[76] Nor did the situation change after 1984 because there was no significant improvement in the tax legislation. In fact, post-1984 inequalities caused by the tax system increased.[77]

Individual income tax rates suggest that the tax system became less progressive over time. As an example, according to data for fiscal year 1955, the individual income tax rate ranged from 5 percent to 59 percent for incomes of up to DRS 1 million (see Table 2); above that, there was a

Table 2 Income tax scale (1955–85)

1955		*1965*		*1975*		*1985*	
Income	*Tax rates*	*Income*	*Tax rates*	*Income*	*Tax rates*	*Income*	*Tax rates*
400,000–1 m	5–59%	500,000–1 m	3–52%	200,000–1 m	3–58%	800,000–900,880	0–60%
>1 m	60%	>1 m	55%	>3 m	60%	>900,880	63%

Source: Sellas, p. 433

Table 3 Tax rates for incomes up to DRS 1 m

Year	*Tax rates (%)*
1975	3–50
1985	0–48
1986	0–37
1989	18–24

Source: Sellas, pp. 433–444

flat rate of 60 percent. Ten years later, this top rate was reduced to 55 percent, and the individual income tax rate ranged from 3 percent to 52 percent. In 1975, tax rates ranged from 3 percent to 58 percent for incomes up to DRS 3 million. Income above that was taxed at a flat rate of 60 percent. There was also a provision that incomes up to DRS 1 million could be taxed at 3–50 percent (see Table 3).

Sellas's study shows in detail the tax structure for each income bracket. The data he presents indicate clearly that progression for the lower incomes was sharper in 1985 than 1955, 1965, and 1975, and in 1985 individual income tax rates ranged from 0 percent to 60 percent. The tax-free threshold probably supported the lower-income brackets. At the same time, the maximum rate for incomes up to DRS 1 million was reduced to 48 percent. In 1986, it was further reduced to 37 percent. From 1989 onwards, the rate was gradually reduced to 24 percent[78] and the maximum tax rate was capped at 50 percent.[79] In summary, the tax system became increasingly regressive. By making the legitimacy and fairness of the tax system worse and the distribution of the tax burden highly unequal, these and similar features contributed to widespread tax evasion, which arguably remains Greece's most serious fiscal problem (for details, see the next section).

Rampant Tax Evasion and Its Causes

One of the weaknesses of the tax system is that in general election years the otherwise upward trend is reversed, as an analysis of the evolution of the rate of tax revenues over GDP shows. According to Tatsos, this indicates that the way the Greek tax system functioned was "adjusted to political circumstances and demands."[80] In other words, in election years governments took measures to relax tax collection in order to woo voters and so increase their chances of being re-elected. Therefore, the tax system was often used for political electioneering rather than for other purposes, such as the implementation of policies that would benefit society or the redistribution of income. This undoubtedly affected the legitimacy of the tax system and the degree of tax compliance.[81]

What also affected the legitimacy of the tax system was the fact that, when the independent state was established after the end of the Second World War, the system's primary scope was to collect revenues, without any significant redistributive or social dimensions.[82] For this reason, people saw the tax system as a mechanism that "drained" money from their pockets and this encouraged them to avoid paying taxes if possible. Moreover, the distribution of the tax burden was considered unfair because, among other things, the burden on the lower-income brackets was significantly higher than on the higher ones.[83] This seems to have added to tax evasion, as the theory suggests.[84]

A further weakness was the very high level of corruption,[85] which reduced even further people's trust in the state and added to the incentive to avoid paying taxes. The first study examining Greeks' perceptions of corruption ("the abuse of public office for private gain")[86] was published in 1996 and was based on an opinion poll conducted at the national level. The survey indicated that 67 percent of respondents agreed with the statement "the state is corrupt," with the tax services characterized as the most corrupt sector of public administration.[87]

Thus, tax evasion indicates taxpayers' lack of belief in the legitimacy of taxes and, by extension, the legitimacy of the state that imposes them. Ultimately, it was an expression of skepticism about the authority of the state itself. In other words, tax evasion expressed lack of trust in the state most directly and explains why tax evasion has been characterized as "the most massive and most tolerable expression of anti-social and illegal behaviour" in Greece.[88]

The literature indicates that Greece continues to suffer widespread tax evasion. According to two studies both published 2012, annual unreported income exceeds €28 billion and the black economy's share of GDP from 1999 to 2010 was approximately 27 percent, compared to an OECD average of 20.2 percent.[89] According to Tatsos, most evasion is detected in personal income taxation. This, he notes, is due to the nature of personal income taxes, which, for example, being direct taxes, are "particularly visible" to taxpayers and therefore "spur … their response [to them]."[90] Other than this, not only is there difficulty in defining what taxable personal income constitutes, but the distinction between personal and business expenses is not always clear. On the whole, personal income taxation is highly convoluted, something that—combined with administrative problems in the tax services, as Tatsos stresses—leads to even higher tax rates. It has also been noted that the proliferation and complexity of tax legislation and the inefficiency of the tax offices encourage evasion.[91]

Something that has made tax legislation complicated is the way the laws are written. One retired tax official interviewed for this research mentioned that when a part of the legislation was repealed, the wording used was of the following type: "Subparagraph x of paragraph y of law z is abolished," with x, y, and z given as numbers only. This made it difficult to determine which part of the law had changed and in what way.[92]

The structure of the economy is yet another factor: the country has fewer salaried employees per capita than the most of the other European countries, and many farmers, most of whom traditionally evade taxation.[93] More tax evasion starting in the mid-1970s was positively related to the number of self-employed, which was also increasing.[94] In the same vein, in late 1979, according to Zolotas, income policies during 1967–1974 (i.e., when the military junta was in power) resulted in a redistribution of income in favor of small business owners and the self-employed. Both had earnings outside the official economy.[95] This added to the illegitimacy of the tax system and exacerbated tax evasion. The chronically high levels of inflation and insufficient indexation of taxes have also led to an unbroken increase in the tax burden, something that again has made more people turn to tax evasion.[96] A further reason, according to a recent IMF report, is "[h]igh dissatisfaction with government services and public goods. If the individual does not perceive that he gets anything in return from the government, the incentives not to pay taxes are high."[97]

It is worth noting that the first relevant studies in Greece appeared in the late 1980s. For this reason, and because the share of tax revenue over

GDP has always been unstable,[98] it is not easy to arrive at a clear view about developments before the late 1980s even after examining the Ministry of Finance's annual reports on the budget. For example, the ratio of difference between declared and collected personal income taxes over the total amount of direct taxes collected can be considered an indication of how much tax evasion occurred in personal income.[99] This ratio, as the Ministry reports suggest, decreased between 1955 and 1965, increased between 1965 and 1975, and then followed a downward trend from 1975 to 1990. As far as corporation tax is concerned, the corresponding ratio (the difference between declared and collected corporate income taxes over the total amount of direct taxes collected) decreased between 1955 and 1965, but then increased between 1965 and 1990.[100] It can be conjectured, therefore, that tax evasion of corporate income was the reason why the total amount of tax evasion increased significantly from the late 1970s onwards.[101] This, however, is mistaken given that corporation tax was a relatively small share of taxation.

It seems that tax evasion was mainly a result of the perception that the tax system was unfair and aimed only at collecting revenue and not concerned with redistribution. Due not only to incomplete reforms but also the preferential tax treatment of certain social groups, tax evasion was seen as a justifiable response to an unfair, untrustworthy, and illegitimate tax system. Characteristic of this is a 1953 article published in one of the oldest economic journals in the country, which noted that some people's salaries were being "decimated by the state each month," whereas others managed to "slip through the fingers" of the tax authorities and was one of the reasons why tax evasion was now "exonerated," taking the form of taxpayers' "just defence."[102]

Conclusion

This chapter analyzes the distribution of tax burden in Greece after the Second World War, focusing on the period from the mid-1950s to the late 1980s. For the most part, the system was prejudiced against the middle- and lower-income groups. That is to say, the burden on low-income earners was significantly higher than that on the high-income earners.

That the poorest bore a disproportionately large part of the tax burden made the system unfair and increased its perceived illegitimacy. The fact that direct taxes, as a source of revenue, were much less significant than indirect taxes had similar implications. The situation is even worse today:

the income tax rate over total tax revenues is currently at the same or even a lower level than what it was more than a century ago in Germany and the United Kingdom, for example.[103]

Added to the perceived unfairness of the tax system were features such as taxes in favor of third parties. The revenue from such taxes was given to the professional classes and organizations in a strong negotiating position and increased the perception of unfair treatment experienced by those who paid them. It has been argued that these forms of taxation, which "disrupted the 'trust' between citizens and the state, encouraging both sides to deceive one another,"[104] were a feature of how Greek society was fragmenting. Here it is suggested that these characteristics contributed to the very high degree of tax evasion burdening it, one of the most severe problems of the country's economy today.

Notes

1. Tax conscience can be defined as the moral sense of right and wrong guiding taxpaying behavior. In the *Oxford Dictionaries* conscience is defined as "[a] person's moral sense of right and wrong, viewed as acting as a guide to one's behaviour." http://www.oxforddictionaries.com/definition/english/conscience. Accessed December 2, 2016.
2. Straw and Glennie, "Third Wave of Globalisation," 23.
3. Kostis, *State and Enterprises in Greece*, 53.
4. Some of the data presented refer to subsequent years; however, for the most part the analysis covers the period up to the late 1980s.
5. For a breakdown of the structure of the tax revenue throughout 1950–2000, see Tatsos, *Shadow Economy*, 281.
6. Giouras, *Taxation and Politics*, 327.
7. Karagiorgas, *Public Finance 2*, 226.
8. *Bulletin of the FGI*, August–September 1987, 493–4, 5–6.
9. Karagiorgas, *Public Finance 2*, 245.
10. Tatsos, *Shadow Economy*, 278–9.
11. Ibid.
12. Ibid., 281.
13. For more information see ibid., 278–9.
14. Ibid., 280–2.
15. Giouras, *Taxation and Politics*, 322 (author's translation).
16. Vovolini Archive, *Viomichaniki Epitheorissis*, 22 (May 1955), 18.
17. The law was introduced in 1919. See Sellas, *Greek System of Taxation*, 38.
18. Glykou, *State and Tax Policy* 147.
19. Giouras, *Taxation and Politics*, 317–18.

20. Glykou, *State and Tax Policy*, 148.
21. Break and Turvey, *Greek Taxation*, 39. OGA = Organismos Georgikon Asfaliseon, the farmers' social insurance organization.
22. Giouras, *Taxation and Politics*, 319.
23. Index of Parliamentary Discussions 1946–67, 56–62, minutes from the sitting of the Special Committee, July 6–26, 1955 (author's translation).
24. *Long-term Statistical Series of the Greek Economy*, 13, 86–7.
25. The Scopes of the Rearrangements, newspaper cutting, CHROTEX archive. From the layout and in comparison to other articles found in the same archive it seems very likely that tit was published in 1957 in *I Naftemporiki* (author's translation).
26. *The Bulletin of Tax Legislation*, 11, 11, January 23, 1957, 46.
27. The Scopes of the Rearrangements.
28. Vovolini Archive, File 30, Eftaxias Family, sub-file 1, Evidence no. 61, 2.
29. Vovolini Archive, *Viomichaniki Epitheorissis*, 22 (May 1955), 18.
30. See e-forologia.
31. Sellas, *The Greek System of Taxation*, 122.
32. Ibid.
33. The tax rate remained at 35 percent until 1973; see Manesiotis, Tax Structure Change, 50.
34. Stathopoulos, *Taxation*, 7.
35. Ibid., 7–8.
36. Ibid., 9.
37. Ibid.
38. Psalidopoulos, *History*, 41.
39. Break and Turvey, *Greek Taxation*, 246–7.
40. Ibid., 243. Laws 3213 and 3765 were introduced in 1955 and 1957, respectively.
41. Ibid., 41. The law was introduced in 1959.
42. Ibid.
43. Ibid., 197.
44. Ibid., 198.
45. Ibid.
46. Ibid., 195.
47. Tatsos, *Public Finance*, 23–34.
48. CHROTEX Archive, "Tax Courts," *I Naftemporiki*, February 28, 1957, 6.
49. Moscholios, *Tax Incentives*, 3–4, in the Library of the Historical Archive of the National Bank of Greece.
50. Ibid.
51. Ibid., 7.
52. Dertilis, *Ineffectual of Effective?*, 40.

53. For more information on the tax treatment of farmers, see ibid., 26, 48–9.
54. Tatsos, *Shadow Economy*, 295–7.
55. Ibid., 299–300.
56. Ibid., 309.
57. Glykou, *State and Tax Policy*, 177. See also Kouros, "The Abolition of Third Party Taxes."
58. Frangos, in Giouras, *Taxation and Politics*, 330.
59. Kalyvianakis et al., *Tax Regime, Shadow Economy and Tax Evasion*, 33.
60. "At least 350 taxes in favor of third parties have been targeted by the government and the troika."
61. Tatsos, *Shadow Economy*, 308–9.
62. Giouras, *Taxation and Politics*, 329.
63. Glykou, *State and Tax Policy*, 177.
64. Tatsos, *Shadow Economy*, 277.
65. Ibid.
66. See Tatsos, *Shadow Economy*, 293.
67. *Statistical Yearbook of Greece*, 1962, 26, 50; 2005, 184; 2009–10, 42, 108.
68. Tatsos, *Shadow Economy*, 290, 293.
69. Ibid., 290.
70. Ibid., 302.
71. Ibid., 302–8.
72. According to the 1981 census.
73. In 1961, pensioners accounted for 2.81 percent of the population; in 1981 their number had risen to 13.3 percent.
74. Ibid., 287.
75. The unequal distribution of the tax burden is also an outcome of the unequal relationship between direct and indirect taxes.
76. Tatsos, *Shadow Economy*, 287.
77. Ibid.
78. Sellas, *The Greek System of Taxation*, 433–4.
79. Ibid.
80. Ibid., 277.
81. Ibid., 74.
82. As Giouras and Psalidopoulos, *Occupation, Nazism and the Greek Economy*, 19–20, 34, 224–46 indicate, this was like the tax policies followed by the German Occupation forces during the war.
83. Tatsos, *Shadow Economy*, 287.
84. See ibid., 20.
85. IMF, *Greece*, 26.
86. IMF, *Corruption*, 3. One of the means by which corruption is facilitated is bribery, "something, usually money, to gain an illicit advantage," given to public officials in this case. See What is Bribery and Corruption?

87. Tatsos, *Shadow Economy*, 247–9.
88. Manesiotis, in Tatsos, *Shadow Economy*, 74.
89. Greece, Selected Issues, 20.
90. Tatsos, *Shadow Economy*, 186.
91. Ibid., 75
92. This tax official asked to remain anonymous.
93. Tatsos, *Shadow Economy*, 75.
94. Ibid.
95. Psalidopoulos, *History of the Bank of Greece*, 293.
96. Ibid., 186.
97. Greece, Selected Issues, 26.
98. Ibid., 277.
99. Greece, Selected Issues, 24.
100. *Annual Reports for the Execution of the Budget*, various issues.
101. Kalyvianakis et al., *Tax Regime, Shadow Economy and Tax Evasion*, 275–9.
102. Vovolini Archive, Notes—Tax Evasion, *Viomichaniki Epitheorissis*, 20 September 1953, 302.
103. Ibid., 282.
104. Giouras, T*axation and Politics*, 330.

References

Unpublished Sources

Interviews

Retired Tax Official Who Asked to Remain Anonymous. 2014, September 9.

Theses

Manesiotis, Vasilios. 1985. *Tax Structure Change During Economic Development: The Case of Greece*. Unpublished Doctoral Thesis. Chicago, IL: Northwestern University.

Primary Sources

Chrotex Archive

The Scopes of the Rearrangements. i*I Naftemporiki* (c. 1955).
Tax Courts. 1957. I Naftemporiki, February 28, p. 6.

Vovolini Archive

Eftaxias Family, file 30, sub-file 1, Evidence 61, 2.
Notes – Tax Evasion, Viomichaniki Epitheorissis, 20 (September 1953), 302.
Viomichaniki Epitheorissis, 22 (May 1955), 18.

Index of Parliamentary Debates, 1946–67

Minutes from the Sitting of the Special Committee (June 26–27, 1955), 56–62.

Secondary Literature

Break, George F., and Ralph Turvey. 1964. *Studies in Greek Taxation*. Athens: Center of Planning and Economic Research.

Dertilis, G.V. 1993. *Ineffectual of Effective? Taxes and Power in the Neo-Hellenic State [Ατελέσφοροι ή τελεσφόροι: φόροι και εξουσία στο νεοελληνικό κράτος]*. Athens: Alexandria Publications (in Greek).

Giouras, Thanasis. 2000. *Taxation and Politics, Political-economic Problematic and Financial Thought [Φορολογία και Πολιτική. Πολιτικο-οικονομική προβληματική και δημοσιονομική σκέψη]*. Athens: Sakis Karagiorgas Foundation (in Greek).

Giouras, Thanasis, and Michalis Psalidopoulos. 2015. *Occupation, Nazism and the Greek Economy – Official Reports and Memoirs [Κατοχή, ναζισμός και ελληνική οικονομία - Υπηρεσιακές εκθέσεις και απομνημονεύματα]*. Athens: Metamesonikties Ekdoseis (in Greek).

Glykou, Ioanna. 2009. *State and Tax Policy, An Historical and Theoretical Approach and the Case of Greece [Κράτος και φορολογική πολιτική: μια ιστορική και θεωρητική προσέγγιση και η πε- ρίπτωση της Ελλάδας]*. Athens: Sakoullas (in Greek).

Kalyvianakis, K., M. Xanthakis, A. Leventis, B. Manesiotis, S. Theodoropoulos, K. Trahanas, and K. Flesiopoulou. 1999. *Tax Regime, Shadow Economy and Tax Evasion in Greece [Φορολογικό καθεστώς, παραοικονομία και φοροδιαφυγή στην Ελλάδα]*. Athens: Papazisis (in Greek).

Karagiorgas, D.P. 1981. *Public Finance 2 – The Fiscal Institutions [Δημόσια Οικονομική 2 Οι Δημοσιονομικοί Θεσμοί]*. Papazisis: Athens (in Greek).

Kostis, Kostas. 2013. *State and Enterprises in Greece, the History of "Aluminium of Greece" [Κράτος και επιχειρήσεις στην Ελλάδα. Η Ιστορία του "Αλουμινίου της Ελλάδος"]*. Athens: Polis (in Greek).

Moscholios, Nikolaos Mich. 1967. *Tax Incentives, Comparative Research, Greece–European Economic Community [Φορολογικά Κίνητρα, Συγκριτική Ερευνα, Ελλάδα – Ευρωπαϊκή Οικονομική Κοινότητα]*. Athens.

Psalidopoulos, Michalis. 2014. *History of the Bank of Greece, 1928–2008 [Ιστορία της Τράπεζας της Ελλάδος, 1928–2008]*. Athens: The Bank of Greece (in Greek).

Sellas, Stephanos Mich. 1989. *The Greek System of Taxation [Το Ελληνικό Φορολογικό Σύστημα]*. Athens: Papazisis (in Greek).
Stathopoulos, Georgios N. 1964. *Taxation of Indigenous and Foreign Companies [Φορολογία Ημεδαπών και Αλλοδαπών Εταιριών]*. Athens: Federation of Greek Industries (in Greek).
Straw, Will, and Alex Glennie. 2012. *The Third Wave of Globalisation*. Institute for Public Policy Research, January. http://www.ippr.org/files/images/media/files/publication/2012/01/third-wave-globalisation_Jan2012_8551.pdf?noredirect=1. Accessed 19 Jan 2017.
Tatsos, Nikos. 1991. *Public Finance in Greece [Τα δημόσια οικονομικά στην Ελλάδα]*. Athens: Sbilias.
———. 2001. *Shadow Economy and Tax Evasion in Greece [Παραοικονομία και φοροδιαφυγή στην Ελλάδα]*. Athens: Papazisis (in Greek).

Official Publications

Hellenic Statistical Authority. *Statistical Yearbook of Greece*, 1962, 26, 50, 50; 2005, 184; 2009–10, 42, 108.
International Monetary Fund. 2013. *Greece, Selected Issues*, Country Report 13/155, 26. http://www.imf.org/external/pubs/ft/scr/2013/cr13155.pdf. Accessed 1 Nov 2015; International Monetary Fund, *Corruption: Costs and Mitigating Strategies*, IMF Staff Discussion Note, May 2016, p. 3. http://www.imf.org/external/pubs/ft/sdn/2016/sdn1605.pdf. Accessed 8 Oct 2016.
Ministry of Finance, *Annual Reports for the Execution of the Budget*, Various Issues (in Greek).

Periodicals

The Bulletin of the Federation of Greek Industries. 1987, August–September.
The Bulletin of Tax Legislation. 1957. 11, 11, January 23.

Web Resources

"At Least 350 Taxes in Favour of Third Parties Have Been Targeted by the Government and the Troika." http://www.unitedreporters.gr/news/GR/Forologika_themata/forologika_themata/Sto_stohastro_kyvernisis_kai_troikas__toylahiston_350_foroi_yper_triton. Accessed 5 Feb 2014 (in Greek).
Oxford Dictionaries Online, s.v. Conscience. http://www.oxforddictionaries.com/definition/english/conscience. Accessed 2 Dec 2015.

e-forologia. *Online Bank*. Legislative Order 3843/1958. http://www.e-forologia.gr/lawbank/document.aspx?digest=48DBD85F893B6FC0.1D031AEA53&-version=1958/09/3. Accessed 3 Oct 2014 (in Greek)

Kouros, Giorgos. 2015. The Abolition of Third Party Taxes Will Deliver a Blow to Insurance Funds', I Naftemporiki. August 3. http://www.naftemporiki.gr/finance/story/986018/i-katargisi-foron-uper-triton-pligma-sta-tameia. Accessed 5 May 2017.

Tackling Bribery and Corruption. What Is Bribery and Corruption? http://www.anticorruption.ie/en/acjs/pages/fq08000018. Accessed 8 Oct 2016.

Limits to Redistribution in Late Democratic Transitions: The Case of Spain

Sara Torregrosa Hetland

Introduction

Inequality increased strongly during the Great Recession (2007–2014) in Spain, rising almost 2.5 Gini points or 7 percent, in contrast with the average of 0.3 percent in the EU-27. At the same time, the country suffered a severe fiscal crisis, with public deficits at an average of 8 percent of gross domestic product (GDP) over the period 2008–2015 (double the EU-27 average). In autumn 2016, experts were still calling for an adjustment on the revenue side.[1] In fact, nearly all measures to curb the deficit during the

This chapter stems from my PhD dissertation, Tax System and Redistribution: The Spanish Fiscal Transition (1960–1990), written under the supervision of Alfonso Herranz Loncán and Alejandro Esteller Moré, to whom I am most grateful. I acknowledge financial support from the Spanish Ministry of Education's scholarship program *Formación del Profesorado Universitario* and Research Project ECO2012–39169-C03-03. I also thank the editors for their comments, which greatly improved this chapter.

S. Torregrosa Hetland (✉)
Department of Economic History, Lund Univerisity, Lund, Sweden
e-mail: sara.torregrosa_hetland@ekh.lu.se

G. Huerlimann et al. (eds.), *Worlds of Taxation*,
Palgrave Studies in the History of Finance,
https://doi.org/10.1007/978-3-319-90263-0_13

recession were expenditure cuts, but tax revenue in Spain is currently well below the EU average—33 percent versus 39 percent of GDP during the crisis years.[2]

Can history help explain the current situation? This chapter provides an affirmative answer. In 1970, Spain collected few taxes, and did so inefficiently and unfairly. Tax revenue was just 16 percent of GDP, slightly over half the level in EU-15 countries. After a series of substantial reforms in 1977–1986, this rose to 80 and 90 percent of the level in these other countries, where it remains to the present. The fiscal system shows a seemingly permanent incapacity on the revenue side, which limits the government's ability to redistribute income.

Nineteenth-century tax principles were in force until democratization was introduced in the late 1970s. Low revenue, rigidity, and reliance on indirect taxation were commonly identified by public finance scholars during General Francisco Franco's dictatorship (1939–1975), but could not be resolved politically. The current system, introduced in 1977, tried to make the country more like its neighbors in this respect: taxes were to be more flexible, guided by the idea of progressivity, and revenue should increase enough to fund a modern welfare state. The fact that these changes were only possible after democratization makes Spain different from the other countries analyzed in this volume. Democracy triggered the tax reform, but the economic context differed from that which saw the initial development of welfare state taxation in the forerunners.

This chapter investigates tax policy in Spain during the political transition (1976–1982), with a focus on the distribution of the tax burden and attitudes toward equality. The fiscal reform has been closely studied, but only a recent quantitative study established the limited results of the new tax system with respect to progressivity and redistribution.[3] Why was tax equity, so widely proclaimed, not achieved? Was it not a social demand, or did it face other obstacles?

This chapter investigates two interrelated aspects: social preferences and the mechanisms for their translation into policy. Demand for redistribution is the result of a complex process, affected, for example, by changing ideas about fairness in the income distribution and the capacity of taxation to impact inequality levels.[4] Economic theory about taxes and the policies followed in leading countries have changed radically since the mid-twentieth century from defending progressivity to severe criticism of it as an obstacle to efficiency, giving rise to the privileged treatment of capital income. Inequality and its various dimensions will also condition social demands and the potential formation of interest coalitions.[5] Understanding how tax equity developed is my first focus, where I consider ideas on distributive justice, progressivity, and income redistribution in sociological surveys, the media, and political debates.

The second question is the translation of citizens' preferences into political measures. During the period covered in this chapter, authoritarianism was replaced by a parliamentary system, based on political parties. Did that mean going from the "only voter" of Francoism to the "median" or "swing" voter of democratic political economy? To what extent were social demands reflected in policies? Which aspects explain continuity in tax incidence despite the extensive fiscal reforms?

I argue that the first years of regime configuration had a long-term impact on the distribution of political power. My focus is on the electoral system. Although formally proportional, its operation deviates significantly from proportionality, favoring conservativism.[6] Differences in political participation would further extend this bias, given that the low turnout of low-income groups generally limits the votes received by the pro-redistribution parties.[7] The activities of pressure groups are also reviewed.

The international context and its implications are then explored. In our globalized world, capital mobility and tax competition are key factors for understanding the pressures at play that are opposed to fiscal progressivity. Spain's economic openness increased during this period, with the milestone of accession to the European Economic Community (EEC) in 1986 and the subsequent construction of the Common Market which liberalized the movement of factors of production.

Inequality and Taxes During the Democratic Transition

The tax reform was a central element in the transition to democracy (1976–1982), and progressivity was declared as its main guiding principle.[8] As we shall see, the resulting system failed, however, to apply this idea generally and effectively.

The roots of tax reform went deep. In the early 1970s, some projects were in accord with Professor Enrique Fuentes Quintana and the Instituto de Estudios Fiscales (Institute of Fiscal Studies), which is part of the Public Finance Ministry. These suggested the adoption of a European taxation model based mainly on personal income taxation, complemented by wealth, inheritance, and value-added (VAT) taxes. The personal income tax did not exist as such in Spain at the time (separate taxes were raised on labor income, capital income, and so on) nor did a wealth tax. Consumption was subject to a turnover tax. The new system was to be fairer, more efficient, and hence more flexible, so that the state could meet the needs of a new stage of development. It also meant convergence with Europe and would thus facilitate integration into the EEC.

However, Franco's government rejected these proposals in June 1973, and the plan was not made public, though the minister was dismissed. After this, Fuentes Quintana and his group were convinced that a modernizing tax reform of this kind would only be possible in a democracy, something that came into effective in 1977, two years after Franco's death.

Another prominent member of Fuentes's group was Francisco Fernández Ordóñez, a high-ranking official at the Ministry of Public Finance and a member of Madrid's upper middle class. He had a background in law and economics, including studying abroad. He had progressive, liberal ideas and as such was one of the founders of the Social Democrat Party in 1976.[9] This party was integrated into the centrist coalition Unión de Centro Democrático (UCD) in 1977, which, headed by Adolfo Suárez, won the first democratic elections that year. Fernández Ordóñez was then appointed Public Finance Minister, while Fuentes Quintana took over the Ministry of Economics.

Fernández Ordóñez presented a comprehensive tax reform project consisting of a set of general anti-tax evasion measures and the complete reorganization of both direct and indirect taxation. In the end, not all of these proposals were passed as planned. The first law presented to parliament, in November 1977, introduced a wealth tax and several regulations to combat tax evasion: the lifting of the veil of banking secrecy, the introduction of tax crime[10] and other related issues. Personal income tax came into force in 1979 as the principal milestone; VAT was also planned then but only introduced in 1986, then as a condition for accession to the EEC. The wealth tax of 1977 had symbolic importance, but only a trivial real impact because of its low revenue-generating capacity; it was transitory until new regulations were set in place in 1991. Similarly, a new inheritance tax was deferred until 1987.

The Public Finance Minister was a proponent of progressivity—or as a minimum of a marked decrease in the regressive nature of the existing system—and an expansion of public services. He also placed huge importance on combating tax evasion, not only by prosecution in the courts but also by encouraging voluntary compliance. He wanted to usher in a new era in the relationships between the (now) citizens and the (now democratic) state, based on responsibility and fair exchange. In his view reducing inequality through the tax system was less contentious than attempting to do it in salary negotiations. This was central to the legitimation of the capitalist economy, particularly in a crisis, which the West was experiencing at the time:

> The fragile Spanish economy is going through difficult times, and we think that adequate restructuring will only be possible if there is fairness in the distribution of sacrifices and the part of effort that we all must share. As much as we respect the market economy as the main instrument for obtaining resources, we firmly demand the public sector's correcting action through the tax system and redistributive expenditure.[11]

Reform of the social security system was also envisaged. It did not, however, fall under the competence of the same minister, but of the Ministry of Health (and later the Labor Department). Contributions to social security were strongly regressive, as they were not assessed on real wages but on a base established for different worker categories. They also imposed a significant tax burden on wages, making labor more expensive for firms and thus probably affected employment rates. The main demand was to integrate social security into the overall budget, increasing general taxation to finance its expenditures or fully funding them with taxes. However, the actual reform did not go that far. Administrative reorganization in 1978 improved transparency, but the contributive system remained largely unchanged until the end of the 1980s.[12]

All in all, the tax reforms made public finances more efficient and flexible, enabling an increase in revenues and the funding of a nascent welfare state.[13] But the overall tax system was not made progressive. The expansion of direct income and wealth taxes was counteracted by onerous social contributions and widespread tax evasion.

Table 1 shows the relationship between taxation and the income distribution. If we compare pre- with post-tax incomes, in all years the inequality index was higher for post-tax incomes, which shows that the income distribution was made worse by taxes. Throughout the period, inequality in disposable income fell only slightly, and final post-tax-and-transfer incomes, which include benefits received by households, were slightly more unequal at the end.

Total tax rates were higher in the second decile than in the top percentile. The tax system became less regressive over time, but the value of the

Table 1 The impact of taxation on inequality in Spain, 1970–1990

	1970	*1982*	*1990*
Inequality (Gini index) across phases of income			
Pre-tax income	38.0	42.1	42.5
Post-tax income	41.4	44.5	49.2
Disposable income	34.7	33.0	32.9
Post-tax-and-transfer income	36.2	34.5	37.3
Average effective tax rates on selected Quantiles of the income distribution			
2nd decile	28.3	43.6	70.7
Top decile	20.0	34.9	46.5
Top percentile	16.4	32.3	44.4
Tax progressivity and redistribution indices			
Progressivity (Kakwani)	−0.0849	−0.0274	−0.0485
Redistribution (Reynolds-Smolensky)	−0.0332	−0.0239	−0.0667

Source: Torregrosa (2015b)

Notes: The Gini indices are calculated using the OECD equivalence scale and individual weighting. Average effective tax rates are obtained adding all taxes paid by households, including indirect taxes and social contributions. The progressivity and redistribution indices also refer to the joint tax system

indices never turned positive.[14] So why was a progressive tax system not attained? Was it not demanded, or did preferences not result in political measures?

Public Opinion

An extensive literature has analyzed collective attitudes with respect to taxes. The evidence starts in the mid-1960s. Early inquiries generally focused on tax legitimacy and evasion in an effort to provide insight for tax administration design. The evidence is disjointed and heterogeneous across time; nevertheless, we can reach some general conclusions.[15]

The Spanish were strongly in favor of redistribution, and a large majority did not believe their tax system was effective in this respect. Both before and after the 1970s reforms over half of the survey respondents considered the distribution of the tax burden unfair. They wanted more progressivity, but also lower overall taxation at the same time as better public services.[16] This can be related to framing inconsistency, which is a problem found in similar studies.

Across the following decades, citizens came to believe increasingly that they had become heavily taxed since the changes made to public revenues. This perception started to fall though around 1990, coinciding with the stabilization of the tax-to-GDP ratio. During the 1980s, the sense of bearing a heavy tax burden can be traced to a perceived disequilibrium with respect to services due to delays in building the welfare state and also to the regressivity of taxation in general. An "anti-fiscal" atmosphere seems to have been developing, which comes through in these indicators and other sources. At the same time, fiscal drag was increasing income tax for the low- and middle-income strata.[17] This seems to have negatively affected its legitimacy owing to greater increases in the tax than in real earnings for several years.[18] Moreover, it coincided with economic distress and indebtedness, creating an impression of poor management and wastefulness.

Tax evasion was also a key topic in the surveys. In general, fraud was considered disturbing and unfair, but social sanctions against it were lax. Throughout the period, the perception seems to have been that tax evasion was widespread, persistent, and possibly increasing. We might venture (as the literature has shown) that a slight improvement coexisted with growing concern among the public, which is evident in more recent surveys.

These conclusions are similar to those reached by studies on other OECD countries in the closing decades of the twentieth century, but the Spanish seem to be comparatively strongly in favor of redistribution.[19] For example, the French, Germans, Spanish, and Italians showed strong support in 2000 for the status quo, but more Spanish preferred an increase in both taxes and benefits (30 percent of respondents, versus 14–17 percent in the other countries), which is consistent with the incomplete harmonization in welfare provision levels.[20]

With the democratic transition, both employers' and workers' associations were legalized in spring 1977. Albeit illegally, trade unions had existed under the dictatorship and had played an important role in opposing late Francoism. However, in the first years of democracy, with high inflation and rising unemployment, they were mainly concerned with maintaining the purchasing power of wages and pensions; tax objectives ranked low on their agenda. Support for the unions, furthermore, decreased during the 1980s, with membership lower than in other European countries.

Business associations, by contrast, started to organize in the late 1970s and were quite aggressive in their defense of economic liberalization and their opposition to welfare expansion and tax progressivity. According to Carlos

Ferrer Salat, president of the Confederación Española de Organizaciones Empresariales, the main employers' association, tax reform was "going to put an important brake on investment."[21] Small firm owners, on the other hand, were more in favor of the proposed changes as they were suffering from the old system through presumptive assessments and the weight of social contributions for labor-intensive establishments. A small business owner from the metal sector told the press in June 1977:

> I don't mind the tax reform, what matters to me is that it is done taking into account the economic capacity of each firm and that it prevents that the most powerful ones get benefited. I hope that this democracy makes things go that way.[22]

Editorials in the journals depict interests and opinions for and against the reform. The most popular newspaper, *El País*, conducted a series of interviews in 1978 with the politicians negotiating the proposed taxes in parliament; these interviews informed readers about some of the main issues. The interviews make clear the extent to which the principle of progressivity was generally accepted at the time. The Center and Left-leaning parties generally defended it, notwithstanding some differences between them. Those on the Right, however, represented conservative voters and so were not in favor of progressivity. This became apparent only in their concrete proposals on detailed issues concerning tax exemptions, allowances, or credits, and not as a general statement or challenge to increasing tax rates.[23]

The Political Transition: Malapportioning the Party System

Given the results from surveys, it would seem that attitudes to progressivity were not translated into effective policy-making. Why was that? My conclusion takes in a national and an international story. The first looks at the consequences of the democratic transition for the policy process and how the new system was institutionalized. The second focuses on international economic circumstances and how they changed in the period when the tax model was originally designed. The two stories are not mutually exclusive. The internal context helps us to consider the nature of the regime itself as it now emerged. The external context is addressed in Section "International Integration".

The transition to democracy was not the result of a revolution, but came about only after Franco's death in November 1975. By then, the political elite was no longer a homogeneous bloc, as some had adopted a slightly reformist stance. Nor was the opposition united in spite of efforts, headed by the Communist Party, to achieve a regime breakdown and have a provisional government, formed by all democratic forces, call for the first elections. Significant social unrest was observed too, with labor disputes and mobilization at various levels.

The usual conclusion is that neither the Francoists nor the opposition were sufficiently strong or united to impose their views, so a compromise had to be reached. The transition took the form of a reform conducted from above, that is to say, from Adolfo Suárez's government, who himself had been appointed by King Juan Carlos, Franco's designated successor. The new regime did not break legal continuity with the dictatorship, but the strength of the political and social opposition made it possible to obtain some aspects of a breakthrough. Were those enough to ensure a democratic tax policy in the sense that the tax system expressed the preferences of the electorate?[24]

Different institutional settings have been found to be more or less favorable to redistribution. Centralized, parliamentary, and proportional systems would be more redistributive than their federal, presidential, or majoritarian counterparts.[25] For Spain, Fernández-Albertos has argued that proportional elections had a positive effect on redistributive policies as well as the existence of large and cohesive parties, and a socialist government from 1982 to 1996.[26] But was parliamentary representation actually proportional?

The elections show very low levels of proportionality when compared to other European countries. One of the reasons was district malapportionment. This term refers to the disproportionality found in territorial representation, which generally favors less populated regions where more conservative voters are found, and so decreases the changes of redistribution, but potentially favors establishing democracy in a transitional context.[27] A number of studies have underlined the interests evident in the design of the electoral system during the transition.[28] Whereas nominally proportional in its operation, it leads to both a majoritarian and a conservative bias (i.e., Right-leaning parties benefit more from the first than Left-leaning ones). Spain's malapportionment value was 0.0963 in 1996, 16th of a sample of 78 countries.[29]

During the first years of democracy, the electoral system especially benefited Suárez's party, the UCD (see Table 2). It won a significant number of seats in parliament of 1977, although not an absolute majority. The UCD was also the most successful in the 1979 election. The impact of the first elections on the party system was very significant: parties obtaining representation not only gained institutional power but also reinforced access to public opinion, and last but not least funding from the state budget. The ones that did not—and they were many—were dissolved or were disadvantaged in the next elections. In that way, elections were an active element in the configuration of the party system during the first years of the new regime.[30] Similarly, because of the foundational moment for many aspects of political life, the majorities enjoyed by the UCD had a long-term impact on public policy.

After 1982, the most successful party was the Socialist Party (Partido Socialista Obrero Español, PSOE), which won the most parliamentary seats. PSOE's absolute majority in 1982 enabled it to expand the welfare state and complete the tax reform, including anti-fraud measures and the introduction of VAT. Both the party and the context, however, had by then changed in many respects. A review of its electoral manifestos shows how, by 1986, tax progressivity had all but disappeared as a means of redistribution, which now focused on social expenditure.

Table 2 Parties benefiting from the electoral rules, 1977–1986

	UCD			*PSOE*		
	% votes	*% seats*	*Diff.*	*% votes*	*% seats*	*Diff.*
1977	34.5	41.1	6.6	24.4	29.4	5.0
1979	35.1	48.0	12.9	30.5	34.6	4.1
	AP coalitions			*PSOE*		
1982	26.5	30.6	4.1	40.8	50.6	9.8
1986	26.1	30.0	3.9	37.9	46.6	8.7

Source: Author's calculations using data from *Junta Electoral Central*

Note: From 1982, the main party on the right was Alianza Popular (forerunner of the Popular Party), which headed coalitions in the two next general elections

The Tax Positions Taken in Parliament

If malapportionment meant that UCD's vision was overrepresented, what ramifications did this have for policy? Which tax positions were reinforced and which weakened? I have studied in-depth the parliamentary debates on the tax laws and the proposals defended by each party (see Table 3).

Only the first two tax proposals, presented by the government in 1977–1979, were approved. These were debated during a period of political consensus among the main parties. The consensus period is clearly expressed in the Moncloa Pacts of October 1977, which set an agreed policy response to the economic crisis. These included several points on taxation.[31] The tax debates coincided with debates on the new constitution, which was the main focus. After its enactment in late 1978, the scenario became more confrontational; at the same time a crisis within UCD unfolded. The remaining tax reforms did not make it through parliament and the delay made it possible for those against them to come up with alternative models in the 1980s.

The first reform of Minister Fernández Ordóñez was LMURF, passed in November 1977. It included the creation of a number of provisional taxes—a wealth tax and a surcharge on high-income taxation—and a set of anti-evasion measures—a tax amnesty, tax crime, and lifting the veil of

Table 3 Main tax proposals, 1977–1979

Law	*Proposal presented*	*Sanctioned*	*No. amendments*
LMURF: Wealth tax, anti-fraud measures	July 1977	November 1977	139
Personal income tax	January 1978	September 1978	202
Net wealth tax	January 1978	–	82
	April 1979	–	115 (incl. 57 prev.)
Inheritance and gift tax	January 1978	–	64
	April 1979	–	80 (incl. 46 prev.)
VAT	July 1978	–	54
	April 1979	–	81 (incl. 48 prev.)

Source: Archive of Congress, Public Finance Commission: Folder 12, Legs. 1069, 1696–2, 1698–3, 1700, 1714–8, 1715–1

Notes: LMURF: Ley de Medidas Urgentes de Reforma Fiscal, Law of Urgent Measures of Fiscal Reform. A net wealth tax was finally passed in 1991, inheritance and gift in 1987, VAT in 1985. (incl. ... prev.): how many amendments from the previous parliamentary process were reintroduced by the parties in the next debate banking secrecy. These were expected to usher in a fresh start in relationships between taxpayers and the tax administration.

With respect to the initial project, the law as finally approved shows an increase in the progressivity of the tax rates on wealth, following quite closely some socialist proposals. This was, however, accompanied by a reduction in revenue-generating capacity, since rates were lowered in the initial brackets, where the majority of estates would be found. By contrast, the structure put forward by the Communist Party was less progressive on paper, but would have brought in more revenue from the propertied classes.[32]

The parliamentary debates focused on two especially contested issues. The Socialists pushed for the inclusion of legal entities in the wealth tax, arguing that leaving them out introduced inequality among firms with respect to individuals, the very reason why they had been included in the first government project. This point was important, according to the socialists, because the wealth tax was meant to serve as a register of the estates for the rest of the prospective reform; thus, wealth held by legal entities should also be registered, together with that held by individuals. UCD justified the change because of concerns about double taxation and a negative impact on investment. The socialist proposal was backed by the Communists, but nevertheless rejected by 164 votes to 147.

Also discussed was the starting date of the duty of financial entities to cooperate regarding the lifting the veil of bank secrecy. Catalan socialists suggested that this principle should be backdated to June 1977, that is, before the law was enacted but notably after the principle had been made public. They argued that during the year important capital movements had gone through and the government ought to be able to investigate these, since the law would not change the legality of their owners' actions. The Right argued against this, defending the principle of non-retrospective action. The point was also rejected, but only by 147 to 142 votes.

Next came the cornerstone of the reform: personal income tax. Members of the government party presented 19 percent of the amendments (38 out of 202). In all, Center-Right groups, UCD included, put forward 70 percent of the amendments. They were also more critical, proof that the Public Finance Minister had taken a more progressive position than many in his own party.

Remarkably, the structure of rates received very little discussion, with a progressive schedule accepted by all parties, at least in theory. Resistance is shown in the debate on tax credits and allowances, when the conservative parties defended significant increases. Some of their suggestions were accepted at least in part, which entailed moderating the law during its passage through parliament.[33] How tax credits are designed profoundly affects progressivity, but it does so in a less transparent way than the tax rates.

Amendments presented by the Left failed, among them strict limits on the application of presumptive taxation.[34] The discretionary power left in the hands of the government was criticized by almost all parties in this respect and also, notably, the capacity to alter the schedule and credits by annual decree. Several groups demanded compulsory adjustment in line with the annual inflation rate, which was high at the time. This had had a strong fiscal drag effect during the 1980s.

The new regulations included an obligation on the Ministry to publish fiscal data at the individual level, a transparency measure which had the aim of exposing tax evaders and improve general tax compliance. It was, however, the object of considerable controversy. The principal argument against it was the threat posed by the Basque terrorist organization ETA: publishing detailed information about taxed incomes would have made it easier for them to target wealthy individuals for extortion and kidnapping. It was finally resolved in 1981 with the publication of aggregate statistics, before it had been applied to the data from the new tax.[35]

In order to make taxation of wealth and capital incomes effective, withholding and third-party information from the banks had to be generalized. The lifting of the veil of banking secrecy in the November 1977 Act, however, was met with a fierce opposition campaign, which argued that the right to personal autonomy was being threatened, and that the measure would have negative economic consequences. The progressive journal *Cuadernos para el Diálogo* denounced the strong pressure being exerted on the reformers.[36] Conservative *ABC*, on the other hand, voiced the concerns of Rafael Termes, president of the Bankers' Association, who showed a willingness to cooperate, but complained about the onerous task of supplying information on all its clients.[37] Under the law, however, detailed data about amounts and transactions were requested only when a tax inspection was undertaken. This was appealed in court in 1983 by one taxpayer. He lost the case in November 1984 in the Supreme Constitutional Court. In 1985, the government published new legislation on the obligation to inform the tax administration about each individual's withholdings. This was appealed by 116 financial entities, which lost their case the following year.[38] In short, during this period the banking sector was unwilling to cooperate.

The tax reform leaders blamed the partial derailment of the initial plan on the opposition exerted by pressure groups. For example, Fuentes Quintana asserted in 1996: "The reform measures were effectively stopped. A big part of the tax changes were paralyzed by vested interests. [...] I am certain that there were [business] interferences to address what should be done."[39]

Fuentes resigned in October 1978, one year after the tax reform came in, when the personal income tax had just been approved. He quit politics owing to vehement resistance to his economic plan, of which Fernández Ordóñez's tax measures were only a part. Fuentes had backed the Moncloa Pacts, which included a range of liberalization measures as well as the stabilization program. Some of these were opposed by the banking and energy sectors, as well as by fellow members of the government who wanted a more conservative policy, which reflected the uneasy coexistence of different tendencies within UCD.[40]

Fernández Ordóñez stayed in government until April 1979, but left before he could complete his program. A year later, he denounced the reactionary character of resistance to the reform:

> In Spain, where public spending has not yet reached the levels of industrial countries, and where the tax system has very recently taken its first steps toward justice, a conservative phenomenon has been born, fueled not only by the international process, but by nostalgia for the past. ... This has strengthened the pressure of conservative forces, from public manifestations against the tax reform and the Moncloa Pacts, to a greater control of government policy.[41]

The 1977 wealth tax was supposed to be temporary, and was therefore called an "extraordinary" measure. In the event, it stayed in force for 14 years. The proposal to replace it was presented to parliament in January 1978, but was not approved before the dissolution of the government. A similar process took place April 1979, again with respect to inheritance tax and VAT (see Table 3).

Among the main issues in the debates on the new wealth tax was the socialist suggestion of annual adjustments to the local government's estimation of the value of property (the cadastral value), in line with the price of rental property. This was intended to tackle the widely known problem of under-valuation, which was used as a reference for other taxes as well.[42] On the other hand, the parties of the Center-Right strove for individual rather than joint taxation, an increase of the exempted threshold, and annual adjustments to inflation, all of which would negatively affect public revenue.

The main modification in the 1978 inheritance tax proposal concerned the recipient, whose other property would be taken into account to calculate the tax levied on him or her. This had the effect of making the tax more progressive and so was rejected by representatives of the Right. It was finally approved in 1987. The same parties again proposed an increase in exempted thresholds and annual adjustments to inflation. Left-wing parties, on the other hand, suggested higher or more progressive rate structures.

Finally, VAT was hotly debated in what is a clear example of special interest politics, with representatives of the different parties aiming for more complexity by granting exemptions or reduced rates for more activities.[43] VAT has been considered a "revenue-raising machine," and as such has many advantages. It is efficient, which encourages compliance among businesses and favors savings with respect to consumption. It also represents a significant improvement in neutrality when compared to turnover tax. Ultimately, however, two aspects made it difficult to introduce: the anticipated impact on prices at a time of double-digit inflation; and the fact that it meant bringing an end to covert protectionism.[44] VAT finally came into force in 1986 with other changes related to accession to the EEC.

Social Security Reform

By 1977, social security contributions represented half of public revenues, and 11 percent of GDP. These contributions were administered by several institutions introduced during the twentieth century. Several problems had resulted in the call for reform: the complexity of the system, small pensions, inequalities among various groups of workers, the high regressivity of the contributions, and the negative effects on employment.

Reform proposals were found in the 1977 programs of the main political parties. There was little difference between those proposed by the Right and the Left: they called for universality, collective control, and government funding (or at least an increase in general participation).[45] The government had appointed a commission to design a new model, which appeared in the *White Book of Social Security* in April 1977. However, over the following years electoral platforms continued to raise the same issues because they had not been translated into practice.[46]

Universalization and pensions, in a context of rising unemployment, had to be funded with larger transfers from the government's general budget. This, however, could not in reality be achieved before the tax reform had accomplished what it was intended to do in terms of revenue and progressivity.[47] In 1978, institutional reorganization improved the administration of social security, but the main reform—health expenditure and non-contributory pensions assumed by the general budget—would not become a reality until 1989–1990, when VAT came into force and simultaneously the economy improved. It is in this sense that continuity during the transition years has been emphasized. Government's participation in its funding increased largely due to growing expenditures on unemployment benefit, and minimum pensions grew faster than those in the top bracket. But the basic nature of the regime, with differentiated categories of workers, was maintained and even bolstered.[48]

The contributory system was simplified in 1978, ending a long transitory period starting in 1972 which attempted to bring the tax bases progressively closer to the wages paid, which had been at a much lower level in the 1960s.[49] Starting in 1978, the government set minimum and maximum caps each year. Maximum caps have the effect of exempting a fraction of the higher salaries; it has a regressive impact. The official explanation was that caps were being increased especially for the higher-paid workers, thus reducing regressivity. In hindsight, however, it does not seem to have been like that. The increase was indeed higher for the top categories in absolute terms, but during 1976–1988 all groups saw their bases grow by the same percentage. Moreover, the caps only increased in real terms in 1977/1978 and slightly in 1983. In the other years, growth seems to have been impeded by the crisis and the desire not to drive up the cost of labor. Compared to the average wage, tax caps were lowered (except in 1983/1984). Of course, to the extent that higher wages experienced above-average rises during the decade, regressivity with respect to wages increased.

This lack of thorough updating of the tax caps was consistent with the position taken by the business sector, which lobbied for a lower fiscal burden in light of the economic crisis, and expressed serious concern about the possibility of any increase in social contributions. Around 80 percent of the total amount of these was paid nominally by employers. Although the statutory regulation does not necessarily reflect the economic incidence of the tax, relaxation of these payments constituted potentially appreciable relief for firms.

International Integration

We now turn to the external factors. Arguably, and despite domestic democratization, the international context made it increasingly difficult to introduce and maintain progressive taxation. Spain's economic openness increased along with political liberalization, eventually culminating in integration with the EEC in 1986 and the subsequent commitments in trade, population, and financial movements.

That economic openness is an obstacle to progressive taxation has been long established in the literature. This arises from the exit option given in a common market to the holders of moveable tax bases—mostly capital, as opposed to labor. Openness would entail a falling tax burden on the factors of production that can be moved to prevent their relocation overseas.[50] Therefore, an open economy might reduce the feasibility of relying on progressive taxes to fund welfare state services.[51]

Why did European countries not reach an agreement on harmonization to get around these problems? The issue formed part of the Common Market talks within the European Commission (EC), but the results were highly uneven: While there was considerable unification in criteria concerning indirect taxes, the same was not reached with respect to direct taxation. Corporation tax rate harmonization had been proposed by the EC in 1975, but deferred by the need to define a common tax base—a complicated issue, which is still underway. As early as 1991, however, a decision reached prevented double taxation of dividends across national borders.[52]

Unification of criteria in personal income taxation has not been on the table in full, but some initiatives were intended to reduce the anticipated downward pressure on capital revenues. These incomes were easily subject to fraud if there were no automatic information-sharing and/or homogeneous withholding, thus giving their recipients more leverage to obtain tax privileges in advance and after the lifting of controls in July 1990. The EC's proposal in 1989 would have set a uniform 15 percent minimum withholding tax on the interest income of EEC residents, but this was abandoned in favor of cooperation. These decisions required unanimity. Scholars claim that interests in the United Kingdom and Luxembourg prevented the adoption of general agreements on an automatic information exchange and uniform withholding at source, and that, for Spain, "this situation is forcing, in order to avoid massive outflows of domestic savings, to put taxation of capital incomes and capital gains in line with that existing in the rest of countries of the Community."[53]

Of course, these developments are an epilogue to our story. They might, however, be a very relevant one. Even though Spain entered the EEC in 1986 and free circulation of capital was not a reality until 1993, the prospect of these events existed long before that. Furthermore, even if actual capital flows were not that big a hole in the tax base, the relevant issue here is that their possibility was seen as such in the economic literature and featured as an argument in tax debates starting in the mid-1980s.

The failure to harmonize thus gave way to competition and national adjustments in tax regulations. In the Scandinavian countries, as is well known, globalization pressures finally resulted in dual taxation of personal income (i.e., differentiated for capital and labor incomes). In Spain, the path to reinforcing capital taxation was "nipped in the bud." Subsequent reforms in the 1990s reduced the top marginal tax rates and granted privileged treatment to capital gains. Finally, steps toward dualization were taken at the beginning of the twenty-first century.

Changes in economic theory occurred too.[54] The tax model introduced in Spain in the late 1970s was a product of the postwar era and the supremacy of Keynesianism. General, progressive, and redistributive taxation peaked in the 1960s and 1970s, with the Carter Report 1966 favoring a system of personal taxation which would be as integrated and comprehensive as possible. A proliferation of allowances and credits, however, made real tax systems different from the ideal, and riddled them with horizontal and vertical equity problems. The proposed solutions rested on new theoretical approaches related to the optimal tax theory developed during the 1970s, which focused on the behavioral effects of taxation: a disincentive to work or save, and thus the negative impact of tax rates on the tax base. Policy proposals have since tended to reduce progressivity, especially at the top, and to prioritize neutrality over equity considerations.

All this coincided with Spain's catch-up to the developments of earlier decades. Whereas there was no strong alternative at the end of the 1970s, soon these new ideas figured in public debates across the country and hindered the full realization of the reform. Pan-Montojo has described a program for "reform of the reform" in the early 1980s, which called for savings and investment to be protected.[55] It was put forward by Alianza Popular in the 1982 elections, but its influence can be found at both ends of the political spectrum too. That the Socialist Party evolved in a similar sense is clear from reforms undertaken by them when they held power in the 1990s and beyond. The tide had changed.

Conclusion

Conditions surrounding tax reform in Spain in 1970–1986 were different from those that saw the development of the European welfare states in the postwar period. In spite of popular demand for progressivity and redistribution, as well as extensive regulatory changes, these objectives were not fulfilled. Public revenue increased and was raised more efficiently, but the overall burden remained regressive. Capital incomes managed to escape from taxation to a large extent. All in all, general redistribution was trapped at comparatively low levels.

Opinion in the 1970s was highly favorable to progressive reform, which initially had no clear alternative to it. Survey respondents, politicians, and commentators across the political spectrum declared themselves favorable to progressivity and a system in which the income tax played a central role. A policy alternative, however, first appeared as a supply-side program at the beginning of the 1980s.

Political institutions and the external context influenced how citizens' demands were translated into policies. Several constraints limited achievement of this reform. Malapportionment in parliament was one: the design of the electoral law during the transitional period was made under significant right-wing influence and gave rise to a system that benefits the rural, conservative districts. The importance of this should not be dismissed as it contributed to the formation of the party system after the first democratic elections of 1977. Successful parties gained access to power in the constitutional talks, prominence in the media, and public funds for their subsequent activities.

Economic distress and changes in public finance theory were closely related. Rising unemployment and sluggish growth made it difficult to increase taxation. Social security reform was delayed by resistance to increased labor costs. Finally, the introduction of VAT was also deferred, owing to its inflationary effects. The model aimed at was the product of postwar Keynesian economics, a period of unprecedented growth and social harmony in Western democracies. The oil shocks ushered in a different context, one in which emphasis would be on the promotion of personal savings and investment. Finally, international openness reinforced this process by affording capital owners a credible exit option.

How does our case fit into the pattern identified by the literature, according to which large, redistributive welfare states rely on regressive taxation (e.g., Sweden), while progressive tax systems give rise to limited redistributive government (e.g., the United States)?[56] Was the Spanish experience a result of a compromise, where the expansion of social expenditures in the 1980s and 1990s could be funded only by the recently introduced VAT and persistently heavy social contributions?

Certainly, as much as the expansion of public revenues in the late 1970s could only be achieved by increasing the burden at the top, where economic capacity was concentrated and very lightly taxed, a sustained further expansion during the economic crisis seems to have been politically feasible only if it also limited progressivity.[57] But we should not overlook the insights provided by the comparison of effective levels of redistribution attained in different countries: by 1990, the joint tax-and-transfer scheme in Spain remained less redistributive than those in the United Kingdom and United States—the prototype of small, liberal welfare states.[58]

The experience of the southern European periphery might therefore not fit into a dichotomous model. Welfare state laggards resorted to regressive taxation to expand social spending, as the leaders in redistributive policies had done before them. But lower revenue from personal taxes, higher inequality, and slow growth impeded the establishment of a highly redistributive tax-and-transfer system.

Notes

1. See, for example, the opinions expressed in *El País,* October 2016: http://economia.elpais.com/economia/2016/10/22/actualidad/1477122682_243716.html
2. All data cited in this paragraph come from Eurostat.
3. Comín, *Reaching a Political Consensus*; Pan-Montojo, "Larga e inconclusa transición"; Albi, *Hacienda Pública en Democracia*. For social expenditures, see Espuelas, *Evolución del gasto social.* Torregrosa, "Did Democracy…?" offers an evaluation of the redistributive incidence of the old and new systems.
4. Steinmo, "Evolution of Policy Ideas."
5. Lupu and Pontusson, "Structure of Inequality."
6. According to Persson and Tabellini, *Economic Effects*; and Iversen and Soskice, "Electoral Institutions," proportional systems would favor the introduction of redistributive policies. For studies on the Spanish electoral system and its design, see Gunther, "Electoral Laws"; Montero and Riera, "Sistema electoral".
7. Montero, "Vuelta a las urnas."

8. The specific dating of the transition to democracy has been the subject of some debate. Franco died in November 1975, but regime change can only be dated to early July 1976, when Adolfo Suárez became prime minister. 1986 signals the first democratic change of party in government, when the Socialists succeeded Suárez's centrist group.
9. For more information about him, see Serrano Sanz, "Francisco Fernández Ordóñez."
10. Until then, tax evasion was an administrative infraction only. The introduction of tax crime meant that, starting at a given amount, tax evasion could be prosecuted in the criminal courts, and thus lead to a longer prison sentence.
11. Fernández Ordóñez, *España necesaria*, 60. Author's translation. When he wrote "we" he meant the Social Democratic Party.
12. Non-contributory pensions were introduced in 1990. Currently, whether survivors' and orphans' pensions should be funded by general taxation is under discussion.
13. Elasticity in the context of tax revenues means that public incomes increase when the economy is growing.
14. Torregrosa, "Sticky Income Inequality"; Torregrosa, "Did Democracy…?" For more information on the data shown in Table 1, see the latter. These impacts would probably be worse if the impact of fraud could be taken into account. Such is the case in the personal income tax; see Torregrosa, "Bypassing Progressive Taxation." On the other hand, welfare state transfers are not included here; see for them Espuelas, *Evolución del gasto social.*
15. The authors of the surveys and reports of the 1970s summarized their results in three popular critiques: unfair distribution of the burden; excessive complexity; and inequitable impact of tax evasion. See Alvira and García, "Límites de Efectos." My own interpretation adds further points. A more detailed review of these data is available in Torregrosa, "Political Economy."
16. For example, in 1975 89 percent of the respondents agreed with progressivity postulates (versus 11 percent who favored a proportional system). Personal income tax was supported by 68 percent as an acceptable revenue method.
17. Fiscal drag occurs when tax thresholds are fixed in nominal terms and there is high inflation. Increases in nominal incomes drive taxpayers into the higher rates even in the absence of improvements in real purchasing power.
18. A point made in Lagares, "Aceptación Social."
19. For example, Edlund, "Public Attitudes"; Singhal, "Quantifying Preferences." The relatively pro-redistribution stance taken is confirmed by Fernández-Albertos, "Making of Egalitarian Spain."
20. Boeri et al., "Would You Like?"

21. *Cuadernos para el Diálogo*, 233, October 15–21, 1977. These words correspond to a conference about the situation of businesses.
22. *Cuadernos para el Diálogo*, 216, June 18–24, 1977.
23. The same conclusion is reached in Pan-Montojo, "Larga e inconclusa transición," 286.
24. Albertus and Menaldo, "Gaming Democracy," discuss the importance of the transition process for new democracies in the sense that redistribution would only come through strongly if the elite's control had been hampered by revolutionary threat.
25. Steinmo, "Political Institutions"; Persson et al., "Comparative Politics"; Iversen and Soskice, "Electoral Institutions."
26. Fernández-Albertos, "Making of Egalitarian Spain."
27. Samuels and Snyder, "The Value of a Vote."
28. Gunther, "Electoral Laws;" Lago and Montero, "Todavía no sé quiénes."
29. Samuels and Snyder, "The Value of a Vote." This means that nearly 10 percent of the seats are allocated to districts that would not receive them under proportionality.
30. Gunther et al., *Sistema de partidos.*
31. Comín, *Reaching a Political Consensus.*
32. In fact, this may be part of the explanation for the distance between the initial revenue estimate in the project (39,649 million pesetas, of which the government's objective was to reach 20,000 million pesetas) and the actual revenues in 1978 (8589 million compared to 15,000 million in 1979).
33. Family allowances, new tax-deductible investments, reduction in imputed incomes from home ownership, and a cap on effective taxation at 40 percent.
34. Presumptive taxation uses indirect means to approximate the tax base and/or tax liability, instead of being based on calculation of actual incomes. In Spain it is called *estimación objetiva* and was widely used, resulting in low taxation and regressive results.
35. Lists of taxpayers corresponding to 1977 and 1978 were on public display at the Ministry of Public Finance in 1979 and 1980, with the press commenting on some dubious cases. These were data from the old, pre-reform tax.
36. *Cuadernos para el Diálogo*, 221, July 23–29, 1977.
37. *ABC*, December 29, 1977, 51.
38. Castillo, *Fraude fiscal.*
39. From an interview with A. Missé, reproduced in Fuentes Quintana, "Pactos de la Moncloa." Author's translation.
40. *El País* was quite clear in this respect: "The pressures of the financial sector against the reform and the manifestations of the more conservative flank of business, along with the maneuvers to form a big right-wing party outside

UCD, undoubtedly frightened the party's political cadres and Suárez himself," *El País*, Editorial, October 25, 1978.

41. Fernández Ordóñez, *España necesaria*, 137. Author's translation.
42. Cadastral values can be found in the Public Finance Ministry's land registry (*cadastre*). Because of lack of adequate updating, cadastral values in Spain have often been found to be far below the values that the same properties would have if they were on the market. Since real estate property is taxed according to its cadastral value, this means that the tax base remains significantly smaller than the economic capacity it is supposed to capture. Furthermore, such undervaluation will introduce inequities between taxpayers, according to the share of these assets in their portfolios. This is also relevant for the income tax when imputed rents from owner-occupied housing are taxed.
43. For example, health services, insurance, cars, fashion, wine, perfumes, even shotguns.
44. Rojo, "Economía española."
45. The Left also insisted on increasing minimum pensions to the minimum wage level, annual adjustment to inflation, and improved conditions for agricultural workers.
46. The main exception was the proposals of the right-wing Alianza Popular, which by 1982 had evolved toward a two-pillar model, with basic-public and complementary-private levels (private institutions also cooperated in the first one too).
47. In the words of the *White Book*, the objectives could only be attained "with more active government involvement. But this leads to the need for a more sufficient and progressive tax system. It would be vain to base redistributive action on regressive government contributions" (author's translation).
48. Guillén, *Construcción política*.
49. Monasterio, "Financiación de las pensiones."
50. Bates and Lien, "Note on Taxation"; Persson and Tabellini, "Politics of 1992"; Boix, *Democracy and Redistribution*; Freeman and Quinn, "Economic Origins."
51. Beramendi and Rueda, "Social Democracy Constrained." Similarly, Genschel, "Globalization, Tax Competition," contends that, in the absence of international tax competition, taxes are higher and more progressive, with stronger burdens on capital and lower burdens on labor and consumption.
52. Kopits, "Overview."
53. Lasheras, "Percepción social," 59. Author's translation.
54. Slemrod, "Professional Opinions"; Steinmo, "Evolution of Policy Ideas."
55. Pan-Montojo, "Larga e inconclusa transición."

56. Steinmo, "Political Institutions"; Kato, *Regressive Taxation*; Lindert, *Growing Public*. For empirical analyses, see Piketty and Saez, "How Progressive"; Prasad and Deng, "Taxation and Worlds"; Bengtsson et al., "Lifetime versus Annual."
57. Timmons, "Fiscal Contract."
58. Torregrosa, "Did Democracy…?"

References

Albertus, Michael, and Victor Menaldo. 2014. Gaming Democracy: Elite Dominance during Transition and the Prospects for Redistribution. *British Journal of Political Science* 44: 575–603.

Albi, Emilio, ed. 1990. *La Hacienda Pública en la Democracia. Estudios en homenaje al profesor Enrique Fuentes Quintana*. Barcelona: Ariel.

Alvira, Francisco, and José García. 2005. Los límites de los efectos redistributivos de la política tributaria. In *Políticas Públicas y distribución de la renta*, ed. J. Ruiz-Huerta, 757–796. Bilbao: Fundación BBVA.

Bates, Robert H., and Da-Hsiang Donald Lien. 1985. A Note on Taxation, Development, and Representative Democracy. *Politics and Society* 14: 53–70.

Bengtsson, Niklas, Bertil Holmlund, and Daniel Waldenström. 2016. Lifetime Versus Annual Tax Progressivity: Sweden, 1968–2009. *Scandinavian Journal of Economics* 118 (4): 619–645.

Beramendi, Pablo, and David Rueda. 2007. Social Democracy Constrained: Indirect Taxation in Industrialized Democracies. *British Journal of Political Science* 37 (4): 619–641.

Boeri, Tito, Axel Börsch-Supan, and Guido Tabellini. 2001. Would You Like to Shrink the Welfare State? A Survey of European Citizens. *Economic Policy* 16 (32): 7–50.

Boix, Carles. 2003. *Democracy and Redistribution*. Cambridge: Cambridge University Press.

Castillo, José Manuel. 1994. *El fraude fiscal en España*. Granada: Comares.

Comín, Francisco. 2007. Reaching a Political Consensus for Tax Reform in Spain: The Moncloa Pacts, Joining the European Union and the Rest of the Journey. In *Fiscal Reform in Spain. Accomplishments and Challenges*, ed. J. Martínez-Vázquez and José F. Sanz, 8–58. Cheltenham: Elgar.

Edlund, Jonas. 2000. Public Attitudes Towards Taxation: Sweden 1981–1997. *Scandinavian Political Studies* 23 (1): 37–65.

Espuelas, Sergio. 2013. *La evolución del gasto social público en España, 1850–2005. Estudios de Historia Económica, vol. 63*. Madrid: Banco de España.

Fernández Ordóñez, Francisco. 1980. *La España necesaria*. Madrid: Taurus, Freeman.

Fernández-Albertos, José. 2011. The Making of Egalitarian Spain: Growth, Demographics, Politics and the Income Distribution, 1960–1990. *Revista Española de Sociología* 16: 47–72.

Fuentes-Quintana, Enrique. 2004. Los Pactos de la Moncloa y la Constitución de 1978. In *Economía y economistas españoles*, ed. E. Fuentes Quintana, vol. 8, 163–238. Barcelona: Galaxia Gutenberg: Círculo de Lectores.

Genschel, Philipp. 2002. Globalization, Tax Competition and the Welfare State. *Politics and Society* 30: 245–275.

Guillén, Ana. 2000. *La construcción política del sistema sanitario español: de la posguerra a la democracia*. Madrid: Exlibris Ediciones.

Gunther, Richard. 1989. Electoral Laws, Party Systems, and Elites: The Case of Spain. *American Political Science Review* 83 (3): 835–858.

Gunther, Richard, Giacomo Sani, and Goldie Shabad. 1986. *Sistema de partidos políticos en España: génesis y evolución*. Madrid: CIS Siglo XXI.

Iversen, Torben, and David Soskice. 2006. Electoral Institutions and the Politics of Coalitions. *American Political Science Review* 100 (2): 165–181.

John, R., and Dennis P. Quinn. 2012. The Economic Origins of Democracy Reconsidered. *American Political Science Review* 106: 58–80.

Kato, Junko. 2003. *Regressive Taxation and the Welfare State: Path Dependence and Policy Diffusion*. New York: Cambridge University Press.

Kopits, George. 1992. Overview. In *Tax Harmonization in the European Community*, ed. International Monetary Fund, 1–21. Washington, DC: International Monetary Fund.

Lagares, Manuel José. 1990. La aceptación social del sistema tributario: el Impuesto sobre la Renta de las Personas Físicas. In *La Hacienda Pública en la Democracia. Estudios en homenaje al profesor Enrique Fuentes Quintana*, ed. E. Albi, 109–132. Ariel: Barcelona.

Lago, Ignacio, and José Ramón Montero. 2005. Todavía no sé quiénes, pero ganaremos: Manipulación política del sistema electoral español. *Zona Abierta* 110 (111): 279–348.

Lasheras, Miguel Ángel. 1990. Percepción social y politica fiscal en España. Historia de un compromiso. In *Sistema Fiscal y Administración Tributaria. Análisis de dos realidades. España y Argentina*, ed. R. Dornbusch, 43–68. Madrid: Instituto de Estudios Fiscales.

Lindert, Peter. 2004. *Growing Public. Social Spending and Economic Growth since the Eighteenth Century*. New York: Cambridge University Press.

Lupu, Noam, and Jonas Pontusson. 2011. The Structure of Inequality and the Politics of Redistribution. *American Political Science Review* 105: 316–336.

Monasterio, Carlos. 1992. La financiación de las pensiones públicas en España. In *Los sistemas de Seguridad Social y las nuevas realidades sociales*, ed. Ministerio de Trabajo y Seguridad Social, 207–233. Madrid: Ministerio de Trabajo y Seguridad Social.

Montero, José Ramón. 1986. La vuelta a las urnas: participación, movilización y abstención. In *Crisis y cambio: electores y partidos en la España de los años ochenta*, ed. Juan Linz and José Ramón Montero, 71–124. Madrid: Centro de Estudios Constitucionales.

Montero, José Ramón, and Pedro Riera. 2009. El sistema electoral español: cuestiones de desproporcionalidad y de reforma. In *Desafíos de la igualdad, desafíos a la igualdad*, ed. Alfonso Ruiz and Andrea Macía, 225–270. Madrid: Universidad Autónoma de Madrid.

Pan-Montojo, Juan Luis. 1996. Una larga e inconclusa transición: la reforma tributaria, 1977–1986. In *Historia de la transición. 1975–1986*, ed. Javier Tusell and Ángel Soto, 264–304. Madrid: Alianza.

Persson, Torsten, and Guido Tabellini. 1992. The Politics of 1992: Fiscal Policy and European Integration. *Review of Economic Studies* 59 (4): 689–701.

———. 2003. *The Economic Effects of Constitutions*. Cambridge, MA: MIT Press.

Persson, Torsten, Gerard Roland, and Guido Tabellini. 2000. Comparative Politics and Public Finance. *Journal of Political Economy* 108 (6): 1121–1161.

Piketty, Thomas, and Emmanuel Saez. 2007. How Progressive Is the U.S. Federal Tax System? A Historical and International Perspective. *Journal of Economic Perspectives* 21 (1): 3–24.

Prasad, Monica, and Deng Yingying. 2009. Taxation and the Worlds of Welfare. *Socio-Economic Review* 7: 431–457.

Rojo, Luis Ángel. 2002. La economía española en la democracia (1976–2000). In *Historia económica de España, siglos X–XX*, ed. Francisco Comín, Mauro Hernández, and Enrique Llopis, 397–436. Barcelona: Crítica.

Samuels, David, and Richard Snyder. 2001. The Value of a Vote: Malapportionment in Comparative Perspective. *British Journal of Political Science* 31 (4): 651–671.

Serrano-Sanz, José María. 1997. Francisco Fernández Ordóñez. In *La Hacienda en sus ministros: franquismo y democracia*, ed. E. Fuentes Quintana, 127–166. Zaragoza: Prensas Universitarias de Zaragoza.

Singhal, Monica. 2013. Quantifying Preferences for Redistribution. Mimeo, Harvard University and NBER.

Slemrod, Joel. 1995. Professional Opinions about Tax Policy: 1994 and 1934. *National Tax Journal* 48 (1): 121–147.

Steinmo, Sven. 1989. Political Institutions and Tax Policy in the United States, Sweden, and Britain. *World Politics* 41 (4): 500–535.

———. 2003. The Evolution of Policy Ideas: Tax Policy in the 20th Century. *British Journal of Politics and International Relations* 5 (2): 206–236.

Timmons, Jeffrey. 2005. The Fiscal Contract: States, Taxes, and Public Services. *World Politics* 57 (4): 530–567.

Torregrosa Hetland, Sara. 2015a. Bypassing Progressive Taxation: Fraud and Base Erosion in the Spanish Income Tax, 1970–2001. *IEB Working Papers* 2015/31.

———. 2015b. Did Democracy Bring Redistribution? Insights from the Spanish Tax System (1960–1990). *European Review of Economic History* 3 (19): 294–315.

———. 2016. Sticky Income Inequality in the Spanish Transition (1973–1990). *Revista de Historia Económica/Journal of Iberian and Latin American Economic History* 34 (1): 39–80.

———. 2017. The Political Economy of Peripheral Tax Reform: The Spanish Fiscal Transition. *Lund Papers in Economic History: General Issues* 156: 44.

Index[1]

NUMBERS & SYMBOLS
2 trillion-yen tax cut, 228, 232
1950s, 11, 19, 22, 51, 60–61, 66, 84, 102, 132, 133, 142, 144, 157, 161, 189, 190, 217, 271, 275, 284, 290, 305
1980s, 7, 8, 10, 12, 57, 101, 103, 105, 110–117, 121, 155–177, 230, 240n56, 254, 309, 325, 327, 331, 333, 339, 340

A
Abe, Shinzo, 234, 245–249, 262
  administration, 10, 235, 240n54, 250, 263
Abenomix, 234, 248
Acemoglu, Daron, 41n14
Ageing population, 247, 248
Aidt, Toke, 41n4, 41n14
Aizawa, Hideyuki, 231
Alliance Nationale, 133
Allix, Pierre, 137
American aid, 136
American "exceptionalism," 176–177
Anderson, Martin, 167
Asian Financial Crisis, 233
Atkinson, Athony B., 4, 40
Australia, 19, 26, 40, 253, 256

B
Bad debt reserves, 204
Baker, James A., 202
Base-broadening measures, 190, 192, 199, 200, 205
Benefits principle, 32
Bensel, Richard, 41n11, 43n49
Beramendi, Pablo, 56, 57
Biko-chochiku system, 219
Birth rate, 112, 133, 148
Blot, Robert, 137, 139–143
Blumenthal, Michael, 196
Bonney, Richard, 3

[1] Note: Page numbers followed by 'n' refer to notes.

G. Huerlimann et al. (eds.), *Worlds of Taxation*, Palgrave Studies in the History of Finance, https://doi.org/10.1007/978-3-319-90263-0

Bonn Summit, 229
Bracket creep, 103, 159, 162, 163, 166, 195, 198
Bradley, Bill, 201
Brannon, Gerald M., 194, 210n45
Brazer, Harvey E., 190, 208n20
Bretton-Woods Agreement, 162, 285
Brownlee, W. Elliot, 4, 5, 8, 178n8, 204, 284
Bubble economy, 115, 118, 125n80, 233
Buchanan, James, 165, 180n28
Burgin, Angus, 158
Burman, Leonard, 173, 180n22, 182n46
Bush, George H. W., 170–173, 175, 176
Bush, George W., 9, 173
Business interests, 37, 60, 62–65, 191, 273
Byrd, Harry, 193

C

Canada, 26, 40, 65
Canton of Aargau, 274, 275
Canton of Lucerne, 279
Canton of Zurich, 275
Capital flight/capital mobility, 12, 50, 52, 56, 57, 284, 323
Capital formation, 168, 195, 197, 199–201, 206, 220
Capital gains, 157, 159–161, 166, 173, 192–194, 197, 199, 200, 202, 204, 205, 211n63, 306, 337, 338
Carter, Jimmy, 163–166, 171, 196–200, 206, 207, 229
  administration, 196, 198–200
  tax reform program, 196–199
Cascade effect, 63
Catholic-Conservatives (Swiss), 276
Cato Institute, 164
Centralization effect, 271
Child allowance, 62, 234, 257, 262
Class tax, 17, 18, 21, 23, 34, 35
Clinton, Bill, 170–172, 175, 176
Cold (tax) progression/fiscal drag, 11, 142, 191, 272, 283–290, 309, 327, 333, 341n17
Colm, Gerhard, 191
Competition, 2, 6, 19, 50, 63, 67, 68, 84, 157, 233, 249, 280, 289, 291, 323, 338
Comprehensive National Development Plan, 221, 222
Conable, Barber, 199
Congressional Budget Office (U.S.), 163
Conservative Party (Denmark), 32, 34, 119
Construction bonds, 229
Construction State, 10, 218
Consumption tax, 6, 11, 17, 23, 31–37, 49–69, 80, 88, 90n1, 134, 147, 230, 234, 235, 240n55, 262, 263, 279
Coolidge, Calvin, 36
Corporation tax, 139, 140, 305, 313, 337
Corporatism, 50, 56, 60, 93n33
Council of Economic Advisers (CEA) (U.S.), 37, 161, 190–193, 196–200, 209n22
CPI adjustment tax cuts, 218
Crisis mobilization, 6, 18, 23–26, 35, 36, 38, 54
Crisis-mobilization model, 18, 23, 31
Crisis tax, 270
Cumulative sales tax, 66
Cusack, Tom, 41n2, 41n6, 42n16

D

Danish Conservative Folk Party (Right Party), 32, 33, 42n38
Danish Finance Ministry, 33
Danish foundational tax act in 1922, 32
Danish income tax act of 1903, 32
Danish Liberal Party, 32, 33, 42n38, 84, 86, 103
Danish Radical Liberal Party, 106
Danish revenue system (Denmark), 32–34
Daunton, Martin, 4
de Gaulle, Charles, 133, 138–141, 145
Debt-financing bonds, 229, 238n33
Decommodification, 253, 261
Deficit Reduction Act of 1984 (DEFRA), 169, 175, 201
Democratic Party (Japan), 234, 246, 250, 257
Democratic Party (US), 35
Democratic-Statism, 157, 158
Democratization, 12, 22, 322, 337
Deng, Yingying, 41n2, 41n8, 42n16, 69n1, 344n56
Denmark, 5–7, 18, 19, 26, 28, 31–40, 66, 78–83, 85, 88–90, 92n17, 146, 253, 254, 257–259, 261
Direct democracy, 269, 273
Displacement effect, 271
Domesticated Keynesianism, 193–195
Domesticated Keynesians, 193, 199
Double taxation on corporate income, 211n63

E

Earned Income Tax Credit (EITC), 172, 175, 195, 204, 205
Economic and Social Committee, 141
Economic development, 13, 32, 54, 278, 301, 303
Economic efficiency, 50, 52, 90, 157, 205, 207
Economic growth, 9, 12, 17, 33, 36, 49, 50, 56, 60, 69, 120, 156, 159, 160, 164, 190–192, 200, 218, 222–226, 228, 231, 233, 248, 284
Economic openness, 21, 323, 337
Economic Policy Group (EPG), 196, 197
Economic Recovery Tax Act of 1981 (ERTA), 158, 159, 166–171, 174, 178n8, 201, 202
Eisenhower, Dwight D., 190
Electoral systems/political structure, 4, 53, 323, 329, 330, 340n6
Employees, 41n8, 74, 76, 83, 93n33, 103, 104, 106, 116, 120, 131–149, 160, 203, 226, 233, 249–252, 254, 255, 264n33, 278, 280, 285, 286, 290, 302, 305, 307–309, 312
Employer coordination, 18, 38
Esping-Andersen, Gøsta, 61, 253, 261
European Economic Community (EEC), 55, 140, 323, 324, 335, 337, 338
European-style welfare state, 231, 234

F

Family Quotient Income Tax system, 143, 144, 149, 174
Federal
- defense tax, 270–272, 276, 278, 280, 291n3
- financial regime, 278, 281, 282, 288–290
- income tax, 34, 160, 161, 163, 165, 169, 174, 179n12, 179n15, 179n17, 180n26, 180n30, 187, 190, 195, 200, 204, 207, 208n13, 270, 272, 274, 276–281, 283, 287, 290, 291
- turnover tax, 270, 271, 273, 276, 278–282, 289–291
- withholding tax, 270, 271

Federalist/federalism, 11, 27, 42n31, 269, 270, 274, 290
Federation of Danish Employers (DA), 33, 34, 42n38
Fernández Ordóñez, Francisco, 331, 334, 341n9, 341n11
Fifth Republic, 132, 133, 138, 144, 148, 149
Finland, 26, 83
Fiscal drag, 11, 142, 191, 272, 282–290, 294n66, 309, 327, 341n17
Fiscal equalization, 291
Fiscal Investment and Loan Program (FILP), 224, 227–232, 237n23
Fiscal-social contract, 274
Flexicurity, 115–117, 122
Ford, Gerald D., 164, 195, 196, 200
Fourth Republic, 132, 133, 138–140, 149
France, 2, 5, 8, 14n7, 26, 40, 54, 67, 75, 76, 78, 131–149, 253, 261, 294n73
Free Democrats (Swiss), 276, 279, 280, 282, 283, 290, 292n30
Friedman, Milton, 157, 158, 164, 165, 167, 178n7, 180n31
Fuentes Quintana, Enrique, 323, 324, 334, 342n39
Fukuda, Takeo, 228, 229, 232, 238n37, 239n38, 239n50, 246
Fukushi Gannen (first welfare year), 226, 228
Furst, André, 138, 142, 150n36, 151n50

G

Ganghof, Steffen, 41n2, 42n16, 56, 57, 94n47
General sales tax, 51, 55, 59–63, 65, 69
German occupation, 81, 82, 135, 136, 316n82
Germany, 5, 7, 14n7, 26, 35, 40, 65, 67, 77, 79–82, 89, 91n16, 92n17, 117, 135, 136, 140, 141, 143, 146, 147, 177n1, 198, 207n3, 229, 252, 253, 259, 261, 283, 285, 293n52, 294n73, 314, 316n82
Giscard d'Estaing, Valéry, 146
Glistrup, Morgens, 105–107, 111, 124n28
Goldscheid, Rudolph, 3
Greece, 5, 11, 301–314
Greenspan, Alan, 168
Grünbaum, Henry, 85–87

H

Hansen, H.P., 82, 85, 86, 88, 93n36, 189, 193
Harvey, David, 156, 178n2, 190, 208n20
Heller, Walter, 37, 161, 190, 191, 193, 209n25
Heritage Foundation, 164
Hertel-Fernandez, Alexander, 6–8, 54, 149
Hetland, Sara Torregrosa, 12
Household income, 122, 234, 235, 252, 257–259
House Ways and Means Committee (U.S.), 165, 208n13, 209n33
Housewives, 217, 230, 233
Huerlimann, Gisela, 11
Huret, Romain D., 5, 14n11

I

Ide, Eisaku, 9, 10, 236n3, 236n4, 236n7, 238n35, 239n44
Ikeda, Hayato, 218–221, 224, 236n10, 237n18, 237n24, 237n25
Income disparity, 218, 234, 235
Income-Doubling Plan, 222

Income redistribution, 100, 249, 252–254, 261, 262, 323
Income tax, 2, 5, 8, 10, 17–19, 22, 26, 28–36, 38, 40, 62, 73–90, 100, 103, 105–107, 111, 112, 115, 116, 119–121, 123n18, 131–149, 158–161, 163–165, 168–174, 179n18, 187–190, 193, 195, 197, 199–204, 207, 209n38, 211n63, 218, 220, 221, 224, 225, 228, 230, 234, 237n21, 255, 257, 259, 270, 274, 276–277, 281, 283, 287, 290, 291, 292n19, 305, 309, 310, 312–314, 323, 324, 339, 343n42
  expansion of 1916, 34, 35, 270
Independent Party (Swiss), 275
Indirect taxation, 11, 61, 62, 67, 144, 302, 322, 324
Industrialization, 21, 27, 32, 307
Industrious labor, 10, 219–221, 236n9
Industrious State, 10, 217–235
Inflation, 6, 8, 33, 80, 85, 103, 105, 111, 112, 142, 144, 146, 156, 159, 160, 162–164, 167, 169, 171, 189, 195, 199, 200, 218, 272, 278, 279, 281, 283–288, 292n32, 309, 312, 327, 333, 335, 341n17, 343n45
Institutions, 4, 6, 12, 18, 23, 25, 26, 29, 30, 32, 33, 35, 36, 38, 50, 54, 56, 74, 81, 102, 104, 177, 178n8, 233, 248, 287, 335, 339, 343n46
Institut National des Études Économiques (INSEE), 143
International competition, 50, 67, 68
Introduction, 7, 8, 55, 58, 61, 103, 110, 111, 116, 119–121, 123n16, 138, 219, 262, 271, 273, 303, 324, 330, 339, 340n6, 341n10
Inspection effect, 290
Italy, 26, 40, 77, 140, 141, 147
Iversen, Torben, 41n6, 340n6, 342n25

J

Japan, 5, 8–11, 54, 77, 182n50, 198, 217–220, 222, 226, 228, 229, 232, 235, 250, 253–259, 261, 262
Japanese Ministry of Health, Labor and Welfare, 223, 250, 262, 264n16, 264n22, 265n43
Japanese-style welfare society, 218, 230, 232, 237n12, 239n43
Jensen, Peter, 41n4, 41n14
Johnson, Lyndon B., 161, 194, 210n40
Joint Committee on Internal Revenue Taxation (U.S.), 160, 210n45, 211n56
Jones, Daniel Stedman, 158, 178n2

K

Kachi, Hakuichi, 220, 236n8
Kato, Junko, 54, 239n40
Kemp, Jack, 165–167
Kennedy, John F., 161, 179n15, 190, 209n25, 209n27, 209n28, 209n29, 284
Kennedy-Johnson tax cuts, 9, 161, 164, 193, 284, 294n67
Kenworthy, Lane, 41n8
Keynesian, 11, 74, 80, 110, 161, 193, 222, 284, 339
Keynesianism, 193–195, 338
Kildeskat (Denmark), *see* Pay-As-You-Earn
Kinro, 219, 220, 236n9, 250
Kishi, Nobusuke, 220
Korean War, 160, 278
Korpi, Walter, 91n6

Krag, Jens Otto, 86, 93n36, 93n39, 93n40, 93n41, 93n42, 93n44
Kurachi, Shintaro, 7, 125n79

L
Labor movement, 51, 53, 58, 61, 177, 217
Labor relations, 23, 35
Lantz, Gunnar, 6, 7
La Plus Grande Famille, 133
Laxan, Max, 142–145
Legitimacy of taxes, 311, 312
Liberal Center (Denmark), 86
Liberal Democratic Party (LDP), 9, 220, 223, 226–232, 234, 235, 237n12, 257, 262
Liberal/liberals (Swiss), 61, 270, 276, 282, 290
Liberal Party (Denmark), 32, 84
Lindert, Peter, 49–51, 56
Livelihood security system, 248, 249, 263
London Summit, 229
Long, Russell, 165, 170, 196
Lynch, Frances M. B., 8, 55, 70n13, 147, 148

M
Macro-corporatism, 23, 25, 38
Majoritarian system, 18, 132
Malapportionment, 329, 331, 339
Marginal taxes, 40, 62, 64, 106, 111, 116, 173, 205, 276, 281, 282, 338
Market competition, 67, 249
Market forces, 247
Martin, Cathie Jo, 6, 13n5, 53, 149, 181n34
Martin, Isaac W., 4, 5, 7, 8
Mass tax, 18, 21, 23, 32, 34, 132, 269
McKinley, William, 35
Medicare (U.S.), 170, 174, 175
Mehrotra, Ajay, 4
Michelmore, Molly, 5, 182n47
Ministry of Finance, 80, 133, 142, 231–233, 313
Miyazawa, Kiichi, 232, 239n50
Moms Tax (Danish predecessor to VAT), 34
Mozumi, Seiichiro, 9
Multipartism, 6, 18, 19, 25, 30, 38, 78
Murauke system, 219
Musgrave, Richard, 3, 191

N
National Association of Manufacturers (NAM), 25, 35, 36
National Council on Social Security System (Japan), 246, 247
National sales tax, 34, 36
Netherlands, 26, 40, 77, 117
New Deal, 5, 8, 157–159, 162, 170, 174, 176
New Zealand, 26, 40
Nominal fiscal lag, 285
Non-regular workers, 247, 250
Norway, 5, 7, 26, 40, 78, 81, 89, 92n17
Norwegian Workers' Party, 89

O
O'Brien, Patrick K., 3, 91n9
OECD Taxing Wages, 255
Ohira, Masayoshi, 229, 230, 232, 236n12
Okun, Arthur, 41n1
Okura, Masataka, 232
Ordinary worker, 249, 250

Organisation for Economic Cooperation and Development (OECD), 5, 8, 12, 13, 20, 26, 39, 41n8, 51, 52, 62, 111, 131, 134, 146, 178n9, 225, 246, 252–256, 259, 261, 308, 312, 326, 327
Ormrod, W. Mark, 3
Osawa, Mari, 10

P
Palme, Joakim, 100
Papon, Maurice, 146, 151n46
Parliamentary politics, 51, 59, 61, 100
Part-time worker, 250, 251
Pay-As-You-Earn (PAYE), 7, 73–78, 80–90, 93n36, 103, 123n15, 132, 138
Piketty, Thomas, 4, 173
Pinay, Antoine, 136
Pittaki, Zoi, 11
Pluralism, 23, 25, 35
Political economy, 19, 155, 178n8, 231, 323
Pompidou, Georges, 144–146
Popular initiative, 273–275, 279, 288
Population migration, 228
Post-Second World War tax reforms, 303–308
Post-war boom, 272
Poujade, Pierre, 136
  Poujadism, 75
Poverty rate, 252–255, 261, 262
Poverty reduction rate, 252–255, 261
Prasad, Monica, 4, 91n6, 178n8, 181n34
Production and Sales Tax Reliance, 26, 28–31
Professors' Commission (Denmark), 80
Progressive taxation, 17, 19, 22, 31, 38, 56, 103, 156, 159, 160, 182n47, 206, 274, 278, 279, 295n99, 337
Progressive tax/Impôt sur le revenu des personnes physiques (IRPP), 5, 8, 26, 35, 139, 142, 145, 149, 171, 261, 285, 337
Progressivity, 8, 9, 19–22, 26, 30, 31, 35, 38, 39, 50, 61, 63, 68, 134, 141, 143, 159, 162, 172, 189, 192, 199, 205, 207, 246, 255–262, 264n34, 301–303, 322–324, 326–328, 330, 332, 333, 336, 338–340, 341n16
Proportional representation, 27, 28, 30
Proportional tax/complementary tax, 135–137, 139, 142, 145
Public Finance Law, 229
Public policy, 23, 25, 177, 330
Public works, 6, 10, 217–235, 238n37

R
Radical Party (Denmark), 106
Real fiscal lag, 285, 288
Redistribution, 1–13, 19, 32, 40, 65, 156, 175, 199, 207, 218, 249, 252–254, 261, 262, 272, 281, 289–291, 303, 311–313, 321–340
Referendum vote, 273, 276, 282, 293n53
Regressive taxation, 22, 23, 51–53, 56, 57, 339, 340
Repeated tax cutting policy, 234, 252
Republican Party (U.S.), 9
Retail-level sales tax/ Retail sales tax, 63, 65–67
Revenue Act of 1935, 34, 36
Revenue Act of 1962, 37, 179n15
Revenue Act of 1964, 37, 161, 194
Reverse-functioning, 10, 245–263
Robinson, James A., 41n14, 43n48
Rodrik, Dani, 41n11
Rueda, David, 56, 57

S
Saez, Emmanuel, 4, 173
Scheve, Kenneth, 26, 27, 31, 40
Schumpeter, Joseph, 3, 271
Selectivism, 99
Self-employed, 11, 84, 132, 135–141, 145, 148, 149, 249, 252, 254, 264n33, 275, 302, 305, 309, 312
Single parent, 254–260, 262, 263
Skocpol, Theda, 3, 13n2
Social Assistance Act, 7, 102–110, 112–114, 116, 121
Social Democratic Party (Denmark), 78, 84, 86, 87, 89, 102, 106
Social Democrats (Swiss), 58, 82, 274
Socialist People's Party (Denmark), 85, 87
Social security
  burden, 252, 255–261, 263
  contributions, 8, 41n8, 55, 56, 131, 145, 249, 252, 255, 262, 335
Soskice, David, 41n6, 340n6, 342n25
Spain, 5, 12, 321–340
Stamp duties, 270, 271, 303, 306
Stasavage, David, 26, 27, 31, 40
State-building model, 18, 23, 38
State Tax Law of 1903 (Denmark), 79
Steinmo, Sven, 4, 6, 53, 55, 56, 68
Streeck, Wolfgang, 42n18
Suzuki, Zenko, 230, 231
Swank, Duane, 39
Sweden, 5, 7, 19, 26, 40, 49–69, 80, 81, 146, 252–254, 257, 261, 339
Swiss Bankers Association, 276, 295n84
Switzerland, 5, 11, 26, 76–78, 253, 254, 269, 270, 273, 282–284, 287, 294n73

T
Taft, William Howard, 34
Takagi, Fumio, 232
Tanaka, Kakuei, 218, 226–229, 231, 232, 238n30
Tax
  burden, 7, 21, 23, 26, 31, 36, 62, 64, 65, 67, 88, 93n47, 100, 102, 103, 105–107, 111, 112, 115–118, 121, 123n16, 137–139, 141–143, 145, 146, 188, 189, 192, 195, 196, 200, 202, 206, 219, 221, 224, 228, 230, 238n28, 252, 255, 265n34, 269, 272, 274–275, 278, 279, 281, 285–290, 302, 303, 305, 307–313, 325, 327, 337
  burden distribution, 18, 141, 143, 146, 274, 287, 301–314, 316n75, 322, 326
  Collection Working Group (Sweden), 82
  Commission of 1946 (Norway), 89
  Committee of 1936 (Norway), 89
  conscience, 301, 314n1
  deductions, 61, 62, 86, 87, 93n47, 105, 111, 116, 120, 156, 158, 197, 203, 218, 224, 256, 275, 278, 281, 288
  evasion, 11, 111, 221, 271, 287, 301–314, 324–327, 341n10, 341n15
  expenditures, 5, 37, 39, 107, 158, 160, 162, 163, 167–169, 171, 173, 176, 180n22, 182n46, 187, 193–195, 197, 198, 201, 205–207
  fraud, 134–136, 271, 287, 288
  incidence, 323, 336
  Law Commission (Denmark), 82
  progressivity, 9, 19–22, 26, 30, 31, 39, 41n8, 159, 261, 327, 330
  rebates, 198, 279–282, 288, 289, 302, 307
  reform 1948, 134–136
  reform 1959, 132, 138–142, 148, 190
  relief, 11, 62, 64, 164, 166, 211n63, 269–291, 302, 307

revolts, 7, 75, 89, 100, 101, 111, 121
welfare paradox, 19
Tax-at-source election (kildeskattevalget), 86
Taxes in favor of third parties, 11, 308, 314
Technocratic rationality/technocracy, 52, 68
Thorndike, Joseph, 177n1, 179n13
Thrift, 9, 219, 221, 222, 235
Tilly, Charles, 41n12, 90n4
Top Income Tax Rate, 18, 26, 28–31, 40
Treasury Department, 9, 36, 210n48
Treaty of Rome, Article 99, 140
Two-party system, 25, 35

U
United Kingdom (UK), 2, 26, 40, 53, 67, 147, 256, 294n73, 314, 337, 340
United States (U.S.)
Chamber of Commerce, 25, 36
congress, 9, 34, 37, 160, 161, 163–166, 168–171, 175, 190, 192, 193, 195–198, 200, 201, 206, 207, 284, 307
revenue system, 34–38
Universalism, 7, 99–122

V
Value-added tax (VAT), 2, 6, 7, 22, 34, 49–69, 88, 90n1, 100, 103, 107, 115, 123n16, 140, 144, 165, 291, 303, 323, 324, 330, 334–336, 339, 340
Vertical integration, 63, 65
Vichy regime, 133

W
Wage growth, 288
War
mobilization, 18, 19, 22, 27, 29, 31, 35
tax, 270
Weber, Max, 276, 280, 281
Welfare state, 2, 4–9, 12, 17–19, 22, 38, 49–69, 82, 84, 85, 88, 102, 103, 116, 117, 134, 176, 177, 217–235, 253, 270, 322, 325, 327, 330, 337, 339, 340, 341n14
White-collar employees, 278, 285, 286, 295n81
White House Domestic Policy Staff, 196
Wilensky, Harold, 41n2, 41n9
Withholding, 73, 74, 76, 77, 81, 84–86, 88, 89, 103, 104, 221, 270, 271, 287, 333, 337
Workers, 11, 22, 23, 25, 38, 51, 57, 58, 60, 61, 75, 77, 83–86, 88, 89, 91n6, 92n32, 104–107, 109, 114, 115, 131, 133, 136–139, 142, 143, 147–149, 166, 221, 225, 226, 228, 237n26, 247, 249–251, 254, 274, 280, 284–286, 290, 325, 327, 335, 336, 343n45
Working class power, 7, 73–90
Working class strength, 22
World War I, 8, 32, 65, 131, 134, 135, 144, 162, 163, 270–272
World War II, 3, 5, 7–9, 11, 12, 22, 32–34, 36, 51, 59, 75–77, 79, 82–84, 93n33, 131, 133, 134, 136, 138, 148, 149, 156, 158–163, 169–171, 177, 178n8, 188–190, 204, 205, 208n17, 208n20, 219, 220, 222, 269, 270, 273, 274, 308, 311, 313

Y
Yoshikuni, Jiro, 231
Yoshise, Shigeya, 231

Z
Zero-ceiling, 232

The manufacturer's authorised representative in the EU is Springer Nature Customer Service Centre GmbH, Europaplatz 3, 69115 Heidelberg, Germany. If you have any concerns regarding our products, please contact ProductSafety@springernature.com

Printed and bound by CPI Group (UK) Ltd, Croydon, CR0 4YY
30/09/2026
02225653-0016